Network Management Fundamentals

Alexander Clemm, Ph.D.

Cisco Press

800 East 96th Street
Indianapolis, IN 46240 USA

Network Management Fundamentals

Alexander Clemm, Ph.D.

Copyright© 2007 Cisco Systems, Inc.

Published by:
Cisco Press
800 East 96th Street
Indianapolis, IN 46240 USA

Printed in the United States of America 1 2 3 4 5 6 7 8 9 0

First Printing   November 2006

LIBRARY OF CONGRESS CATALOG CARD NUMBER: 2004110268

ISBN: 1-58720-137-2

Warning and Disclaimer

This book is designed to provide information about network management. Every effort has been made to make this book as complete and as accurate as possible, but no warranty or fitness is implied.

The information is provided on an "as is" basis. The authors, Cisco Press, and Cisco Systems, Inc., shall have neither liability nor responsibility to any person or entity with respect to any loss or damages arising from the information contained in this book or from the use of the discs or programs that may accompany it.

The opinions expressed in this book belong to the author and are not necessarily those of Cisco Systems, Inc.

Corporate and Government Sales

Cisco Press offers excellent discounts on this book when ordered in quantity for bulk purchases or special sales. For more information, please contact: **U.S. Corporate and Government Sales**   1-800-382-3419   corpsales@pearsontechgroup.com

For sales outside of the U.S. please contact: **International Sales**   1-317-581-3793   international@pearsontechgroup.com

Feedback Information

At Cisco Press, our goal is to create in-depth technical books of the highest quality and value. Each book is crafted with care and precision, undergoing rigorous development that involves the unique expertise of members from the professional technical community.

Readers' feedback is a natural continuation of this process. If you have any comments regarding how we could improve the quality of this book or otherwise alter it to better suit your needs, you can contact us through e-mail at feedback@ciscopress.com. Please make sure to include the book title and ISBN in your message.

We greatly appreciate your assistance.

Trademark Acknowledgments

All terms mentioned in this book that are known to be trademarks or service marks have been appropriately capitalized. Cisco Press or Cisco Systems, Inc., cannot attest to the accuracy of this information. Use of a term in this book should not be regarded as affecting the validity of any trademark or service mark.

Publisher: Paul Boger

Executive Editor: Mary Beth Ray

Managing Editor: Patrick Kanouse

Development Editor: Betsey Henkels

Project Editor: Tonya Simpson

Copy Editor: Krista Hansing Editorial Services, Inc.

Team Coordinator: Vanessa Evans

Book and Cover Designer: Louisa Adair

Compositor: Mark Shirar

Indexer: Larry Sweazy

Cisco Representative: Anthony Wolfenden

Cisco Press Program Manager: Jeff Brady

Technical Editors: Prakash Bettadapur, David M. Kurtiak, Lundy Lewis

CISCO

Americas Headquarters	Asia Pacific Headquarters	Europe Headquarters
Cisco Systems, Inc.	Cisco Systems, Inc.	Cisco Systems International BV
170 West Tasman Drive	168 Robinson Road	Haarlerbergpark
San Jose, CA 95134-1706	#28-01 Capital Tower	Haarlerbergweg 13-19
USA	Singapore 068912	1101 CH Amsterdam
www.cisco.com	www.cisco.com	The Netherlands
Tel: 408 526-4000	Tel: +65 6317 7777	www-europe.cisco.com
800 553-NETS (6387)	Fax: +65 6317 7799	Tel: +31 0 800 020 0791
Fax: 408 527-0883		Fax: +31 0 20 357 1100

Cisco has more than 200 offices worldwide. Addresses, phone numbers, and fax numbers are listed on the Cisco Website at **www.cisco.com/go/offices.**

About the Author

Dr. Alexander Clemm, Ph.D. is a Senior Architect with Cisco Systems. He has been involved with integrated management of networked systems and services since 1990. Alex has provided technical leadership for many network management development and engineering efforts from original conception to delivery to the customer. They include management instrumentation of network devices, turnkey management solutions for packet telephony and managed services, and management systems for Voice over IP networks, broadband access networks, and provisioning of residential subscriber services. Alex has approximately 30 publications related to network management and 15 patents pending. He is on the Organizing Committee or Technical Program Committee of the major technical conferences in the field, including IM, NOMS, DSOM, IPOM, and MMNS, and he served as Technical Program Co-chair of the 2005 IFIP/IEEE International Symposium on Integrated Network Management. He holds a Ph.D. degree from the University of Munich and a Master's degree from Stanford University.

About the Technical Reviewers

Prakash Bettadapur is a Senior Engineering Manager at Cisco Systems. He has been with Cisco since 1999, working in various network management and IOS manageability programs. Before Cisco, Prakash worked in Bell Northern Research (BNR) in Ottawa, Canada, and in Nortel Networks in Santa Clara, California, for 14 years. While in BNR/Nortel, Prakash worked in DMS–Service Control Point, Data Packet Networking (DPN), Magellan Passport, and Meridian PBX product lines, focusing on the areas of software development and network management. Prakash holds a Master's degree in computing science from the University of Alberta, Canada; a Proficience Certificate in computing systems from the Indian Institute of Science, Bangalore; and a Bachelor's degree in electronics and telecommunications engineering from Karnataka Regional Engineering College, India. Prakash currently lives in San Jose, California.

David M. Kurtiak is a Principal Engineer for Loral Skynet, where he currently architects systems and network infrastructure and provides tier 3 support for the company's global IT organization. In a previous role at Skynet, Dave led a team of technical professionals responsible for managing the daily operations of the company's IT and data network infrastructure. Before joining Loral, Dave was a senior data communications specialist for AT&T. David has more than 18 years of experience in the IT and telecommunications industry, working in many telecommunications technologies. He is recognized as the resident expert in TCP/IP networking, with specialization in end-to-end network analysis, planning, troubleshooting, and performance tuning. David has a Master's degree (M.S.) in telecommunications from the University of Colorado at Boulder and a Bachelor's degree (B.S.) in information systems from the University of North Carolina at Greensboro.

Lundy Lewis is the Chair of the Department of Information Technology at Southern New Hampshire University. He has worked in the area of network management since the early 1990s. He holds 22 U.S. patents and has written three books on network and service management. He is a member of the technical committees for the major IEEE conferences on network management.

Dedications

To my wonderful wife and kids—Sigrid, Clarissa, and Christopher. Thank you for making me complete.

Acknowledgments

At various stages of writing this book, I had interesting discussions, support, and valuable feedback from many friends and colleagues. In particular, I would like to acknowledge Ron Biell, Steve Chang, Eva Krüger, Victor Lee, Dave McNamee, Fred Schindler, Hector Trevino, Eshwar Yedavalli, and Ralf Wolter. A very special "thank you" goes out to my dad, Helmut Clemm, who, in fact, read through the entire manuscript and, although not a "network manager," provided many useful insights.

I also want to acknowledge this book's production team, which is the finest anyone could ask for. Specifically, I would like to acknowledge the people I interacted with the most—Jim Schachterle, who first got the ball rolling; Raina Han and Mary Beth Ray, who accompanied me through most of the writing stage; and Betsey Henkels, whose development edits were of great help during the "crunch time" of the book; and Tonya Simpson, my project editor. The team also includes my technical editors, Prakash Bettadapur, David Kurtiak, and Lundy Lewis, whose excellent comments and suggestions undoubtedly helped to significantly improve the book.

Last but not least, I would like to thank my family for their understanding and support throughout this project, which, by the nature of things, meant sacrificing many weekends; nonetheless, they never stopped cheering me on. We did it!

This Book Is Safari Enabled

The Safari® Enabled icon on the cover of your favorite technology book means the book is available through Safari Bookshelf. When you buy this book, you get free access to the online edition for 45 days.

Safari Bookshelf is an electronic reference library that lets you easily search thousands of technical books, find code samples, download chapters, and access technical information whenever and wherever you need it.

To gain 45-day Safari Enabled access to this book:

- Go to http://www.ciscopress.com/safarienabled

- Complete the brief registration form

- Enter the coupon code FDGI-KXRF-ARYB-BVF5-CXGN

If you have difficulty registering on Safari Bookshelf or accessing the online edition, please e-mail customer-service@safaribooksonline.com.

Contents at a Glance

Contents

Icons Used in This Book

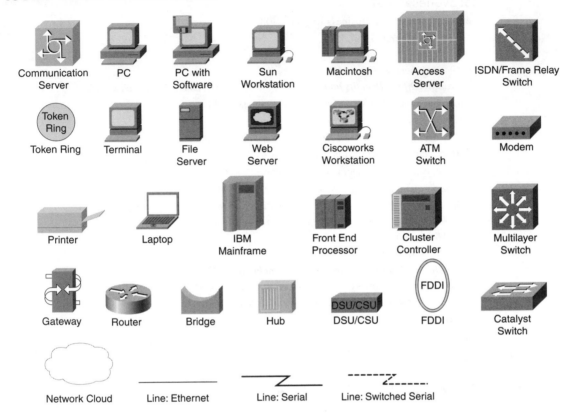

Command Syntax Conventions

The conventions used to present command syntax in this book are the same conventions used in the IOS Command Reference. The Command Reference describes these conventions as follows:

- **Boldface** indicates commands and keywords that are entered literally as shown. In actual configuration examples and output (not general command syntax), boldface indicates commands that are manually input by the user (such as a **show** command).

- *Italics* indicate arguments for which you supply actual values.

- Vertical bars (I) separate alternative, mutually exclusive elements.

- Square brackets ([ ]) indicate optional elements.

- Braces ({ }) indicate a required choice.

- Braces within brackets ([{ }]) indicate a required choice within an optional element.

Introduction

Network management is an essential factor in successfully operating a network. As businesses become increasingly dependent on networking services, keeping those services running becomes synonymous with keeping the business running.

Properly performed, network management ensures that services provided over a network are turned up swiftly and keep running smoothly. In addition, network management helps to keep networking cost and operational cost under control. It ensures that networking equipment is used effectively and deployed where it is needed the most. It increases the availability and quality of the services that the network provides. At least in the case of service providers, it is also a significant factor in the generation of revenue from networking services. On the other hand, ineffective management can lead to deterioration and disruption of networking services, poor utilization of investment made in the network, and lost business. Network management is hence key to getting the most value out of a network and can be absolutely business critical.

Despite its significance, network management is without much doubt one of the lesser understood topics in the otherwise well-charted world of networking. Reasons for this include the fact that network management looks deceptively simple, whereas it can be difficult to master, and that it is overshadowed by the networking technology itself that it is supposed to manage.

In some ways, managing a network is like throwing a party: Most people enjoy going to a party (read: the services provided by the network) but do not want to deal with the hassle of setting it up, keeping everything flowing smoothly, and cleaning up the mess afterward (read: network management). Yet this is essential to the party's success (and ensuring that there will be another one). As with network management, many technical disciplines are involved: Food needs to be cooked, rooms decorated, invitations printed, and electrical equipment and lighting set up. And as with network management, organizational and business questions abound: Do I throw it at my home, or do I lease a location? Where will I put the coats? How many drinks do I need? Can I do it all by myself, or at what point does it make sense to use a caterer?

Network Management Fundamentals aims to provide an accessible introduction to this important subject area. It covers management not just of networks themselves, but also of services running over those networks. It explains the fundamental concepts and principles that network management is based on. It attempts to provide a holistic system perspective of network management and explains how different technologies that are used in network management relate to each other. This system perspective aims to convey a sense of the forest rather than of the individual trees. Hopefully, the resulting understanding will put you, the reader, in a position in which you can successfully navigate the subject area of network management and apply its concepts to your particular situation.

Who Should Read This Book?

This book is intended as an introduction and guide to network management for anyone interested in the topic, whether that person has only a basic understanding of networking technology and is only casually interested in the subject, or whether that person is an experienced networking professional looking to expand his or her core competencies. The book tries to avoid overloading the reader with unnecessary complexity and details that would distract from these fundamentals and key concepts, yet provide a solid technical foundation for the practitioner.

The target audience includes network operators, development engineers, test engineers, operations planners, project managers, and product managers who need to deal with network management in some way as part of their jobs. It also includes executives who need to understand the impact of network management on their organization, as well as engineering students who want to round off a networking curriculum.

The emphasis in this book lies on fundamentals and general principles in network management rather than technical details and "how-to" instructions. Accordingly, if you are interested in the details of a particular management protocol or in the specifics of a particular management application, this is not the right book for you. If, on the other hand, you want to understand the foundations of network management and how management technology really works, this book should prove useful to you.

How This Book Is Organized

This book is intended to be read cover to cover because later chapters build on concepts and principles that earlier chapters introduce. Nevertheless, many chapters are relatively self-contained, which should make it fairly easy to move between chapters.

The chapters of this book are grouped into four parts:

■ **Part I, "Network Management: An Overview,"** provides an overview of what network management is about and why it is relevant. It also conveys an informal understanding of the functions, tools, and activities that are associated with it. Part I consists of three chapters:

Chapter 1, "Setting the Stage," provides an informal overview of what network management is all about, from both a business and technical perspective. It explains how one can benefit from network management and what basic challenges are associated with it.

Chapter 2, "On the Job with a Network Manager," takes a glimpse at typical activities that people who run networks for a living are involved with, using three example scenarios. It also provides an overview of the types of tools they have at their disposal to support them in their jobs.

Chapter 3, "The Basic Ingredients of Network Management," discusses the basic components in network management and the roles they play. This includes the network and the devices in it that need to be managed, the systems and applications that are used for their management, and the network that connects them for management purposes. It also includes the organization behind it that makes it all happen and that is ultimately held responsible for ensuring that the network is run properly.

■ **Part II, "Management Perspectives,"** dissects the topic into its various aspects in a more systemic manner. In the tradition of the analogy of the elephant and the blind man, it illuminates network management from several different angles. This culminates in a discussion of how these aspects are combined into management reference models. Specifically, it includes the following chapters:

Chapter 4, "The Dimensions of Management," presents different orthogonal (unrelated) yet complementary aspects in network management. An understanding of those aspects will help you divide and conquer network management problems that you might face. This includes different hierarchical levels of network management concerns, from dealing with equipment in the network to managing your business as it relates to networking. It includes the phases in the management lifecycle, from planning your network to decommissioning equipment. It includes the aspect of how to represent information about the managed network, how managing and managed systems can communicate, and how to set up a management organization. Last but not least, it includes the management functions that are needed for network management in the first place.

Chapter 5, "Management Functions and Reference Models: Getting Organized," takes an in-depth look at the function dimension of network management—specifically, the range of different functions that management systems need to cover. It proceeds along the lines of several well-established *management reference models*, such as the FCAPS model, that do an excellent job of organizing these functions.

- **Part III, "Management Building Blocks,"** dives further into different building blocks of network management, picking up on various aspects encountered in conjunction with the management dimensions that Part II introduces.

Chapter 6, "Management Information: What Management Conversations Are All About," discusses what lies at the core of all communication between managing and managed systems—namely, how to establish a common understanding of what is being managed and different ways to represent this information for management—how it is modeled, how it is represented (for example, as part of a Management Information Base), and how it is encoded over the wire.

Chapter 7, "Management Communication Patterns—Rules of Conversation," dives into the various patterns in which managing and managed systems interact. These patterns have a profound impact on many areas, from how management communication protocols are designed to how management applications are architected so they can scale.

Chapter 8, "Common Management Protocols: Languages of Management," presents a sampling of what are arguably the most important and widely deployed management protocols today—in effect, languages that managing and managed systems use to communicate with each other and exchange management requests, responses, and event messages. The technologies presented include SNMP, CLI, syslog, Netconf, and NetFlow/IPFIX. In addition to a technical overview, the chapter also explains how they are positioned with regard to the management purposes they serve and what their most important distinguishing characteristics are.

Chapter 9, "Management Organization: Dividing the Labor," takes a closer look at the different ways in which management can be organized from a technical perspective and how management functionality can be divided between different systems. In particular, it explores the "vertical" division of management tasks in which different systems need to collaborate to ultimately achieve a common management purpose.

- **Part IV, "Applied Network Management,"** rounds out the book with a number of management topics of general interest. These topics also combine and put into perspective many of the pieces that were introduced earlier.

  Chapter 10, "Management Integration: Putting the Pieces Together," explores what is considered by many the "Holy Grail" of network management—namely, how to achieve management that is *integrated* and that provides all management functionality in a holistic fashion. The goal of this is to avoid the shortcomings and inefficiencies of management that is provided in the form of multiple islands. The chapter discusses the challenges that are associated with integrated management; articulating what those challenges are is the first step in confronting them successfully. Subsequently, the chapter presents techniques for tackling those challenges, along with their tradeoffs.

  Chapter 11, "Service Level Management: Knowing What You Pay For," presents an introduction to service level management. This topic is of fundamental importance, both to the providers of networking services, who need to ensure that agreed-to service levels are being met, and to their customers, who want to validate that they are indeed getting the level of service they pay for. It also serves as an example of a practical management application area that puts to use many of the concepts that were introduced earlier in the book.

  Chapter 12, "Management Metrics: Assessing Management Impact and Effectiveness," revisits the business proposition of network management that the Introduction initially laid out. It thus closes a circle and provides a fitting conclusion for the book. The chapter examines what factors determine the effectiveness and impact of network management. It also shows how an assessment of network management impact and effectiveness can be methodically approached through use of metrics.

Part I: Network Management: An Overview

CHAPTER 1

Setting the Stage

This chapter sets the stage for the rest of the book. It provides an overview of what network management is all about, how you can benefit from it, and what basic challenges are associated with it. Don't worry—the chapters that follow provide you with a solid foundation to successfully deal with many of those challenges. This chapter gives you the background necessary to understand the remainder of this book and, in general, put you in a network management frame of mind.

After reading this chapter, you should be able to:

- Explain the term *network management*

- Develop a basic sense of what is involved in network management

- Explain the importance of network management and how it impacts cost, revenue, and network availability

- Recognize the different players and industries that have an interest in network management, and understand the different angles from which they approach the subject

- Describe some of the challenges posed by network management, including those that are technical, organizational, and business

Defining Network Management

As is the case with so many words, *network management* has many attached meanings. Therefore, some clarification is in order regarding what is meant by the term in this book.

Speaking informally, *network management* refers to the activities associated with running a network, along with the technology required to support those activities. A significant part of running a network is simply monitoring it to understand what is going on, but there are also other aspects.

What network management is all about is perhaps best conveyed using some simple analogies.

Analogy 1: Health Care—the Network, Your Number One Patient

A network is not unlike a complex living organism. Let us therefore compare a network with a patient who is in an intensive care unit in a hospital. The patient, of course, is under intensive scrutiny, just as your network should be. After all, the network could be the lifeblood of your enterprise.

In an intensive care unit, monitoring the patient's pulse is constantly required. A slowing or missing pulse, after all, requires an immediate response. Other health functions of the patient are monitored as well, such as temperature and blood pressure. Because they do not require as constant attention as the pulse, it is sufficient to measure them only once an hour or so. Curves are often plotted to detect trends over time, to answer not just questions such as "What is the patient's current temperature?", but also questions such as "Is the temperature dropping or rising?" In addition, on a more exceptional basis, blood samples are taken and analyzed, and under special circumstances an MRI is performed.

In response to the patient's symptoms, doctors prescribe a set of medications and treatments. Again, through monitoring, the patient's response is observed and diagnoses are confirmed or alternative paths of treatment are considered if the response is different than expected. Needless to say, an extensive hospital staff, expensive equipment, and millions in R&D dollars to develop effective drugs are required to provide the best possible care for the intensive care patient.

Likewise, a network must be monitored. In fact, people often refer to the "network health" when they are discussing network performance and its capability to provide service. As with the pulse of a patient, critical functions of network equipment that could lead to service outages need to be monitored constantly and malfunctions alarmed immediately to react as quickly as possible when trouble occurs. As with the temperature or blood pressure of a patient, other parameters could be indicators of impending trouble, such as increasing rates at which packets are dropped or utilization on a link that is approaching 100 percent. These parameters must be closely monitored, and changes and trends must be heeded. For example, a rising packet-drop rate could be an indication of impending failures, whereas rising link utilization could be an indication that additional network capacity is required.

Under certain circumstances, extensive troubleshooting and diagnostic procedures must be run. Some of those procedures can be costly because they require, for example, that network devices spend precious cycles running diagnostics instead of routing packets, or because, in extreme cases, a device or a port must be taken offline to run a test. Therefore, those functions would not be run constantly, but only when called for, just as special circumstances are required to run an MRI on a hospital patient.

To remedy failures and react to signs of trouble, networking parameters must be tuned and devices might need to be reconfigured—in some cases, even replaced. This is the equivalent of "medicine" for the network. The effect of the actions taken is again monitored to ensure that the desired result is reached; otherwise, alternative methods of treatment are attempted. And as with the hospital patient, effective organization and management tools are all required to keep things running smoothly.

Analogy 2: Throwing a Party

Running a network has much in common with running events. Think for a moment of a network as analogous to a big party—not a party you attend as a guest (that is, an end user), but one that you are hosting (that is, managing).

Depending on the type of party and the number of guests, throwing a party involves many different activities. Long before the date of the party, planning begins: Invitations need to be designed, printed, and sent out. Organizational questions abound. Do you throw it at your home, or should you rent a spot at another location (and which one)? What external circumstances do you need to consider? Depending on the season and where you live, you might need to think about where to put the coats. Food must be prepared and rooms decorated. You need to decide whether to throw the party all by yourself or at what point you would rather use a caterer. Of course, it is also a question of money. How many drinks will you need? You don't want to run out, but on the other hand, you don't want to be wasteful by serving too much. Electrical equipment and lighting need to be set up. During the party, you want to make sure your guests are feeling comfortable. Do you need to bring more drinks? Is the volume of the music at the right level? Finally, after the party, there is the cleanup to take care of.

Likewise, many activities are involved with running a network. As in the case of the party, you begin with planning: What services do you intend to provide over your network, and what service capacity will be needed? What circumstances will influence your network topology—for example, do you need to connect many small branch offices, or are you planning a network for one large campus? The answer likely influences the choice of equipment and dimensioning of links. Equipment, in turn, must be commissioned and turned up. In many cases, special configuration activities and tuning of configuration parameters might be required—not an easy feat, given the multitude of knobs that can be turned, the technical interdependencies, and the many different types and versions of equipment in the network.

Business questions need to be answered as well. Should you use the equivalent of a caterer and simply buy a set of communication services and outsource operation of the network, or should you manage your own network? Do you have the expertise to do so? Budget might be limited, forcing you to make hard choices. Furthermore, unlike throwing a party, the task of running the network never ends. This complicates matters further. You need to be able to continually make adjustments as you go and introduce new services. You might need to decommission and replace old equipment without affecting end users. And, of course, all along you need to make sure that everything is functioning properly so that the end users of your communication services will be happy, just as you want the guests at your party to feel comfortable.

A More Formal Definition

Given the previous examples, this definition sums up a little more formally what's involved in managing a network:

> Network management refers to the activities, methods, procedures, and tools that pertain to the operation, administration, maintenance, and provisioning of networked systems.

Operation deals with keeping the network (and the services that the network provides) up and running smoothly. It includes monitoring the network to spot problems as soon as possible, ideally before a user is affected.

Administration involves keeping track of resources in the network and how they are assigned. It deals with all the "housekeeping" that is necessary to keep things under control.

Maintenance is concerned with performing repairs and upgrades—for example, when a line card must be replaced, when a router needs a new operating system image with a patch, when a new switch is added to the network. Maintenance also involves corrective and preventive proactive measures such as adjusting device parameters as needed and generally intervening as needed to make the managed network run "better."

Provisioning is concerned with configuring resources in the network to support a given service. For example, this might include setting up the network so that a new customer can receive voice service.

The following figures illustrate the role that network management plays. Figure 1-1 depicts the task of running and monitoring a network that the organization responsible for the network is faced with. Figure 1-2 depicts where network management fits in to help organizations responsible for managing a network with their task. Figure 1-3 depicts what is included in network management—namely, the systems and applications used to manage networks, as well as the activities and operational procedures that those systems support.

Figure 1-1 *An Organization and Its Network*

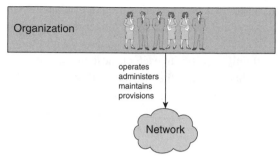

Figure 1-2 *The Role of Network Management*

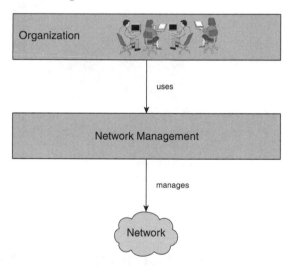

Figure 1-3 *What Constitutes Network Management*

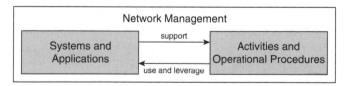

A narrower definition of network management would not refer to "networked systems" in its generality, but simply to "communication networks." Sometimes a distinction is made among the management of the networks themselves, the management of the end systems that are connected to networks, and the management of (networked) applications running on the systems connected to the networks. This distinction separates the terms *network management*, *systems management*, and *application management*, as depicted in Figure 1-4. In addition, networks, systems, and applications might all be involved in providing a service. Management of the service is therefore often distinguished as well and subsumed under the term *service management*.

Although there are certainly specifics to each of those management disciplines, they have much more in common than what separates them. Unless otherwise noted, we use the term *network management* in its broader sense, encompassing all of these very closely related disciplines.

Figure 1-4   *Network, Systems, and Application Management*

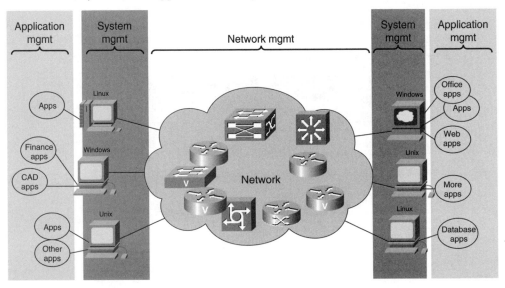

The Importance of Network Management: Many Reasons to Care

Wouldn't it be nice if, to run a network, you just had to buy a bunch of networking equipment, wire it and hook it up, flip a switch, and, voilà—the network just works. You can turn off the lights and basically forget about it and simply enjoy the services that it provides, kind of like an entertainment center in a living room. Well, although you might wish it were that simple, you can't quite get away with so little effort.

A network is a complex structure that requires a great deal of attention. It must be carefully planned. Configurations of network devices must be modified without adversely affecting the rest of the network. Failures in the network do occur and need to be detected, diagnosed, and repaired. Service levels that were guaranteed to customers and end users—for example, a certain amount of bandwidth—need to be monitored and ensured. The rollout of services to customers and end users—making service offerings available to them and turning up services quickly when they are requested—must be managed.

Many telecommunications and Internet service providers (ISPs) are finding that the communication services they offer—long-distance telephone service, Internet access, digital subscriber line (DSL)—are becoming commoditized. As a consequence, in many cases not only the base offering itself determines success or failure in the marketplace. Other factors are becoming increasingly important:

- Who can operate the network at the lowest cost and pass those cost savings on to customers?

- Who provides better customer experience by making it easy to order communication services and service those orders with minimal turnaround time?

- Who can maintain and guarantee the highest quality of service?

- Who can roll out services fast and efficiently?

Operating a network is hence truly at the core of the business for service providers. (Service providers are sometimes also referred to as *network operators*. However, we prefer to use the term *operator* for personnel who operate and maintain the network, not for the organization that they are part of.)

Similar factors apply to businesses and enterprises that run their own networks: Cost savings in operating the network benefit the enterprise that the network serves; fast turnaround time to deploy new services and maintain a high quality of service can translate into important competitive advantages. All these factors are ultimately economic success factors, and they are all intricately linked to network management. Therefore, network management is a key factor for the economics of running a network. The significance of network management to that regard cannot be overemphasized.

This section provides a closer look at the benefits that effective network management and management tools can provide—reduced cost, improvements in the quality of service that the network provides, and increased revenue. From now on, we refer to the organization that is running a network simply as the *network provider*. In some cases, we also use the term *service provider* in reference to the services that those organizations provide over the network. Unless mentioned otherwise, we do not limit use of the term to "classical" service providers such as telecommunications carriers or Internet service providers, but we include also enterprise IT organizations. After all, they provide communication services to the enterprise that they are part of.

Cost

One of the main goals of network management is to make operations more efficient and operators more productive. The ultimate goal is to reduce and minimize the total cost of ownership (TCO) that is associated with the network. The TCO consists essentially of the equipment cost, as well as the cost to operate the network (see Figure 1-5). Equipment cost is typically amortized over several years, to take into account the lifetime of the equipment. Operational cost includes cost such as operating personnel, electricity, physical space, and cost for the operations support infrastructure.

The cost savings that result from a lower TCO make the service provider more competitive from an economics perspective. In addition, the service provider can pass the cost savings on to its customers, thus making them more competitive. The expectation is that network management can help accomplish this.

Figure 1-5   *Total Cost of Network Equipment Ownership*

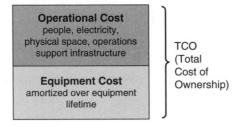

To put things in perspective, the cost of operations can be higher than the cost of amortizing the network equipment itself, in some cases by as much as a factor of 2 or more. To illustrate, assume for a moment that an equipment vendor charges $300,000 for a set of network devices, which are amortized at $100,000 per year over 3 years. Assume furthermore that for a given service provider, the associated operational cost is an additional $200,000 annualized.

From a service provider perspective, a competitor who manages to realize an operational efficiency gain of 25 percent will enjoy a competitive cost advantage of $50,000 per year, or half the entire equipment amortization cost. From an equipment vendor perspective, a vendor whose management capabilities result in a mere 25 percent operational efficiency gain will be capable of charging 50 percent more for equipment as a premium for its superior operations capabilities, or $150,000 instead of $100,000, at the same TCO. Figure 1-6 illustrates this fact. (Unfortunately, it is not always easy to come up with definitive numbers for TCO and crisp models for return on investment on network management. Chapter 12, "Management Metrics: Assessing Management Impact and Effectiveness," presents more information on how management effectiveness can be assessed and translated into monetary values.)

Figure 1-6 *The Significance of Lowering Network Equipment Operational Cost*

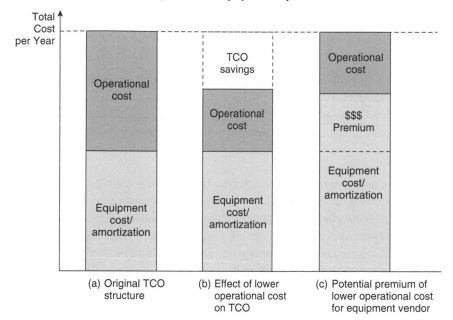

The following are examples of how the application of network management tools can help increase operational efficiency and lower cost:

■ Network testing and troubleshooting tools. These tools enable operators to more quickly identify and isolate problems and thereby free themselves up for other tasks. Automating troubleshooting for routine problems enables operations personnel to focus on the really "tough" issues.

■ Systems that facilitate turn-up of services and automate provisioning. By automating most of the steps that are required to enable a service for an end user, fewer operational steps must be performed by an operator. This also reduces the potential for human error.

■ Performance-reporting tools and bottleneck analysis. This enables service providers to allocate network resources to where they are needed most, minimizing the required investment in the network and maximizing the "bang for the buck."

Another cost benefit of network management tools, besides operator productivity, is that such tools potentially reduce the skill level that is required to manage the network. This reduces investment in training. It also increases the pool of qualified labor that is available, making hard-to-find skill sets less of a bottleneck and limiting factor in the service provider's business. One of the most critical hurdles in operating a network—and, therefore, an incentive to increasing efficiency—is that, in many cases, it might simply not be possible to hire and train sufficient numbers of skilled engineers.

Quality

Other operational aspects are not related to cost but are equally important. One such aspect concerns the quality of the communications and networking services that are provided. This includes properties such as the bandwidth that is effectively available, or the delay in the network, which, in turn, is a factor in the responsiveness a user experiences when using services over a network.

Quality also includes the reliability and the availability of a communications service: As an end user, can I rely on my service, or do I need to often retransmit data because I experience interruptions in the middle of my communication session, such as timeouts and no response from the remote end because of a dropped communication session? Is the service always available when I need it, or do I sometimes (in the case of voice service) get no dial tone? Availability is not simply nice to have; lives can literally depend on it. For example, think of a 911 service in a telephone network, or connectivity for critical equipment in a hospital.

Reliability and availability are attributes that are typically associated only with the network itself. Accordingly, and rightfully so, much emphasis is given to engineering networks in a way that makes them carrier class. This involves developing network equipment with redundant hardware so that if a component fails, a hot failover to a spare can occur. In addition, networks themselves are carefully engineered to allow for redundant communication paths, in many cases ensuring network availability that is overall higher than the availability of any single element in the network. Intelligent capabilities are introduced to automatically reroute communication traffic around faults or fiber cuts. The list goes on.

One aspect that is easily overlooked, however, is the fact that network management is also a key ingredient in this equation. Here are some examples:

- Systems for the end-to-end provisioning of a service automate many of the steps that need to be performed to configure the devices in the network properly. Those systems help make operations not only more efficient, but less error prone as well because they provide fewer opportunities to make mistakes. Misconfigurations, in which some devices or network parameters are not set up properly, result in lower network and service availability. They can be hard to troubleshoot and slow to fix. Through end-to-end provisioning, many such misconfigurations can be avoided in the first place, providing an important contribution to increased network availability.

■ Performance trend analysis can help network managers detect potential network bottlenecks and take preventive maintenance action before problems occur and before services and users are negatively impacted. This can also help improve the level of service being delivered, such as the bandwidth that is effectively available to users or delay that is introduced in the network.

■ Alarm correlation capabilities enable faster identification of the root cause of observed failures when they occur, minimizing the time of actual outages.

Even more than with cost, it is difficult to quantify the return on investment in network management with respect to quality. One possibility is to consider opportunity cost, the cost if quality is *not* met. Examples for opportunity cost are listed here:

■ Lost revenue from customers taking their business elsewhere if quality objectives are not met.

■ Increased networking cost from inefficient utilization or networking resources, which potentially leads to more networking equipment and capacity being deployed to support a certain level of service than would otherwise be necessary. This results in higher equipment cost and a larger footprint—for example, space for all that equipment.

■ Higher operational cost that is spent on fixing problems and having to monitor additional equipment that would not be necessary if quality would meet required levels and existing equipment were better utilized.

Revenue

Network management is not just related to cost and quality. Network management can also be a revenue enabler that opens up market opportunities that would not exist without it. Here are some examples:

■ Service provisioning systems enable service providers to reduce the time that elapses from the time a service is ordered to the time the service is actually turned up. The capability to turn up a service quickly translates into quicker time to revenue generation. A management system that automates the complete workflow, from ordering the service to turning it up, obviously provides greater speed than workflows that involve human operators who need to key data into multiple systems redundantly along various steps of the way. Also, if a service cannot be provisioned and turned up quickly, a customer might decide to take his business elsewhere.

■ In some cases, network management enables a service provider to augment a service offering with management-related capabilities that attract more customers. For example, to a customer, the capability to track accounting charges online and to configure service features over the Web (examples for voice: caller ID, follow-me services) and have them take effect immediately constitutes a valuable service feature.

■ Cost savings made possible through network management might make certain services feasible in the first place. For instance, a new communications service for residential customers might not be feasible if it takes several hundred dollars in operational cost per subscriber just to turn up that service. Residential customers might not be willing to pay such amounts, and service providers might not be willing or able to absorb them. (This is what happened in the early days of digital subscriber line [DSL] service, for example.) An efficient management system that reduces or eliminates truck rolls might be the prerequisite to economically offer a service in the first place and open up a whole new market. (A truck roll refers to the need to send operations personnel to a customer site, which typically involves "rolling a truck" and is associated with high cost.)

The Players: Different Parties with an Interest in Network Management

Network management is a whole industry that involves many players. Different players are concerned with different aspects of network management, depending on their particular perspective. In this section, you learn who the players are and what role network management plays for them. Roughly, the players fall into the categories of users of network management and providers of network management (see Figure 1-7).

Figure 1-7 *Players in the Network Management Space*

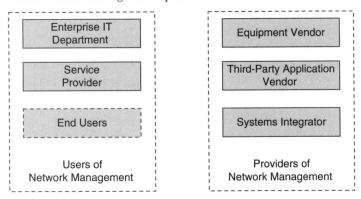

Network Management Users

The Service Provider

As their name indicates, service providers are in the business of providing services to their customers. Those services can be any communication and networking service, such as telecommunication services (telephone, voice mail) and data services (leased lines, Internet connectivity). In some cases, service providers host applications—they are then also called application service providers.

Many different types of service providers exist, categorized along different criteria—for example, according to what services they provide (telecommunications service providers, Internet service providers, application service providers, and so forth) or whether they are regulated by government (regulated incumbent service providers; local exchange carriers; Post, Telegraph, and Telephone administrations [PTTs]; or unregulated "competitive" local exchange carriers).

What all those service providers have in common is that they make a living out of running networks—running networks is the core of their business, their sole purpose of existence. Network management is accordingly of existential importance to them—and they are not interested in it just for its cost-saving potential, although, of course, given their massive operations, they also need to keep cost at bay. Even more important, service providers are interested in network management as a guarantor for their revenues. How they manage their networks is a key competitive differentiator. In particular, in an environment where many communication services are being commoditized (basically, anybody can offer long-distance voice service or a connection to the Internet), other factors make or break a service provider—and many of those factors are directly related to network management. Again, the winner in the marketplace is the service provider that can turn up services and roll them out to customers the fastest, that can offer the best service level guarantees, that knows how to be the quickest to recover from failures and how to limit their impact to a minimum, and that can best utilize its equipment and get the most mileage out of it. Because it is of such utmost importance, service providers are willing to invest heavily in network management—in development of efficient operational procedures to give them the upper hand, and in custom tools that best support those procedures.

The Enterprise IT Department

Enterprise IT departments are in charge of running the network inside an enterprise, providing the enterprise with all its internal communication needs. They are often thought of as mini service providers of communications services for the enterprise that they are part of. Although this is correct, some important differences exist:

■   Generating revenue and making money are not important for the enterprise IT department. Instead, it is essentially a cost center, so the focus is on how to provide the communication services the enterprise needs at the lowest cost possible. Enterprise IT departments don't generate revenue; to some degree, they might be concerned with making sure enterprise departments get charged for their consumption of communication services, but, in many cases, this not a critical function. Not so for the service provider: It provides communications services for a living, so making sure that dollars are charged and collected is top priority.

■   Enterprise IT departments have one customer: the enterprise. End users within the enterprise have no choice in who provides their service. (Of course, enterprises might choose to outsource many or most of their communication services to a service provider, again, to control cost.) Likewise, the enterprise IT department couldn't attract customers from outside the enterprise even if it wanted to. Service providers, on the other hand, have many customers, and those customers do have a choice. This puts a different emphasis on how customer relationships are managed and tied into operations.

■   Because communications services are not the core business of the enterprise, how to manage and run their networks is not a primary competitive differentiator. In fact, enterprise IT departments might be forced to outsource much of their operations to a service provider (then called a managed service provider), to minimize distraction for the enterprise from their core business.

■   Enterprise IT departments are not regulated, whereas, in many cases, service providers are. (However, the adoption of Sarbanes-Oxley legislation in the United States is changing that and, in fact, does have a certain regulatory effect on enterprise IT departments.)

Interestingly, network size isn't really a defining difference. Although it is true that the largest networks are owned by service providers, some very large enterprises—in particular, global Fortune 500 companies—own networks that, in size, number of end users, and communications volume, are on par with and, in many cases, even larger than those of many service providers.

Because network management, while important, isn't as differentiating and as critical a factor for large enterprises as it is for service providers, the investment in management applications and tools might be more restrained. The enterprise might be more willing to settle for generic applications and standard tools to save cost. It generally avoids investing in expensive custom network management development when possible.

The End User

Finally, there is the end user. With end users, here we are referring not to the users of the communication service—to them, network management is invisible; it is simply part of the infrastructure that keeps it all running. We are instead referring to the persons who keep the network running—the network managers. They are the ones who are ultimately the users of the various management systems and applications, and who rely on them as tools to get their jobs done. Collectively, network managers are often also referred to as operators, although, in fact, many different responsibilities and roles can be differentiated, depending on the organization. These roles include network administrators who can configure and tune routers and switches remotely, and who know how to troubleshoot the network when things aren't going right. They include the craft technicians, who are dispatched to fix problems that can't be fixed remotely, or to commission and decommission equipment. They include the help-desk representatives, who take user calls and complaints, and support personnel, who monitor the network. They include the network planners who design the network, plan the topology, dimension links and nodes, and select the network equipment.

In fact, the roles of network managers vary greatly, depending on the organization. In the cases of smaller enterprises, the same person might be responsible for it all and wear many different hats, being a very sophisticated Jack-of-all-trades. In the case of large service providers, an entire army of personnel might be involved in running the network, which results in much greater specialization and myriad roles and job descriptions.

Network Management Providers

The Equipment Vendor

Equipment vendors are primarily in the business of selling networking equipment, not network management applications. Hence, traditionally equipment vendors have shown a tendency to limit investment in management application development. In general, they have been willing to settle for the minimum management capabilities that customers would allow them to get away with. That means that generally they would provide just the level of management capabilities needed to not inhibit equipment sales. Of course, they might have heard an occasional complaint as a result. However, if at the end of the day the vast majority of their customers made their purchasing decisions based on the capabilities of the equipment, not the management that comes with it, and if on top of that many customers expected any management capabilities to be thrown in essentially as a freebie without being charged extra, who could blame them?

In recent years, however, a subtle shift has started to occur in which people think of networking equipment less in terms of "boxes," but more in terms of end-to-end systems. Management, while not a part of the box, is certainly a part of that system. At the same time, there is an increasing awareness that TCO of a network includes not only the cost of buying or leasing the equipment, but the cost of managing it as well. Increasingly, that total cost is being factored into purchasing decisions. In addition, equipment vendors face constant pressure to avoid commoditization of their equipment. If everyone offers the same basic set of features, it becomes hard for vendors to charge a premium for their equipment, and margins suffer. On the other hand, when a particular vendor's equipment offers additional features and functions that are useful to end customers and that the competition doesn't have, this constitutes a positive competitive differentiator that the vendor might even be able to charge a premium for.

The capability to manage networking equipment is therefore increasingly being recognized as one such competitive differentiator. Hence, equipment vendors are paying increasing attention to network management. This includes management applications that equipment vendors make available for the equipment. In some cases, basic management software might come bundled with the equipment, not unlike a vendor of digital cameras that throws in additional photo-editing software. But at least as important, this also includes the management interfaces of the equipment that allow the equipment to be easily supported by management applications and to be easily integrated into operations support environments.

The Third-Party Application Vendor

Third-party management software application vendors fill the management application gap that equipment vendors leave open. For one, management application software developed by an equipment vendor tends to support only equipment of that particular vendor. Even if multivendor support is provided, preferential treatment is given to the vendor's own equipment, in terms of both available features and the timeline at which the support becomes available. At the same time, as stated previously, in some cases management application software provided by equipment vendors delivers merely the minimum functionality that is required to keep network management from becoming a deal-breaker for equipment sales. The result in those cases is not always the best possible application.

In addition, many network providers have management needs that are not tied as much to any particular equipment in the network, but to operational tasks and workflows. In addition, many management needs are related to the particular communication services that network providers supply on top of the equipment to their own customers. Because those aspects are more removed from the equipment itself, the equipment vendor is less likely to be able to help network providers with those aspects.

This provides an opening that independent (third-party) management software application vendors are trying to fill. For simplicity, we refer to those vendors simply as management vendors. Management vendors try to make a living of selling management software. They have to make money from it and, therefore, charge a premium. In return, they need to offer features that network providers—service providers and enterprise IT departments—will be willing to pay for. Often one of those features is vendor independence—or perhaps, more precisely, multivendor support, meaning that the application will work well across equipment from different vendors.

The Systems Integrator

Organizations that run large networks, whether enterprise IT departments or service providers, eventually find that no one tool or application can do it all. Instead, over time they end up with a multitude of applications for different purposes. Nevertheless, the applications must, at least to a certain degree, be integrated with the overall operations support environment. They might have to operate from the same set of data—for example, inventory data of the network. They must be tied into the same workflow and many of the same procedures. Also, they must manage different aspects of the same network. Unfortunately (or fortunately, if you are a systems integrator), things don't always work together as seamlessly out of the box as the network provider would like. In addition, in many cases, network providers need additional pieces of functionality, tailored to their specific needs, that their management systems do not provide and that they cannot buy from an independent management vendor.

This is where the systems integrator comes in. Systems integrators provide services to integrate a set of management applications with a specific network and operations support environment, often plugging functional gaps and providing interface adaptations that might be necessary to turn a set of independent applications into a turnkey solution that is customized for a specific network provider. So, like the management vendor, the systems integrator makes a living from network management. However, unlike management vendors that aim to make an off-the-shelf product of management applications that they can sell to multiple network providers, the systems integrator performs custom-tailored development.

Network Management Complexities: From Afterthought to Key Topic

A little earlier, we compared network management to running a big party. This analogy is actually appropriate in more ways than one: When deciding to throw a party, no one thinks at first of the effort that goes into planning the party, the logistics, the cleanup—you think of the party itself and how much everyone will enjoy it. And certainly no one throws a party just for the sake of the work that it involves, but for the fun they expect out of it.

This is not unlike the situation with networking and network management. When you first set out to deploy a network, chances are, at the center of attention initially is the network itself and the communication services that it provides, not how to run it. Network management is little more than an afterthought at first. One thing is sure: No one deals with network management just for network management's sake.

However, as the complexity of your network increases, so does the relevance of network management. More devices are added. Different types of devices are introduced, and different versions of the same type of equipment start to appear. At the same time, more users get connected to the network and use an ever-greater variety of communication services. You will soon find that it is hard to keep up with all that. In fact, the number of new users to add and new services to introduce might start to outpace your capability to do so.

Eventually, things start to break—they are not supposed to, but once in a while, they do. Even worse, you don't even realize it initially until some of the users on your network start complaining. Now you are quickly starting to become really overwhelmed.

At the same time, your competition seems to have a better handle on their network. Their network is utilized better; they accomplish more with less. This helps keep their cost down, while yours is spinning out of control. They can turn up new services for their users faster and more quickly reap their benefits, while you have trouble just keeping things running as they are. Suddenly, it becomes strikingly clear to you that network management is much more than an afterthought. It is, in fact, the key topic. It is the difference between the network running you and you running the network, between failure and success, between tailgating with a six-pack in a parking lot (not that this wouldn't be some fun once in a while, too) and feasting at an elegant restaurant.

This is the type of experience for quite a few organizations that run networks. The sudden realization of its importance eventually moves network management to the center of attention as far as the communications infrastructure is concerned. At the same time, it becomes quickly clear that network management isn't really that trivial after all. Indeed, it comes with plenty of challenges that are interesting, exciting, and very rewarding to deal with. The sections that follow are intended to illustrate where some of those challenges lie. Developing a sense of those challenges is important for a number of reasons:

- It implies a sense of what the underlying problem domain is all about. Therefore, it is an important prerequisite for its understanding.

- It is a key to dealing with those challenges successfully. Challenges that are not recognized imply risks. Risks need to be dealt with because they have the nasty habit of sneaking up on you and jeopardizing your success if they are ignored. Recognizing a challenge is usually the first step in successfully dealing with it.

The following discussion makes no claim of completeness—in fact, it is highly likely that you will experience different network management challenges that pertain to your particular context. However, the examples are representative of what to expect and think about.

Technical Challenges

The first and perhaps most obvious set of challenges is of a technical nature. It deals mostly with how to build applications that help with the management of networks and how they communicate with the devices in the networks they help manage. Many of these challenges are familiar to people who have experience in building complex software systems, and many of the same general software-engineering techniques can be applied to help address these challenges. A discussion of general software-engineering techniques is not specific to network management and, therefore, is beyond the scope of this book. However, other aspects are specific to the management domain. Let's take a look at a few of them! Don't worry—by the end of the book, you will have a good sense of how to confront most of these challenges. Later in the book, we dedicate entire chapters to some of those challenges, such as the topic of integration.

Application Characteristics

Typically, management systems have to support many different functions. As it turns out, many of those functions really need to be supported through their own (sub)applications. Many of these applications have characteristics with certain architectural implications.

We discuss management applications and tools in greater detail in the next chapter. However, let us preview some typical and important types of network management applications to illustrate the wide range of application characteristics that are involved. Each of them is associated with its own set of challenges. In addition, many of these applications impose different requirements on the supporting management systems, which, from a software engineering point of view, sometimes can be difficult to reconcile. In particular, this concerns characteristics that management applications share with transaction-based systems, interrupt-driven systems, and number-crunching applications.

Transaction-Based System Characteristics

Provisioning applications are concerned with driving desired configurations down to network devices; for example, to turn up a service for a customer in the network. Using network management parlance, we also refer to network devices as network elements, as depicted in Figure 1-8. To perform provisioning, a management system typically sends a request, or a number of requests, to a network element, or a set of network elements, and processes the responses returned from the network to make sure everything is in order. These interactions with the network devices constitute transactions that are conducted with the network.

Figure 1-8 *Network and Network Elements*

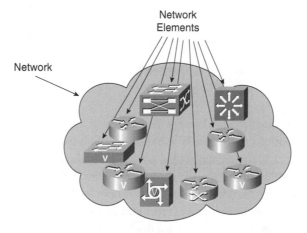

This means that a provisioning application shares many characteristics with transaction-based systems in other areas, such as banking. As with a transaction-based system in those other areas, a provisioning application must be good at dispatching requests, processing responses, managing jobs, and keeping track of the workflow. (Of course, some differences also exist. For example, unlike in a banking application, the provisioning application needs to deal with devices in a network that in some sense have a life of their own. Changes in the network element's state can occur unexpectedly, outside the control of the operations support infrastructure. Likewise, unlike with bank transactions, some of the operations that are performed might have effects that are potentially impossible to undo, such as when a reset occurs or a line is blocked that causes a glitch in service for some customer.)

Figure 1-9 depicts the role of a management application used for provisioning in simplified fashion. Roughly speaking, the application first confirms that the request for a new service is filled out correctly and identifies which pieces of network equipment are needed to fulfill the request. It then sends a series of configuration commands to the devices that are involved. Finally, it confirms that the newly provisioned service is working. If any errors occur during execution of the transaction, the provisioning application must perform any needed rollback operations to bring the network back to a well-defined state.

Figure 1-9 *Network Provisioning*

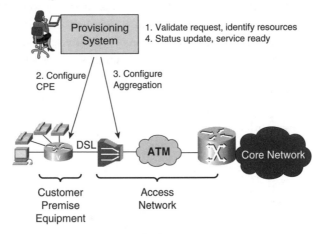

Few people would consider a bank transaction system that must serve automatic teller machines in thousands of locations for hundreds of thousands of customers and their associated bank accounts to be trivial. Compare this with a provisioning application that must serve hundreds of operators for tens of thousands of network elements. The numbers for the provisioning application might be an order of magnitude smaller, but consider now that the network elements might comprise dozens of different equipment types and technologies, and support service for hundreds of thousands of customers, each requiring a distinct set of parameters to be configured properly to obtain service.

Interrupt-Driven System Characteristics

An important aspect of network management concerns keeping track of the health of the network. In particular, this involves monitoring the network for any alarms that network elements emit. Network elements emit alarms whenever unexpected events occur that might require management attention. In many cases, this involves unusual conditions or failures in the network that require immediate action to avoid degradation of service to customers. With communications services, time is money quite literally—after all, every second of service outage leads to loss of productivity of users in an enterprise and lost revenue to service providers. Alarm monitoring applications can receive and process such alarms, enabling the network manager to get an accurate view of the current state and health of the network, and alerting the network manager to take action when it is required.

Figure 1-10 sketches the function of an alarm monitoring system. Alarms that are received, for example, are displayed on a graphical user interface (GUI) and icons animated with color indicate whether a device is healthy or whether it is currently experiencing problems.

By their nature, alarm monitoring applications call for interrupt-driven systems with real-time or near-real-time characteristics. In a way, they share characteristics with stock-brokering applications that need to keep users updated in real time with constant fluctuations in the prices of thousands of different stocks and alert them of any unusual stock movements because failure to react quickly can result in large amounts of money lost. Again, most people agree that building such a stock-brokering application is not trivial. Compare this with the need to reliably keep network operators up-to-date with the state of thousands or tens of thousands of network devices and service for hundreds of thousands of users.

Figure 1-10   *Alarm Monitoring*

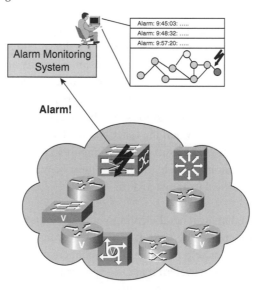

Number-Crunching System Characteristics

Service providers need to analyze networks for their performance for many reasons: to identify bottlenecks, assess whether service levels are being met, evaluate utilization of network resources and efficiency of the network, understand traffic patterns, and analyze trends for planning future network rollout. Generally, this requires collecting and sifting through large volumes of data, including large numbers of data points collected continuously over different periods of time.

The comparison, in this case, is with weather-forecasting systems that need to sift through and analyze large amounts of data as well, collected at periodic intervals from many sensors, to identify weather patterns. Again, by most accounts, building such systems is not trivial. Similarly, network management applications that perform statistical analysis constitute number-crunching applications that must be highly efficient in dealing with large amounts of data and applying complex algorithms for statistical analysis on top of that.

Scale

Parents of young children should be able to relate to the following scenario: Try babysitting a toddler for a few hours. When she is hungry, she requires something to eat; you should make sure she drinks enough so she doesn't get dehydrated; perhaps she needs her diaper changed once in a while and a little entertainment to keep her occupied, so you read her a story and offer her some Legos. Doable. Now imagine a toddler birthday, with 20 toddlers and no one there to help you, and things become a little more challenging. While you are changing one child's diaper, another cries that he is hungry, two are fighting over a toy, and you see from the corner of your eye that someone is just about to fall off the sofa and bang his head. Now imagine a football stadium full of toddlers, with you alone in charge. You'll have to start thinking about how to organize things a little differently. The point is, scale matters.

The functionality that a management system provides might not involve rocket science in many cases. However, to be able to build the system so that it doesn't break down as you have to support networks of a very large scale, often much larger than originally anticipated, requires careful architecting and rigorous design discipline. A system that can support a network with a few hundred network elements and a few thousand end users is one thing, but to support tens of thousands of network elements and millions of subscribers, a system might have to be built very differently from the ground up, even if the functionality that the system provides is the same. What it takes to develop a system that can successfully support very large scales is often underestimated. Scale doesn't happen randomly as a byproduct; it must be taken into account at every stage of design and must be specifically architected for.

It must be emphasized that, in general, dealing with scale in applications is a software problem, impacting how the system must be built. It is not a hardware problem, per se. Although it is true that servers are becoming more powerful, relying on increasing hardware performance alone to increase network management system scale is a serious pitfall: For starters, the bottleneck of the system might not lie in CPU power or even disk I/O. More important, as hardware power doubles, network size and complexity are likely to more than double, making Moore's law of doubling CPU price/performance every 18 to 24 months possibly work *against* network management applications, not for them (see Figure 1-11).

Figure 1-11   *Network Management Scale Crunch and Moore's Law*

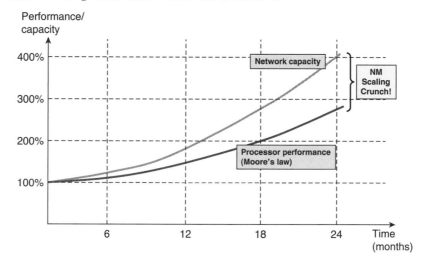

The following aspects need to be considered when designing network management applications for scale:

■ **Operations concurrency**—How to maximize concurrency in communications to network elements, to maximize management operations throughput. For example, instead of sending a request to a network element, waiting for the response, and then sending the next request to the next network element, it is preferable to send several requests to network elements at once, collecting the responses successively (see Figure 1-12). This way, the management application uses the time of the communication delay productively, and network elements can process requests by management applications concurrently instead of sequentially. As a result, more gets done over the same period of time.

Figure 1-12 *Impact of Operations Concurrency on Operations Throughput*

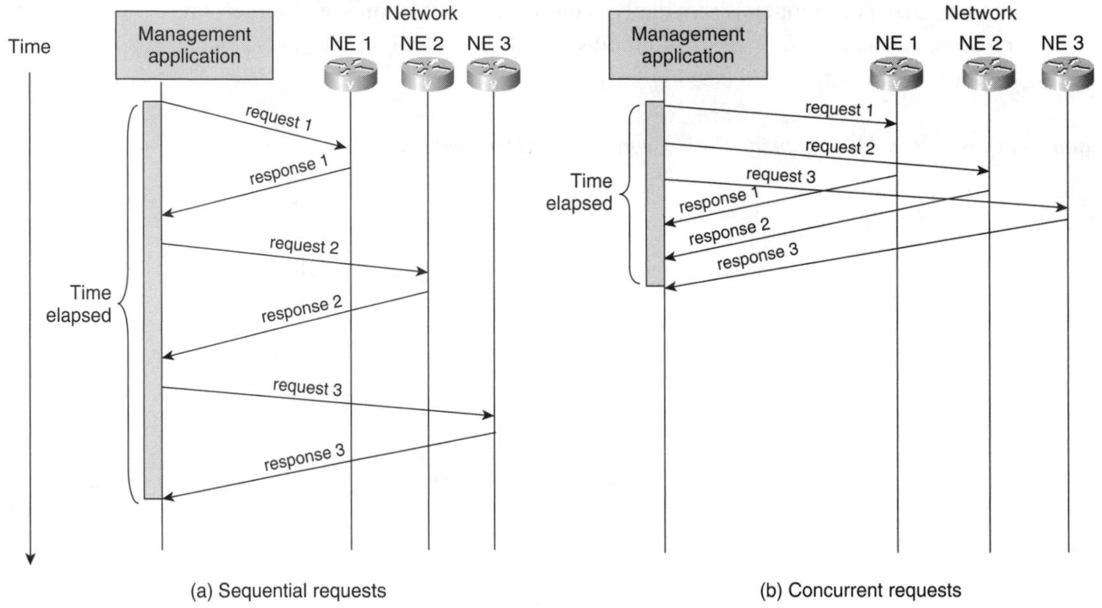

(a) Sequential requests   (b) Concurrent requests

- **Event propagation**—How to allow events to propagate efficiently to the system and update state. For example, when an event is received from the network, the management application needs to quickly identify where the event belongs (to which device, which card, which port), what its implication is (does the event call for intervention, or can it be ignored?), and what else might be affected (does the event mean that other devices are impacted, are communications interrupted, are customers experiencing a degradation in service?).

- **Scoping**—How to access and manipulate large chunks of management information efficiently and through single operations, without the need for tedious incremental operations (see Figure 1-13). Compare this to the analogy of network management and throwing a party—it scales much better to carry a tray with dishes between kitchen and guests instead of shuttling back and forth to carry every item individually.

Figure 1-13   *Impact of Bulk Operations on Management Efficiency*

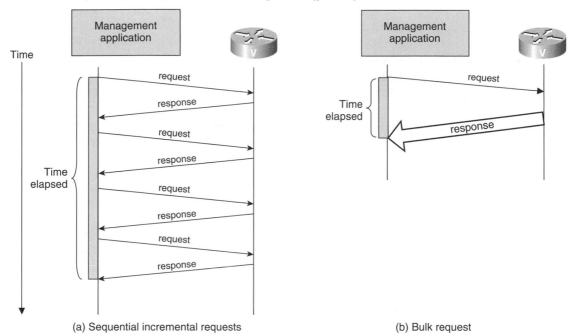

(a) Sequential incremental requests   (b) Bulk request

■ **Distribution and addressing**—How to allow processing to be distributed across different systems to allow the introduction of additional hardware horsepower when required, and how to provide for location transparency and efficient addressing to shield application logic from such distribution. Again using the party analogy, when you unexpectedly go beyond a certain number of guests, you would like to be able to increase your food preparation capacity. If you have only one caterer and one oven, you might be out of luck. To increase your cooking capacity, you would like to be able to add a new oven quickly and thus "distribute" the cooking across several ovens and pots and pans instead of having to upgrade to a larger oven and larger pots and pans, which, beyond a certain size, becomes impractical. Ideally, your caterer will be able to handle increased capacity accordingly. If you had to add a second caterer, it would require you to coordinate between them and keep track of which caterer is responsible for what, which you would rather not do. This means that you want to keep the fact transparent that distribution has even occurred.

One final word concerning how to measure scale: Most network management providers claim that their management applications are scalable. Statements such as "supports millions of objects" are often made. But what does that mean? Do those objects consist of a Boolean true/false flag, or do they represent entire devices in the network? Would they be synchronized with the network resources that they represent up to the minute or once per week? Does the application require a supercomputer to run on, or will a PC do? Clear metrics, such as those in the list that follows, are required. Of course, to be comparable, claims for scale must all be based on clearly defined hardware configuration and system load:

- Management operations throughput (per time unit, with stated assumptions on the nature of the operations, the number and complexity of parameters, and the number of network elements involved)

- Event throughput (per time unit, maximum throughput [a burst over a short period of time] and sustained, raw receipt of events; or including some kind of processing, again with a predefined scenario)

- Network synchronization capacity (for example, how many network elements an application can synchronize with—that is, retrieve information from—in a given unit of time)

As a side note, it should also be mentioned that, in addition to scale from a technical standpoint, service providers and enterprise IT departments expect a management system to realize economies of scale. This means that the incremental network management cost to introduce more capacity and network elements to the network should get smaller with the size of the deployment. On the flip side, not only large scale, but also small scale can be an issue. For instance, before going to large-scale network deployments, field trials of much smaller scale generally are conducted to verify the soundness of a network solution. For these scenarios, it is important that the cost of the management solution does not become prohibitive.

Cross-Section of Technologies

Building network management systems involves many different technical areas, each requiring its own specific subject matter expertise. Therefore, a firm grasp of a wide array of technologies is required to build effective nontrivial network management systems. This makes network management a technically demanding discipline because it requires a significant amount of breadth in technical expertise.

Let us take a look at some of the technologies that are typically used in network management.

Information Modeling

The centerpiece of any management application is how the application domain is modeled—that is, how network devices, cards, ports, connections, users, services, and dependencies and relationships among them are represented. The resulting models are abstractions of the real world that management algorithms and network managers have to operate on. Ideally, management applications are model driven to a certain extent. This makes them easier to extend and maintain, which is very important, given the constant technical evolution of networks and services that need to be managed.

Successful information modeling requires expertise with object-oriented analysis and design techniques and methodologies, such as the Unified Modeling Language (UML). To avoid reinventing the wheel, it is helpful to be familiar with the many models that industry consortia and standards bodies have previously defined so that they can be leveraged. Perhaps most important are good modeling heuristics and plain common modeling sense. Modeling, like design, is a creative activity. Often there is no objective "right" or "wrong" way to model, but models surely differ in how adequate they are for a particular problem domain, affecting greatly how effective, at what cost, management applications ultimately are. This requires good technical judgment and a good sense for design trade-offs.

Databases

Management systems typically require persistent storage. For instance, they need to store configuration information with which to provision the network and services. Often they also cache information from the network. This way, they avoid needing to query the network element each time someone asks for it, which improves management application performance and scalability. In many cases, management applications also need to store information that augments the information from the network with application-specific data that is not of interest to (and, therefore, not kept in) lower-level systems and network devices, such as customer information.

Of course, management systems generally use and leverage existing database management systems instead of developing their own custom ones. In addition, modern development tools shield applications developers to a certain degree from database intricacies. However, aspects such as performance tuning (disk I/O frequently is a bottleneck) and efficient mapping of information models that are often object oriented into databases that are usually relational (rather than object oriented) still require familiarity with database technology.

Distributed Systems

By definition, management applications are distributed applications because they involve systems that manage and systems that are being managed. In addition to that, to meet requirements for scale as well as requirements for reliability and availability, it is often required to allow the managing system to be distributed itself. For instance, if a server runs out of horsepower to support a network of a given size, it is desirable for additional hosts to be added to increase management capacity. Likewise, reliability and availability requirements often extend from the network to the management systems, requiring a capability to fail over between systems, resulting in graceful degradation instead of a sudden failure of management capabilities. Maintenance requirements might require that individual systems be taken out of service, allowing others to take over their management duties. Similar requirements exist for the support of global management operations that follow the sun, shifting the main management load, for instance, among operations centers in Los Angeles, California; Barcelona, Spain; and Bangalore, India.

None of these requirements can be addressed simply through hardware. For instance, a reliable server does not protect against outage resulting from, say, flooding of the building it is located in or a terrorist attack. Likewise, there is typically a limit to what scale can be addressed simply by using larger servers. Instead, these issues need to be addressed through software. Therefore, many management applications need to be architected as distributed software systems that can distribute and reassign processing load between servers that can be geographically distributed.

Communication Protocols

By definition, management applications communicate with other systems—the network elements they manage, as well as possibly other management applications. At least as far as network elements are involved, this communication occurs using management protocols. Management protocols define the rules by which the systems that are involved in management communicate with each other. The technical properties of those communication mechanisms and their impact need to be well understood because they can have a profound influence on how management applications should be built. For example, is communication reliable, or can pieces of information get lost? How are pieces of information in the device identified and retrieved? What information throughput can be achieved? As with other networking applications, communications trade-offs need to be well understood to arrive at a sound overall system design.

For example, an event-oriented communication paradigm in which the management application can rely on the network element to inform it of any relevant events and changes in the network has an impact on the required complexity of network elements. In this case, network elements have to be capable of storing and retransmitting events in case they cannot be sent at the moment, they are lost, or their receipt not confirmed. This is considerably harder than having the network element merely try to send an event and then allow it to forget about the event, not knowing or caring whether it ever reached its destination. On the other hand, if a management application cannot rely on being automatically informed by network devices when something important happens, it must poll the device whenever it needs information about the network and find out by itself what, if anything, has changed. This results in higher management communications overhead and has implications on the management application's capability to scale—after all, in many cases, nothing will have changed, meaning that much of the communication is wasted.

User Interfaces

Last in this list, but not least, human factors need to be considered. Networks can be of enormous scale and complexity. Hence, vast amounts of management information need to be visualized and navigated in an efficient manner. Consideration must be given to how to make operators efficient in performing their tasks: The user interface needs to make the operator productive, as measured, for instance, in terms of the number of operations performed per time unit or the number of network elements that a single operator can safely monitor, while preventing operational errors. In addition to human factors, there is the technical aspect that the user interface back end on a server must scale well. In many cases, hundreds of operators need to be supported simultaneously, requiring large amounts of information to be exchanged between server and user interface clients, to keep information that is displayed to operators up-to-date.

Figure 1-14 depicts a typical screenshot for a network management application GUI. The network and its topology are depicted on a map, with icons color-coded to immediately give an overview of the overall health of the network. Different ways to navigate the map and zoom into different portions are provided, including a listing of what's in the network that follows a file explorer metaphor. Tabs are used to switch between tasks, and subscreens provide the user with the most recent noteworthy events in the network or the status of management tasks that were recently issued.

Figure 1-14   *A Typical Screenshot of a Network Management Application*

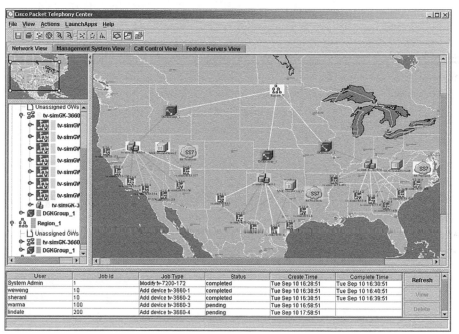

Other Considerations

In addition to the technologies that are required to build a management system, a good understanding of the managed technology itself is required—that is, of the managed network and services. Specifically, an understanding of what aspects are unique about the network and services that need to be managed is required, along with an understanding of what aspects are fairly generic and might be common to other managed technologies. For example, management of a voice network and management of an optical transport network have many aspects in common—for example, topologies need to be displayed on a map, devices must be monitored for alarms, and inventory must be tracked. Other aspects are completely different—for example, the voice network requires management of the dial plan that allows voice calls to be directed to their destination according to the phone number dialed, whereas management of the optical network might involve managing how optical links that carry different wavelengths of light can be cross-connected.

Finally, an understanding and appreciation of the network provider's workflow are required, along with how the management system fits in with the overall operational structure—what the management system is intended for in the first place. A thorough understanding of the system's purpose and how it fits in with the larger context of overall network operations is of tremendous value because it facilitates prioritization between requirements and provides guidance when trade-offs between certain system aspects are required.

Integration

One of the major themes in network management concerns integration. We already hinted at the fact that different applications can be used to monitor a network and to provision services over a network. Likewise, a network probably contains equipment from different vendors, each of which may come with its own set of management software. This leads to an undesirable situation in which the organization running a network must deal with many different applications, as Figure 1-15 depicts. Users need to be trained on all of these applications, and shifting between different tasks might be awkward because the user must switch back and forth between different applications. Often this leads to the so-called swivel-chair syndrome, named after an operator who sits in a swivel chair to move more easily between different terminals, each providing access to a different application. Of course, we don't even want to mention the task of having to administer all the different hosts to support the different applications, each running its own different operating system and database version.

Figure 1-15 *Many Different Applications to Manage a Network*

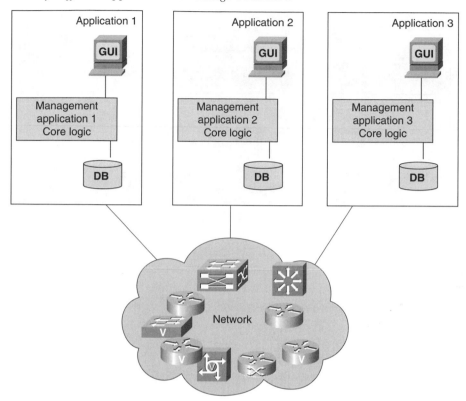

This situation leads to the demand for integration—that is, the requirement to make all the various applications and systems needed to manage a network work together as if they were one "system"—resulting in a seamlessly integrated operations support infrastructure, as shown in Figure 1-16. Probably one of the biggest complaints that network management providers hear is that the technical solution offered to manage a network is not "integrated" enough. This is a requirement that is very easy to state but that can be very hard to meet; in fact, it is one of the most important reasons why network management can be hard. The need for integration is one reason why standardization is an important topic in network management. Much of the standardization work—for example, standardization of the information that must be exchanged between systems—aims at making integration between different systems easier.

Figure 1-16 *Management Integration—System View*

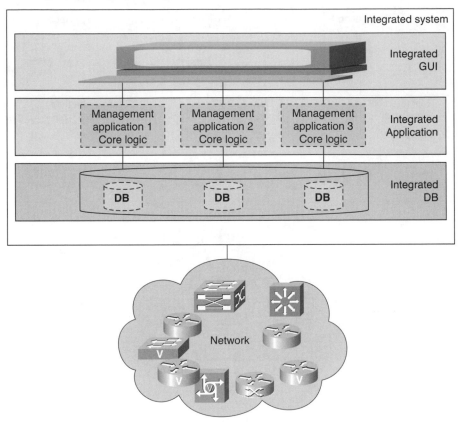

We do not dive deeper into this topic here. Instead, an entire chapter later in the book is dedicated to this topic (see Chapter 10, "Management Integration: Putting the Pieces Together").

Organization and Operations Challenges

Small networks, such as those deployed by small businesses, might be run by a single person or network administrator as a part-time job. In those cases, how to run the network isn't much of an organizational issue: The network administrator is in charge, and if problems arise that the network administrator cannot solve (or if the network administrator is out sick), customer support by a third party, by the equipment vendor, or by a consultant is only a phone call away. In addition, many communication services such as web hosting or voice services are simply purchased from an outside service provider.

However, running larger networks is different. As outlined in the previous section on technical challenges, scale matters. Also, larger networks might incorporate a much larger variety of different types of equipment and network technologies, making it a lot more difficult to find the combined expertise to deal with running a network all in a single person. Additional dimensions of running the network begin to appear: Help desks have to be introduced. Network technicians need to be dispatched to the field to deploy equipment. Billing disputes need to be resolved.

This indicates that management tools and technology are just one aspect of network management. Running a large network is in many ways an organizational task, truly a management task in the more general sense of the word. Running a network has a lot in common with running any other business and shares many of the same challenges. It is not unlike running a railroad, running a production line, or running a catering business. Although general principles of business administration are outside the scope of this book—this is, after all, a book on network management technology—you should keep in mind that there is an entire other dimension that is an important part of successfully running a large network as well.

In the following section, we point out just a few of the organizational aspects that need to be addressed when running a large network.

Functional Division of Tasks

Question: How do you swallow an elephant? Answer: One little piece at a time. The way to deal with a task of significant complexity is to divide it up into smaller parts. Already the Romans knew *divide et impera.* (Divide and rule.) When you can get your hands around each of the subtasks, you have a good handle on the entire problem. In some cases, of course, the subtasks still need to be divided up further, but you get the idea.

Now there remains only one little detail: *how* to divide the task of running a network. There is no single way to do it, and different organizations find different answers to which way works best for them. However, it is important to keep in mind the different functions that need to be performed and be accounted for. (We dive into this particular aspect in Chapter 5, "Management Functions and Reference Models: Getting Organized.") Identifying what those functions are and organizing around them is a useful first step in identifying a proper division of tasks. An important additional aspect concerns identifying the interdependencies between these functions. The interdependencies determine how different roles and functions need to interact and coordinate, and what interfaces between them are required. Clear interfaces, clear ownership of tasks, and minimization of interdependencies are hallmarks of many successful organizations, and organizations that run networks are no different.

Typical functions and tasks to consider include the following:

- Network planning, for example to determine network topology, dimension nodes and links, and plan for proper network rollout

- Network deployment, to install and commission equipment into the network

- Network operations, to monitor the network for any problems, failures, and issues with performance

- Network maintenance and maintenance planning, to perform equipment and software upgrades, provision services, and tune network parameters

- Workforce management and truck dispatching, to manage maintenance and deployment personnel, which might need to visit remote sites when performing tasks remotely is not possible

- Inventory management, to keep track of what is and what should be in the network, and to maintain spare equipment

- Order management, to take orders for services from customers, dispatch requests to get the services provisioned, and track their execution

- Customer help desk, to provide a front end to customers and provide level 1 support—that is, take calls from customers, answer simpler questions, and, if needed, direct customers to the proper contact for help

- Billing, and billing dispute resolution, to charge customers and collect revenue (very important if you are a service provider because ultimately this pays your bills)

Geographical Distribution

Large networks can be geographically distributed around the globe, along with their users. The network must be managed and users supported globally and around the clock. Often this occurs in follow-the-sun fashion. This means that operational responsibilities get handed off at the end of an 8-hour workday from a network operations center in Europe to a center on the U.S. West Coast, then to Asia, and then back to Europe. The organization itself also must be equipped to handle such rotating responsibilities for different tasks.

Operational Procedures and Contingency Planning

A network provider needs to ensure that the network is managed in an orderly fashion and must stay in control of the functions that keep the network running at all times. To this end, introducing comprehensive and consistent operational procedures and guidelines and documenting is an important tool. This establishes a process that helps ensure that activities can be tracked in an orderly fashion and that tasks do not fall through the cracks. Examples include ensuring that issues that require responses to customers are not lost and that, for example, equipment configurations are not changed without anyone knowing, which might cause problems later. Documented guidelines ensure a consistent way of dealing with network management tasks and problems, which facilitates a certain level of quality in network operations. Accordingly, these are an important prerequisite to be able to certify quality (think of process quality standards such as the ISO 9000 suite of standards) of network operations.

Part of the operational procedures should deal with contingency planning. What should be done in case of a virus outbreak inside the network or if the network is under a denial-of-service attack? Planning for these types of contingencies and establishing action plans beforehand is an important factor in being able to deal with them successfully and swiftly if they occur.

In a similar way, operational procedures need to be designed to establish a system of checks and balances. For example, authorizations of who is allowed to perform what task need to be carefully managed. This also helps limit vulnerability to sabotage from the inside. Given that people in a network operations organization have access to the network in a way that hackers can only dream about, this is a reasonable consideration in this age of security concerns.

Business Challenges

Technical and organizational network management challenges are there to be conquered. As in most other areas, when the business proposition is sufficiently clear and there is lots of money to be made, the motivation and commitment to overcome those hurdles will become high enough that good solutions eventually follow. However, there are also aspects in the business environment that make network management and, specifically, the development of network management applications, challenging. This is especially the case when application functionality is closely tied to the network equipment instead of, for instance, service management.

Of course, network management encompasses a broad range of functionality. It encompasses management of individual network elements as well as management of business processes surrounding the operations of the enterprise providing network services as a whole. The business proposition for providing management support depends to a large degree on the particular management function. Challenges vary in terms of which aspect of the network management value chain is addressed by a network management application, a targeted market segment, and so on.

In the following subsections, we take a look at some of the more common business challenges. The challenges presented do not constitute a comprehensive list, but they point out some areas that need consideration.

Placing a Value on Network Management

Although network management is vitally important, there is also a flip side: Network management costs money. The amount of investment in network management must be justified, and this ultimately is a business decision. It must be justified by expected cost savings or increased revenues. Ideally, the value proposition must be quantifiable in dollars. Return-on-investment models for network management are needed. Unfortunately, such models can be hard to come by.

In general, service providers expect that no more than a certain fraction of a networking investment should go into network management; as much as 90 percent might go into the equipment itself, and 10 percent into the operations support infrastructure—almost a 10-to-1 ratio. (This includes management of both network and services; the ratio can be even more pronounced for the portion of the infrastructure that manages just the equipment itself.) In many cases, this does not reflect the actual cost structure of network equipment development and management system development, nor the value proposition that network management offers to service providers:

- To an equipment vendor, the development of network management capabilities might cost more than the 10-to-1 ratio indicates. (Of course, unlike equipment, the incremental cost of goods sold is marginal for management software.) This means that, in terms of direct revenue opportunity, it can be more difficult to recoup investment in management application development than investment in networking feature development. Of course, there are other benefits of providing good management support, but they are less tangible and more difficult to measure.

- On the other hand, the operational cost of a service provider might actually exceed the cost for amortization of the equipment. It is often a lot higher than a 10 percent ratio of investment in network management might indicate. This means that limited gains in operational efficiency translate into disproportional gains in terms of overall cost. Statements such as this are not unheard: "As much as 25 percent of the workforce of typical large service providers could be redeployed if it were not for the inefficient operational support provided by the available management solutions." On top of that, in many cases, it is difficult to obtain personnel with the required skills, making the lack of effective management applications a bottleneck to the overall business, thereby implying additional cost from lost opportunity.

So where does the discrepancy come from that leads to a lower business valuation of network management than might be expected? One can speculate about the reason, but some of the discrepancy probably has to do with the fact that it is apparently difficult to quantify the actual value that a management system provides. This is particularly true for many of the "soft" properties of a management system, such as scalability and reliability. Scalability and reliability are the types of properties that can significantly increase technical complexity and, thereby, development cost, as much as an order of magnitude. At the same time, those properties can dramatically drive down a service provider's operational cost. However, unlike with networks in which one might apply measures such as a cost per bit or cost per port, the value of a particular management system and the properties that it offers are often hard to assess and to prove in a quantifiable manner.

Network providers are thus understandably hesitant to pay a premium. In turn, vendors can find network management investments hard to recuperate and, hence, to justify. This is particularly true for investments in premium features that would have to result in a premium price tag, when in many cases people have difficulty understanding and appreciating even the difference between a simple device viewer and a complex operations support system.

The difficulty of accurately quantifying network management's value proposition can hence lead to significant business challenges. We revisit this topic in Chapter 12.

Feature vs. Product

Traditionally, network equipment vendors have been interested primarily in one thing: selling iron. This is what drives their revenues, profits, and, ultimately, their valuation as a company. Of course, other aspects generate revenue and profits for them, such as services. However, at the end of the day, the success of the vendor comes down to how well the network equipment products do in the marketplace.

Of course, to drive the vendor's business, it is not sufficient to develop world-class network equipment alone. Other aspects have to be offered as well to keep customers satisfied and coming back, such as services, training, and network management. This means that the motivation for network management is, in many cases, not only to make it a self-sustaining business in its own right, but, just as important, to have it serve as a business enabler for the core business. In many cases, it is difficult to sell network equipment by itself. The customer expectation is to get a complete system, which includes network management capabilities offered with it. In that sense, it is easy to view the network management system as a "feature" of the equipment. Of course, network management applications should still generate profit, but this is not the only reason for making a network management–related investment in the first place.

The most tangible business case is still rooted in the revenue contribution made by network management products. However, when viewing network management applications from the perspective of being an enabler of equipment sales, the challenge concerns how to determine the "right" level of investment. Two possible perspectives exist: The first perspective views the development of network management capabilities merely as a cost factor for those other products. Under this perspective, clearly the investment in management applications must be kept to the minimum that is necessary to keep the customer just happy enough to not break the deal. The goal, in that case, is to keep cost as low as possible because additional cost is viewed as simply reducing overall profitability. The business challenge here lies in finding the sweet spot at which investment in network management is just enough to not jeopardize equipment sales.

The second perspective is to recognize network management as a positive competitive differentiator. This changes the business proposition somewhat because development of network management capabilities shifts from being a cost factor to being a revenue enabler. The business challenge in that case lies in being able to articulate the corresponding business case because network management's true business benefit and impact on the bottom line can be intangible and difficult to assess.

Uneven Competitive Landscape

When network equipment vendors offer management applications that are less than perfect, network providers could end up with operational inefficiencies. In general, this should provide an excellent business opportunity for other companies to step in. In most cases, network equipment vendors welcome third-party management vendors who offer network management applications for the equipment vendor's products, and even encourage them to do so: Network management is not the equipment vendor's core product offering, so a competing network management offering is considered less threatening. On the contrary, a third-party offering can help the equipment vendor's customers better leverage their investment and thus buy more equipment. Network providers, on the other hand, gain additional advantages that an independent network management offering might provide, such as support for network equipment from multiple vendors that equipment vendors themselves might not provide. The result can be a win-win situation for everybody.

One business challenge for the management vendor arises from the fact that, in many cases, the equipment vendor will still be pressed to have its own network management offering, for several reasons: to avoid being too dependent on third-party vendors, to avoid having to disclose information on planned products when they are still confidential, or to ensure that a management offering will be available in time when the network equipment is brought to market instead of six months later. As a result, the business proposition for an independent management vendor is often not as attractive as it might otherwise be, for several reasons. Those reasons have to do with the fact that the competitive landscape can be a bit uneven:

- **Timing**—Ideally, a management application should be ready to go to market at the same time as the network equipment that it manages. However, a third-party management vendor tends to lag behind the equipment vendor in offering device support. The equipment vendor often cannot share development plans with an outside company until those plans mature, unlike an internal division developing management applications, which might be cued in from the very beginning. This makes it less likely that the management vendor will be ready when the equipment vendor is ready to deploy. Also, the management vendor might want to wait until it is reasonably sure that the equipment vendor's product will indeed be successful in the marketplace to justify the investment that is required to develop management support for it.

The management vendor cannot afford to chase every lead; it has to use development resources economically, at the risk of coming somewhat late to market. Of course, this means that the first customers of network equipment have to select the equipment vendor's management offering because of a lack of alternatives. As a consequence, they will get accustomed to it even if it has shortcomings and will invest in aspects such as training and even systems integration. By the time a management vendor's product finally goes to market, it might already be too late because network providers will not be willing to switch easily from the system they already have. When an application is deployed in the field, even if it has weaknesses, it becomes very hard to replace it. This results in a high business hurdle for a third-party management vendor to overcome.

- **Economics**—As discussed previously, to the equipment vendor, management software in many cases constitutes a feature of an overall system that also includes the networking equipment. From that perspective, as long as the system as a whole makes a profit, things are fine. The situation is different for a management vendor that considers management software not a part of a larger system, but an independent (and perhaps only) product. The management vendor therefore must generate a profit from the network management application alone to stay in business. Of course, to be competitive, the management vendor's product should provide additional value that sometimes can be more difficult for the equipment vendor to provide, such as support for multiple vendors.

- **Customer expectation**—Customers of network equipment rightfully expect economies of scale. As far as network management is concerned, this means that the incremental cost of management support for the 10,000th network element should be less than the incremental cost for the first. The equipment vendor, on the other hand, will still be able to charge substantially for the 10,000th piece of equipment. Hence, the equipment vendor that views network management as an extended equipment feature can amortize the network management development cost over a substantial volume of networking equipment—a possibility that the third-party management vendor does not enjoy.

All said, the result is a business environment in which it can be fairly hard to make money, particularly when management applications are closely tied to the actual network equipment. This is somewhat paradoxical because management is such an important factor in decreasing cost and increasing revenue, as discussed earlier.

However, the situation is different for management software that is more removed from and less dependent on the network equipment itself. This includes management software that ties together business processes or, for example, billing software. Those are the areas where the playing field shifts more in favor of the management vendor.

Chapter Summary

In this chapter, to set the stage for the remainder of the book, we provided a brief overview of network management. Network management refers to the activities, methods, procedures, and tools that pertain to the operation, administration, maintenance, and provisioning of networked systems. In other words, network management is about running and monitoring networks. Many analogies can be drawn between network management and other areas where complex systems are monitored or where complex operations are run. We discussed the analogy of monitoring the health of a human body, but we could also have used examples involving monitoring nuclear power plants or airplanes in flight. Likewise, we used the example of running a party as an analogy for running a network but could have used other examples as well, such as running operations at an airline or a factory.

Network management should not be just an afterthought to the network itself. Network management plays a significant role in saving cost, making operation of a network more efficient, and ensuring effective use of resources in the network. It is also vital to service providers in generating revenue—for example, by allowing new services to be rolled out more quickly. In addition, it plays an important role in preventing network outages and, if they occur, keeping their duration to a minimum and limiting their effect.

Different players have an interest in network management for different reasons, and therefore approach it from slightly different angles. There are users of network management, particularly service providers and enterprise IT departments that run networks for a living. Some subtle differences exist in their perspective on network management: For service providers, the focus is on maximizing profits; for enterprise IT departments, it is generally on minimizing cost (of course, while maximizing benefit of network ownership). Then there are providers of network management. Equipment vendors provide network management capabilities to enable and complement their communications equipment business, whereas management vendors build best-of-breed systems for particular management functions that equipment vendors do not address, or that they do not address in the vendor- and technology-neutral fashion required by organizations that run networks. In addition, system integrators provide custom-tailored integration of a multitude of otherwise independent applications and network equipment technologies.

Finally, we provided an overview of important challenges that are often faced in conjunction with network management. Many of those challenges are of a technical nature and relate to the fact that management applications tend to be complex systems with stringent requirements in terms of scale, robustness, extensibility, and maintainability. Other challenges are of an organizational nature, including how to best divide the day-to-day operations of running a network, and of a business nature, involving how to create a business environment in which the development of network management capabilities can flourish. To be sensitized to those challenges is often the first step in dealing with them successfully.

Chapter Review

1. Explain the term *network management* in one sentence.

2. We used a patient in intensive care as one analogy to explain network management. Can you think of areas in network management that this analogy does not capture?

3. Can you think of other areas in which you would expect analogies to network management to apply?

4. Give two examples of how network management can help an enterprise IT department save money.

5. Give two examples of how network management can help a service provider increase revenue.

6. A famous requirement for availability is "five nines." This refers to the requirement that a device or a service must be available 99.999 percent of the time. Assume that you have a device with hardware availability of 99.9995 percent. Now assume that an operational error is made that causes the device to go offline for 5 minutes until the error is corrected. Calculated over a period of a month, how much has the operational error just caused availability to drop?

7. How does the perspective under which network management is approached often differ for an enterprise IT department compared to a service provider?

8. Name at least two factors that can be important to the business success of a third-party management application vendor that potentially has to compete with a network management offering of a network equipment vendor.

9. What does the term *swivel-chair syndrome* refer to, and why is this undesired?

10. Name two or more reasons for network management applications to be approached as distributed systems.

CHAPTER 2

On the Job with a Network Manager

This chapter presents a number of scenarios to give an impression of the types of activities that are performed by people who run networks for a living. We refer to them collectively as network managers, although they perform a wide variety of functions that have more specialized job titles. In fact, strangely enough, the term *network manager* is rarely used for the people involved in managing networks. Instead, terms such as *network operator, network administrator, network planner, craft technician,* and *help desk representative* are much more common. Each of those terms refers to a more special function that is only one aspect of network management.

The chapter also provides an overview of some of the tools network managers have at their disposal to help them do their jobs. The intention is to give you a taste of the kinds of tasks and challenges that network managers face and how network management tools support their work.

Ultimately, the network management technology introduced in this book exists in an operational context. Although this idea might seem self-evident, it must be understood and emphasized, particularly for people who are not themselves users but are providers of network management technology—application providers, equipment vendors, and systems integrators. Network management involves not just technology, but also a human dimension—how people use management tools and management technology to achieve a given purpose, and how people who perform management functions and who are ultimately responsible for the fact that networks and networking services are running smoothly can best be supported. In addition, the organizational dimension must be considered—how the tasks and workflows are organized, how people involved in managing a network work together, and what procedures they have in place and must follow to collectively get the job done.

Reading this chapter will help you understand the following:

- The types of tasks that people involved in the day-to-day operations of networks face

- How network management technology supports network operators in those tasks

- The different types of management tools that are available to help people running a network do their job

A Day in the Life of a Network Manager

Let us consider some typical scenarios people face as they run networks. No single scenario is representative by itself. Scenarios differ widely depending on a number of factors. One factor is the type of organization that runs the network. We refer to this organization as the *network provider*. The IT department of a small business, for example, runs its network quite differently than the IT department of a global enterprise or, for that matter, a global telecommunications service provider. Another factor is the particular function that the network manager plays within the organization. An administrator in an IT department, for example, has different responsibilities than a field technician or a customer-facing service representative. To cover the diversity of possible scenarios, this chapter examines the roles of several network managers.

The examples in this chapter are intended to be illustrative. Therefore, they are by no means comprehensive. The examples contain simplifications, and, in reality, the details described differ widely among network providers. Even people who have the same job description might perform their job functions in different ways. Ultimately, how they manage their networks differentiates network providers from one another, hence the presented scenarios should not be expected to be universally the same. Finally, don't worry if you are not familiar with all the networking details that are contained in the examples; they constitute merely the backdrop against which the storylines play out.

Pat: A Network Operator for a Global Service Provider

Meet Pat. Pat works as a network operator at the *Network Operations Center* (NOC) of a global service provider that we shall call GSP. She and her group are responsible for monitoring both the global backbone network and the access network, which, in essence, constitutes the customer on-ramp to GSP's network. This is a big responsibility. Several terabytes of data move over GSP's backbone daily, connecting several million end customers as well as a significant percentage of global Fortune 500 companies. Even with the recent crisis in the telecommunications industry, GSP is a multibillion-dollar business whose reputation rests in no small part on its capability to provide services on a large scale and global basis with 99.999% (often referred to as "five nines") service availability. Any disruption to this service could have huge economic implications, leading to revenue losses of millions of dollars, exposing GSP to penalties and liability claims, and putting jobs in jeopardy.

Pat works directly in command central in a large room with big maps of the world on screens in front, showing the main sites of the network. Figure 2-1 depicts such a command central.

Figure 2-1 *An Example of a Command Central Inside a NOC*

(Figure used with kind permission from ish GmbH&Co KG)

In addition to the big maps, several screens display various pieces of information. For example, they show statistics on network utilization, information about current delays and service levels experienced by the network's users, and the number of problems that have been reported in different geographic areas. This gives everybody in the room a good overall sense of what is currently going on—whether things are in crises mode or whether everything is running smoothly.

Normally, everything on the map appears green. This means that everything is operational and that utilization on the network is such that even if an outage in part of the network were to occur, network traffic could be rerouted instantly without anyone experiencing a service outage. The network is designed to withstand outages and disruptions in any one part of the network. However, Pat still remembers the anxiety that set in on a couple occasions when suddenly links or even entire nodes on the map turned yellow or red. Once, for example, a construction crew dug through one of the main fiber lines that connect two of GSP's main hubs. And who could forget 9/11, when suddenly millions of people wanted to call into New York at the same time, while at the same time seemingly every news organization in the world requested additional capacity for their video feeds?

On Pat's desk is an additional, smaller screen that shows a list of problems that have been reported about the network. Pat has been assigned to monitor a region of the southeastern United States for any problems and impending signs of trouble. Pat sees on her screen a list of so-called *trouble tickets,* which represent currently known problems in the network and are used to track their resolution.

Those trouble tickets have two sources: problems that customers have reported and problems in the network itself. Let's start with customer-reported problems.

For every call that is received from a customer about a network problem, one of the customer service representatives at the help desk in building 7 opens a trouble ticket. The rep provides what GSP refers to as "tier 1 support." Those service reps have their own procedures. The person who first answers the call records a description of the problem, according to the customer, and asks the customer a series of questions, depending on the type of problem reported. If the service rep cannot help the customer right away, the customer is transferred to someone who is more experienced in troubleshooting the problem. That person is part of the second support tier. If this more experienced rep cannot solve the problem, or if it takes him or her too long to do so, the ticket is assigned to the people in Pat's group and shows up on Pat's screen. Pat's group provides the third tier of support.

The tickets contain a description of the problem, who is affected, and contact information. At least, this is what they are supposed to contain; sometimes Pat's group gets tickets with little or no information. In those cases, someone from Pat's group must call the service rep who first entered the ticket and find out more, which is always painful for everyone involved. It can be embarrassing when, in the worst case, Pat's co-workers need to call the customer back and the customer realizes that GSP is only starting to follow up on a serious problem hours after it was reported.

The second source of tickets is the network itself. These tickets are reported by systems that monitor alarm messages sent from equipment in the network. The problem with alarm messages is that they rarely indicate the root cause of the problem; in most cases, they merely reflect a symptom that could be caused by any number of things. Pat doesn't see every single alarm in the network—that would be far too many. For this reason, the alarm monitoring system tries to pre-correlate and group alarm messages that seem to point to the same underlying problem. For each unique problem that alarm messages seem to point to, the alarm monitoring system automatically opens a ticket and attaches the various alarm messages to it, along with an automated diagnosis and even a recommended repair action. Ideally, the underlying problem can be corrected and the ticket closed before customers notice service degradation and corresponding customer-reported trouble tickets are opened.

Seeing messages grouped in this way is much more practical than having to deal with every single alarm individually. The sheer volume of alarms would quickly overwhelm Pat and her group. Also, tickets that are system generated are typically issued against the particular piece of equipment in the network that seems to be in distress. This makes system-generated tickets a little easier to deal with than customer-generated tickets, which often leave Pat's group feeling puzzled over where to start.

Pat remembers that tickets generated by alarm applications were problematic in the past. Often many more trouble tickets were generated than there were actual problems, so Pat sometimes saw 20 tickets that all related to the same problem. However, GSP has made significant progress in recent years—system-generated trouble tickets have become pretty accurate, with redundant tickets generated only in a small portion of cases. GSP's investment in developing better correlation rules for their systems paid off. Although Pat is an operator, not a developer, she knows that she was an important part of the development process because she provided much of the expertise that was encoded into those correlation rules. She still remembers being interviewed by a group of consultants for that purpose. During numerous sessions over the span of several months, they asked about how she determined whether problems that were reported separately were related.

Of course, despite all the progress made, many tickets still relate to the same underlying root cause. Many of those are tickets that were not automatically generated but instead were opened by customers. Perhaps a particular component in the access network through which customers were all connected to the network has failed, causing all of them to report a problem.

When clicking on a trouble ticket, Pat can see all the information associated with it. Pat must first acknowledge that she has read each ticket that comes in. If she does not acknowledge the ticket, it is automatically escalated to her supervisor. In busy times, this feels almost like a video game: Whenever a new ticket appears on the screen, she effectively "shoots it down" to stop it from flashing. Of course, acknowledging is only the first step. Next, Pat must analyze the ticket information. For the most part, her tasks are fairly routine. First she checks whether there are other tickets that might relate to the same problem. If there are, she attaches a note to the ticket that points to the other ticket(s) already being worked on. The system is intelligent enough to update the information in the other ticket to cross-reference the new one, thereby providing additional information that could prove useful in resolving it. This effectively leads to a hierarchy of tickets in which the original ticket constitutes a master ticket and the new ticket becomes a subordinate to the master. Pat then tables the resolution of the subordinate ticket until the master ticket that is already being worked on is resolved. At that point, she revisits the ticket to see whether the problem still exists or whether it can be closed also.

If she does not identify an existing ticket that might be related, she starts diagnosing the root cause of the problem. Let us assume that, in this case, the ticket was opened by a customer. Pat brings up the service inventory system to check which pieces of equipment were specifically configured to help provide service for that customer. With this knowledge, she brings up the monitoring application for the portion of the network that is affected to see for herself what is going on. This application offers her a view with the graphical representation of the device from which she can see the current state of the device, how its parameter settings have been configured, and the current communications activity at the device. She begins troubleshooting, starting with verifying the symptoms that are reported in the network.

In some cases, Pat eventually decides that a piece of equipment needs to be replaced, such as a card in a switch. In those cases, she brings up another tool, a work order system. She creates a new work order and specifies which card needs to be replaced. She enters the identifier of the trouble ticket as related information. This automatically populates the fields in the work order that identify the piece of network element, and also where it is located. Pat considers this to be a particularly nice feature. In the old days, she had to manually retype this information and also look up the precise location of the network element in the network inventory system. Now all those back-office systems are interconnected. She enters additional comments and submits the work order, and off it goes. This is all that she has to do for now.

It is not Pat's responsibility to dispatch a field technician or to check the inventory for spare parts; this is the job of her colleagues in the group that processes and follows up on equipment work orders. Actually, there are several groups, depending on where the equipment is located. Sometimes the equipment is in such a remote location that people have to physically get out there—"roll a truck," they call it. This is often the case for equipment in the access network. As mentioned earlier, the access network is the portion of the network that funnels network traffic from the customer sites to GSP's core network. In other cases—specifically, when the core network is affected—the equipment is at the NOC, in an adjacent building. Pat was once able to peek inside a room with all the equipment—many rows of rack-mounted equipment, similar to Figure 2-2.

Figure 2-2   *Rack-Mounted Network Equipment*

Pat's friends tell her that the NOC equipment is more compact than it is used to be, but Pat still finds it very impressive, especially the cables (cables are shown in Figure 2-3). Literally hundreds, if not thousands, of cables exist; taken together, they would surely stretch across many miles. You would never want to lose track of what each cable connects to. Although it all looks surprisingly neat, Pat can only imagine what a challenge it must be to move the NOC to a different location if that ever becomes necessary.

Figure 2-3 *Cabling and Equipment Backside*

(Figure used with kind permission from ish GmbH&Co KG)

Pat knows that the groups that do equipment work orders operate in similar fashion to her own group. The workflows are all predefined, and their work order system takes them through the necessary steps, autoescalates things when necessary, and generally makes sure that nothing can fall through the cracks—for example, it ensures that a work order does not sit unattended for days. It's impressive how integrated some of the procedures have become. For example, Pat has heard that when the technicians exchange a part, they scan it using a bar-code scanner that automatically updates the central inventory system. The system then warns them right away if they are scanning a different component than the one they are supposed to enter with the work order. In the past, occasional mismatches occurred between the equipment that was deployed and the equipment that was supposed to be there. This could lead to all kinds of problems—for example, equipment might be preconfigured in a certain way that would then no longer work as planned, or the installed equipment had different properties than expected. Those were rare but nasty scenarios to track and resolve.

Pat notes in the trouble ticket what she did and enters the identifier of the work order and when resolution is expected. For now, she is finished.

When the work order is fulfilled, Pat will find in her in-box a notification from the work order system identifying the trouble ticket that was linked to the work order and that should now be resolved. When she receives this notification, she does a quick sanity check to see if everything is up and running, and then closes the ticket for good.

When Pat first started her job, she was sometimes tempted to close the tickets right away without doing the check. Her department kept precise statistics on the number of tickets that she processed, the number of tickets that she had outstanding or was currently working on, the average duration of resolution for a ticket, and the number of tickets that had to be escalated. Of course, Pat wanted those numbers to look good because they were an indication of her productivity. Therefore, it was seemingly rewarding to take some shortcuts. It appeared that even in the unexpected case that a problem had not been resolved, someone would simply open a new ticket and no harm would be done. However, Pat soon learned that any such procedure violation would be taken extremely seriously. She now understands that procedures are essential for GSP to control quality of the services it provides. Doing things the proper way has therefore become second nature to her.

Chris: Network Administrator for a Medium-Size Business

Meet Chris. Together with a colleague who is currently on vacation, Chris is responsible for the computer and networking infrastructure of a retail chain, RC Stores, with a headquarters and 40 branch locations. RC Stores' network (see Figure 2-4) contains close to 100 routers: typically, an access router and a wireless router in the branch locations, and additional networking infrastructure in the headquarters and at the warehouse.

The company has turned to a managed service provider (MSP) to interconnect the various locations of its network. To this end, the MSP has set up a Virtual Private Network (VPN) with tunnels between the access routers at each site that connects all the branch locations and the headquarters. This means that the entire company's network can be managed as one network. Although the MSP worries about the interconnectivity among the branch offices, Chris and his colleagues are their points of contact. Also, the contract with the MSP does not cover how the network is being used within the company. This is the responsibility of Chris and his colleagues.

Figure 2-4   *RC Stores' Network*

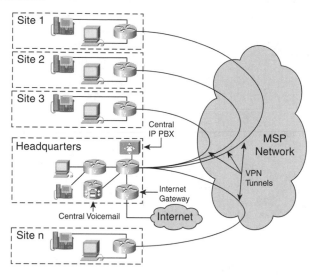

Chris has a workstation at his desk that runs a management platform. This is a general-purpose management application used to monitor the network. At the core of the application is a graphical view of the network that displays the network topology. Each router is represented as an icon on the screen that is green, yellow, orange, or red, depending on its alarm state. This color coding allows Chris to see at first glance whether everything is up and running.

Even though the network is of only moderate size, displaying the entire topology at the same time would leave the screen pretty cluttered. Chris has therefore built a small topology map in which multiple routers are grouped into "clusters" that are represented by another icon. Each cluster encompasses several locations. In addition, there is a cluster each for the headquarters and the warehouse. This configuration enables Chris to display only the clusters and thereby view the whole network at once. Chris can also expand ("zoom into") individual clusters when needed to see what each consists of. As with the icons of the routers, the icons for the clusters are colored corresponding to the most severe alarm state of what is contained within. This way, Chris does not miss a router problem, even though the router might be hidden deep inside a cluster on the map. As long as the cluster is green, Chris knows that everything within it is, too. Figure 2-5 shows an example of a typical screen for such a management application.

Figure 2-5 *A Typical Management Application Screen (Cisco Packet Telephony Center)*

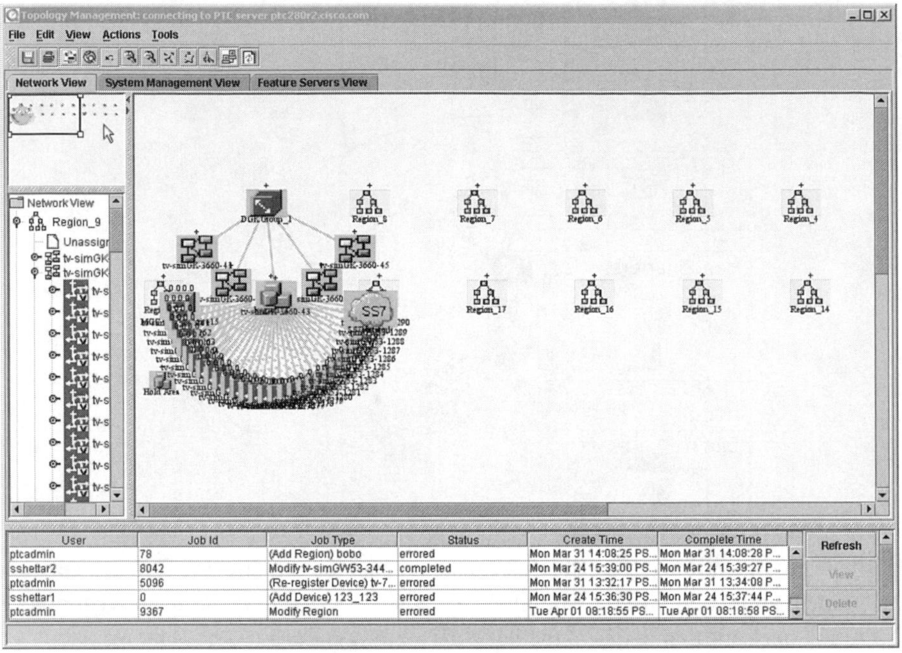

Mike calls from upstairs. Someone new is starting a job in finance tomorrow and will need a phone. Chris notes this in his to-do list. He will take care of this later. First, he is trying to get to the bottom of another problem.

Chris received some complaints from the folks at the Richmond branch that the performance of their network is a little sluggish. They have been experiencing this problem for a while now; they first complained about it ten days ago when access to the servers was slow. At the time, Chris wondered whether this was really a problem with the network or with the server. As an end user, there was really no way to tell the difference. Eventually, the problem went away by itself and Chris thought it might have been just a glitch. Then three days ago, the same thing happened, and it did this morning again. This time Chris tried accessing the server himself with the Richmond people on the call but did not notice anything unusual.

Chris thinks that perhaps it really is a problem with the network. He wonders whether the MSP really gives them the network performance that they have promised. The MSP sold Chris's company a service with 2 Mbps bandwidth from the branch locations and "three nines" (99.9%) availability from 6 am until 10 pm during weekdays, 98% during off hours. The people from the MSP did not contact Chris to indicate that there was a problem on the MSP's side, but maybe they don't know—and besides, why would they worry if they didn't get caught? Chris wonders whether he should have signed up for MSP's optional service that would have allowed him to view the current service statistics, as seen from the MSP's perspective, in near-real time over the web. Although Chris doesn't think the MSP can be entirely trusted, this would have provided an interesting additional data point.

From his management platform, Chris launches the device view for the router at the edge of the affected branch by clicking the icon of the topology map. The device view pops up in a window and contains a graphical representation of the device from which the current state, traffic statistics, and configuration parameter settings can be accessed. Currently, not much traffic appears to be going across the interface. From another window, Chris "pings" the router, checking the round-trip time of IP packets to the router. Everything looks fine.

Chris decides that this problem requires observation over a longer period of time, so he pulls up a tool that enables him to take periodic performance snapshots. He specifies that a snapshot should be taken every 5 minutes of the traffic statistics of the outgoing port. Chris also wants to periodically measure the network delay and jitter to the access router at company headquarters and to the main server. The tool logs the results into a file that he can import into a spreadsheet. Spreadsheets can be very useful because they can plot charts, which makes it easy to discover trends or aberrations in the plotted curves. (Of course, sometimes management applications support some statistical views as well, as shown in Figure 2-6.)

Figure 2-6   *Sample Screen of a Management Application with Performance Graphs (Cisco Works IP Performance Monitor)*

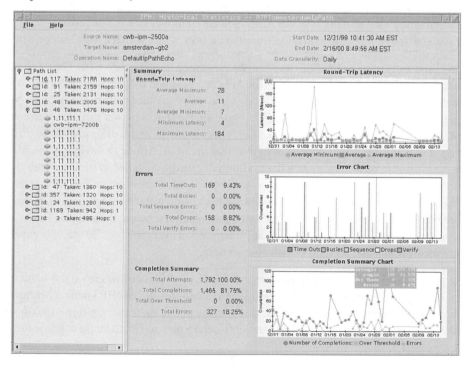

For now, that seems all that he can do. Chris takes a look at his to-do list and decides to take care of the request for the new phone. He doesn't know whether they have spare phones, so he goes to the storage room to check. One is left, good. He will have to remember to stock up and order a few more. He then peeks at the cheat sheet that he has printed and pinned in his cubicle, which has the instructions on what to do when connecting a new user. Most phones in RC Stores' branch locations are assigned not to individual users, but to a location, such as a cashier location, so changes do not need to be made very often.

RC Stores recently replaced its old analog private branch exchange (PBX) system with a new Voice over IP (VoIP) PBX. This enables the company to make internal phone calls over its data network. It also has a gateway at headquarters that enables employees to make calls to the outside world over a classical phone network, when needed. Chris remembers that, to make phone calls, the old PBX worked just fine, but programming the phone numbers could be a pain. Phone numbers were tied to the PBX ports, so he had to remember which port of the PBX the phone outlet was connected to so he could program the right phone number. Because RC Stores had never bothered documenting the cabling plan in the building, there were sometimes unwelcome surprises. Connecting one new user wasn't that bad, but Chris would never forget when they were moving to a new building and he and his colleague spent all weekend to get the PBX network set up to ensure that everyone could keep their extensions.

Now it is a simpler. Chris jots down the MAC address from a little sticker on the back of the IP phone and brings up the IP PBX device manager application. He also gets his sheet on which he notes the phone numbers that are in use. His method to assign phone numbers is nothing fancy. He has printed a table with all the available extensions. Jotted on the table in pencil is the information on whether a phone number is in use. Chris selects a number that is free, crosses it out, and notes the name of the new person who is assigned the number, along with the MAC address of the phone.

Chris then goes into the IP PBX device manager screen to add a new user. The menu walks him through what he needs to do: He enters the MAC address and the phone extension, along with the privileges for the phone. In this case, the user is allowed to place calls to the outside. Now all that remains to be done is to add voice mail for the user. He starts another program, the configuration tool for the user's voice-mail server. RC Stores decided to go with a different vendor for voice mail than for the IP PBX. Chris often moans over that decision. Although having different vendors resulted in an attractive price and a few additional features, he now has to administer two separate systems. Not only does he need to retype some of the same information that he just entered, such as username and phone number, but he also needs to worry about things such as making separate system backups. Chris leaves the capacity of the voice mail box at 20 minutes, as the application suggested for the default; it is the company's policy that everyone gets 20 minutes capacity except department heads and secretaries, who get an hour.

The phone extension is now tied to the phone itself, regardless of where on the network it is physically plugged in. Chris walks over to the Human Resources (HR) person upstairs and asks where the new employee will sit. He carries over the phone right away, plugs it into the outlet, and makes sure that it works. He must remember to send a note to HR to let them know the number he assigned so they can update the company directory. Chris has been intending for some time to write a script that provisions new phones and automatically updates the company directory at the same time. Unfortunately, he has not gotten around to it yet. Maybe tomorrow.

Chris goes back to his desk and checks on the performance data that is still being collected. Things look okay; he will just let it run until the problem occurs again so that he has the data when it is needed. In addition, he decides that he wants to be notified right away when sluggish network performance is experienced. He goes again into his management platform and launches a function that lets him set up an alert that is sent when the measured response time between any two given points in the network exceeds a certain amount of time. He configures it to automatically check response time once per minute and to send him an alert to his pager when the response time exceeds 5 seconds. He hopes that this will give him a chance to look at things while the problem is actually occurring, not after the fact.

Chris realizes that the response time is needed for two purposes—once for the statistics collection function, once for the alerting function. Currently, there is no way to tie the two functions together. Therefore, the response times will simply be measured twice. Although this is not the most efficient method, there is no reason for Chris to worry about it.

Thinking about it, Chris suspects that the problem is related to someone initiating large file transfers. Perhaps an employee is using the company's network to download movies from the Internet. If this is the case, it would be a clear violation of company policy. Not only does it represent an abuse of company resources, but, more important, it also introduces security risks. For example, someone could download a program containing a Trojan horse from the outside and then let it run on the company network. Of course, Chris has set up the infrastructure to regularly push updates of the company's security protection software to the servers, but this alone does not protect against all possible scenarios. All the efforts to secure the network against attacks from the outside do not help if someone potentially compromises network security from the inside. Chris thinks that this hypothesis makes sense. The gateway that connects the company to the Internet is located at headquarters, and from the remote branch someone would have to go first via the company's VPN to that gateway to go outside. The additional traffic on the link between the remote branch and headquarters might be enough to negatively affect other connected applications. So maybe the problem resides with RC Stores after all, not with the MSP.

In any event, Chris knows that when the symptom occurs again, he will be able to find out what is going on by using his traffic analyzer, another management tool. He will be able to pull up the traffic analyzer from his management station to check what type of data traffic is currently flowing over a particular router—the gateway to the Internet, in that case—and where it originates.

Before Chris leaves in the evening, he forwards his phone extension to his mobile, in case something comes up. Also, he brings up the function in the alarm management portion of his management platform application and programs it to send him a page if an alarm of critical severity occurs, such as the failure of an access router that causes a loss in connectivity between a branch and headquarters. Chris has remote access to the VPN from home and can log into his management application remotely, if required.

Sandy: Administrator and Planner in an Internet Data Center

Meet Sandy. Sandy works in the Internet Data Center for a global Fortune 500 company, F500, Inc. The data center is at the center of the company's intranet, extranet, and Internet presence: It hosts the company's external website, which provides company and product information and connects customers to the online ordering system. More important, it is host to all the company's crucial business data: its product documents and specifications, its customer data, and its supplier data. In addition, the data center hosts the company's internal website through which most of this data can be accessed, given the proper access privileges.

F500, Inc.'s core business is not related to networking or high technology; it is a global consumer goods company. However, F500, Inc. decided that the functions provided by the Internet Data Center are so crucial to its business that it should not be outsourced. In the end, F500, Inc. differentiates itself from other companies not just through its products, but by the way the company organizes and manages its processes and value supply chains—functions for which the Internet Data Center is an essential component.

Sandy has been tasked with developing a plan for how to accommodate a new partner supplier. This will involve setting up the server and storage infrastructure for storing and sharing data that is critical for the business relationship. Also, an extranet over which the shared data can be accessed must be carved out. The extranet constitutes essentially its own Virtual Private Network that will be set up specifically for that purpose.

Sandy has a list of the databases that need to be shared; storage and network capacity must be assessed. Her plan is to set up a global directory structure for the file system in such a way that all data that pertains to the extranet is stored in a single directory subtree—perhaps a few, at most. She certainly does not want the data scattered across the board. Having it more consolidated will make many tasks easier. For example, she will need to define a strategy for automatic data backup and restoration. Of course, Sandy does not conduct backups manually; the software does that. Nevertheless, the backups need to be planned: where to back up to, when to back up, and how to redirect requests to access data to a redundant storage system while the backup is in progress.

Sandy's main concern, however, is with security. Having data conceptually reside in a common directory subtree makes it much easier to build a security cocoon around it. Security is a big consideration—after all, F500, Inc. has several partners, and none of them should see each other's data. A major part of the plan involves updating security policies—clearly defining who should be able to access what data. Those policies must be translated into configurations at several levels that involve the databases and hosts for the data, as well as the network components through which clients connect.

Several layers of security must be configured: Sandy needs to set up a new separate virtual LAN (VLAN) that will be dedicated to this extranet. A VLAN shares the same networking infrastructure as the rest of the data center network but defines a set of dedicated interfaces that will be used only by the VLAN; it allows the effective separation of traffic on the extranet from other network traffic. This way, extranet traffic cannot intentionally or unintentionally spill over to portions of the data center network that it is not intended for. The servers hosting the common directory subtree with the shared data will be connected to that VLAN. Sandy checks the network topology and identifies the network equipment that will be configured accordingly.

Figure 2-7 shows a typical screen from which networks can be configured. This particular screen allows the user to enter configuration parameters for a particular type of networking port.

Figure 2-7   *Sample Screen of a Management Application That Allows the Configuration of Ports (Cisco WAN Manager 15.1)*

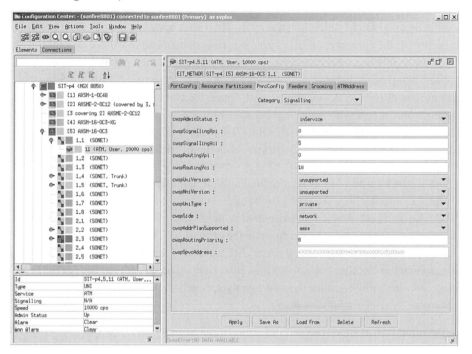

In addition, access control lists (ACLs) on the routers need to be set up and updated to reflect the new security policy that should be in effect for this particular extranet. ACLs define rules that specify which type of network traffic is allowed between which locations, and which traffic should be blocked; in effect, they are used to build firewalls around the data. This creates the second layer of security.

Finally, authentication, authorization, and accounting (AAA) servers need to be configured. AAA servers contain the privileges of individual users; when a client has connectivity to the server, access privileges are still enforced at the user and application levels. Any access to the data is logged. This way, it is possible to trace who accessed what information, in case it is ever required, such as for suspected security break-ins.

However, before she can proceed with any of that, Sandy needs to assess where the data will be hosted and any impact that could have on the internal data center topology. After all, without knowing what servers should be connected, it is premature to configure anything else. When the partner comes online, demand for the affected data is sure to increase.

Sandy pulls up the performance-analysis application. She is not interested in the current status of the Internet Data Center because operations personnel are looking after that. She is looking for the historical trends in performance and load. Sandy worries about the potential for bottlenecks, given that additional demand for data traffic and new traffic patterns can be expected. She takes a look at the performance statistics for the past month of the servers that are currently hosting the data. It seems they are fairly well utilized already. Also, disk space usage has been continuously increasing. At the current pace, disk space will run out in only a few more months. Of course, some of the data that is hosted on the servers is of no relevance to the partnership; in effect, it must be migrated and rehosted elsewhere. This should provide some relief. Still, it seems that, at a minimum, additional disks will be needed. Given the current system load, it might be necessary to bring a new server with additional capacity online and integrate it into the overall directory structure. Sandy might as well do this now. This way, she will not need to schedule an additional maintenance window later and can thus avoid a scheduled disruption of services in the data center.

Of course, the fact that data is kept redundantly in multiple places will be transparent (that is, invisible) to applications. All data is to be addressed using a common uniform resource identifier (URI). The data center uses a set of content switches that inspect the URI in a request for data and determine which particular server to route the request to. The content switch can serve as a load balancer in case the same data and same URI are hosted redundantly on multiple servers. The content switch is another component that must be configured so it knows about the new servers that are coming online and the data they contain. Sandy makes a mental note that she will need to incorporate this aspect into her plan.

Observations

This should suffice for now as an impression of the professional lives of Pat, Chris, Sandy, and many other people involved in running networks. At this point, a few observations are key:

- Pat, Chris, and Sandy handle their jobs in different ways. For example, in Pat's case, there are many specialized groups, each dealing with one specific task that represents just a small portion of running the network. On the other hand, Chris more or less needs to do it all. Sandy is less involved in the actual operations but more involved in the planning and setup of the infrastructure. This work includes not just network equipment, but computing infrastructure as well. There is no "one size fits all" in the way that networks are run.

- Pat, Chris, and Sandy all have different tools at their disposal to carry out their management tasks. We take a look at some of the management tools in the next section. Not all tools that they use are management systems; in Chris's case, we saw how a spreadsheet and a piece of paper can be effective management tools.

- A major aspect of Pat's job is determined by guidelines, procedures, and the way the work is organized. Systems that manage operational procedure and workflows are as much part of network management as systems that communicate with the equipment and services that are being managed. Their importance increases with the size and complexity of the network (and network infrastructure) that needs to be managed.

- Some tasks are carried out manually; some are automated. There is no one ideal method of network management, but there are alternative ways of doing things. Of course, some are more efficient than others.

- Management tasks involve different levels of abstraction and, in many cases, must be broken down into lower-level tasks. Chris and Sandy both were at one level concerned with a service (a voice service in one case, an extranet in the other case), yet they had to translate that concern into what it meant for individual network elements. Sandy had to worry about how security policies at the business level, that state which parties are allowed to share which data, could be transformed into a working network configuration that involved a multitude of components.

- Many functions are involved in running a network—monitoring current network operations, diagnosing failures, configuring the network to provide a service, analyzing historical data, planning for future use of the network, setting up security mechanisms, managing the operations workforce, and much more.

- Integration between tools affects operator productivity. In the examples, we saw how Pat's productivity increased when she was supported by integrated applications, which, in that case, included a trouble ticket, a work order, and network monitoring systems. Chris, on the other hand, had to struggle with some steps that were not as integrated, such as needing to keep track of phone numbers in four different places (company directory, number inventory, and IP PBX and voice-mail configuration).

Later chapters will pick up on many of the themes that were encountered here, after discussing the technical underpinnings of the systems that enable Pat, Chris, and Sandy do their jobs. Before we conclude, however, let us take a look at some of the tools that help network providers manage networks.

The Network Operator's Arsenal: Management Tools

We conclude this chapter by taking a look at some of the tools that assist people who manage networks for a living—people like Pat, Chris, and Sandy. Ultimately, it is the goal of network management technology to provide tools that make people efficient. Having an impression of what such tools can do provides a helpful context for material covered in later chapters.

We start with simple and relatively basic tools and move progressively toward tools of greater complexity, concluding with tools that are typically found only in large-scale network operations.

The list is by no means complete but covers many of the most important tool categories. It illustrates the kaleidoscope of different functionality that is available to network providers. Perhaps it also explains why it is not uncommon to find literally hundreds of different management applications at large service providers. Don't worry, though. Many environments use far fewer applications, as with enterprise IT departments of medium-size businesses like the one encountered in the example with Chris. In addition, although the breadth of tools and functions might seem overwhelming at first, in later chapters we discuss how to bring order to all of this. For example, in Chapters 4, "The Dimensions of Management," and 5, "Management Functions and Reference Models: Getting Organized," we discuss systemic ways of categorizing and organizing management functionality; Chapter 10, "Management Integration: Putting the Pieces Together," picks up on the challenge of how to integrate different tools into one operational support environment.

Device Managers and Craft Terminals

Craft terminals, sometimes also referred to as device managers (not to be confused with element managers, discussed shortly), provide a user-friendly way for humans to interact with individual network equipment. Craft terminals are used to log into equipment one device at a time, view its current status, view and possibly change its configuration settings, and trigger the equipment to execute certain actions, such as performing diagnostic self-tests and downloading new software images. Frequently, craft terminals provide a graphical view of the equipment that shows the physical configuration of the equipment with its different cards and ports, viewed from both the front and the back sides. Figure 2-8 shows an example of such a view. The view might even be animated to show which LEDs will be currently lit or blinking, depending on the device's status.

Contrary to most other management tools, craft terminals generally do not retain any information about the managed equipment in a database, nor do they offer electronic interfaces to other management applications. All they provide is a remote real-time view of the equipment you want to look at, one at a time. In some cases, managed equipment might already provide a "built-in" craft interface, for example, by way of a mini-web server that renders a device view. In this case, separate craft terminal software is not needed because all that a user needs to do is point a web browser at the device.

Craft terminals are often used by field technicians, who might have craft terminal software loaded onto their notebook computers with which they connect to the device that needs to be managed through a universal serial bus (USB) or serial interface, much as you find on most PCs. In general, craft terminal functionality can also be launched from other management applications, such as from management platforms (see the section, "Management Platforms"), to provide a remote graphical view of the managed device. This was also the case in the earlier scenario, when Chris was using the function of a craft terminal that he launched from a management platform to take a look at the router at the edge of the branch that was having a performance problem.

Figure 2-8 *Sample Screen of a Device Manager Offering a Graphical Device (Chassis) View (CiscoView for Catalyst 6500)*

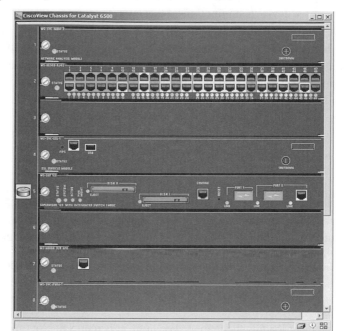

Network Analyzers

Network analyzers come under many different names, including packet sniffers, packet analyzers, and traffic analyzers. They are used to view and analyze current traffic on a network, generally to understand the way in which the network is behaving and to diagnose and troubleshoot particular problems. Network analyzers capture or "sniff" packets that flow over a port of a network device, such as a router or switch, and present them in a human-readable format that an experienced network operator can interpret. In the earlier example, Chris was planning to use a network analyzer to analyze the type of traffic that occurred during times when the network performance problem was observed.

Element Managers

Element managers are systems that are used to manage equipment in a network. Typically, element managers are designed for equipment of a specific type and of a particular vendor; in fact, they are often provided by an equipment vendor. Element managers are similar to craft terminals, in that they allow operators to access devices to view their status and configuration, and possibly modify their parameter settings. The functions of element managers, however, far exceed the functions of craft terminals. For example, element managers typically include a database in which they retain information about all the various devices (at least, for those that are supported) in the network.

This enables users to view how devices are configured without the devices themselves needing to be repeatedly queried. More important, it enables users to back up and archive how devices are configured, to restore device configurations if that ever is required, and to manage the distribution of software images to the devices. In addition, element managers can receive event messages from the devices, which enables users to monitor the various pieces of equipment across the entire network, not just one device at a time. Element managers might also be able to automatically discover equipment that is deployed on the network. The tool that Chris used in the earlier example to manage the IP PBX was an element manager.

Element managers also often offer an electronic interface to other applications. This allows other applications to manage the equipment through the element manager instead of having to interface to the equipment directly. This can have important advantages:

- Less possibility exists that data about the network will run out of synch between different applications. The element manager not only serves as an authoritative data store about the device, but also coordinates management requests that applications might issue concurrently.

- The interface that the element manager offers might be easier to use and, hence, build to than the interfaces offered by the devices themselves. The element manager can also shield applications from minor variations in device interfaces.

- The management load on the managed equipment is reduced. Not only can the element manager coordinate requests that are received from other management applications, but, in many cases, it can respond to requests by providing information about the device from its own database instead of needing to talk to the device.

Management Platforms

Management platforms are general-purpose management applications that are used to manage networks. The functionality of management platforms is generally comparable to that of element managers. However, management platforms are typically designed to be vendor independent, offering device support for equipment of multiple vendors. Typically, the primary task of a management platform is to monitor the network to make sure it is functioning properly. Therefore, it was also the main tool that Chris used in the earlier example. Management platforms are often accompanied by development toolkits. Those toolkits enable users, systems integrators, and third-party management application developers to adapt and extend the management platform. Its functionality can be customized and adapted to different environments, it can be extended with new capabilities, and it can be integrated with additional management applications whose functionality is made accessible through the management platform.

These capabilities can make management platforms resemble a sort of "operating system" for management applications. Indeed, in some ways, analogies between a management platform and a PC operating system can be drawn.

For example, the PC operating system includes basic functionality such as a file explorer and Internet browser, and might come bundled with a basic word-processing program and spreadsheet, with an abundance of additional applications available that run on top of it and make the PC operating system more useful. Those applications leverage certain operating system infrastructure, such as the file system. The management platform, on the other hand, provides out-of-the-box support for basic management needs such as network monitoring and discovery, with additional add-on applications available to cater to more advanced needs. Those applications use management platform infrastructure. An example are functions that allow applications to communicate with network devices, as well as functions that keep an inventory of the equipment in the network and that cache their configuration in an internal database. Also, where a PC operating system offers plug-in support for additional device drivers, management platforms need to support similar capabilities to support additional networking equipment.

Collectors and Probes

Collectors and probes are auxiliary systems that offload applications from simple functions.

Collectors are used to gather and store different types of data from the network. An example is Netflow collectors, which collect data about traffic that traverses a router. Such data can be generated by routers in high volumes and is commonly represented in a format known as Netflow. Another example is loggers, which collect so-called syslog messages from network equipment that provides a trail of the processing and activities that occur at a router.

Probes are similar to collectors but are "active," in the sense that they trigger certain activities in the network and collect the responses—for example, they perform periodic tests. In the earlier scenario, Chris used a probe to take periodic measurements of the network response time over a certain link.

In each case, the data that is collected is made available to other applications, such as a management platform.

Intrusion Detection Systems

Intrusion detection systems (IDSs) help network providers to detect suspicious communication patterns on the network that might be indicative of an ongoing attack. Attacks include attempted break-ins into routers or, much more common, into servers, and denial-of-service (DoS) attacks that could be caused by Internet worms designed to overload and, hence, effectively shut down a service. IDSs use a wide variety of techniques, including analyzing traffic on the network, listening to alarms, inspecting activity logs, and observing load patterns. IDSs help operators quickly recognize such threats and mitigate their effects—for example, by shutting off network ports through which attacks occur.

Performance Analysis Systems

Performance analysis systems enable users to analyze traffic and performance data, with the goal of recognizing trends and patterns in that traffic. They have to deal with massive amounts of data that has been collected over long periods of time; hence, they frequently involve data mining (techniques to recognize common patterns in large amounts of data), as well as advanced visualization techniques to display data in the form of graphical patterns that make sense to a user. Users such as Sandy from our earlier scenario use this information for a variety of activities, such as for network planning. Sandy can use information she gathers from a performance analysis system to anticipate where additional capacity will be needed in the near future and to tune data center performance based on an analysis of bottlenecks. Information gathered from performance analysis might even be helpful for tasks such as the development of pricing structures that will encourage communication behavior that helps "even out" the communications load on the network. Recognizing which services lead to a disproportionate load and frequently cause congestion in portions of the network might cause a service provider to charge extra for them.

Alarm Management Systems

Alarm management systems are specialized in collecting and monitoring alarms from the network. They help users to quickly sift through and make sense of the volumes of event and alarm messages that are received from the network. Often alarm management systems have additional capabilities to group ("correlate") alarms that are likely to belong together, to offer initial diagnoses for the root cause of an alarm, or to provide impact analysis to forecast the fallout that an alarm might have. Sometimes, based on their analysis, alarm management systems generate additional synthetic event messages that aggregate and interpret the findings from a set of raw alarms. In many cases, alarm management systems also serve as preprocessors for other management applications, such as trouble ticket systems, like the one that we encountered in the earlier scenario with Pat.

Of course, other tools, such as management platforms and element managers, already include a certain degree of alarm management functionality. Dedicated alarm management applications, however, generally offer functionality that is more sophisticated and goes above and beyond what more general-purpose applications are offering.

Figure 2-9 shows a view of a screen of a typical alarm management application, displaying a list of alarm messages that can be expanded or searched and filtered for various purposes. For each alarm message, the screen shows a brief summary of what the message is about, along with information on which device it originated from, what category of alarm it belongs to, when it occurred, and (through its color coding) how severe the condition is.

Figure 2-9   *Sample Screen of an Alarm Management Application (Cisco Info Center)*

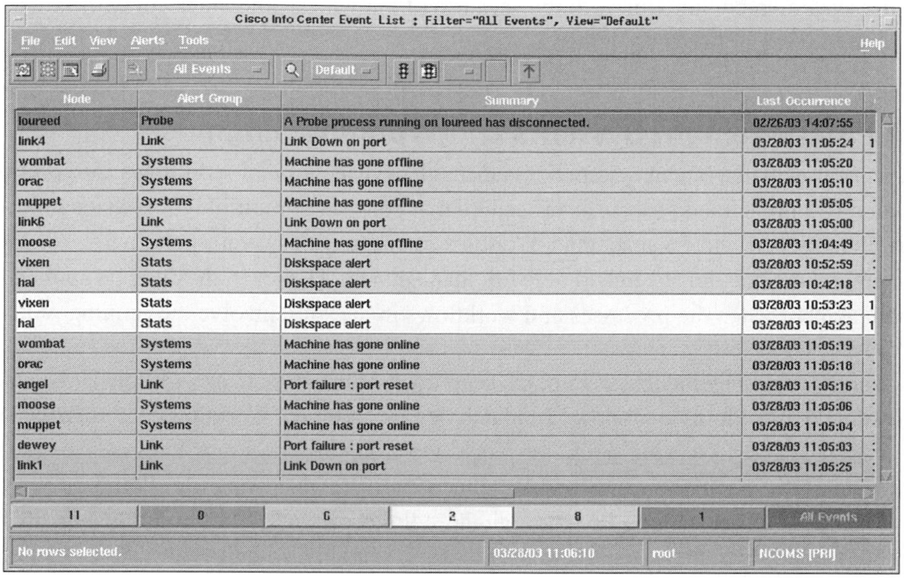

Cisco Info Center Event List : Filter="All Events", View="Default"

File   Edit   View   Alerts   Tools   Help

All Events   Default

Node	Alert Group	Summary	Last Occurrence	
loureed	Probe	A Probe process running on loureed has disconnected.	02/26/03 14:07:55	
link4	Link	Link Down on port	03/28/03 11:05:24	1
wombat	Systems	Machine has gone offline	03/28/03 11:05:20	
orac	Systems	Machine has gone offline	03/28/03 11:05:10	
muppet	Systems	Machine has gone offline	03/28/03 11:05:05	
link6	Link	Link Down on port	03/28/03 11:05:00	
moose	Systems	Machine has gone offline	03/28/03 11:04:49	
vixen	Stats	Diskspace alert	03/28/03 10:52:59	
hal	Stats	Diskspace alert	03/28/03 10:42:18	
vixen	Stats	Diskspace alert	03/28/03 10:53:23	1
hal	Stats	Diskspace alert	03/28/03 10:45:23	1
wombat	Systems	Machine has gone online	03/28/03 11:05:19	
orac	Systems	Machine has gone online	03/28/03 11:05:18	
angel	Link	Port failure : port reset	03/28/03 11:05:16	
moose	Systems	Machine has gone online	03/28/03 11:05:06	
muppet	Systems	Machine has gone online	03/28/03 11:05:04	
dewey	Link	Port failure : port reset	03/28/03 11:05:03	
link1	Link	Link Down on port	03/28/03 11:05:25	

| 11 | 0 | 6 | 2 | 8 | 1 | All Events |

No rows selected.   03/28/03 11:06:10   root   NCOMS [PRI]

Trouble Ticket Systems

Trouble ticket systems are used to track how problems in a network (such as those that are indicated by alarms) are being resolved. Note that this is different from managing the alarms themselves. Trouble ticket systems are used to capture information about problems that were observed in the network and to track the resolution of those problems. In many cases, trouble tickets are generated by users of the network who experience a problem, although they might also be created proactively by an application that monitors the network and detects a problem.

A trouble ticket system supports the resolution of problems in many ways. For example, the trouble ticket system can automatically assign trouble tickets to a ticket owner who has to take responsibility, or it can automatically escalate tickets that take too long to resolve. The trouble ticket system can also report statistics about the resolution process and generally ensures that problems are followed up on. Of course, the scenario that featured Pat was centered heavily on the use of a trouble ticket system.

Work Order Systems

Work order systems are used to assign and track individual maintenance jobs in a network. They also help organize and manage the workforce that carries them out. For each job, a work order is assigned whose resolution is then tracked. Similar to trouble ticket systems, work order systems offer a myriad of functions to capture information about jobs, to manage the assignment of jobs to a work force, to make sure those jobs are properly taken care of, and, in general, to track what the work force that is maintaining the networking infrastructure is doing. We encountered a work order system in conjunction with the scenario of Pat when someone needed to be dispatched to replace a piece of faulty equipment.

Workflow Management Systems and Workflow Engines

A workflow management system helps manage the execution of workflows. A workflow is basically a predefined process or procedure that consists of multiple steps that can involve different owners and organizations. Workflow management systems pertain to business processes in general and are not specific to network management. However, they can be applied to network management when the processes and workflows in question involve the running of a network.

A workflow management system helps keep track of the steps in a workflow and ensures that predefined procedures are followed and policies are enforced. Workflows are usually defined using a concept called *finite state machines*. Each step along the way constitutes a state, and transitions between states occur according to well-defined interfaces and when well-defined events occur. The individual tasks are then pushed through these finite state machines as applicable, managed through the core of the workflow management system, the so-called *workflow engine*.

Both trouble ticket and work order systems can, in fact, be considered specialized examples of workflows. However, a workflow management system is more general in nature and highly customizable, to allow for the incorporation of any type of workflow.

Inventory Systems

Inventory systems are used to track the assets of a network provider. They come in two flavors:

- Network inventory systems track physical inventory in a network, mainly the equipment that is deployed, but sometimes also spare parts. Inventory information includes the type of equipment, the software version that is installed on it, cards within the equipment, the location of the equipment, and so forth. We encountered a network inventory system in the scenario involving Pat when the network technicians replaced a part in the network and the work order system automatically updated the network inventory accordingly.

- Service inventory systems track the instances of services that have been deployed over the network and that can be traced to individual users and end customers. For example, this could be DSL and phone services for residential customers of a telecommunications service provider. They might also include information on which network equipment and which ports are used to physically realize the service. Knowing this information makes it easier to assess who will be affected in case maintenance operations need to be performed or in case of a network failure.

In addition to inventory systems, facility management systems are used to document and keep track of the physical cable and ducts in buildings that are used to interconnect networking equipment.

Service Provisioning Systems

Service provisioning systems facilitate the deployment of services over a network, such as Digital Subscriber Line (DSL) or telephone service for residential customers of large service providers. Service provisioning systems translate requests to turn on or to remove a service into a series of steps and configurations that are then driven into the network.

Service provisioning systems are typically very complex applications that can be found only in operational support environments of large service providers; we did not encounter any in our earlier scenarios. They allow service providers to roll out services on a very large scale, often at a rate of tens of thousands of service requests per day. In many cases, service provisioning systems do not even interact with human operators, except possibly in case of exceptions that require human intervention. For this reason, perhaps surprisingly, they often offer no graphical user interface (GUI) or only a very rudimentary one. Instead, requests are issued from another system, for example from a service order management system via an electronic application programming interface (API). Such an interface allows another system to automatically interact with the system without user involvement, for example to request a piece of information or to hand off a request. For example, a service order management system (which we encounter in the section that follows) might use the API to automatically dispatch a request for provisioning a service to the service provisioning system when the order for the services becomes due.

Service Order–Management Systems

Service order–management systems are used to manage orders for services by customers of large service providers. (As with service provisioning systems, such systems are generally not encountered in enterprise environments.) They are part of a larger category of systems that deal with customer relationship management (CRM), which, for example, also includes help-desk functions.

Managing service orders involves a set of specialized workflows, similar to managing work orders or trouble tickets. Service order management systems help service providers track and fulfill orders for services and automate many, if not most, steps along the way. This includes identifying needed equipment, locating required ports, performing customer credit checks, scheduling the fulfillment of service orders, and eventually dispatching requests to turn up services to a service provisioning system.

Note the distinction between service order management systems and service provisioning systems. The former help manage workflows and processes of an organization. The latter are applications that interact with a network to configure it in a certain way. Compare this to the earlier distinction between trouble ticket systems and alarm management systems.

Billing Systems

Last in our list, but not least, are billing systems. We did not discuss billing systems in any of our earlier scenarios, but we should not lose sight of the reason many network providers (service providers, in particular, not enterprise IT departments) are in the business of running networks in the first place: to make money. Billing systems are essential to the realization of revenues. They analyze accounting and usage data to identify which communication services were provided to whom at what time. Subsequently, a tariffing scheme that defines how services need to be charged for is applied to that data to generate a bill.

Many other functions than billing systems themselves are associated with billing. For example, fraud detection systems help detect suspicious patterns in activity that could indicate that services are being stolen. Billing systems might also need to interface with other systems that are used for customer relationship management so that, for example, customer databases can be updated with information on which customers are past due.

Chapter Summary

In this chapter, we took a look at a few scenarios that illustrate how networks are being managed in practice and the variety of tasks that are involved. We followed three fictitious network operators and administrators: Pat in the Network Operations Center of a large service provider, Chris in the IT department of a medium-size business, and Sandy in the Internet Data Center of a large enterprise. The three scenarios represented operational support environments that differ greatly, as do the daily routines of the persons involved.

The service provider scenario emphasized workflows, processes, and interactions. In fact, in service provider environments, a significant part of the management infrastructure is dedicated to managing those organizational aspects, not just the technologies deployed in the networks themselves. The medium-size enterprise scenario was characterized by a great variety of tasks that had to be performed by the individual and a greater reliance on the individual expertise and intuition of the operator. The Internet Data Center scenario, finally, was geared at a different part of the network's life cycle, the planning phase. Also, it showed how the boundary between managing a network and managing the devices, servers, and applications that are connected to the network can become blurry.

The scenarios are representative of some of the environments in which management technology is ultimately applied. The scenarios also illustrate that network management is not just a topic of management technology; there are other significant factors in the equation, such as organizational aspects and human factors.

In each case, the personnel were supported by a variety of tools. In the end, management technology is tasked with building such tools, which are supposed to facilitate to the greatest extent possible the task of running a network. A wide variety of different tools exist for a great variety of purposes, so it comes as no surprise that running the largest, most complex networks can involve literally hundreds of management systems and applications. Of course, many scenarios are much simpler; it all depends on the particular context.

Chapter Review

1. Is running a network only a matter of network management technology, or are there other considerations?

2. What does Pat's employer use to track the resolution of problems in the network?

3. How does the integration of the work order system with the trouble ticket system make Pat's job easier?

4. Which network provider do you think will be more vulnerable to human failures by operations personnel, Pat's or Chris's?

5. Which of the following can be used as management tools? A. alarm management system, B. spreadsheet, C. pencil and piece of paper, D. all of them.

6. In how many different places does Chris need to maintain the same phone number, and why could this be an issue?

7. When Chris is worried about compromised security of his company's network, does the threat come from outside attackers or from within the network?

8. Connectivity between different company sites is provided by an outside MSP. Why is Chris nevertheless concerned with monitoring traffic statistics across these outside connections?

9. When Sandy wants to implement a security policy for the Internet Data Center, at what different levels does she take security into account?

10. Why is Sandy interested in "old" performance data and traffic statistics, even though she is not monitoring actual network operations?

CHAPTER 3

The Basic Ingredients of Network Management

Chapters 1, "Setting the Stage," and 2, "On the Job with a Network Manager," explored what network management does, why it is important, where its challenges lie, and what kinds of activities and tools are associated with it. But what does network management, at a very basic level, really consist of? First, there is, of course, the network that is to be managed, consisting of a multitude of interconnected devices that collectively shuffle data (for example, web pages, e-mails, voice packets of phone calls, and video frames) across the network. Second, there are the systems and applications that are used to manage the network, many of which were described in Chapter 2. In those systems the management logic resides, helping network managers to monitor the network and collect data from it, to interpret and analyze the data, and to send commands to the devices to affect the network's behavior—for example, to configure a port in a certain way or to shut down an interface.

So far, so good—we fully expected that it would take two to tango. But we are not quite finished. Third, the network that is to be managed and the managing applications must be interconnected so they can communicate with each other. Network management itself is a networking application, which creates an almost paradoxical situation: To work properly, network management needs a network that works properly so that management applications and managed network can talk to each other. Without this, it would be impossible to exchange management commands and management information. Of course, for the network to work properly, it needs to have proper network management in place!

Last but not least, beyond the technical components of network management, there is the organization behind it that makes it all happen and that is ultimately responsible for the proper running of the network. In the end, all the management applications and management infrastructure are merely tools that support an organization in managing its network.

In this chapter, we look at each of these basic components in a little more detail; they are depicted in Figure 3-1.

Figure 3-1 *Basic Components of Network Management*

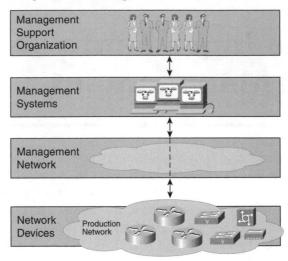

After you have read this chapter, you should be able to do the following:

■   Explain the terms *manager* and *agent*

■   Describe what Management Information Bases (MIBs) are about

■   Explain how management agents, managed devices, and MIBs relate to each other

■   Explain the difference between in-band and out-of-band management communications

■   State the pros and cons of dedicated management networks

■   Describe the role of a Network Operations Center (NOC)

The Network Device

The first main component in network management consists of the device that must be managed. Of course, in general, there will be not just one, but many devices. In network management parlance, we also call the managed devices *network elements* (NEs). To be properly managed, they must participate in the management process. Therefore, let us look at the network elements more closely from this point of view.

Management Agent

To be managed, a network element must offer a management interface through which a managing system can communicate with the network element for management purposes. For example, the management interface allows the managing system to send a request to the network element. This could be, for example, a request to configure a subinterface, to retrieve statistical data about the utilization of a port, or to obtain information about the status of a connection. Likewise, the network element can send information to the managing system, such as a response to a request, but also unsolicited information, such as when an unexpected event (for example, the failure of a fan or a buffer overflow) has occurred. Accordingly, during network management, management communication occurs.

Management communication is inherently asymmetrical: A managing application plays the role of a "manager" in charge of the management, and the network element plays the role of the "agent" that supports the manager by responding to its requests and notifying it proactively of unexpected events (see Figure 3-2).

Figure 3-2   *Manager-Agent Communication*

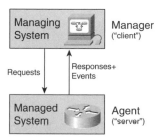

Manager and *agent* are important terms in network management parlance; they refer to the systems that manage (manager) and the systems that are managed (agent). Client/server is another well-known asymmetric communication relationship that the reader might already be familiar with; therefore, a few words on the relationship between manager/agent and client/server are in order. As shown in Figure 3-2, the agent corresponds to a server, and the manager to a client. Of course, client/server–based systems typically imply that a small number of servers must service a large number of clients. For example, one bank transaction system (server) must serve thousands of ATMs and bank terminals (clients), as well as hundreds of thousands of online users. In network management, the situation is reversed, as depicted in Figure 3-3; typically, large numbers (perhaps tens of thousands) of servers—that is, agents—serve a small number of clients—that is, managers.

Figure 3-3 *Manager/Agent Versus Client/Server*

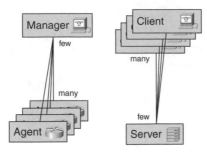

Network elements must provide a piece of software that implements the management interface. This software effectively provides the intermediary between external manager and managed device. We refer to this software generally as the *management agent*. In fact, this means that we are slightly overloading the term *agent*. *Agent* is used to refer both to the agent role that a network element plays in network management and to the software component, called the management agent, that allows the network element to play that role, that provides the management interface, and that represents the managed device to the manager. In general, the meaning of the term should be clear from the context in which it is used. For the remainder of this section, the term *agent* refers to the management agent, not the agent role.

The management agent conceptually consists of three main parts: a management interface, a Management Information Base, and the core agent logic. All three are explained here:

- The management interface handles management communication.

  The management interface supports a management protocol that defines the "rules of conversation" for communication between the managed network element, as represented by the management agent, and the managing application. It allows the managing application to open (and tear down) a management session with the network element. It also allows managing applications to make management requests to the network element and receive responses. Many types of management requests are conceivable—for example, requests to retrieve a piece of statistical information such as the network element's current utilization, or requests to change a configuration setting, such as the size of a buffer allocated to a particular port. Through the management interface, the management agent can also send unsolicited event messages that the managing application can receive. Event messages enable the manager to be alerted of certain occurrences at the network element, such as the unexpected loss of communication with another network element.

■ The Management Information Base (MIB) is a conceptual data store that contains a management view of the device being managed. The conceptual data contained in this data store constitutes the *management information*.

Management operations are directed against this conceptual view. For example, the network ports of a network element could be represented as a table in an imaginary database, with each port having a corresponding entry in the table. Columns in the table contain conceptual attributes that refer to actual properties of the port. Examples of such attributes are the type of communication protocol supported by the port and the number of packets that have been transmitted.

The MIB should not be confused with a real database. It is a way to view the device itself, not a database in which information about the device is stored. This view is a proxy for the network element that is being managed, which is an actual device that is a part of the real world. For example, when a managing application modifies an entry in the conceptual table, in reality, the actual configuration of the network element is changed and the communication behavior of the network element is impacted.

Management information in a MIB does not necessarily always have to resemble a conceptual table. Alternative representations include Extended Markup Language (XML) documents or even simply a set of command-line parameters. It all depends on the management agent.

■ The core agent logic translates between the operation of the management interface, the MIB, and the actual device. For example, it translates the request to "retrieve a counter" into an internal operation that reads out a device hardware register that contains the desired information. In fact, many counters of the same type might exist inside the network element— for example, one per communications interface. Therefore, the agent logic must be capable of mapping the name by which the counter is referred to in the MIB to the actual register whose contents are being requested.

In addition to those core functions, agent logic can include added management functions that offload the processing required by management applications. In marketing jargon, those functions are often referred to as "embedded management intelligence." A typical example is the capability to pre-correlate raw events before they are sent out so that the management application does not need to sift through a large volume of events that turn out to be irrelevant because they are all symptoms related to the same root cause. Another example is a function that allows an application to schedule a periodic test function to validate proper functioning of the device instead of needing to send a new test request each time.

Figure 3-4 illustrates the components of a management agent and how the management agent interacts with the managing system and the underlying device that it represents.

Figure 3-4 *Anatomy of a Management Agent*

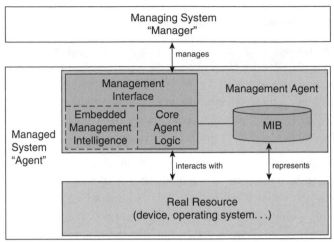

Although a network element plays only one agent role, it can actually contain several management agents, each with its own management interface. Just as different views can be defined on the same underlying database, each management agent can offer its own MIB that is its own abstraction of the underlying network element. A network element can provide different management agents for a number of reasons. One common reason is to give management applications a choice of management interfaces. Another reason is that the different management agents might each serve different functions. For example, one management agent might be dedicated to reporting performance statistics through a special interface that is tuned for that particular purpose, whereas another management agent might be dedicated to configuring a device, offering a different kind of interface for that purpose.

We talk extensively about management interfaces and the details of management communications in Chapters 7, "Management Communication Patterns: Rules of Conversation," and 8, "Common Management Protocols: Languages of Management." For now, let us continue by focusing on the aspect of management information.

Management Information, MOs, MIBs, and Real Resources

In general, many aspects of a network device (such as a router or a switch) are important for its management. For example, the device has a network address, it is of a certain type, and it has software installed of a certain revision. If the device is a router, it might be running a variety of routing protocols. The device might consist of a rack-mountable chassis with a fan for cooling, a central processor module, and a set of expansion slots. Furthermore, the device might contain a set of line cards or service modules that are plugged into the device's chassis. Each of these cards has a certain number of ports, on which different kinds of interfaces are supported.

All these aspects exist independently of whether the device is being managed. They are simply "there" because of the nature of the device, necessary for the device to provide its communications function in the network. Many, but not all, of these aspects are of interest to network management:

■ The version of installed software must be remotely determined, to decide which devices need to have a new software patch installed.

■ Utilization of ports must be assessed, to determine whether capacity upgrades are necessary or whether surplus capacity could be redeployed.

■ Environmental data is monitored to determine temperature and voltages, to ensure that a device is not overheating.

■ Fans are monitored to help remotely determine what is causing device temperature to rise.

■ Packet counters for different interfaces must be monitored; for example, sudden jumps in certain types of packet counts could indicate that a network is under a certain type of attack, such as a so-called denial-of-service (DoS) attack.

■ Protocol timeout parameters must be configured to fine-tune network communication performance.

■ Firewall rules that define a security policy must be configured (for example, "Discard packets of a certain type unless they originate from an address with a certain prefix").

Management information that is provided by a management agent provides an abstraction of these real-world aspects for management purposes. We refer to a chunk of management information that exposes one of these real-world aspects as a *managed object* (MO). An MO could represent a device fan along with its operational state, a port on a line card along with a set of statistical data, or a firewall rule. As you shall see later, many management protocols, including the Simple Network Management Protocol (SNMP), use their own flavor of MO, but for now, we refer to an MO in its more general sense—that is, not tied to any particular management protocol. An "MO" could thus be a MIB object in SNMP, a parameter in a command-line interface (CLI) command, or an element of an XML document in a web-based management interface.

Management information does not model every aspect of the real world; it omits certain details. For this reason, it is an abstraction. For example, for management purposes, it might be irrelevant to know whether a piece of equipment is blue, green, or black—accordingly, this information is unlikely to be included in the management information that a management agent provides.

Sometimes it is necessary to distinguish between the management abstraction of an MO and the underlying thing that it represents. The real-world object that an MO represents is generally referred to as the "real resource." The same real resource can be abstracted in different ways. Therefore, it is possible for different MOs to exist, sometimes concurrently, that all refer to the same thing. Figure 3-5 illustrates this. In this example, the same dog can be referred to as dog in English (this is how agent Dale refers to it), chien in French (that's what it's called by agent Jacques), and Hund in German (the way it is referred to by agent Friedrich). However, independent of what you call it and how many names you have for it, ultimately, a dog is a dog is a dog.

Figure 3-5 *Different Abstractions of the Same Real Resource*

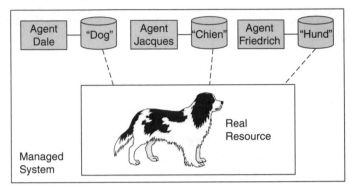

The collection of all management information that is exposed by a network element to managing applications is referred to as the network element's Management Information Base (MIB). The concept was mentioned in the previous section, but because it is so central to network management, it is briefly revisited here: The MIB constitutes a conceptual data store, an abstraction that contains all the information that management applications need to know about a device. In essence, a management application can treat the MIB like a conceptual database that contains data about the network element. This database can be queried for information, and as far as the information represents configuration information that is subject to be changed by a manager, the conceptual database can be modified, inserted, and deleted.

Of course, unlike in a database, the MIB is connected to the device that it represents. The management information in the MIB represents real resources, which seemingly have a life of their own in terms of their function in the communications network, as opposed to passive pieces of informational items. When querying the MIB for an MO representing a packet counter three times, the value returned will be different each time because the real resource—for example, the device register in which the count is kept—will have changed. Likewise, when modifying information in the MIB to perform certain updates, the effects of this will be felt in the real world. For example, an interface might be shut down, which, in turn, changes the way that data packets flow across the network.

Basic Management Ingredients—Revisited

Now that the notion of real resources and the distinction between the network device and the management agent is in place, we can briefly revisit our original picture of the basic management components to include that distinction. Figure 3-6 refines Figure 3-1. At the most basic level, there are really only two components, depicted at the top and at the bottom: the network provider's operational support organization and the "real world" that it wants to manage.

However, technical means are required to connect the operational support organization to the real world, and that connection comes through management technology. The management agent acts as a proxy that represents the real world for management purposes. Likewise, the management system acts as a proxy for the operational support organization. Management interfaces and protocols define their rules of engagement. Communication between them is carried over a management network.

Figure 3-6 *Basic Parts of Network Management—Refined*

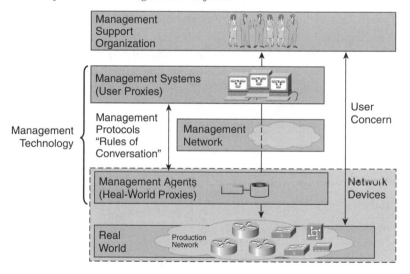

The Management System

Management systems provide network providers with the tools to manage the network. These tools include applications to monitor the network, service provisioning systems, craft terminals, and so forth—that is, all the applications that were introduced in the previous chapter.

Strictly speaking, the terms *management application* and *management system* should be differentiated. The same management system can run one or more management applications. However, for practical purposes, this distinction is largely irrelevant, and therefore we use the terms *management application* and *management system* synonymously in this book. Note that, as with other software systems, a management system is not the same as a host: A management system can run on one or more hosts—that is, it can be distributed across several hosts. The capability to be distributed allows the system to scale because more hosts provide for greater processing, I/O, and storage capacity. It can make the system also more robust—even if one host fails, the system can still keep running.

Management System and Manager Role

The terms *manager* and *management system* are often used synonymously. Strictly speaking, this is not quite correct, and, in general, care should be taken to distinguish a manager (the role) from a management system (the application). This is because, for various reasons, it might make sense for the same system to play both agent and manager roles. For example, one network element might act as a management proxy to another. In this case, the network element plays the agent role in interacting with the management system, but it plays the manager role in interacting with the other network element. Likewise, two management systems might be part of a management hierarchy, with one management system directing management requests at another, which then turns around to pass on the request to a third system or a network element (see Figure 3-7). In that case, the management system in the middle acts in an agent role when it receives management requests from the first management system, in addition to playing its more conventional role of manager with respect to the network element. In our discussion here, we generally assume that the managed system—and, hence, the system in the agent role—is a network element. It should be realized, however, that, in general, the system in the agent role does not always have to be a network element—it can be also another type of system in a management hierarchy.

Figure 3-7 *A Management Hierarchy*

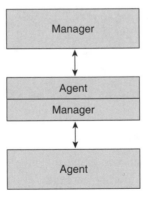

To provide their functionality, management systems must communicate with the network elements they manage. In the communication that takes place, management systems assume the manager role.

The management system is ultimately the consumer of the management interface that is offered by the system in the agent role—the managed system, generally a network element. The manager sends requests to the agent, receives responses from the agent, and asks the agent to be notified of events. It operates on the abstraction of the managed system provided through the agent's MIB.

Figure 3-8 illustrates how a manager and agent relate to each other. Although the figure is simplistic, you should keep it in mind because the relationship between manager, agent, and MIB is a fundamental concept in network management.

Figure 3-8 *Manager/Agent Reference Diagram*

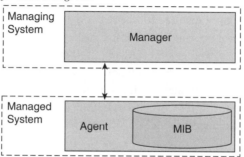

Of course, for efficiency reasons, many management systems build their own database in which they cache information about the network. They do this to avoid having to go back to the network element repeatedly for the same information, when it is much more efficient to retain that information locally. Of course, as with any system that employs caching strategies, the system needs to resolve the trade-off between risking that data in the cache is stale, versus the cost involved in updating the cache too frequently. Sometimes application vendors refer to this cache as the management system's MIB. This, of course, is a misnomer. The management system might have an internal database that it can refer to as a shadow MIB or a MIB cache, but the actual MIB always resides with the agent, not the manager, as depicted in Figure 3-9.

Figure 3-9 *The MIB Always Resides with the Agent*

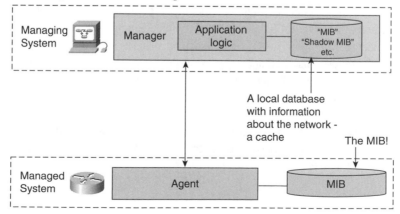

Finally, a side note on a duality between management systems and management agents: As mentioned earlier, the purpose of an agent is to provide a representation of a real-world entity that is to be managed. The management agent can thus be considered to be a proxy for the managed device. As far as the management system is concerned, the management agent *is* the managed device. Similarly, as far as the managed device is concerned, the management system in effect serves as a proxy for the real-world organization that is responsible for managing the network.

A Management System's Reason for Being

Unlike the network element, a management system exists only for the purposes of network management. It is not per se required for the network to function. If you have a management system that manages your network, and disaster strikes so that from one moment to the next, the management system stops working, the network itself should be completely unaffected. Ongoing phone calls that run over your network will not be disrupted, and it will even be possible to place new phone calls. Data will continue to be transferred. Users can continue to surf the web. In short, communication services will still work just as before, and users and networking applications will not even notice what just happened.

Of course, losing your management system also means that you can no longer easily monitor and maintain your network. If something in the network fails, chances are, the failure will go undetected and not be fixed quickly, as it should. The quality of the services provided by the network will drop. New services will become difficult to deploy, and new users will be hard to add. Eventually, users will be affected and will notice. But that does not change the fact that the network per se functions independently of its need to be managed.

The Management Network

Now we understand that managers and agents refer to different roles in which management systems and network elements communicate with each other for management purposes. But how do they communicate? The answer is, over a network, of course. At the end of the day, network management is just another distributed application. The different systems that need to communicate in this case just happen to involve management systems and the network elements that they manage. Managing systems and managed systems need to be interconnected. The network that provides this interconnection is referred to as the *management network*. In contrast, when referring to the network that carries the traffic of subscribers and end users, we use the term *production network*.

A management network and a production network can be physically separate networks, or they can share the same physical network. Both deployment alternatives are discussed later in the chapter.

For the network element that is being managed, one important difference between management traffic and other types of communication traffic is that management traffic is one of the few types of traffic that involve the network element itself. The network element serves as a conduit for communication traffic all the time. A typical scenario is that of IP packets entering through one port, having their header inspected and processed, and exiting through another port. Here, the situation is different: The network element itself is one of the participating parties in the communication where traffic is terminated or originated; it is not merely a point of transit. It can be the destination of the management communication traffic that arrives from a management system, and the origin for traffic carrying responses and event messages that are generated by the network element and sent to the management system. Management traffic that is directed at the network element carries as its destination address the address of the network element (NE) itself, not of an end system that is connected to the edge of the network. Of course, for other routers and switches that lie on the path between management system and network element, the management traffic is just another type of application traffic.

Management agents are applications that run on the network element, just like, for example, routing software. As with other applications, management agents typically have their own ports that they are associated with. For example, an SNMP agent listens on port 161 of the IP stack for management requests. When the NE receives an IP packet that contains its own address as the destination, it inspects the payload within it. SNMP is carried over the User Datagram Protocol (UDP), so in this case, the NE would find a UDP packet that specifies port 161 as the destination port. The NE then knows to pass the packet to its own SNMP agent process, which processes it further.

With this in mind, let us take a look at the different options with which a manager can connect to a network element.

Networking for Management

One way in which network elements can be connected to a management system is through the network element's management port.

For most routers, this is a serial interface. It is possible to connect a terminal, such as a notebook computer, directly to that serial interface using a serial cable, as illustrated in Figure 3-10. The terminal thus connected to a network device is typically referred to as a *craft terminal*, in reference to the craft technician who typically uses it. The craft terminal then functions as a console through which a user (a craft technician) can interact with the device. For example, the craft technician can enter CLI commands to configure and troubleshoot the network device.

Figure 3-10 *Connecting a Craft Terminal to a Managed Device*

Of course, if you are a craft technician, in most cases, it soon becomes impractical to go from device to device, connecting and disconnecting the craft terminal as you go along. You need to continuously fumble around with the plugs and the cables, and, worse, you need physical access to the network elements and must work in spaces that can be quite confined. For these reasons, a terminal server can be introduced, as illustrated in Figure 3-11.

Figure 3-11 *Connecting to Multiple Devices Through a Terminal Server*

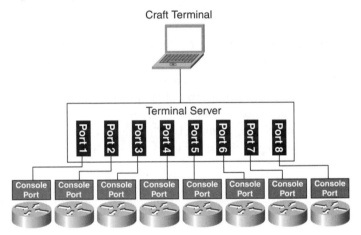

The terminal server takes the place of an intermediate "switch" between the actual craft terminal and the network element. The terminal server has a whole set of serial interface ports through which it can connect with many network elements simultaneously, one through each port. In addition, it has a port for the craft terminal to connect to. You can connect your craft terminal to the terminal server to connect to every device that is hooked up to the terminal server. When connecting, your console initially opens a session with the terminal server. You can then specify which port you want to be switched to. From that point on, the terminal server relays all communication between your craft terminal and network element connected to that port. Thus, you can communicate with the network element behind the terminal server's port, just as if you were directly connected through its console port. When you are finished with that network element and want to switch to a different device that is connected to a different port, you typically enter a special command that is prefixed with a special escape parameter. This allows the terminal server to recognize that it itself is the intended recipient for the command and can switch you to another port.

To make matters even better, the terminal server also has an IP address and an Ethernet interface. This enables you to connect to the terminal servers through a network, such as a local-area network (LAN). This way, your craft terminal no longer needs to be directly connected to the terminal server, as long as it connects to the same network. Accessing the network element works exactly the same as when you access the terminal server through its local port: You specify which port you want to be connected to and are dropped into a terminal session with the device that is connected to that port. Because it is, of course, possible to address different terminal servers over the network by merely using their respective IP address, it is no longer required to physically connect and disconnect between different terminal servers just to be connected to network elements that are connected to different terminal servers. After all, terminal servers have only a finite number of ports, usually no more than a few dozens. Instead, the craft terminal can reach any terminal server on the network and, with it, any network element connected to a port of the terminal server. In fact, the craft terminal can be a management application, for all practical purposes; it does not need to be a human craft technician interacting with the device.

Of course, what you have just introduced and barely noticed is an actual management network—a network to interconnect managing application (your craft terminal) and managed devices.

Of course, the management network that we have just built has one big drawback: Although we can connect to any network element, it is necessary to keep track of which network element is connected to which terminal server, and through which port. It is easy to lose track of this information, especially as the number of network elements, terminal servers, and, thus, complexity of the management network grows. Wouldn't it be easier if you could just address the network elements directly, instead of through a port of a terminal server? This leads us to another way in which to connect to the network elements directly.

The second method of connecting to an NE is through its Ethernet port. Most NEs offer such a port through which they can be addressed directly from the network. The NE does not use the port to route traffic; the NE uses it to attach to a network like any other host. Now the NE no longer needs to be addressed in terms of a serial port of a terminal server through which it connects. Instead, it has its own IP address—used for management purposes—that allows the NE to be treated and addressed like any host on a network. In addition, this Ethernet port, not the console port, is the interface of choice to interact with the device using methods other than the CLI, such as a management protocol like SNMP. The console port, after all, is intended mainly as an easy means for craft technicians and, thus, human users who need to interact with the device, not for management systems over a network.

The third method of connecting to an NE is to simply use a port that is shared with other traffic—traffic that does not terminate at the NE, but that is routed or switched. In this case, management traffic is carried "in band" instead of "out of band," as with the other options.

The Pros and Cons of a Dedicated Management Network

Carrying management traffic out of band can quickly result in building a fairly sophisticated network that is dedicated just to network management. This network can exist in addition and in parallel to the network that you are trying to manage—a dedicated network that allows your management systems to communicate with the network elements that they are managing. However, using out-of-band management communications does not necessarily imply the use of a dedicated management network that is physically separate and distinguished from the production network. Although a dedicated management port is used, the traffic to and from that port could also be carried through the same network that carries the rest of the traffic. Instead of being a dedicated network, the management network is, in effect, overlaid on top of the production network.

Figure 3-12 depicts the two alternatives of having a network that is shared for both management and production traffic (Figure 3-12a) and keeping management and production networks physically separate (Figure 3-12b). Which option makes the most sense? The answer is, it depends. Like so much in engineering, it is all about trade-offs.

Figure 3-12 *Dedicated Versus Shared Management and Production Networks*

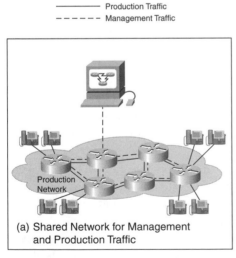
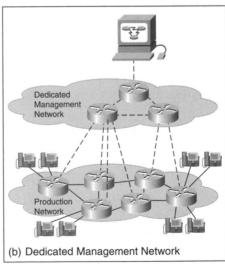

(a) Shared Network for Management and Production Traffic

(b) Dedicated Management Network

The advantages of using a dedicated management network are numerous:

- **Reliability**—With a dedicated management network, management traffic is carried independently of traffic over the production network, making management significantly more reliable. For example, picture a situation in which a network failure or network congestion occurs and makes a certain segment of the network hard to reach. In this situation, management is absolutely critical to finding out what happened, and possibly to subsequently instructing the network to perform certain reconfigurations to remedy the situation. However, unless you have a dedicated management network, chances are, management traffic will be just as incapable of getting through as any other communications traffic. As with an ambulance that is stuck in traffic, you will not be able to get to the scene easily to determine exactly what has happened (in fact, the call to alert you might have trouble getting through), let alone provide first aid or clean up the mess. This means that management might effectively be unavailable just when it is needed the most. Of course, with a dedicated management network, all of this is a nonissue.

- **Interference avoidance**—When carried over the production network, management traffic competes with other networking traffic. This includes data application traffic as well as traffic with high quality of service (QoS) requirements, such as voice or streaming video, which is sensitive to fluctuations in bandwidth and delay. Although management traffic is not very high in volume compared with other applications, it can be bursty and still of non-negligible volume. For example, it might involve downloading large files with new configurations or software images to network elements, or transferring statistical data that was collected over a longer period of time at the network element. The amount of traffic can be sufficient to interfere with other applications. For example, it can cause load conditions on the network that can lead to noticeable degradations in the QoS that is provided to other applications. This is not a recipe for keeping network users and customers happy; in the worst case, it can translate into lost revenue to the network provider. Interference between management and production network traffic can also make certain problems harder to diagnose. Again, with a dedicated management network, all of this is a nonissue.

- **Ease of network planning**—Avoiding interference as described in the previous bullet requires careful network planning that takes into account the effects of unpredictable network management traffic. Network planning for the production network becomes easier if there is no need to consider management traffic, as is the case when a dedicated management network is used. Of course, the price to pay is that the management network also must be planned for. However, a dedicated management network runs only a single application—network management—so this problem becomes simpler.

■ **Security**—A dedicated management network is harder to attack and easier to secure. End users and subscribers will never come into contact with it; its devices are on a completely separate network. This makes it less prone to hackers and less vulnerable to, for example, DoS attacks on the production network.

On the other hand, there are a variety of reasons not to use a dedicated management network and to use management communication exchanges over a shared network:

■ **Cost and overhead**—Despite its advantages, a dedicated management network requires a separate network to be built. This comes with a huge price tag that results in significant additional cost. A shared network does not require additional devices, additional space, and additional cabling.

■ **No reasonable alternative**—In quite a few cases, a shared network might realistically be the only option. For example, equipment that is deployed at the customer premises might be reachable only through one network. One scenario involves a Digital Subscriber Line (DSL) router that is located at the site of a customer. The service provider provides DSL connectivity to this router, but it does not make sense to provide separate management connectivity. Instead, any required management communication occurs over the same physical network. Of course, at the logical level at least, a separate channel can be used.

What about management of the dedicated management network? Shouldn't this be a consideration as well? Will we now also need a "management management network" to manage the management network as well? And who would manage that? Will it ever end? This is a good point, and for the truly paranoid, it is well worth considering. However, in general, the answer is that the management network will also provide management connectivity for its own devices. One management network is enough. The management network will be considerably less complex than the production network that it actually must manage; it has only a very small set of services and users. Also, the environment in which it is deployed is very controlled. Finally, the production network can provide backup to the management network in case it is needed, as explained in the discussion that follows.

In summary, a dedicated management network has undeniable advantages. For areas of a network in which management is critical—for example, the backbone at a service provider or even a large enterprise—this is the implementation of choice. Its big drawback is cost, which is the main reason dedicated management networks are found only in the most critical network deployments. Hybrid solutions also are possible, with management traffic traveling in part over a dedicated management network and in part over the production network.

As for in-band and out-of-band management communications at the network element itself, typically network elements are configured to support both. The out-of-band communications path normally is used, using a dedicated port for management traffic. However, if problems arise in the management network, the option exists to fall back on the secondary in-band—and shared management network—option. This way, the production network itself is used to provide critical backup for the management network when needed. This is perhaps an ironic twist, considering that management traffic was deemed so critical that the production network couldn't be relied on to carry it to begin with.

The Management Support Organization: NOC, NOC, Who's There?

The ingredients that we have introduced so far—network elements and management agents, management systems, and management network—are all that is required to make network management work from a technical perspective. However, if we really want to successfully run a network, we are not quite finished. Missing is the organization that will be responsible for running the network—ultimately, the people who use all that management technology. Unless you are a small business that has few devices that can all be managed by a jack-of-all-trades system administrator and that buys everything else that is needed from an outside service provider, chances are good that some consideration will have to be given this aspect as well.

In this section, we briefly discuss some of these nontechnical aspects. You can think of the organizational aspects as a separate problem dimension in network management. This dimension exists in parallel and in addition to the technical dimension. Of course, there is a mutual dependency between the two—at the end of the day, the sole purpose of all the technical management infrastructure that is put in place is to support the organization that is running the network in the best possible manner. For this reason, telecommunications service providers quite fittingly refer to management systems often as operational support systems (OSS). By this, they mean that systems must blend in with their operational support environment and be used to provide operational support functions.

At the same time, the organization must account for and accommodate certain technical realities that come with the nature of running a communications network. In some cases, the organization must adapt to what is technically possible as well. How to best organize the management organization is a significant topic in itself, and we can only touch the tip of the iceberg in this chapter.

Managing the Management

The management support organization ultimately is responsible for making sure that the network is being run effectively and efficiently. It needs to perform such tasks as were presented in the previous chapter, including but not limited to these:

- Monitoring the network for failures

- Diagnosing failures and communication outages if they occur, and planning and carrying out repairs

- Provisioning new services, and adding and removing users to and from the network

- Keeping an eye on performance of the network, taking preventive measures when service levels appear to slip, and taking note of early indications when, for example, the network is running low on communication capacity

- Planning network upgrades, such as installation of new line cards to increase capacity or distribution of software patches

- Planning network topology and network buildout, to ensure that the network will continue to meet future communication demands

One way of structuring the management support organization involves analyzing the different tasks that must be accounted for and the workflows that they involve. The organization is then divided into different units that each perform a distinct function, taking into account workflows to minimize interactions that are required between different units and, specifically, dependencies that might lead to finger-pointing situations. Responsibilities of the different units and the organizational interfaces between them, procedures, and workflows must be clearly defined. For example, one way to structure an organization might result in distinctive organization units for the following:

- Network planning, responsible for analyzing network usage and traffic patterns, and planning network buildout and service rollout.

- Network operations, responsible for keeping the network running and monitoring the network for failures.

- Network administration, the only organization allowed to actually physically "touch" the network, responsible for deploying the network and services on it. This group includes field technicians who are dispatched to commission new equipment into the network, replace line cards, and so on.

- Customer management, responsible for interacting with the customers. This group takes orders for new services and provides various forms of customer support.

Each of the organizations has its own personnel, with their own distinct roles. The most generic term that describes the role of a staff member is *network operator*, but this term includes network operators, network administrators, network planners, craft technicians, service order operators, workforce dispatchers, customer support personnel, and many more.

The various organizations are not entirely independent. For example, network planning must interact with customer management for demand forecasts that indicate areas in which further network buildout is needed. Network operations must provide work orders to network administration, instructing them to fix things that were diagnosed as broken. Customer management must inform network operations of customer-perceived problems with network services and must get information from network operations about the current status of the network so that they can provide technical assistance to users who call.

Of course, organizational structures in large service provider organizations are much more sophisticated than this, but the preceding description should suffice to sketch the picture. In fact, telecommunications service providers have perfected the art of building the most suitable operational support organization. They are the ones who manage the largest networks and most diverse sets of services out there, and their whole business success depends to a large part on their capability to optimize the organization of their operations. Being the most successful in the marketplace is directly correlated with being the most efficient to run the network, the fastest to roll out new services, the most effective to deal with unforeseen events in the network, and so on. At the same time, telecommunications service providers are being subjected to a significant amount of public and regulatory scrutiny that forces them to, for example, guarantee high levels of service and maximum availability. The requirement to have telephone service available 99.999% of the time, which allows only for downtimes per year that are measured in seconds, not minutes, is one such example. E911 service is another example. With E911 service, emergency phone calls made to the 911 phone number must always be put through, no matter how congested the network.

However, many of the same organizational concepts are also being applied in large enterprises and, for example, Internet data centers. Of course, in some cases, smaller and less sophisticated structures must suffice. For a small business, for example, often a single person acting as administrator manages all the communications equipment, possibly in addition to end systems and hosts that are connected. Any other arrangement would be uneconomical and would distract from the core business. Of course, in such an environment, many communication services are simply bought from the outside from a service provider that has a large support organization in place. All that really needs to be administered is perhaps a few routers and a private branch exchange (PBX).

In addition to a good organizational structure and clear network management responsibilities, many other things need to be considered to be able to run the network smoothly. These include but are not limited to the following:

- **Establishment of process and operational policies, documentation of operational procedures**—This helps make management of the network consistent and efficient, and facilitates meeting a consistently high standard of operations. One aspect of this is well-defined workflows, to make sure that things that are supposed to happen do not fall through the cracks. Another aspect concerns well-defined escalation procedures to ensure responsiveness. Also, in case of emergencies or situations that a network operations staff is not prepared for, this provides invaluable guidance.

- **Collection of audit trails**—Automatically logging the activities of operations support staff—who initiated what action, at what time—makes it easier to reproduce what happened and recover from situations in which human error or omission led to operational hiccups.

- **Network documentation**—Make sure not just your procedures and policies, but also your network itself is well documented—that is, documentation must be accurate and up-to-date. This is important for activities such as network planning and the planning of software upgrades. It also enables you to identify discrepancies between what is supposed to be in the network and what actually has been deployed. Clearly, you want to avoid people hooking up devices to the network that you are unaware of, whether intentional or unintentional (for example, someone accidentally hooked up the wrong piece of equipment or inserted the wrong line card).

- **Reliable backup and restore procedures**—This provides your network operations with an invaluable lifeline that lets you bring the network back up in case of disasters and emergencies. If you cannot immediately figure out what's wrong, the best course of action might be to restore the last configuration that was known to work properly.

- **Security emphasis**—Security threats in networking have received a lot of attention in recent years. The most significant threat to your network might not be hackers from the outside, but disgruntled employees on the inside. On the inside, employees have physical access to the networking equipment, as well as to the tools to mess with it. Hence, your network is potentially most vulnerable from the inside. Therefore, in addition to keeping your operations staff happy, make sure that the amount of damage that any one person can cause is limited and can be recovered from. Some of the items of the previous points (audit trails, dependable backup and restore procedures) are important tools for that.

Inside the Network Operations Center

One important aspect of the management support organization concerns where it is physically located. This might not be a consideration for a small business running a few routers in one or two locations, but it does matter for a service provider with a global presence, interconnecting thousands of sites.

The place from which large networks is managed is generally termed the Network Operations Center (NOC). From here, the bulk of management-related activities is carried out, from monitoring the network to provisioning services, from backing up network configurations to collecting accounting data used for billing customers. You might have seen pictures of NOCs with large command rooms of telecommunication service providers. These photographs show screens in front displaying world maps with pictures of the global network and blinking icons, with numerous operators sitting at consoles. These photographs might remind you of the command center of a NASA space mission. The previous chapter showed one such NOC in Figure 2-1.

In addition, the NOC might house the communications equipment itself. Communications equipment is often housed in rooms that are filled with large floor-to-ceiling racks in which network elements are mounted with their LEDs blinking and masses of wiring and cabling coming out of the back. Cabling, in fact, is another issue that can quickly become a problem. Network management must be accompanied by good facilities management that keeps track of the "passive" components of the network, such as cables, that do not have agents associated with them but that are important physical aspects of the network. Again, you saw pictures of that in the previous chapter, in Figures 2-2 and 2-3.

For large and global organizations, a central NOC might not be enough. In those cases, several NOCs acting as peers that can back each other up, if required, are introduced. For example, NOCs can be deployed on a global basis to realize a "follow the sun" strategy: one NOC in London, one on the U.S. West Coast, and one in India, for example. At any one time, only one NOC is in charge, with the other NOCs providing emergency off-hours support. When the sun sets and it is time for the local personnel to go home, the responsibility for running the network is handed off and the next NOC where the sun is just rising takes over. Obviously, to be realized successfully, sophisticated organizational procedures and operational policies are required, along with stringent requirements imposed on management systems to support them.

Likewise, in some cases, "regional NOCs" are used to divide a central responsibility into several domains, such as U.S. West Coast and U.S. East Coast. Here, the responsibility is split between different NOCs.

In addition to NOCs, you might hear service providers sometimes refer to another geographical unit, a Central Office (CO). A Central Office is much less central than its name implies—the central operations center, after all, is the NOC itself. A CO terminates local lines. It is a local outpost that typically houses access network communication equipment that local business or residential dwellings are physically connected to. Typically, there are many COs, with numbers that can reach into the thousands. Unlike NOCs, COs might not be staffed. *Central Office* is fundamentally a telecommunications service provider term that is unknown to enterprise organizations. An equivalent in an enterprise is a room at a remote branch office that houses the local communications equipment, such as local routers, switches, and PBX.

Chapter Summary

In this chapter, we took a closer look at the basic parts of network management.

The network device plays the role of the managed system, also referred to as an agent. Agents provide a management interface through which they can communicate with the outside world and respond to management requests. They provide an abstraction of the device that is being managed, referred to as a MIB. The MIB constitutes a conceptual data store. The real resources of the device that are to be managed are represented as managed objects—that is, data items inside the MIB.

As the managing system, the management system or application plays the role of the manager with regard to the network elements it is managing. It is the counter piece to the role of the agent.

The management network is the network through which management systems and network devices are connected. The management network can be its own dedicated network, which offers significant advantages specifically in the case of complex networks for which high availability is a key concern. However, it results in significant additional cost. Management communications can also be carried over the same network that is being managed, in which case the management network is shared.

In addition to the technical parts, a support organization is required to successfully run a network. One way to organize is along the lines of the different functions that are required to manage the network, taking into account the required interactions between those functions. Having proper processes and procedures in place is another key ingredient of a successful support organization. The location from which the network is managed is referred to as the Network Operations Center (NOC).

Chapter Review

1. Name the two contexts in which the term *agent* is used in network management.

2. Compare the manager/agent and client/server paradigms. What are the commonalities and what are the differences?

3. The chapter stated that a network element can contain more than one management agent and that a management agent can contain embedded management intelligence. Taking these statements literally can lead to the conclusion that the same management intelligence might have to be implemented redundantly in a network element, once for each management agent. Clearly, this would be a wasteful approach. What would be an appropriate refinement of the model of a management agent?

4. Explain the term *MIB*—what does the acronym stand for, what is it, and who provides it?

5. Name one difference between a MIB and a database.

6. Tell whether the following statement is true: "If a network is required to have availability of 99.999%, its management systems need to also be 99.999% available." Why or why not? Please elaborate. For extra points, factor in the influence of the type of application that the management system is used for.

7. Management traffic is different from other communication traffic, in that the NE itself is a destination and originator of traffic. However, it is not the only type of traffic for which this is true. Name an example of other network traffic that the NE does not just switch or route, but actively participates in.

8. What could be the most important reason for using a dedicated management network instead of a shared one?

9. Which other term do service providers use to refer to management systems?

10. Would you expect a management system to provision services to be located at a NOC or at a Central Office? Why?

Part II: Management Perspectives

CHAPTER 4

The Dimensions of Management

Many readers will be familiar with the story of the elephant and the blind men. It goes something like this: A group of blind men goes to the zoo to learn about elephants. Each man goes up to an elephant and touches a part of it. When asked to describe it, the first one responds, having felt its legs: "An elephant is like a group of trees." The second one responds, having examined its trunk: "No, it's like a snake." The third one, having touched its ears, compares it to a large sheet of paper. Every one of the men is right from one particular point of view. However, only the combination of these different aspects ultimately reveals the complete picture.

Like an elephant for a blind man, network management can be a big topic to grasp. When dealing with a particular network management problem, we are often like one of the blind men—grasping one of its aspects, yet not realizing the big picture. Sometimes that is sufficient, sometimes it is not. The descriptions in the earlier chapters indicated that network management is a broad subject. It involves building applications that help monitor networks or provision services. It involves how the underlying real world is represented in a data model, as well as establishing management protocols that allow managing and managed systems to interact. It involves organizational aspects of running a network. After those introductory chapters, we are ready to drill deeper into the subject area. But where do we start, and how will we know that we have covered the subject thoroughly? In other words, how is the subject area best decomposed into its different aspects?

This chapter tries to answer those questions. In doing so, it provides the foundation for dividing and conquering the network management problems that you might face. While the concepts covered in this chapter are clearly more theoretical in nature than those ones in previous chapters, they lay a systemic conceptual groundwork for dealing one at a time with different aspects of management.

After reading this chapter, you will be able to do the following:

- Differentiate between different orthogonal (unrelated) yet complementary aspects in network management, which will help you to divide and conquer network management problems.

- Describe the different phases in the network management life cycle, from the planning stages to the decommissioning of network equipment.

■ Distinguish different layers in network management that build on top of each other, from dealing with equipment in the network to managing your business as it relates to networking.

■ Explain the relevance of network management standards.

■ Separate different types of interoperability concerns in network management, from function to information to communication.

Lost in (Management) Space: Charting Your Course Along Network Management Dimensions

If we think of network management as a multidimensional space, the question arises as to which dimensions or axes span that space and what coordinates will be defined for each axis. This is important because, when faced with any problem, it can be tremendously helpful to know how to divide the problem into different aspects. Each aspect corresponds to one of the dimensions. If the dimensions are identified in such a way that they are independent of each other, we call them *orthogonal*. When those dimensions are clear, it becomes much easier to define a systemic approach to the problem and deal with its different aspects one at a time.

Figure 4-1 depicts a set of orthogonal dimensions for network management. We take a closer look at each dimension in the following sections.

Figure 4-1 *Network Management Dimensions*

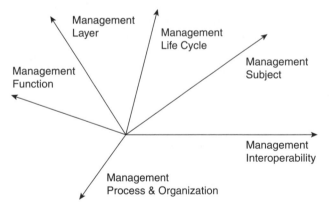

Management Interoperability: "Roger That"

Management is a distributed application that involves different systems—management applications and network devices. For management to work, those systems must communicate with each other for management purposes. In other words, they need to be interoperable. A central aspect of network management deals, therefore, with how management interoperability between different systems can be ensured. For a managing system and a managed device to interoperate, it is not sufficient for the systems to be merely "connected"—that is, to have a physical or a Layer 3 connection that allows them to exchange data packets. This, of course, is a prerequisite. But much more is required. They need to speak the same management language. When the manager sends a management message, the agent needs to understand the message. For example, the agent needs to understand that the manager is trying to make a specific request and must be able to provide a response that the manager can understand. The agent needs to support the functionality that the manager requests in the management message and that the manager requires to do its job. When the management messages involve the exchange of management information about the device, there needs to be a mutual understanding between manager and agent about how information is represented and how it needs to be interpreted.

Management interoperability can hence be divided into several subdimensions, as illustrated in Figure 4-2:

■ The *communication viewpoint*, dealing with what kinds of messages are exchanged between parties engaging in management communications

■ The *function viewpoint*, dealing with the management functions that either party can provide

■ The *information viewpoint*, dealing with how management information that needs to be exchanged is being represented

Figure 4-2   *Aspects of Management Interoperability*

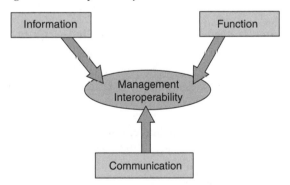

To give a real life analogy, for two persons to successfully conduct a business interaction with each other, it is not sufficient for them to merely hear each other when talking over the phone. In addition, they need to speak the same language—English, for example (communication viewpoint). They also need to know what services they can provide. For example, are you speaking to someone in a ticket office for a theater, or are you talking to someone from the Internal Revenue Service (function viewpoint)? Finally, you need to be clear about what you are talking about. If you want to order a ticket for a play, you need the following: Know the name of the play, refer to a common seating chart to know what seats you are buying, and have a common way to refer to the starting time—for example, know whether "9 o'clock" refers to 9 a.m. or 9 p.m. (information viewpoint).

Communication Viewpoint: Can You Hear Me Now?

As mentioned, the communication viewpoint deals with what kinds of messages are exchanged between managers and agents. Those messages generally constitute the core of a management protocol. An example of a management protocol is the Simple Network Management Protocol (SNMP).

So why is it not sufficient for manager and agent to simply have IP connectivity? "IP connectivity" means that they can exchange IP packets; "IP," of course, refers to the Internet Protocol, which defines basic rules that are used for all data exchanges in the Internet. In fact, IP connectivity in general is one of the prerequisites to exchange management messages. But by itself, it is not sufficient. Again, IP connectivity just ensures that manager and agent can hear each other; it does not mean that they speak the same language, let alone that they can understand each other.

Some of the aspects that must be addressed in addition to establishing basic data connectivity include the following:

■ **How is a management session established?**—In other words, how does a manager contact an agent to tell it that it would like to manage it (and how is the agent supposed to answer to this request)? How is the management session later torn down?

■ **How does a manager need to authenticate itself to the agent (or, for that matter, the agent to the manager)?**—In other words, how does the agent know that the manager is indeed who he says he is? Clearly, with all the security threats that loom over the Internet, you want to make sure that the configuration of your networking equipment can be modified only by those who are authorized to do so.

■ **How does a management message that carries a request identify the type of request that is being made?**—For example, how does the message indicate whether the manager wants to get information on the current utilization of a port, versus telling the agent to reset itself? What kinds of parameters need to accompany the request? Is there a separate type of request for each function—that is, does the management protocol need to be extended when new requests are to be supported, or is the type of request identified as a parameter inside the request itself?

■ **How does the manager recognize a message as a response to the request?**—How will the manager know that a message that the agent later sends it is a response to this particular request, as opposed to a response to another request or to an unrelated unsolicited message?

- **Is a time stamp required?**—Is the format of this time stamp yyyy:mm:dd:hh:mm:ss, is it dd/mm/yy:hh-mm-ss, or is it something else? How is information about the time zone represented?

- **How is management information carried inside a management message encoded?**—Does it use the Western alphabet, does it use Extensible Markup Language (XML) format?

In addition to the messages themselves, certain rules that govern their interchange need to be defined. For example, consider what is to happen in situations such as the following:

- **How is the agent supposed to react if two messages that seemingly contain the same request are received?**—Is the second message to be rejected and a separate error response to be sent, is it sufficient to ignore the second request and simply send one response, or should the same request be carried out a second time?

- **Who can initiate the tearing down of a management session?**—Effectively, this means that a manager is "logged out" and any system resources that are reserved at the agent to service the manager are released—no more event messages will be sent to the manager nor management requests be accepted until a new management session is established. Is this the responsibility of the manager, or can the agent tear down the session as well? What happens when an agent receives a request to tear down a management session, but there are still outstanding requests to be serviced? Should the session be torn down immediately, or should responses still be sent?

- **What should happen when a response to a management request is not received after a certain amount of time?**—Should the same request be sent a second time? Should a new request be issued? Can the manager find out whether the first request has actually been received and serviced already, but the response got lost?

Some management protocols define additional aspects, such as what management functions need to be supported. However, the communication viewpoint is at the core of any management exchange. It defines the language that manager and agent need to speak.

Much as in real life, a successful interaction between different parties requires more than just speaking the same language. For example, managers and agents need to have the same understanding of the domain they are talking about. Just because a medical doctor and a hardware engineer both speak English does not mean that one will understand the other when explaining a medical diagnosis or a technical detail in integrated circuit design. However, that is a different problem and, hence, a different aspect of management interoperability.

Function Viewpoint: What Can I Do for You Today?

The function viewpoint establishes what functions are supported—that is, what services a manager can expect from an agent. This includes the type of requests that a manager can make and that the agent supports. It also includes capabilities that an agent has to send event messages to notify a manager of certain event occurrences.

At this point, we've covered the need to establish connectivity, as well as the need for rules for the exchange of management messages. Some additional aspects that must be addressed are part of the functional viewpoint and include the following:

- What functions are provided to enable a manager to retrieve information from the agent? Is it necessary to get one item at a time, or can many items be retrieved "in bulk" at once?

- How can a managed system's configuration be modified? Again, is it necessary to modify it one item at a time, or can multiple updates be packaged into the same request?

- Are "transactions" supported—that is, is there an option for sending a list of configuration changes that will either all take place at the same time or none at all, in case a failure occurs? Or do the functions support only so-called "best effort" semantics, which means that some of the changes might succeed while others might fail?

- Is there a function that allows a manager to sign up to receive only specific types of events? (We refer to this as an *event subscription* capability.)

- Does the agent provide functionality that allows events to be replayed in case a management application missed an event, perhaps because it was offline?

- Does the agent provide *introspection* capabilities that enable a manager to find out from the agent itself what functions the agent supports, or does the manager need to know all functions beforehand?

- Can the agent be programmed to perform certain test functions at predefined intervals, or do those functions need to be invoked explicitly every time?

Clearly, the functions that are provided have a great impact on how management applications interact with the agent and even how they are built. For example:

- Agents that provide introspection capabilities facilitate and even suggest a data-driven design in the management application. The management application can dynamically discover the capabilities of the agent. For the management application to fully take advantage of this introspection capability, it should not be hard-wired with regard to the functions that the management application expects to use on the agent. As a result, it can leverage functionality of the agent even if that functionality was originally not available at the time the management application was first written. The management application becomes easier to maintain and might not need to be upgraded as often.

■ Transaction capabilities offload applications from complicated exception handling. Without transaction capabilities, management applications need to apply complicated logic in case operations start failing in the middle of a sequence of commands. The reason is that earlier commands that had succeeded might need to be "backed out of" and their effects undone, which is not always a simple thing to do. Without it, the network might be left in an inconsistent state and precious networking resources might be wasted that could be reclaimed for a productive purpose. If the agent supports transaction capabilities, much of this logic is no longer needed.

■ An agent that offers an event subscription capability allows applications to subscribe to very specific categories of events. This imposes less strain on the management application's performance because events that the application is not interested in are not forwarded and, hence, do not need to be received and filtered. This, in turn, makes it easier for the application to scale.

Often the management protocol already defines many of the management functions. For example, functions to retrieve management information ("get") and to update configuration information ("set") are often built into the protocol. Nevertheless, there is clearly a distinction between the function and the communication viewpoints: One defines the functions themselves, and the other defines the messages that are being exchanged to perform the function. These include messages for a default set of functions, sometimes referred to as *primitives*. Those primitives can be built on to compose and communicate more advanced functions. The function viewpoint defines the capabilities that an agent is offering that a manager can rely on, as opposed to the language used between manager and agent.

The independence of different viewpoints is a central point of this chapter, which is why it is stressed one more time: The functions that a management agent provides are essentially independent of the management protocol they map into. The management protocol determines one particular way in which the functions are mapped into the actual message exchanges between managers and agents. Of course, the function that is being requested and the parameters of the function need to be encoded and carried using the protocol. However, the fact that functions and protocols can be mixed and matched enables us to discuss communication and function aspects separately because they constitute independent viewpoints. Here is how the earlier examples of different management functions could be supported through different protocols (management protocols are discussed in detail in Chapter 8, "Common Management Protocols: Languages of Management"):

■ The introspection capability could provide information about an agent's capabilities, for example, in the following forms: an XML document, an SNMP MIB (retrievable through SNMP "get" commands), or a custom-formatted output of a CLI **Show** command.

■ The transaction capability could be communicated through a set of CLI commands delineating the beginning and end of a transaction, by emulating a specific type of MIB that is manipulated through SNMP "set" commands, or by using a custom transaction protocol that is applied to management operations.

■ Event subscription could happen through a special CLI command, through setting MIB variables in a special SNMP MIB, or through a custom protocol that encodes the event subscription as an XML document.

Information Viewpoint: What Are You Talking About?

The information viewpoint, finally, defines a conceptual model of the domain of discourse—for example, the device, or the service provided by the network. This model is an abstraction of the real world, introduced for management purposes, that enables manager and agent to communicate about the real-world entities that are being managed. It defines the management information that is carried as part of the management message exchanges and that is subjected to the management functions. It establishes a common terminology between manager and agent. For example, how do you refer to a specific card in a device? To a particular port? To an interface? To a software function? To an instance of a voice service?

In addition to modeling a particular system, the rules according to which the system is to be modeled need to be established. This is, in effect, a meta model—a model of a model, used to define the actual models themselves. Here are some of the options that a meta model could provide for defining a model:

■ Do you provide abstractions that allow the managed system to be modeled as a collection of objects, following rules of object-oriented design?

If so, will methods need to be defined as part of those objects, or will there be a well-defined set of operations implicitly available to operate on those objects—for example to retrieve information about an object and to create, delete, and update objects?

■ Do you provide abstractions that allow the managed system to be modeled as a set of tables, reminiscent of tables used in databases?

■ Do you simply define rules by which to define a set of command parameters that need to be sent in conjunction with commands to achieve the desired effect?

Again, these information-related questions are independent of the other viewpoints. Of course, the information needs to be ultimately encoded and carried over a management protocol. But the meaning of what is being encoded is, in general, completely irrelevant to the protocol, just as the telephone wire does not care whether it carries a conversation in English or French. Vice versa, the same information can be carried over multiple protocols, just as a conversation in French about nuclear physics could occur over the telephone or over letters exchanged via carrier pigeons.

The Role of Standards

For managers and agents to interoperate, quite a few elements need to be aligned: In addition to being interconnected, they need to speak the same management language—that is, protocol. The manager needs to understand precisely which functions the agent supports and to interpret the results that are returned. Furthermore, manager and agent need to be on the same page concerning the management information carried in the management messages. Otherwise, to pick up on the earlier example, those tickets you order at the mezzanine level are bound to lead to disappointment when you expected to be sitting in the middle of the orchestra section.

A typical manager needs to manage much more than a single agent. Although it is possible for a manager to manage a network consisting of identical devices with the same agent on each device, this is much more the exception than the norm. It is much more likely that the manager has to manage a network with many different kinds of devices and many different kinds of agents, as Figure 4-3 illustrates. For example, the devices can vary in terms of the following:

- **Capabilities of the device and, hence, device type**—For example, this could entail routers and switches, voice gateways, directory servers, and more.

- **Size and capacity of the device**—For example, this could mean a low-end versus a high-end router, differing numbers of ports, different switching and routing capacity.

- **Vendor**—Many service providers, in particular, have a conscious policy to have several competing equipment vendors as suppliers for their network, to keep them "on their toes."

- **Operating system version**—Even devices of the same make and model can differ in terms of the operating system version and patch level they are running, resulting potentially in differences between their agents.

Figure 4-3 *Differences in Network Equipment*

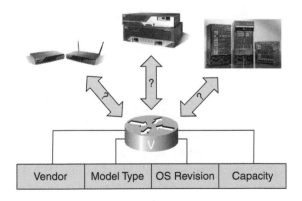

If each agent requires a set of different interoperability rules, the manager will be confronted with an exploding number of language variants, different flavors of management functions, and alternative representations of management information. This makes the job of management application developers difficult and results in high development cost and slow time to market. In turn, it hampers the capability of network providers to manage networks effectively because fewer tools are available. In addition, application developers and system integrators might pass costs on to the network provider. Think about how difficult things would be if you needed to speak to everyone you interacted with—your spouse, your child, your teacher at school, your grocery clerk, your boss, your friends—in a different language. Luckily, there are standards. Just as many countries have an official language, management standards are a way of ensuring that different systems speak the same management language.

The role of standards is to establish common rules that everyone adheres to. For management, standards address all aspects affecting interoperability:

- The rules for management message exchange, and the way in which management messages encode information

- A complete and consistent set of basic management functions with well-known meaning, parameters, and function return codes

- The way in which the entities that are being managed are modeled as management information

Standard management protocols address the first aspect (standardizing management messages and rules that guide their exchange). They also include a set of base functions, addressing the second aspect.

The third aspect—management information—is often the most tricky to standardize. Many of the entities that need to be managed are in fact different—they have different features that need to be represented and might even have different physical characteristics. This can lead to a monumental amount of information that needs to be standardized, and to standards that are in constant need of update and extension. Any particular piece of information, perhaps with the exception of a few very general aspects, might apply in only a few cases, which makes a potential standard less widely applicable and, by the same token, decreases the pressure on getting this information standardized. For this reason, in general, standards merely state what means are available for modeling entities to be managed, instead of standardizing the models themselves. They standardize the so-called "schema"—the language in which a model is expressed—as opposed to the model itself. Standardization of the model, if it is addressed at all, typically occurs in additional, separate standards that address very focused, specific aspects. (Of course, as always, there are exceptions—the Desktop Management Task Force [DMTF] has published a comprehensive model called the Common Information Model [CIM] that is designed to provide what amounts to universal model coverage. Likewise, the Digital Subscriber Line Forum [DSL Forum] has published a management protocol standard called TR-69 that includes management information as an intrinsic component, albeit for a very specific and focused area—DSL management.)

Because they establish the common rules that allow managing and managed systems to communicate, management standards play a central role in network management wherever interoperability between systems is concerned—between managers and agents, and specifically between management applications and devices in the network being managed. Management standards are a prerequisite for making management economical and for supporting new services and devices in a network.

Of course, no rule or law states that a management agent must adhere to a standard. Every vendor is free to decide which, if any, standards should be supported by its equipment, or whether the management interfaces offered should be strictly proprietary. No standards police exist to fine an equipment vendor for not supporting a standard; the marketplace forces that. (There are a few exceptions to this statement in areas where the communications industry is regulated. For example, most countries have laws that require telecommunications service providers and, by extension, equipment vendors to support certain interfaces that allow for the collection of call records and wiretapping by government agencies.) Having said that, every vendor clearly wants its equipment to easily integrate with management applications and existing operations environments. Customers shopping for equipment might require support for certain management standards as a crucial purchasing criteria and put pressure on equipment vendors accordingly. All these factors lead to the spread of standards.

One word of caution: As in many other areas, network management encompasses many standards, and many standards organizations exist that publish management-related standards. This includes organizations sponsored by governments or international bodies such as the International Telecommunications Union (ITU-T) or the International Standardization Organization (ISO). It also includes industry forums or associations whose mission it is to advance the industry as whole or a segment thereof, for which standards are an important aspect. Examples include the TeleManagement Forum (TMF), the DSL Forum, the Institute for Electrical and Electronic Engineers (IEEE), the Desktop Management Taskforce (DMTF), and, of course, the Internet Engineering Task Force (IETF). In addition, there are proprietary "standards," which are not standards at all, but specifications that are simply published by a company that might or might not gain a wider following. Coordination between standards organizations is generally limited. As a result, some standards complement each other, others compete, and others are completely unrelated. No piece of equipment supports every standard, but a few standards, such as SNMP, are pretty universal.

In the end, the success of a standard depends not on what it does on paper, but whether it is actually adopted in the marketplace. As a general observation, standards tend to be successful if they meet the following criteria:

■ They are "universal," in that they stick to a least common denominator in terms of functions that everyone will have to support anyway. Their scope may therefore be somewhat limited, but within that scope, they are complete.

- They are extensible, or offer a platform on which extensions are possible to meet new requirements. This makes the standard future proof, to an extent.

- They are easy to implement. This facilitates their acceptance and is a prerequisite to obtaining the critical mass for a standard to become not just a *de jure* standard (that is, a standard on paper only), but a *de facto* standard (that is, a standard that has actually caught on, that is widely implemented, and that the industry has generally accepted).

Management Subject: What We're Managing

As mentioned and depicted in Chapter 1, "Setting the Stage," in Figure 1-4, there are different kinds of networked systems that require management. Network management is often categorized into different subdisciplines to reflect that distinction:

- Network management, in a narrower sense, deals with the management of communication networks and the resources in the network that are required to establish end-to-end communications. For example, this includes the routers and switches in a network, or the communications backbone of a service provider.

- System management deals with the management of end systems that are connected to networks. For example, this includes hosts and servers in a data center, or personal computers on users' desktops.

- Application management deals with the management of applications that are deployed on systems that are interconnected over a network. For example, this includes corporate e-mail applications and security software that is supposed to be running on computers.

In terms of their management needs, networks, systems, and applications have much more in common than what separates them. Configurations need to be displayed, alarms have to be communicated and logged, operations have to be executed remotely, information about the entities that are being managed needs to be modeled and represented. The broad management themes are generally shared, which means that, in general, the same management principles and paradigms apply across the board. However, certain aspects and requirements are unique to each. For this reason, it can be important to be clear about the subject of management. There might be only specific details in which network, system, and application management differ, but as the saying goes, the devil is in the details. Hence, attention to those details is required. For example:

- Network management must deal with end-to-end connections, making sure that the configurations of routers and switches across the network are coordinated. This does not concern application or system management.

■ Systems management deals with aspects such as memory utilization and hard disk capacity. Systems management is somewhat similar to dealing with individual routers and switches in the network, but it does not involve the end-to-end considerations.

■ Application management is largely concerned with aspects that relate to the deployment of software, such as keeping track of software licenses and ensuring that the operating system version is compatible with a given patch. Although similar tasks apply to software that runs on routers in a network, general-purpose application management generally involves a far greater set of dependencies and degree of sophistication for those tasks.

For further specialization, each of these disciplines can be further subdivided into an arbitrary number of subcategories, becoming more specialized in the process. Let us look at network management as an example. Here, we can distinguish between the management of transmission systems, switching equipment, and communications at Layer 3 and above. We can furthermore distinguish between the types of technology being managed, for example depending on the transmission media—such as wireless, cable, or hybrid fiber coax—and the switching and routing technology used—such as ATM, IP, or MPLS. Another distinction that can be made concerns the services that are to be supported by the network to be managed—management of a data network versus a voice network, versus a video or perhaps a cable TV network. With the appearance of converged networks, the latter distinction has actually started to disappear at the networking level, although it still matters at the service management level.

Each communication technology and each class of applications has some management requirements that are specific and unique, even if they have much in common from a high-level perspective. For example, for voice networks, one aspect that requires management concerns dial plans. Dial plans determine where voice calls are routed depending on the phone numbers that are dialed. For ATM networks, an important category of management requirements concerns the management of permanent virtual circuits (PVCs). The list goes on.

Management Life Cycle: Managing Networks from Cradle to Grave

Typically, network management is associated with keeping a network running. However, this assumes that a network is already in place. But how did it get there? How are networks "born," and how do they—and the components in them—"die"? These different stages are referred to as the life cycle of a network and the services running over it. This life cycle is accompanied by a management life cycle. At inception, networks require planning. After planning comes deployment—new equipment needs to be installed and properly turned up. Only then do regular operations ensue. As the network matures, upgrades must be planned and performed. Finally, equipment must be decommissioned and network traffic cut over to new equipment or to a new generation of networking technology. Figure 4-4 depicts these different phases. Clearly, this is a very basic life cycle; more sophisticated life cycles entail additional life cycle phases, such as maintenance cycles, network upgrades, and the provisioning of services over the equipment.

Figure 4-4 *A Basic Management Life Cycle*

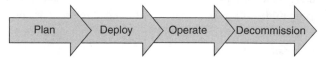

The management life cycle forms another dimension of management. It is independent of how managers and agents interoperate, and it applies regardless of whether management involves networks, networked systems, or applications. Let's explore different stages in the management life cycle in more detail.

Planning

Before any actual operations can take place, networks must be planned. Based on current and forecasted user needs, network equipment is selected, and its placement in the network and location for installation determined. The topology must be planned, taking into account resilience and redundancy. Lines might have to be leased to interconnect different sites. Capacities must be determined, and the possibility of future growth must be taken into account. An enterprise also must decide which aspects of the network to run itself and which services to buy from outside service providers. In all of this, cost and budget constraints must be considered.

Good planning has a tremendous impact on the business and competitiveness of the organization running the network. It ensures proper planning of capital spending, and directing capital investment in the network to areas in which the highest business impact is achieved. It greatly increases the likelihood that situations are avoided in which shortages in communication capacity exist in one place while excess bandwidth lies idle in other places. Supporting tools allow network topologies to be designed and simulations to be performed to analyze the network's capacity, its resilience to fault conditions, and its performance properties.

Network planning does not occur only upon initial deployment. It should occur on an ongoing basis to ensure that the network is kept up-to-date. Planning should accordingly be supported not only by offline planning tools, but by management systems that feed back information about actual utilization and performance data in the current network. This type of information can provide important data points for planning subsequent network buildout.

Deployment

When planning is completed, networks need to be deployed. This means that equipment must be installed and turned up. Deployment can involve its own unique set of management procedures. For example, when a piece of equipment is first installed, it generally does not have an IP address. This means that, at first, it cannot be reached remotely, including from remote management applications. If the device is installed by a network technician, this is not much of a problem because the initial configuration steps can occur through a console directly connected to the device.

However, in other cases, such as with customer premises equipment, the equipment is physically located at the premises of a customer, not the organization that actually runs the network. Sending a technician to a customer costs money and inconveniences end users. It is much better to have the customer simply "plug in" the device and perform whatever other operations are required from the Network Operations Center (NOC). For this to be possible, bootstrapping mechanisms are required that allow a device to obtain an IP address and have Layer 2 and Layer 3 connectivity established automatically. When the device is connected to the network, configuration files that contain the initial set of equipment, parameter settings need to be generated and delivered to the network equipment.

In some cases, management systems might be required to allow network operators to configure network resources before they are actually deployed. The purpose of this is to allow services to be configured in advance and have them be automatically turned on the moment the network equipment is actually deployed, instead of starting the process of generating configurations to provision services only after the equipment has been turned on, which would result in delays. In those cases, the management system keeps track of a fictitious network that is planned but has not actually been built, and reconciles the two as the planned network actually comes online.

After the equipment is physically deployed and initial management connectivity has been established, the configuration that had been prepared in advance can be delivered to the device. The trigger can be automatic, as part of a bootstrap procedure, or manual, requiring an operator to explicitly take a device into commission. If turn-up occurs in the context of a network upgrade, additional functionality could be required to manage the cutover while keeping impact to services to a minimum.

Operations

After turn-up and installation, the regular operation of the network follows. This is where many of the most typical activities that are associated with network management take place: monitoring the network, troubleshooting, conducting performance tuning, collecting performance statistics and accounting data, and so forth.

Decommissioning

Eventually, network equipment might have to be decommissioned in an orderly manner. There can be many reasons for decommissioning. For example, new technologies replace old ones and lead to a general network upgrade, or requirements might have changed and certain types of network equipment are no longer needed. For example, as Internet dialup through modems is being replaced by Digital Subscriber Line (DSL), equipment that terminates telephone lines might be retired, giving way to other types of equipment, such as DSL access multiplexers (DSLAMs). Even decommissioning needs to be carefully carried out; it is not as easy as simply switching off power and hauling the old equipment to the dump. For example, switching existing traffic and users from the old to the new needs to be planned carefully so that the actual cutover causes as little disruption as possible.

Management Layer: It's a Device… No, It's a Service… No, It's a Business

Network management is not just a multidimensional but also a multilayered problem space. At one layer, the concern is with managing individual devices. For example, each device must have the right software patch installed and must be monitored to make sure that it is running properly. These tasks apply regardless of what devices are actually used for in the network—for example, whether they route IP traffic in the core of the network, whether they connect end users to the network, or whether they provide voice-mail service to the employees at a remote branch office. At another layer, the concern is with the management of services that run over the network, such as ensuring that orders for a service that are received from end users or customers are properly tracked and that resources in the network that are required to support the service—such as ports, bandwidth, telephone numbers, and IP addresses—are properly allocated. Those tasks, in turn, can occur largely independent of the specifics of how to manage the individual devices, even if ultimately the service runs over the device.

Although in both cases the "network" is being managed, the functions that are needed to address these different layers of concern are quite different. Ultimately, both layers need to be dealt with. To provide services over the network, it is, of course, necessary to manage the service, but at some point, the individual devices also have to be managed. After all, services are carried over networking equipment, and if that equipment is not properly managed, this eventually has a negative impact on the service. Accordingly, management can be structured into a hierarchy of layers, each building on another. The layers range from lower layers that involve managing details of individual pieces of network equipment, to higher layers that are closer to the running of the business that the network supports. A well-established categorization of management layers for the management of networks is the TMN hierarchy.

TMN refers to a set of standards by the International Telecommunications Union (ITU-T) for the specification of a Telecommunications Management Network (hence, the acronym TMN). TMN covers a wide range of topics related to the principles for how networks used to manage tele-communication networks are to be constructed and which standards they should adhere to. These principles vary according to which networks are being constructed, as well as the standards that they should adhere to. Although the commercial relevance of TMN remains limited and is, in fact, decreasing, it is widely established as a reference framework. One of TMN's benefits is that it provides a clear and widely accepted terminology that facilitates talking about management-related topics.

TMN specifies a wide range of topics. One of them is the TMN hierarchy, a reference model that specifies a set of management layers that build on top of each other and address different abstractions of the management space, as illustrated in Figure 4-5. In practice, those layers are not always clearly separated in the systems that implement the corresponding functionality. However, as a reference, the layer concept is invaluable. We therefore take a closer look at each of the layers in the following subsections.

Figure 4-5   *TMN Layers: A Management Hierarchy Reference Model*

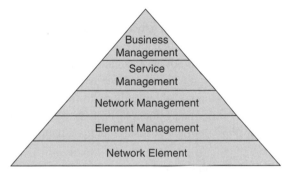

Element Managment

The element management layer involves managing the individual devices in the network and keeping them running. This includes functions to view and change a network element's configuration, to monitor alarm messages emitted from elements in the network, and to instruct network elements to run self-tests.

In this book, we use many terms to refer to the network element, including *device* and *piece of equipment*. Unless specifically noted, all these terms are used synonymously.

Network Management

The next layer in the TMN hierarchy is the network management layer. In the context of TMN, *network management* refers just to this one layer. In this section, the term is accordingly used in a narrower sense than elsewhere in this book, where it refers not only to one of several management layers, but to the discipline of managing networks as a whole.

The network management layer involves managing relationships and dependencies between network elements, generally required to maintain end-to-end connectivity of the network. It is concerned with keeping the network running as a whole. In contrast, although element management enables the management of every element in the network, it does not cover functions that deal with ensuring overall network integrity. It is possible, for example, to have a network with individual element configurations that are perfectly valid but that do not match up properly. As a consequence, the network does not work as intended. For example, to configure a static path across the network, each element along the path must be configured properly. Otherwise, the path is broken and data cannot reach its destination. Likewise, timer values need to be tuned to avoid excessive timeouts and retransmissions. Monitoring tasks at the network management layer involves ensuring that data flows across the network and reaches its destination with acceptable throughput and delay. Policies that control which kinds of calls to admit at any given entry point into the network need to be coordinated across the network to be effective.

These kinds of tasks are addressed at the network management layer. It takes into account the networking context of the individual devices and involves managing the end-to-end aspects of the network. It offers the concept of a forest, as opposed to individual trees. An example of a network management task is the management of a network connection as a whole—for instance, setting it up and monitoring it. As mentioned earlier, this involves managing multiple devices in a concerted fashion. Such management includes not only managing how devices are configured individually, but also ensuring that their configurations are coordinated in certain ways and monitoring for cross-network connectivity, instead of and in addition to simply ensuring that individual elements are up and running. The network management layer makes use of functionality provided by the element management layer, providing additional functions on top.

Again, it is important to realize that *network management* is a term that is seriously overloaded. Depending on the context, it is used to refer to the general discipline of management as a whole, to the type of technical systems that are being subjected to management, and to a particular layer within the "greater" network management.

Service Management

Service management is concerned with managing the services that the network provides and ensuring that those services are running smoothly and functioning as intended. For example, when a customer orders a service, the service needs to be turned up. This might be required for a new employee in an enterprise who needs phone service. Turning up phone service might, in turn, result in a number of operations that need to be carried out across the network so that the service is activated: A phone number must be allocated. The company directory must be updated. Voice mail servers and IP PBXs need to be made aware of the new extension. Later, the user might call the service help desk and complain that the service is not working properly. Problems could include poor voice quality and calls that disconnected unexpectedly. Troubleshooting the service is required to identify the root cause of the problem and solve it. These are all examples of typical tasks in managing a service. These tasks build on functionality that is provided by the network management layer underneath and provide additional value on top, applying them to the context of managing a service.

At the end of the day, networks exist to provide services to users. Services generate revenue for a service provider; they are the reason networks exist in the first place. Services range from the basic—such as providing simple data connectivity or telephony service—to the more sophisticated—such as hosting large-scale enterprise websites that require balancing of load across servers and transparent setup of virtual LANs. In practice, network and service management are often addressed together, and the boundaries between them are blurred. However, at least conceptually, the difference between service and network management is significant: The latter is technology dependent and driven by the implementation of the network. The former is concerned with concepts that end users and customers relate to and the value that they derive from a network—namely, the service, not the networking infrastructure per se.

Business Management

Business management deals with managing the business associated with providing services and all the required support functions. This includes topics as diverse as billing and invoicing, help-desk management, business forecasting, and many more.

Network Element

A fifth layer of the hierarchy is often forgotten: the network element itself—the management agent, in effect. The network element is involved with the management functionality that the network element itself supports, independent of any management system. The network element is in the bottom of the management hierarchy, everything else builds on top of it. As you will see later, in Chapter 7, "Management Communication Patterns: Rules of Conversation," this layer is actually of tremendous importance to the effectiveness of management systems.

Additional Considerations

A few aspects of the TMN hierarchy shown in Figure 4-5 should be noted. First, different management layers are often handled by different organizations—and sometimes even by different service providers. This way, the technical layering can influence how a business is vertically layered and can define the actual business relationships. For example, a transport provider might provide raw transmission services—physical lines and transmission equipment. Network service providers provide networked services, such as voice or data services, using the transmission services of a transport provider. The customers of the (network) service provider do not realize that the service provider, in turn, relies on a transport provider, nor do they care. This is simply part of a value chain, similar to the value chains between vendors and suppliers in other industries.

Another aspect concerns the criticism of the TMN hierarchy as a "multilayered cake." Presumably, multiple management layers result in inefficiencies because management operations trickle down layer after layer until they finally hit the network element. Just as important, the number of layers presumably results in complicated overall management solutions that consist of multiple systems, each restricted to a particular management layer, with a multitude of mutual dependencies. This can result in an integration nightmare, costly system administration, and slow time to deployment that makes the underlying network inflexible and hard to change. At this point, we do not explore this criticism further. For now, it should suffice to mention that although integration and efficiency concerns are valid, much of the criticism results from a literal interpretation of the hierarchy as mandating a particular method of deployment. The criticism, thereby, loses sight of the primary intention and value of TMN as simply a reference model. It is certainly possible for management systems to provide functionality that spans multiple layers of the TMN hierarchy without violating the framework.

As with the other management dimensions, note that the management layer is independent of other dimensions. For example, the different management functional areas apply at each of the management layers. Consider fault management: You must deal with equipment faults at the element management layer, with configuration mismatches at the network management layer, and with defective services that affect end users at the service management layer. Likewise, the way in which managers and agents interact is independent of the management layer, although, of course, different management information is of interest at different layers.

Management Function: What's in Your Toolbox

At each layer of management, different management functions need to be performed. It is possible to categorize those functions, with the same categories applying across management layers.

For example, one category of management functionality might deal with activities that relate to faults—in other words, rainy-day scenarios when things go wrong. Of course, in an ideal world, things would never go wrong; in reality, however, faults are just a fact of life. Instead of unrealistically assuming that they can be avoided, it is better to know how to deal with them when they occur. At the network element layer, equipment and software malfunctions need to be detected and alarms sent to management applications. At the element management layer, equipment needs to be monitored for outages and subsystem malfunctions, which must be diagnosed and resolved when they occur. At the network management layer, faults can involve disruptions in network traffic that must be dealt with. For example, the network might need to be dynamically reconfigured, and connections and routes adjusted to direct network traffic around parts of the networks where failures have occurred.

A second category of management functionality might deal with configuration—configuring individual devices at the element management layer, provisioning end-to-end network connectivity at the network management layer, and provisioning services at the service management layer. A third category of management functionality might deal with accounting— that is, tracking consumption of communication resources.

The three categories described in the preceding paragraphs follow the Fault, Configuration, Accounting, Performance, Security (FCAPS) model, which is another topic that has been standardized as part of TMN. Other categorizations are certainly possible. At this point, however, we do not discuss the functional viewpoint further; the next chapter is devoted to this topic and discusses it in much greater detail.

Management Process and Organization: Of Help Desks and Cookie Cutters

Management interoperability, management function, and management layers capture different technical aspects of network management. However, network management also involves a nontechnical dimension: how to organize the management. This includes the processes that are required to ensure that the networks are run smoothly and reliably, as well as the structure of the support organization. Those nontechnical aspects are the topic of the management process and organization viewpoint.

The management support organization can be structured in different ways. One factor is, of course, the size of the network that is being managed. It makes a big difference whether you are a medium-size business that runs a few routers at a remote branch office or whether you are a global service provider with millions of end customers spread over 85 countries across the globe.

In the first case, running the network might simply be part of the system administrator's job; most networking services can simply be bought from outside anyway. In the second case, you need to become more sophisticated. In any case, you need to prepare your organization for scenarios such as when key employees get sick or, worse, when disgruntled employees try to wreak havoc on the network configuration. As mentioned in Chapter 3, "The Basic Ingredients of Network Management," the most severe potential security threats to a network could come from within. After all, there are no firewalls to traverse and no passwords to hack. The very nature of management systems in a NOC represents a potential hacker heaven.

The function, life cycle, and management subject dimensions described earlier in this chapter can actually be used as guidance for organizing the management organization. For example, a service provider might decide to divide responsibilities according to management subject. As a result, one group manages the core transport network, a second group manages the voice network, and a third group takes care of the systems and applications that are connected to the network. Within each of these groups, subteams take on the different management functions. Another service provider might decide to divide responsibilities by the different functions that need to be performed. For example, a group is responsible for the help desk, fault management, and network monitoring. A second group is responsible for equipment deployment and provisioning of services over the network. A third group deals with planning and network inventory. A fourth group deals with customer issues—taking service orders, resolving disputes over bills, and so forth.

In addition to the distribution of responsibilities, processes and procedures that need to be followed must be clear. For example, each time a user in an enterprise notifies the IT department that he needs a new IP telephone service for a new employee, the operator should not need to figure out from scratch what to do. Instead, there should be a standard procedure to follow. The lack of documented, standard operating procedures would be a recipe for disaster for a variety of reasons, such as the following:

■ Different network managers might accomplish the same task with slight variations. For example, the same service might be provisioned in a slightly different way, depending on who happened to be tasked with it. This diversity makes it much harder to troubleshoot services later if problems arise.

■ Problems can arise when configurations need to be changed or services removed. Because there can be many variations in which services have been configured, it can be difficult to determine what exactly needs to be done to remove a service or to determine the effects that a change in a configuration has on services.

■ Quite simply, the lack of documented, standard procedures increases the chance that mistakes are made that could impact end users.

■ Related to the previous bullet, an operator might be unfamiliar with a certain task and might not know how to react in a situation. The organization as a whole gets more dependent on the individual expertise of individual network managers, even for routine tasks.

For all these reasons and more, it is important that processes and procedures get "canned" and prepackaged to the greatest extent possible. Cookbooks on how to deal with different eventualities are required. Common tasks should follow a predefined template. This applies not only to adding a new user, but to all kinds of tasks you can think of: commissioning new equipment, troubleshooting different kinds of problems, backing up network configurations, and more. It is like baking cookies: Instead of carving hearts and stars by hand for each cookie, it is a much better idea to simply use a cookie cutter. It makes the job faster and yields better results—cookies that are shaped just perfectly each time. As an added bonus, even a 3-year-old can do it with decent results. It's true that individually crafted cookies might hold a certain charm, but charm doesn't get you far in operating a network.

Many tools that facilitate implementing consistent procedures exist. An important category of tools is workflow systems. Workflow systems allow the tracking and, to a certain degree, automating of tasks that are performed in a particular order of steps. The way in which those tasks are performed is referred to as workflow.

Simply speaking, a workflow corresponds to a graph. Nodes in the graph correspond to different states in the execution of the task. Edges in the graph correspond to transitions between states. Transitions between events occur according to well-defined rules. They are triggered by certain events, such as when a certain activity is completed. The current state of execution of a particular task can be represented by a token that is placed on the node corresponding to the state that the task is currently in.

The workflow system keeps track of the tokens for individual tasks and helps push those tokens through the graph until the corresponding tasks reach their completion. This helps the organization keep track of individual tasks and greatly offloads users. For each task and at every stage in the process, it is clear where things are and what needs to happen next. Tasks do not fall through the cracks, but are escalated automatically, as required. Progress is logged automatically. At every point, it easy to reconstruct what activities have taken place at which point in time, by whom, and why.

Which type of organizational structure and which set of processes and procedures work best in a given setting depend on many individual factors and require careful planning and consideration. Defining the most effective structure and developing the processes and procedures that work best for an organization is perhaps the area that offers the greatest possibility for differentiation among service providers. Those factors, perhaps more than anything else, determine the effectiveness, efficiency, and, consequently, competitiveness of a service provider. Among the aspects to consider are these:

- **Coverage**—Are all the tasks accounted for, or are there areas in which tasks can fall through the cracks?

- **Clear roles, responsibilities, and interfaces**—Is it clear who has to deliver what to whom? Are there any overlaps in responsibilities? The last thing you want is for everyone to assume that someone else will catch problems. In addition, you want to avoid the possibility of mutual finger pointing, with everyone arguing that it was someone else's fault.

■ **Efficiency and effectiveness**—How effective are the tasks being performed? Are the number of required steps and the number of parties that need to be involved kept to a minimum? Can steps be performed concurrently, or are there dependencies and bottlenecks?

■ **Resilience**—The processes and procedures must cover the unexpected, whether from human error or other unexpected events.

■ **Flexibility**—With all rigor that is required, it is also important to avoid organizational paralysis. The organization must be capable of rapidly adapting to change, when it is required. Such change could involve new networking technology to be supported, new services to be provided, or simply changes to processes and procedures.

Chapter Summary

This chapter explored different viewpoints of network management. Each of those viewpoints, or dimensions, represents a different set of concerns. As in the tale of the elephant and the blind men, like with orthogonal dimensions, the viewpoints complement each other to jointly provide a bigger picture of network management.

From a technical perspective, management interoperability is at the core of network management. It addresses what is required for managers and agents to be able to understand each other, a prerequisite to managing a network from remote. Management interoperability comprises the following:

■ Communication aspects, governing the exchange of management messages between managers and agents

■ Function aspects, establishing the functional capabilities that an agent provides and that a manager can rely on

■ Information aspects, defining how what is being managed is represented—that is, how it is modeled and can be referred to

Management interoperability covers the technical prerequisites that enable management to take place. But it does not cover all of management. Other dimensions do not involve exchanges between managers and agents:

■ The management subject is concerned with identifying management requirements that are specific to the target that must be managed, whether it involves a network, a set of hosts or systems that happen to be connected to a network, or a set of applications that run on systems across the organization.

- The management life cycle differentiates between tasks that occur at different stages in the life of a network being managed, from planning to decommissioning.

- The management layer takes a look at management tasks at different layers in a management hierarchy, starting with management agents at the individual devices and ending with the business that is being managed and that is supported by the network and interconnected devices and applications.

- The management function dimension categorizes functions that apply independent of the layer at which network management takes place.

- Finally, management process and organization deals with the nontechnical aspects of network management—that is, with the management support organization that is running the network, and the processes and procedures implemented by this organization.

Chapter Review

1. What are the different aspects, or "subdimensions," of management interoperability?

2. Why is a management protocol needed between managers and agents, and why isn't mere connectivity between them sufficient?

3. Why is it important for interoperability that a manager understand the functions provided by an agent?

4. Assume that you need to manage a network that contains three different types of devices. To avoid dependence on a particular vendor, you have two suppliers for each type of device. Explain some of the ways in which management standards are important in this situation.

5. What does TMN stand for?

6. Would the layers of the TMN reference model apply to application management? Why or why not?

7. Name three phases in a typical network management life cycle.

8. If an upgrade in a network is not carefully planned, service outages can occur. Name three ways in which upgrade operations might impact network availability.

9. Give three reasons why cookie-cutter procedures can be useful in network management.

10. An enterprise organizes network operations as follows: Group 1 is responsible for telephony services. Group 2 is responsible for interactions with end users. Group 3 is responsible for maintaining the network infrastructure. Can you see potential problems with this organization?

CHAPTER 5

Management Functions and Reference Models: Getting Organized

This chapter picks up right where we left off in our discussion of management dimensions in the previous chapter. Specifically, it takes an in-depth look at the function dimension of network management, a big topic that deserves its own chapter. This concerns the range of functionality that management applications and operational support systems need to cover. We discuss these functions along the lines of several management *reference models*, which do a great job of organizing these functions. Reference models are conceptual frameworks, introduced for the purpose of organizing in a systemic manner the different functions of a system or a technology—network management in this case.

After reading this chapter, you will be able to

- Explain what the most established functional reference model, FCAPS, stands for and what it consists of

- Outline the wide range of management functions in network management and explain what these functions entail

- Describe the OAM&P model, an alternative functional reference model that is popular with telecommunications service providers

- Explain the limitations of reference models

- Describe how different functional reference models relate

Of Pyramids and Layered Cakes

As mentioned previously, management reference models serve as conceptual frameworks for organizing different tasks and functions that are part of network management. The emphasis is on the word *conceptual*. In reality, reference models are, in many cases, not literally followed— management systems and operational support environments can be structured in different ways that, for various reasons, do not reflect the same breakdown in functionality as suggested by any particular reference model. However, a reference model can be used for guidance and helps provide a sense of orientation in the following ways:

■ It makes it easier to check a management system or operations support infrastructure for completeness. It forces the person applying the model to differentiate the different tasks that must be addressed. For the reference models presented here and for the purposes of this chapter, this aspect is the most important.

■ It helps categorize and group different functions, and identify which ones are closely related and belong together and which ones do not.

■ It helps to identify scenarios and use cases that need to be collected, and to recognize interdependencies and interfaces between different tasks. ("Use cases" are a part of use case analysis, a software engineering methodology that is used to derive functional requirements for systems by analyzing in a systemic manner different ways in which the system might be used—hence the term *use case*.)

A few reference models have been widely established. One of them is the Fault, Configuration, Accounting, Performance, Security model, commonly referred to as FCAPS (pronounced: "eff-caps"—rhymes with *snaps*). As its name indicates, it divides management functions into five categories—fault management, configuration management, accounting management, performance management, and security management. It is actually part of a larger management reference model that we introduced in the previous chapter: the TMN reference model. As mentioned earlier, the TMN reference model covers much more than just management layers; the FCAPS categorization of management functions is one of the concepts that it introduces. We can redraw the TMN pyramid from Figure 4-5 with more refinement, as in Figure 5-1, to show the functional dimension in addition to the layering. Whereas the layering dimension of the TMN model was discussed in the previous chapter, this chapter takes an in-depth look at its functional dimension.

Figure 5-1 *TMN Reference Model Refined with FCAPS*

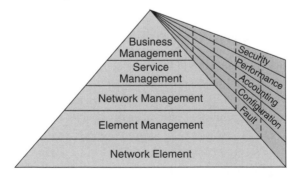

Another reference model is the Operations, Administration, Maintenance, and Provisioning (OAM&P) model. Here, management functions are categorized a bit differently. Ironically, although the FCAPS model originated from TMN and was intended to standardize network management for telecommunications, large telecommunications service providers traditionally favor the OAM&P model. We take a look at this model as well.

Although these are the most prominent reference models, they are not the only ones. Network management can be organized in a thousand ways. Still, discussion of these reference models teaches important lessons regarding established ways to think about network management. Even more important for the purposes of this chapter, discussing reference models provides a great opportunity to explain in detail the different functions that are associated with managing a network.

TMN and similar models are sometimes criticized as being overly complex—looking like multilayered cakes of many slices when perhaps a doughnut would do. However, in many cases, much of this criticism stems from an improper understanding of what these models are all about. A number of points should be kept in mind when considering reference models:

- A reference model is conceptual—that is, an abstract partitioning of a problem space. In general, there is no need for an actual system to follow the structure of a reference model literally.

- A specific application or operational support system may be designed with very specific constraints in mind. A reference model, however, has to be generally applicable and cannot be optimized for any one specific case. Otherwise, there would be a risk that the model might break in other scenarios—that is, the model might lose its generality.

- Generally, it is advantageous to be able to slice up a problem space for many of the same reasons that make component-based systems more attractive than monoliths. Different functions can always be combined later; breaking up is what's hard to do.

FCAPS: The ABCs of Management

To get a handle on the wide range of management functions that are required in an operational support environment, people often group them into a set of broad categories that are known as Fault, Configuration, Accounting, Performance, Security (FCAPS). This is the categorization that we use to go over the various functions.

In many cases, function categories can be addressed independently of each other, in terms of both the systems supporting them and the organization performing these functions. For instance, fault management activities such as monitoring, diagnosing, and troubleshooting devices are very different in nature from configuration management activities that deal with the configuration and turn-up of devices.

The subsections that follow introduce each of the FCAPS function categories in more detail. The subsections contain a number of enumerations that might appear lengthy but that are intended to convey the breadth of the spectrum of functions associated with the management of networked systems. The functions are presented mainly from a user perspective—functionality that is at the disposal of a service provider organization and network managers within that organization.

F Is for Fault

Fault management deals with faults that occur in the network, such as equipment or software failures, as well as communication services that fail to work properly. Fault management is therefore concerned with monitoring the network to ensure that everything is running smoothly and reacting when this is not the case. Effective fault management is critical to ensure that users do not experience disruption of service and that when they do, disruption is kept to a minimum.

Fault management functionality includes but is not limited to the following:

- Network monitoring, including basic alarm management as well as more advanced alarm processing functions

- Fault diagnosis, root cause analysis, and troubleshooting

- Maintaining historical alarm logs

- Trouble ticketing

- Proactive fault management

Network Monitoring Overview

Network monitoring includes functions that allow a network provider organization to see whether the network is operating as expected, to keep track of its current state, and to visualize that state. This functionality is fundamental to being able to recognize and react to fault conditions in the network as they occur.

The most important aspect of network monitoring concerns the management of alarms. Alarms are unsolicited messages from the network that indicate that some unexpected event has occurred, which in some cases requires operator intervention. Those unexpected events can actually be about anything—from a router that detects that one of its line cards is no longer working to (literally) a fire alarm, from a sudden drop in signal quality on a wireless link to a suspected intrusion into the network by an unauthorized user. Like other alarms in the real world, an alarm in a network might actually set off a bell just like a fire alarm or result in the automatic dispatch of operating personnel, similar to alarms set off by home intrusion-detection systems. In most cases, however, they simply result in a message being sent to a management system, which lets an application or an operator decide what to do.

Alarm management is such a large area that the term is sometimes used synonymously with *fault management*, although there is more to fault management than alarms. Alarm management includes many functions that we classify into basic functions, such as alarm collection and visualization, and more advanced functions that involve processing alarms to perform filtering and correlation tasks.

Basic Alarm Management Functions

We start the discussion of alarm management with the more basic functions—collecting alarms, maintaining accurate and current lists of alarms, and visualizing alarms and network state.

The most basic and, at the same time, most important task—the task that everything else builds on—consists of simply collecting alarms from the network and making sure that nothing important is missed. This includes receiving the alarms and storing them in memory so that they can be further processed by an application or a human operator who decides how to react. Basic alarm management functionality also includes persisting alarms—that is, writing them to disk or storing them in a database, to build a historical record of alarms that occurred.

In more sophisticated cases, alarm collection can include additional, more advanced mechanisms that can check that no alarms were lost and that can request replay of alarms, as long as the network provides such capabilities. In practice, alarms can be lost in many ways, even when this is not supposed to happen—after all, in most cases, the event that is being alarmed was not supposed to happen, either. For example, the underlying transport might not be reliable and the alarm information might thereby be dropped on the way to the management application. Another reason alarm information might fail to reach its destination is that the network is congested and alarm messages simply cannot get through (remember that this situation was one of the selling points for a dedicated management network). In a third scenario, the alarm information might actually have reached the host of the management application but was still not properly collected because the application or database was not functioning properly or was being restarted when the alarm message arrived.

After alarms have been collected, an accurate list of current alarms needs to be maintained. This list answers the questions, which current conditions in the network require management attention, and which issues are currently being experienced with the services provided by the network. The alarm list also informs the operator of the current state of each of the various entities that are being managed and whether a particular device, for instance, is having problems. To maintain the alarm list, it is not sufficient to simply append alarms to the list as they occur. Alarms can also clear—

that is, the underlying condition that caused the alarm can be resolved. The current list of alarms needs to be updated accordingly, removing alarms when they no longer apply.

It is also important to understand how the alarms and indeed the network state are visually presented to the user. In its most basic and most important form, visualization can occur simply through textual lists. Each alarm results in an entry in the list, containing information about the alarm. Those lists can be searched, sorted, and filtered according to many different criteria, such as alarm severity, the type of alarm, the network element (or range of network elements) affected, the type of network element affected, the time of day when the alarm occurred, and many more.

However, visualization can occur in many ways. One popular method uses topology maps. Icons on the map represent devices and can be animated to indicate the current alarm state. The alarm state corresponds to the highest severity of any alarm condition on a device, of which there might be several. Likewise, connections can be represented on the topology map, as indicated by lines that connect the icons. Like the icons, the lines can be animated with different colors to indicate the current state of that particular connection. Not all alarms indicate a complete failure of a device or the services running over it. In fact, in most cases, they do not. The severity of an alarm indicates the degree of impact of its underlying alarm condition—the higher the severity, the greater its impact on the network, services, and end users. For example, red might be used for devices on the map with a critical alarm, orange for major alarms, yellow for minor alarms, and green for no alarms. Gray might be used to indicate lost management connectivity to the device. Please note that red would be inappropriate in the case of lost connectivity because the device itself might in fact be functioning properly. Of course, icons can be used not just to represent individual devices, but to represent groupings of devices that can be "zoomed into." In that case, the color for the grouping of devices reflects the most severe alarm of any of the devices contained within it.

Topology maps can make monitoring systems look attractive and, hence, become good sales tools for those systems. In addition, they provide a good overall picture of the health of a network and a good way to indicate geographical "hot spots" and identify where the real problems lie. If everything in area Chicago suddenly turns red, including the single access router through which all those devices are connected to the core network, chances are, the resolution for the problem lies with that router, and that's where the troubleshooting should start. As Figure 5-2 illustrates, this way the graphical representation of topology on a map makes information much easier to correlate than if the same information were merely represented in a flat list of alarms, interspersed with alarms from other parts of the network.

Figure 5-2   *Visualization of Alarm Information (a) Through a List and (b) Through a Topology Map*

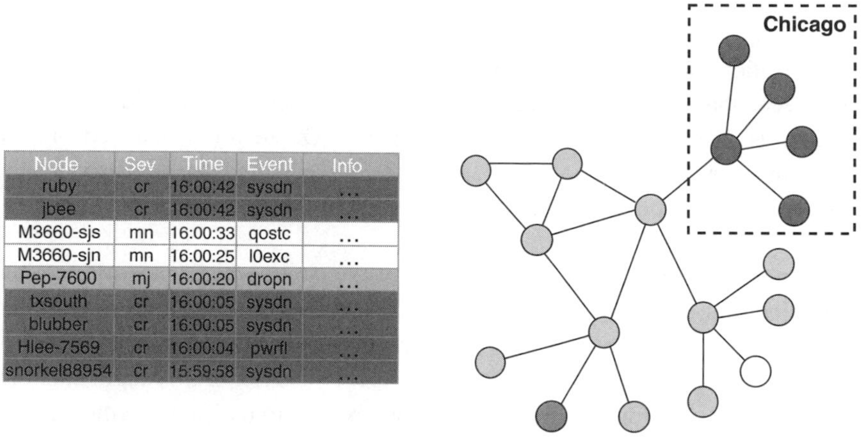

Node	Sev	Time	Event	Info
ruby	cr	16:00:42	sysdn	...
jbee	cr	16:00:42	sysdn	...
M3660-sjs	mn	16:00:33	qostc	...
M3660-sjn	mn	16:00:25	l0exc	...
Pep-7600	mj	16:00:20	dropn	...
txsouth	cr	16:00:05	sysdn	...
blubber	cr	16:00:05	sysdn	...
Hlee-7569	cr	16:00:04	pwrfl	...
snorkel88954	cr	15:59:58	sysdn	...

(a)   (b)

Many reasons exist for maintaining historical alarm data in addition to the list of current alarms. This requires simply logging and archiving alarms as they occur, which is actually simpler than maintaining the current list. After all, items are appended only at the end of the list. Historical alarm data is not required for monitoring the network but is useful in many other ways. For example:

- Historical alarm data can be mined to help with future diagnosis and correlation (we come to these topics in a moment). Basically, this can be helpful to identify alarm patterns that have occurred in similar form on past occasions. Recognizing such patterns and recalling their past resolution can help resolve future problems faster.

- It can be used to establish trends, to see how alarm rates and types of alarms reported have evolved over time.

- It can be analyzed in conjunction with other historical data, such as changes that have been performed on the network—for example, the introduction of new network elements—and its impact on historical alarm patterns, or correlation of alarms with certain usage patterns of the network.

Advanced Alarm Management Functions

Beyond those basic alarm management functions, in any network of meaningful size, additional functions to manage alarms are required.

Some of those functions provide network managers with greater flexibility in processing alarms. For example, an alarm-forwarding function might send alarms to the pager of an operator to allow for an automatic dispatch, much as a home intrusion detection system automatically calls the local police station.

Another function allows network operators to acknowledge alarms, meaning that they confirm that they have seen the alarm and are taking care of it. The function might allow network operators to open a *trouble ticket* (as first mentioned in Chapter 2, "On the Job with a Network Manager," and explained in more detail later in this chapter) that is based not on customer complaints, but on event messages from the network that point to trouble.

A third function handles the clearing of alarms: recognizing when an alarm is no longer current or, more precisely, matching failure onset and failure remission conditions. Most alarms have an underlying alarm condition (if they do not, they belong to a special category of alarms called *transient alarms*). An alarm message is sent to report the onset of this alarm condition. At some later point in time, a second alarm message might be sent to indicate that the alarm condition no longer exists.

It is important to maintain at the management system level accurate lists of the current, or *standing*, alarm conditions, without needing to query the network device for what those conditions are. More often than not, the device does not have such a query capability. Besides, it would be a bad idea to continuously poll the device for information that can be derived from information that it has sent already.

You can think of the alarm condition in terms of a conceptual panel of light emitting diodes (LEDs), one for each distinct alarm condition that exists on the device. (Of course, because the multitude of alarm conditions that exist, providing a comprehensive panel is impractical in reality because it would require too many LEDs.) LEDs light up when the condition comes into effect and remain lit while the condition holds. LEDs go off when their underlying alarm condition no longer holds. An alarm is sent whenever a LED just went on—an operator might not be watching the LED panel all the time because there are so many to watch in the network. Likewise, an alarm clear is sent to indicate that the LED went off again. The list of standing alarms is simply the list of LEDs that are currently lit.

Figure 5-3 illustrates this concept. The left side of the diagram depicts a chronological list of alarm messages. Some messages indicate the onset of an alarm condition of a certain type; others indicate the remission of the same condition—the alarm has cleared. The list of current alarms includes only those messages that have not cleared—that is, those for which no matching "clear" indication has been received. The right side of the diagram depicts a fictitious LED panel that indicates which of the alarm conditions are current, corresponding to the alarm list.

Figure 5-3 *Alarms and Alarm Conditions*

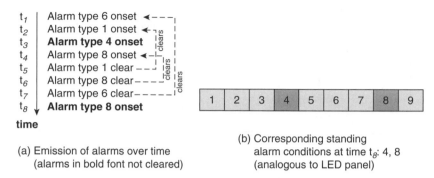

(a) Emission of alarms over time
(alarms in bold font not cleared)

(b) Corresponding standing
alarm conditions at time t_8: 4, 8
(analogous to LED panel)

The concepts of clearing alarms and acknowledging alarms are often confused; sometimes "clearing of alarms" is mistakenly used to mean acknowledging an alarm. When you encounter these terms, make sure you understand how they are being applied.

When an alarm is cleared, it means that the underlying condition that caused the alarm has ended. This is different from acknowledging an alarm. *Acknowledging* merely means that the alarm was noted and, presumably, action is being taken. To use a physical picture, if the alarm sets off a bell that keeps ringing, turning off the bell corresponds to acknowledging the alarm. The problem might still be indicated by a LED that is still lit and that will remain lit until the underlying condition that caused the alarm ends. Only at that point will the alarm be cleared.

Another category of functions that is related to managing alarms concerns trying to reduce the amount of information that human operators and higher-level management applications are exposed to. It is possible in large networks, such as those of large telecommunications service providers, for hundreds of thousands of alarms to occur per day—so many alarms that alarm-processing capabilities of alarm management applications are often measured in hundreds of alarms per second. Of course, not every alarm indicates something major or an impending catastrophe of its own. Most are not really "alarms" in the narrower sense of the word, but event messages. Still, they need to be looked at. The problem is, therefore, how to reduce the volume of information that must be evaluated.

Generally two techniques deal with potential event information overload. One technique is filtering. Its goal is to remove event information that is deemed unimportant or redundant, to allow the receiver to focus on the more relevant event information. The other is correlation. Its goal is to preprocess and aggregate data from events and alarms, and distill it into more concise and meaningful information. Figure 5-4 illustrates and contrasts both techniques. We discuss each of these techniques in the sections that follow.

Figure 5-4   *Alarm Filtering vs. Preprocessing*

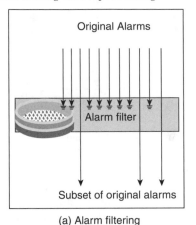

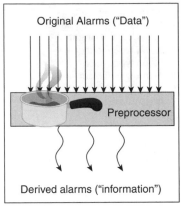

(a) Alarm filtering   (b) Alarm preprocessing

Alarm and Event Filtering

Let us first turn our attention to filtering, not just of alarms, but of events in general. To focus an operator's or a management application's attention on those events that really matter, it is important to block out as many irrelevant or less important events as possible. This is analogous to the way in which the human brain is able to deal with the massive flow of data that it is constantly exposed to, such as sounds, visual images, and sensory data. To focus, it filters out massive amounts of data that would otherwise be distracting, for example, background noise when following a conversation.

One way to enable filtering is to allow users (operators or management applications) to subscribe only to those alarms and events that are of potential relevance to them and what they need to accomplish, as specified by some criteria. This way, users receive only events that meet those criteria. Here are some examples of using this technique effectively: Users might choose to subscribe only to alarms that involve a particular system or subsystem. For instance, they could be concerned with always ensuring that the company's CEO receives excellent communication service and, therefore, subscribe specifically to alarms that affect the port through which the company's CEO's office is connected. Users might also choose to subscribe only to alarms of a certain type. For instance, operating personnel for voice services might be interested only in alarms that indicate problems that are related to voice service. Finally, users might choose to receive only alarms that have a certain severity. They might decide to receive only critical alarms and to have everything else discarded (well, perhaps not discarded, but simply stored in a logfile so that it can be used for analysis when needed, as opposed to being brought directly to their attention). This could be important when high alarm volumes occur, so they can avoid the small stuff and ensure that high-impact items are dealt with.

Another way to filter alarm concerns *deduplication* of alarms. In some cases, the same alarm condition might cause the same alarm to be sent repeatedly. Because each new instance of the same alarm contains no new information, the new instances might simply be thrown away. The process of discarding the redundant alarms is referred to as deduplication. A similar scenario to which similar considerations apply is that of oscillating alarms. In that case, there is an underlying oscillating alarm condition, causing alarms to be sent and then cleared again immediately before occurring again in rapid succession multiple consecutive times. Although oscillating alarms relate to only a singe condition and are hence relatively easy to spot, they can lead to a high overall alarm volume that drowns out other events that are happening in the network. Therefore, the alarms should be turned off.

An infamous example concerns the "door open" alarm. Such an alarm can often be sent by equipment that can be installed in publicly accessible locations whenever a sensor detects that its door is opened. Having a door to a piece of equipment opened can indicate a serious problem because it could mean that an unauthorized person might be tampering with the equipment. The problem in this case is that thousands of alarms could be generated per hour when the sensor on a particular piece of equipment is faulty and mistakenly detects that the door is open, only to correct itself by reporting that it is closed, every other second. Until the faulty sensor is fixed, the oscillating alarms need to be filtered.

Of course, with oscillating alarms, it could still be useful to know the frequency with which oscillation occurs, or, with redundant alarms, how many duplicates there are. For example, is the door reported open three times in an hour? If so, the door might really have been opened three times because someone is in fact tampering with the equipment, perhaps while performing maintenance. Or is the door reported open 3,000 times in an hour, in which case a sensor or contact is probably bad? If the repeated occurrences of the alarm are simply filtered, this information is lost. A better solution is to record the information that duplicates or oscillations have been observed, along with how many there were, but to throw away the alarms themselves. Of course, if the rate at which oscillations or seemingly redundant alarms occur drops below a certain threshold, it might even be advisable to not filter those alarms at all.

For example, here is one technique that can be applied in the case of redundant alarms: The first occurrence of the alarm message needs to be forwarded without delay to the intended recipient. If duplicates of the same alarm occur, at least 1 minute should be allowed to pass before notifying the recipient of the same alarm again. At this point, the alarm message is sent again, annotated with a counter that tells the recipient how many instances of the alarm message have actually occurred.

Figure 5-5 also illustrates this. If alarm A1 occurs in the initial state, S1, of the system, it is forwarded immediately and another state, S2, is entered. If no more alarm A1s are received within the minute time period, the system reverts back to its initial state. However, if additional A1 alarms occur, they are not forwarded immediately. Instead, the system enters another state, S3, in which the duplicate counter is increased for each occurrence of A1. Eventually, the minute timer expires.

At that point, the system enters state S4, in which it sends the alarm A1 along with the count of its number of occurrences. It then immediately enters again state S2, waiting for more duplicates of A1 or, if no more are received within the minute interval, reverts back to the initial state.

Figure 5-5 *Deduplication of Alarms*

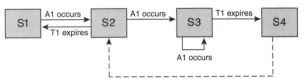

S1: Initial state; wait for A1 to occur
S2: Send A1; start timer T1; initialize duplicate count to 0
S3: Increment duplicate count by 1
S4: Send A1 annotated with number of occurrences

Of course, strictly speaking, we are now no longer simply filtering messages. Although it is true that we throw away many of the duplicates, we maintain a little counter for the number of occurrences and add this counter to the duplicate alarm message that we sent. This means that we have actually started to aggregate and preprocess information across alarm messages—what we have here is really a very simple form of *correlating* alarms, which leads us to the next topic.

Alarm and Event Correlation

Generally, alarm correlation refers to an intelligent filtering and preprocessing function for alarms. Alarm messages are intercepted and analyzed and compared to identify which alarms are likely related. For example, alarms could be related because they report the same symptom or because they probably have the same root cause. Depending on the sophistication of the correlation function, different aspects can be taken into account—information contained in the alarms themselves, context information such as knowledge of the network topology, or time context, such as the delay encountered between different messages.

The idea behind event and alarm correlation is that instead of forwarding and reporting many individual alarm or event messages, only a few (ideally, only one) messages need to be sent that aggregate and summarize the information from across multiple "raw" events. This way, the number of alarm messages that are reported to other alarm management applications and to human users can be significantly decreased, often by orders of magnitude. At the same time, the semantic content of those messages can be dramatically increased—that is, the actual information that is conveyed with each message. This prevents users from becoming overwhelmed and allows them to focus on the most relevant information instead of wasting their energy or processing cycles on alarms that could be easily discounted as noise. To give a simple analogy, instead of sending alarms "There is a funny smell," "The windows are fogging up," "Visibility is getting poor," "More funny smell," "It is uncomfortably warm," "It is really getting hot," "There is a crackling noise," and "There are flames," it is much more efficient to send one correlated message that says "The kitchen is on fire." The correlated alarm might still contain references to the original, uncorrelated, "raw" alarms, in the rare case that this information is still needed. It might also be marked as a correlated alarm so that an end user can distinguish between the conclusions drawn by the alarm correlation function and the original alarm data.

Correlation can have varying degrees of sophistication. Simple forms of correlation can occur at the level of the managed device (for example, if a card fails, let the device suppress alarms indicating that its ports have failed as well). More complex forms of correlation might involve sophisticated algorithms, inference engines, or expert system technology. The use of the term *alarm correlation* easily raises expectations that highly sophisticated and complex correlation is performed, whereas in reality simple forms of correlation are far more common. In fact, *correlation* can be considered an overused term. In many cases, it is incorrectly applied to refer to any function that reduces the volume of alarms, even if that function is not a correlation but perhaps simply a filtering function.

Note that alarm correlation is different from root cause analysis, although, again, sometimes both terms are used liberally and interchangeably. Alarm correlation focuses on identifying which alarms are likely different symptoms that are all related to the same root cause, without actually identifying the root cause that initiated the symptoms. Its goal is to intelligently filter and reduce the amount of alarm information that is reported. The correlated alarm information still must be analyzed for what caused it. This is precisely the subject of root cause analysis.

Fault Diagnosis and Troubleshooting

Alarm management is a significant aspect of fault management—so significant, in fact, that the two terms are often used synonymously. However, there is more to fault management than alarms. One other aspect concerns fault diagnosis and troubleshooting.

Network diagnosis is conceptually not much different from medical diagnosis. The difference, of course, is the type of patient. To reach a medical diagnosis for a set of symptoms (for example, a rash), the doctor might want to take a look at additional monitoring data (for example, by taking the patient's temperature and blood pressure) and might conduct his or her own series of tests, such as testing the reflexes or asking the patient to breathe deeply while listening with a stethoscope.

When a fault occurs in a network, the capability to diagnose the problem—that is, to quickly identify what caused it, is key to minimizing its impact on users. The proper diagnosis then is the basis for selecting the proper repair action. The analysis process that leads to a diagnosis is often also referred to as root cause analysis. An alarm generally alerts you only to a symptom, not what caused it.

For example, assume that you receive an alarm "Device overheating," as Figure 5-6 illustrates. How do you find out what actually caused the alarm? Was it because the device fan failed? Is the room temperature in general too high? Or is the building on fire? Of course, you might simply walk over to the device and check for yourself. But remember that you might be sitting in a network operations center 50 miles away and have to diagnose the problem remotely. And only after it has been properly diagnosed can you determine what the proper repair action should be: Should you dispatch a technician to replace the fan? Do you need to turn up the air-conditioning? Or should you call 911?

Figure 5-6   *Symptom, Root Cause, and Repair Action*

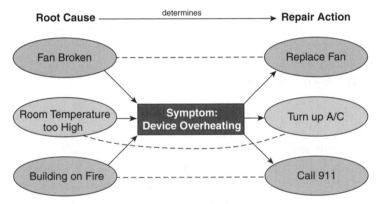

Diagnosis is often supported by troubleshooting functions. Troubleshooting can involve simply retrieving additional monitoring data about a device, data that was not conveyed as part of the alarms. In addition, the capability to inject tests into a network or a device for troubleshooting purposes provides essential support for diagnosis activities. With networks, there are many examples of such tests: For instance, loopback tests are common in telecommunications. Those tests involve setting up a connection to a remote endpoint that is automatically "looped back" to where it originated—short-circuited, if you will. By comparing data that is sent and received over the looped connection, important conclusions can be made. For example, loopback tests can be used to verify that communication paths are indeed intact. As a side benefit, they can also be used to measure certain quality-of-service parameters, such as delay. Likewise, phone calls might be generated to test voice connections.

Tests can be used not only in troubleshooting after a problem has already occurred, but also proactively, to be able to recognize any fault conditions or deterioration in quality of service before it becomes noticeable to a user. The best fault management, after all, is to avoid faults altogether.

Proactive Fault Management

Most fault management functionality, such as alarm management, is, by nature, reactive—it deals with faults after they have occurred. However, proactive fault management is also possible—that is, taking steps to avoid failure conditions before they occur. This includes, for instance, the previously mentioned injection of tests into the network to detect deterioration in the quality of service and impending failure conditions early, before they occur. Proactive fault management can also include alarm analysis that recognizes patterns of alarms caused by minor faults that point to impending bigger problems.

Trouble Ticketing

Another problem to mention concerns management of the fault management process itself, from detection to resolution of problems. A larger network might easily serve tens of thousands of users. In such networks, it is possible for hundreds of problems requiring follow-up to occur daily. Hopefully, none or only very few of the problems will be catastrophic in the sense of large-scale network outages. Nevertheless, individual users might still be experiencing problems that are serious enough for them, such as sluggish network response time or loss of dial tone. Given the scale of today's networks, it is quite easy to lose track of things.

Trouble tickets are one way in which a network provider organization can keep track of the resolution of network (or service) problems that typically require human intervention. Those problems might have been reported by the network itself through certain types of alarms, or they might have been reported by a customer experiencing a problem. When certain problems are encountered or reported by users, a trouble ticket is issued to describe the problem. Trouble tickets are assigned to operators, who are responsible for resolving the trouble ticket—that is, taking care of the problem. The trouble ticket system helps keep track of which trouble tickets are still outstanding. It can automatically escalate a problem if it is not resolved in time. The system can also help communicate a problem between different operators by automatically attaching the entire history of the problem and its resolution to the trouble ticket.

Not every alarm results in a trouble ticket because issuing that many tickets would quickly overwhelm operations personnel. Instead, trouble tickets are issued generally only when the reported alarms and other observed conditions indicate that the capability to deliver service could be affected, and for alarm conditions whose resolution likely requires human intervention that the network provider organization needs to track.

C Is for Configuration

We now turn to the second letter in FCAPS, *C*, which stands for configuration management. For the network to do what it is supposed to do, it might need to be first told what to do—that is, configured. This is similar to having to initially set up a VCR so that it tunes to the proper channels, to select the proper input for connections from a video console, and later needing to program the

VCR to record a particular show. Depending on the type of network equipment, its configuration can be much more involved than that of a VCR. In addition, in a network, you might have a large number of devices, all of which need to be configured in a coordinated manner to be capable of singing in tune, so to speak.

Configuration management includes functionality to perform operations that will deliver and modify configuration settings to equipment in the network. This includes the initial configuration of a device to bring it up—that is, to be properly connected to the network—as well as ongoing configuration changes. For example, to provide a new employee with phone service in an enterprise network, the network needs to be configured so that it will recognize the new user's phone number and be capable of directing calls to that phone, as well as ensure that the collection of billing records associated with the new user is turned on so that his department can be properly charged.

Performing configuration operations alone is not enough; you also need to keep track of what you have in your network. The write operations must be complemented by read operations, so to speak. Although in a small network keeping track of what's in it seems trivial, as you start scaling your network to thousands or tens of thousands of devices and users, it becomes more difficult—how do you know that all equipment is really where you expect it to be? How can you be sure that a user did not unplug one of your routers and plug it in somewhere else, altering your physical network topology that had been fine-tuned to offer well-balanced performance? Or what if someone simply connected another piece of equipment on his own, unwittingly making the network vulnerable to attacks?

By the same token, you need to also know what has been configured—for example, what services are running over which equipment, and which users are associated with the equipment—so that you know who might be affected if you need to perform maintenance operations. Accordingly, configuration management also includes auditing the network to retrieve its current configuration and making sure that the management system's information about the network is current.

Configuration management is at the core of setting up a network so that it can deliver service; it is really at the core of network management in general. Configuration management is fundamentally tied to provisioning and to fulfillment—but those are functions used in other categorizations of the management function space, namely OAM&P, as well as Fulfillment, Assurance, Billing (FAB), discussed later in this chapter. Without effective configuration management, a network provider will have a hard time keeping track of what is actually deployed in a network or providing even basic functions such as turning up a service. However, other management functions depend on configuration management as well. For example, in fault management, many networking problems cannot be properly diagnosed without accurate knowledge of the network's configuration.

We dive into configuration management functions in more detail in the following subsections and cover the following topics:

- Configuring managed resources, whether they are network equipment or services running over the network

- Auditing the network and discovering what's in it

- Synchronizing management information in the network with management information in management applications

- Backing up network configuration and restoring it in case of failures

- Managing software images running on network equipment

Configuring Managed Resources

At the core of configuration management are the activities and operations used to configure what is being managed. Ultimately, this involves sending commands to network equipment to change its configuration settings. In some cases, this involves only one device in isolation, such as configuring an interface on a port. In other cases, configuration operations that are performed on the devices are simply part of a bigger operation at the network level that involves changing the configuration of multiple devices across the network. An example is setting up a connection across the network, such as a static route or an ATM permanent virtual circuit (PVC). This requires configurations to be performed on each hop along the connection to, in essence, cross-connect incoming and outgoing interfaces along the path, as Figure 5-7 illustrates.

Figure 5-7 *Network-Level vs. Device-Level Configuration*

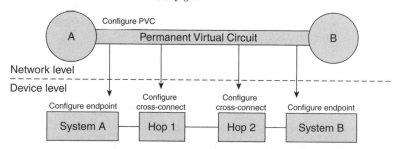

Above the element and network management layers, configuration management also includes functionality to perform configurations that are necessary for the network to provide a service for an end user—the managed resource, in this case, is simply the service. Configuration management at the service level is generally referred to as *service provisioning*, borrowing terminology from the OAM&P reference model that we discuss in the next section.

Provisioning a service involves being able to turn up the service, to modify certain service parameters, and to tear it down. The latter aspect is often forgotten but is just as important as setting up the service. For example, if an employee leaves your company, you do not want that employee to still have access to the company's VPN. Likewise, if you are a telecommunications service provider and have a customer who isn't paying, you want to be able to cut off his service.

It is important to be able to describe the service in terms that relate to the service, not in terms that relate to the network over which the service is provisioned. For example, you might want to be able to order a service that provides a new employee, John, with VPN service, e-mail with a mailbox of certain size, and phone service with voice mail, call forwarding, but no authority to place international calls. It is up to a service provisioning application, not an end user, to break down the instruction to configure this particular type of service into the detailed configuration operations that need to be sent down to the networking equipment so that the service can go into effect. For example, the application would need to assign a phone number and configure the voice-mail servers, e-mail servers, switch ports, and IP PBX accordingly. The capability to provision services rapidly, correctly, and efficiently is of utmost importance to service providers and their competitiveness: Being able to roll out services faster decreases the time to collect revenue and could therefore actually increase revenue. In addition, it minimizes operational cost and increases customer satisfaction.

Auditing, Discovery, and Autodiscovery

Being able to configure your network is important, but not enough. You need to also be able to query the network to find out what actually has been configured—you need a read in addition to the write. This is referred to as *auditing*. Many reasons exist for auditing devices in the network. For example, you might want to verify that the configuration of the network is indeed what you expect it to be. You might want to see if configuration commands that you sent down indeed took. Without this function, a service provider would have a very hard time understanding what is going on in a network and why it is going on.

Closely related to auditing devices for configuration data is querying devices for other data that is not related to configuration. This includes information about the current state of the device as well as performance data, such as the number of packets that are currently being dropped or the current use of device ports. The basic mechanisms to query nonconfiguration data on the device are generally the same as for configuration data. The only difference is that, in the case of configuration data, the queried data is in general persisted on the device (stored in nonvolatile memory or on hard disk), whereas this normally is not the case with state information. State information will not survive a reboot, for example. However, retrieving nonconfiguration data is typically associated with the other FCAPS functional areas, such as fault (used to retrieve monitoring data that helps in troubleshooting a problem), performance (used to collect statistics), or security (for example, to detect suspicious patterns in network usage that could indicate a denial-of-service attack).

In addition to auditing your network, you also might want to be able to discover what is in your network. The need for such a function might not be obvious at first. After all, if you as a network provider keep proper track of your network, you would not expect any surprises. However, discovery is still a very important function for many reasons. For example:

- Inventory records might not be accurate.

- Personnel might change things in the network and might not always record those changes properly.

- Discovering the network might be more efficient than having to enter the information about the network into a management application.

- Finally, depending on the management scenario, in many cases inventory records might not be available because keeping an inventory might not be appropriate in the first place. Consider, for example, system management scenarios that involve devices that are mobile or that roam across the network, with people moving managed end systems such as computer workstations, disconnecting and connecting them to the network at arbitrary locations. Trying to keep an inventory database with information on what is supposed to be connected where in the network might not be a good idea in such an environment. However, managing the network and monitoring those devices is still required, so the capability to discover them is important.

A word of caution: in some cases, auditing functionality is misleadingly dubbed as discovery. However, what is "discovered" in those cases is not a device or something unexpected whose presence in the network was previously unknown. Instead, it is already known that the device is there; information merely is retrieved about its configuration. To be able to refer to actual discovery functionality when the term *discovery* is already occupied for auditing functionality, the term *autodiscovery* is frequently used. So whenever you encounter the claim that an application supports functionality to discover a network, be sure to check that the term is not confused with auditing and that the functionality that is referred to is indeed discovery.

Synchronization

Each time you or your management application needs to know your network's configuration, you do not want to first have to audit the equipment or discover the network. That would be much too inefficient and slow. Instead, you expect your management system to maintain a cache of information about your network, probably stored in a database. At least, this is the case for information that is relatively slow to change, such as which equipment is deployed in the network and how it has been configured. After all, configuration information is not the same as state or statistical information that rapidly changes, in which case you have no choice but to retrieve it on demand when you need a real-time view. However, as with any cache, you run into the problem of how to ensure that your cache does not get stale—that is, how to ensure that the information in your management system is indeed an accurate reflection of the information in the network.

Therefore, functions are needed to help management systems maintain an accurate and consistent management view of the network. Those functions are fundamentally concerned with the notion that there are two representations of management information: the network itself and the management system's view of it. Whenever there are two views of the same information, the question arises how to keep them from contradicting each other and, if contradictions occur, how to resolve them—in other words, how to synchronize the information.

For synchronization to take place properly, a key question is which set of information should be considered the "master" of the information in question. The master is also referred to as the golden store.

- One view is that the network should be considered the master—the network ultimately is the reality, and this reality needs to be reflected by the management system (see Figure 5-8). The management information maintained by the management system is nothing other than a cache that needs to be kept from going stale. This is the more common approach and the approach that enterprises generally apply.

- Another view is that the management system should be considered the master, and the network needs to be built toward the information maintained in the management system (see Figure 5-9). A discrepancy between network and management system indicates that an error occurred in setting up the network and that the network is wrong—well, not wrong, but not what it is supposed to be. This approach is less common but can be found with large telecommunication service providers.

Figure 5-8 *Network as Golden Store*

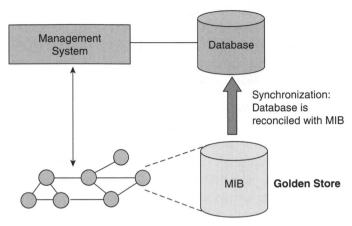

Figure 5-9 *Management System as Golden Store*

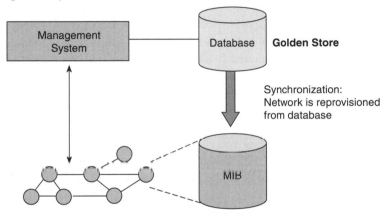

Depending on which view is taken, one of the following functions is used to synchronize management information:

■ **Reconciliation**—The network is considered the master, and the information of the management system should reflect what is actually in the network. Information is therefore synchronized from the network to the management system (management information reflects the network as *built*). As mentioned, this view is the most common; hence, most of the time, synchronization of network information occurs through reconciliation.

- **Reprovisioning**—With reprovisioning, the management system is the master of management information; synchronization flows from the management system to the network, resulting in configuration changes to network devices as needed so that they reflect the information in the management inventory (management information reflects the network as *planned*). Until the network devices report that the appropriate changes have been made, the management system maintains a flag indicating that they are out of synch.

- **Discrepancy reporting**—With discrepancy reporting, discrepancies are simply detected and flagged for the user. The management application does not make a decision about the direction in which synchronization is to take place. This decision is the responsibility of the user and must be performed on a case-by-case basis. When the user decides that the management system should reflect the information that is out there, he will ask for reconciliation. When the user decides that he wants the configuration of the network to correspond to what is currently reflected in the information stored by the management system, he triggers a configuration operation.

Note that sometimes within the same network provider organization, both views of what should constitute the golden store are valid for different management functions: Monitoring certainly needs a view of what is actually in the network; the network, in this case, is clearly considered the master of management information. However, for network inventory functions in a large service provider, what is kept in the inventory should indeed be considered the master as the network is carefully engineered; network devices should not just "pop up" on the network, but should be the result of careful planning.

Of course, you need to keep track of things beyond information that is already reflected in the network—in addition to maintaining a cache of management information, there is a need for a true inventory of information that is nowhere reflected in the network but that is needed for management purposes. For example, you might want to keep track of the tasks you have assigned to the resources in your network, such as which services and end users they should support. This enables you to distinguish between network resources that have already been committed for a particular purpose and those that can still be assigned. With this information, you can avoid situations such as accidentally reassigning a port to a customer when it is already in use by someone else, or assigning the same IP address twice, which leads to all kinds of confusion and can disrupt service for existing users. In addition, keeping track of those assignments enables you to anticipate potential capacity shortages and react in a timely manner. For example, if you keep track of how network ports have been allocated, when the percentage of allocated ports exceeds a certain threshold, you will still have time to increase network capacity before being hit by a shortage. On the other hand, by knowing that sufficient ports have not yet been assigned, you can avoid overcapacities in the network and hence dead capital that would result from adding capacities too early.

Backup and Restore

If you are a PC user (and, chances are, you are), you are aware of the importance of protecting your data by performing regular backups. You never know when your hard disk will bite the dust or whether your PC will contract a virus that could destroy your PC's file system. Having a backup of your data in such cases enables you to recover. With backups in place, contracting a virus or needing to replace your hard drive is still annoying, but it beats by far simply being wiped out.

Likewise, the need for backup and restore functionality applies to your network. Here, your user data is not Word files or Excel spreadsheets, but the configuration data of your network. This data is very critical and needs to be protected, just as you would protect the accounting data and customer database of your company. Imagine some catastrophic event taking down a portion of your network and wiping out configurations, possibly affecting thousands of end users or customers, who might be getting more disgruntled and impatient by the minute. There would be no time to reconfigure network equipment one by one and reprovision every service. This would simply be too inefficient and would take too much time. Instead, the quickest, simplest, and most reliable way to bring things back up would be to simply restore your network to the last working configuration. As with PCs, having to restore the network is a function that you will hopefully never have to invoke. Still, it is a critical function—if you ever encounter a situation in which you need to restore a network, you will be glad to have such a capability in place.

Image Management

As with PCs, network equipment vendors occasionally issue new software revisions. Such revisions might be new feature releases, or they might simply be patches that contain bug fixes. In these cases, you need to be able to upgrade your network. The problem is that now you are not dealing with a single PC, but with hundreds or thousands pieces of equipment scattered across your network. To do so effectively, you need to be able to keep track of which software images are installed on which network devices, and have a way to deliver new images to those devices where the upgrade applies and install them without disrupting service. This functionality is referred to as *image management*. Despite the name, image management has nothing to do with managing your image in the public relations sense of the word; it involves managing software images running on network equipment.

A Is for Accounting

Organizations that offer communication services over a network ultimately need to generate revenue for the services they provide. After all, this is how they make their living. If they do not bill for the services they provide, they will not stay in business for long—notwithstanding some dotcom businesses that might give a service away but compensate for it through some other means, such as advertisements. Even if the organization is not a service provider but, say, an internal IT department providing those services to its own company, measuring the actual services provided and consumed is still required. This is necessary to be able to assess the cost/benefit ratio of running those services, to keep cost under control relative to the services that are actually provided, and to use firm data for decisions on whether to perform services in-house or outsource them. After all, if an outside vendor could provide certain services as well as or better than your IT department at a lower cost, chances are, you will at least consider outsourcing.

Accounting management is all about the functions that allow organizations to collect revenue and get credit for the communication services they provide, and to keep track of their use. It is hence at the core of the economics of providing communications services. Obviously, accounting management needs to be highly robust; highest availability and reliability standards apply. After all, if accounting data is not properly collected, the service provider is actually giving away free services, translating directly into lost revenue.

Earlier we used the analogy of network management and the medical field, comparing the diagnosis of faults in a network with the medical diagnosis of a patient. A cynic might say that the analogy extends to accounting management—after all, the hospital will want to send a bill as well.

On the Difference Between Billing and Accounting

Accounting management is often associated simply with billing, which is actually only one aspect. Billing is a common function that is performed for most businesses, whether they are rental car agencies, house-cleaning services, or restaurants. The business in this case is, of course, providing communication services. Writing the bills themselves, keeping track of customer data, and sending payment reminders is pretty similar for all these business. The domain specifics come in with regards to how to account for use of the service—that is, measuring what was consumed, by whom, and when. After all, unless you provide services at a flat fee ("all you can eat" or "all you can communicate"), you can send someone a proper bill only when you know what they have consumed, how much, and at what time. In other words, you need to *account* for the services and goods that your customer received.

Consider how you would account for rental car services—this would involve knowing the type of car, how many days the customer rented it, and whether the customer returned it with a full gas tank. Of course, this is not enough to write a bill. For this, you also need to know what tariff to apply. The tariff defines the rules on how to charge for the accounted services. In many cases, what to charge is determined not only by the actual service provided (in this case, the duration of the rental and the type of car); it might also depend on when the service was provided (weekday or weekend, for example) and to whom (regular or corporate or gold customer rate). Therefore, to produce a bill, the accounting data needs to be processed and the proper tariff needs to be applied to it. Figure 5-10 illustrates the relationship between accounting data, tariff, and bill.

Figure 5-10 *Accounting vs. Billing*

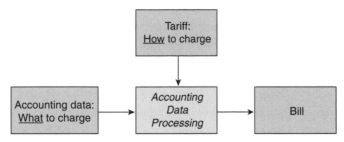

As indicated earlier, it is certainly possible to also simply charge a flat fee (think "all you can eat" in a restaurant, or "all you can communicate" in the networking context). Flat fees for networking services are not uncommon because customers often prefer simple and predictable pricing—think of flat-fee Internet service, for example. It also makes the task of billing easier for communication service providers, although it does not do away with the need to account for service usage entirely, as you shall see when we revisit flat fees in the section after next.

Accounting for Communication Service Consumption

To track the consumption of network services, meters must be set up that collect usage data. In the case of some services, usage data is automatically generated. For example, in the case of voice, call detail records (CDRs) are automatically generated by the network as part of call setup and teardown. Of course, these records still need to be collected, making sure that none are lost. In addition, because communication services often are provided across a network, duplicates must be eliminated. For example, if for a connection or a call the source and the destination each generate their own record, they need to be matched and consolidated into one.

In general, usage data is based on volume, duration, and/or quality. Examples of accounting measures are megabytes of data traffic, minutes of phone calls, number of service transactions, and use of premium or guaranteed services versus best-effort services. The data that needs to be collected must be put in terms and units that are relevant to the particular service and, hence, tend to be service specific. For example, to perform accounting for a voice service, it will not be interesting to know how many bits of voice payload were transported. However, the duration of a call is important. On the other hand, for a database-backup service the volume of data is very important, but not necessarily the duration of the backup. Sometimes other factors need to be taken into account, such as the distance of a phone call—although in recent years, the notion of distance has become much less relevant.

Accounting data is often collected only for offline processing. For example, this is typical if you send a subscriber a monthly bill. However, sometimes accounting data processing is also required in real time or near–real time. A good example is prepaid voice services: calling cards. The calling card customer can talk only as long as her minutes have been paid for. When the prepaid credit runs out, the prepaid voice service provider will want to be able to disconnect the call. Of course, this imposes additional requirements and the need for a feedback cycle between the network that is providing the service and accounting management. In some cases, this blurs the line between management and control—a management function becomes a part of the communication service itself.

Although it should go without saying, it does need to be mentioned that it is not sufficient to merely measure communication service consumption; consumption also must be properly attributed to the user of the service. Therefore security functions, such as authentication to identify a user, often need to accompany and complement the collection of accounting data. This does not require users to provide a login and password each time; it can simply be based on the port through which a user connects to a service—a data port in an office or a phone jack in a home, for example.

Related to attributing communication service to the proper user is another important function of accounting management: fraud detection. Fraud detection is concerned with tracking down and preventing theft of communication services, such as unauthorized users hacking into a network to receive free Internet access or making free phone calls, or—worse—assuming the identity of legitimate users to steal services. Fraud is a big concern to communication service providers. It causes revenue leakage—that is, lost revenue for communication services that were provided but not paid for. It can also impede the quality of the service that legitimate users receive because communication resources are unexpectedly not available. And of course, no customer will accept being billed for services that were not actually received.

Accounting Management as a Service Feature

To simplify accounting and to simplify communication products, in many instances, flat-fee instead of usage-based models are offered. As mentioned earlier, flat-fee Internet service is one example. Of course, although flat fees ease some of the requirements of tracking precise use, other aspects, such as the need to attribute service use to authorized users—who are known to the service provider and not delinquent on their bills—remain.

In addition, accounting management can serve as an additional feature of the service itself, the very service that it provides accounting for. For example, viewing service use and billing information online makes a service more convenient and transparent, resulting in greater customer satisfaction and perceived ease in purchasing and paying for the service. The capability to view service use differentiated by different accounts of the same primary customer (example: wife, husband, and each of the children) constitutes additional service features that could be sold at a premium; at the same time, it opens up new ways to bundle service offerings and target specific market segments.

Flexibility in accounting management can lead to very sophisticated service offerings, such as having different charges for "family and friends" or different charges for calls that are made between customers on the same network versus to customers on other networks (on-net and off-net calls), to name a few examples. These are examples taken from telephony services that can be commonly found today but that were made possible only by advances in accounting management.

P Is for Performance

When you buy a car and look at different choices, you assume that the cars you are looking at can all transport you from point A to point B. Each of the choices might also offer automatic transmission, power door locks, air-conditioning, and perhaps even a navigation system. However, those functional properties alone might not tell the whole story, and you might even take them for granted. To make a decision, you also take a look at nonfunctional properties, most important of which is performance. Does the car accelerate from 0 to 60 mph in 5 seconds, or in 25? Does it get 40 miles per gallon, or only 10? The point is, performance makes a big difference, and it is no different with communication networks.

Performance Metrics

Performance of networks is characterized by a multitude of performance characteristics, measured according to metrics. Some examples of performance metrics are these:

- Throughput, measured by a number of units of communication performed per unit of time. The units of communication depend on the layer, type of network, and networking service in question. Examples are as follows:

  — At the link layer, the number of bytes, or octets, that are transmitted per second

  — At the network layer, the number of packets that are routed per second

  — At the application layer for a web service, the number of web requests that are serviced per second

  — At the application layer for a voice service, the number of voice calls, or call attempts, that can be processed per hour

  As a side note, closely related to throughput is utilization. Whereas throughput is an absolute number (such as number of bytes per second), utilization is a relative number that expresses throughput as a percentage of the theoretical maximum capacity of the underlying system.

- Delay, measured in a unit of time. Again, you can measure different kinds of delay, depending on what layer or networking service you are dealing with. Examples are as follows:

  — At the link layer, the time that it takes for an octet that is transmitted to reach its destination at the other end of the line

  — At the network layer, the time that it takes for an IP packet to reach its destination

— At the application layer for a web service, the time that it takes for a request to reach its destination at the host servicing the request after the request has been issued

— At the application layer for a voice service, the time it takes to receive a dial tone after you have lifted the receiver

- Quality is in many ways also performance related and can be measured differently, depending on the networking service

— At the link layer, the number or percentage of seconds during which errors in transmission occurred

— At the network layer, the number or percentage of packets dropped

— At the application layer for a web service, the number or percentage of web requests that could not be serviced

— At the application layer for a voice service, the number or percentage of voice calls that were dropped or abnormally terminated

As the examples point out, the same performance concept (such as throughput and delay) can be applied at different layers of the communication hierarchy. It should be mentioned that what is measured at each layer is nevertheless fundamentally different and not just a matter of which unit is applied—for example, whether throughput is expressed in kilobytes or megabytes per second. Instead, what is measured at each layer is different, and the measurements observed at one layer give no indication of what might be observed at a different layer. For example, the number of bytes transmitted at the link layer provides no indication of the number of voice calls that are successfully serviced at the application layer, nor can they be computed from one another.

Monitoring and Tuning Your Network for Performance

Performance management deals with monitoring and tuning your network for its performance. This includes a wide variety of functions.

At the most basic level, you want to be able to retrieve a snapshot of the current performance. This corresponds with taking a look at the speedometer of your car to see how fast you are going. Of course, in the case of network management, the speedometer is replaced by packet counters, delay measures, and gauges that indicate utilization percentages.

For a more sophisticated analysis, you might want to observe some of these parameters over time. For example, you might want to plot a histogram of some performance values on a screen, with a new sample taken (and point plotted) every second, or every 5 minutes, or whatever time interval suits you. Doing this gives an absolute reading of a particular value, and you also can observe how the values change over time. This way, you will be able to distinguish between a sudden drop or spike in value from a value that is within the ordinary.

Some patterns might indicate that a problem is about to occur—for example, an increase in utilization of an interface might precede an increase in the number of packets that are dropped, which, in turn, might precede users experiencing application sessions timing out. Monitoring the performance often allows you to anticipate problems and take care of them before they occur.

When observing the values over time, you might be able to determine a trend—whether the utilization continues to go up, for example. In this case, you can get a head start on planning for an upgrade. You might be able to spot bottlenecks in your network—areas that seem to be constantly congested, as well as areas that seem to be underutilized, where equipment might be put to better use elsewhere. All this can be valuable information for adjusting and tuning your network configuration to get the optimum performance and value from your equipment.

Collecting Performance Data

When you sit in front of a screen, you can monitor the performance of only a very small portion of your network—for example, of a hot spot where there appears to be a problem. However, you might be interested in recording performance data from all over the network, even if you cannot constantly monitor it. It can sometimes be useful to have the option of looking at the data later if you discover a problem, to see if there are any indications in the data of how the problem developed, or to just use the data for general analysis. In many cases, such analysis does not have to occur in real time; it is even possible to perform the analysis offline. This means that you need to collect statistical performance data. Periodic snapshots need to be taken and stored somewhere in a file system or database.

Constant polling of performance data from devices can quickly bring a management system to its knees, not to mention the network and devices being polled. Imagine that you have a network with 10,000 devices, and you are interested in 10 performance parameters on each. If you wanted to collect data on a per-minute basis, it would require 100,000 polling cycles per minute! Fortunately, there are more intelligent ways of collecting performance data.

One popular way of obtaining performance data is by having it reported as what amounts to a stream of events—for example, using protocols such as Netflow or IP Flow Information Export (IPFIX). This way, the request to poll performance data is no longer required.

Another option is popular whenever the collection of performance data does not have to occur in real time: The data collection is simply set up at the device. A management application tells the device what type of performance data it is interested in. Internally, the device then takes a snapshot of this data over predetermined time intervals, such as every 15 minutes starting on the hour. The device logs this data in a file on flash memory or hard disk (if it supports this function, it will almost certainly have one). This collects the data into "buckets," dripping in an additional drop of data at every time interval until the bucket is emptied (that is, retrieved by the management application) or until it is full. Once a day, perhaps in the middle of the night, when the overall processing load is low, the management application retrieves the files containing the performance data from the devices. Then management applications that know how to crunch large volumes of numbers go over those files, trying to establish trends or whatever else a user is interested in.

S Is for Security

The final letter in FCAPS, "S, stands for security—that is, management aspects that are related to securing your network from threats, such as hacker attacks, the spread of worms and viruses, and malicious intrusion attempts. Two aspects need to be distinguished: security of management, which ensures that the management itself is secure, and management of security, which manages the security of the network. Those aspects are depicted in Figure 5-11 and are explained in detail in the following subsections.

Figure 5-11 *Security of Management vs. Management of Security*

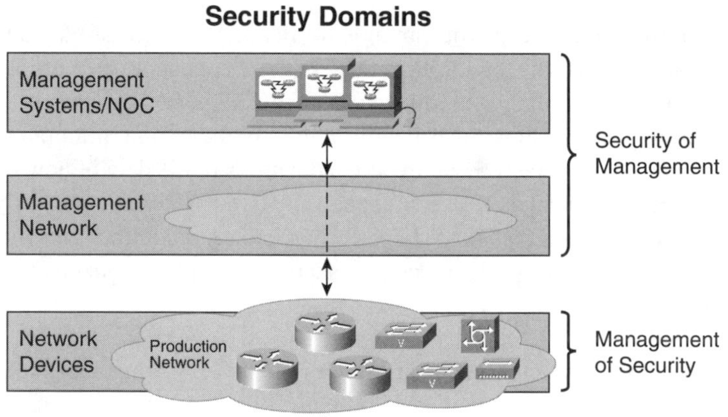

Security Domains

Security of Management

Security of management deals with ensuring that management operations themselves are secure. A big part of this concerns ensuring that access to management is restricted to authorized users.

For example, access to the management interfaces of the devices in the network needs to be secured to prevent unauthorized changes to network configurations. Also, the management network needs to be secured to prevent disruption to management traffic.

In addition, access to the management applications themselves needs to be secured properly—devices generally authorize on the basis of a management application, not on the basis of the user of a management application. Therefore, securing access to the management interfaces and management network without securing the management applications is akin to locking the door of your house to keep thieves out but leaving the windows open. Clearly, improper access to management applications can cause considerable damage. After all, if you can use those applications to modify configurations of devices in the network to provision services and to tune network performance, you could also abuse them to disrupt services, degrade network performance, or provision services illegitimately to give users who are not authorized (or have not paid) access to the network.

Note that management needs to be secured not only against attacks from the outside. You need to also account for the possibility that security breaches occur from within. Accordingly, although managing access privileges properly is a necessary ingredient to ensure secure management, it is not sufficient by itself. Another important function concerns maintaining tamper-proof security audit trails that record any management operations that are performed on the network. If mechanisms to safeguard the network and its management fail, an audit trail enables you to reproduce what has actually happened, possibly identify culprits, and more easily recover from the security breach.

As a general rule, security threats from the inside are harder to defend against than threats from the outside. However, by performing the following tasks, you can go a long way in defending against the worst threats and preventing disruptions to the operation of your network:

- Set up proper processes and procedures to ensure orderly operations

- Assign access privileges only to those who actually need these privileges for their immediate job function

- Require "secure" passwords that cannot easily be cracked

- Require that passwords be changed at regular intervals

- Establish audit trails, themselves secured properly

- Set up proper facilities for backup and restore of critical management data

Management of Security

Management of security involves managing security of the network itself, as opposed to security of its management. Unfortunately, as we all know, in these days, online security threats are all too common. In many cases, security threats target not so much the network, but devices connected to the network—PCs of end users, for example, or systems that host websites for corporations. In addition, the network infrastructure itself might come under attack. Common security threats include but are by no means limited to the following:

- Hacker attacks of individuals who try to obtain improper control of a system that is connected to the network.

- Denial-of-service (DOS) attacks that try to overload portions of a network by generating illegitimate traffic, preventing legitimate network traffic from getting through. A variant is distributed denial-of-service (DDOS) attacks, which coordinate those attacks from multiple sources, making them harder to defend against.

- Viruses and worms that attempt to corrupt and possibly destroy systems along with their file systems, which are connected to the network or which are network devices themselves. Related to this are Trojan horses, malicious code that masquerades as a useful and innocent program that, when opened by a user, can wreak havoc.

- Spam, also considered a security problem because its volume can overwhelm a network and its servers.

Management of security provides functions to deal with and protect against these and other security threats. This involves some of the same functions that provide security for management, such as ensuring that management interfaces of network devices are not open to people from the outside, as well as maintaining security audit trails that record all operations—and attempted operations—on network elements.

In addition, management of security involves other functions. All of those functions can be components of a comprehensive security management strategy. For example:

- Intrusion detection involves monitoring traffic on the network to detect suspicious traffic patterns that could indicate an ongoing attack. One technique that can help guard against the spread of viruses involves inspecting traffic payload to see what is carried inside it, and then discarding or marking content that is apparently intended to compromise the network's security. Methods that involve inspection can sometimes be ineffective, however, because in many cases payload is transported over secure connections that are encrypted. In those cases, inspection fails because it cannot decrypt the traffic that is being transported.

- Another technique that can help protect a network consists of applying policies that limit or allow to only gradually increase the amount of traffic that is geared toward a particular destination or that originates from a particular source. If an attack resulted in a sudden burst of traffic, this technique allows for a more graceful degradation of the network and its services if they come under attack.

- The capability to "blacklist" ports and network addresses at which suspicious traffic patterns are observed and through which suspected offenders may enter the network constitutes another important safeguard. Those ports and addresses can be put under additional scrutiny and monitored for suspicious activity so that they can be quickly shut down if an attack is suspected.

■ So-called "honey pots" are a more recent technique to gather information about security vulnerabilities in a network to help better defend it. A honey pot is a piece of equipment or a host system that appears to be a part of the regular network but that, unbeknownst to the attacker, is actually isolated and specially secured. It serves as a trap. Because the honey pot is not an actual part of the production network, any traffic that is directed at the honey pot can with reasonable certainty be regarded as malicious. Analyzing such traffic yields important information about attacks on the network and allows you to better fend off such attacks.

Limitations of the FCAPS Categorization

The notion of FCAPS is tremendously useful in providing a simple framework that is easy and intuitive to understand. It provides structure to discussions of management functionality and establishes a common terminology. However, it is important to note that it also constitutes somewhat of an oversimplification. Many cases of functionality cannot be easily categorized because they can be used for different purposes that fall under different function categories.

One example is the capability to test the functioning of a given service, often used for troubleshooting—in other words, fault management. However, there are other uses of the same capability, such as to validate that provisioning steps have had the desired effect (configuration management), or to use the same test to simultaneously take performance measurements (performance management).

Another example concerns the capability to log and report events—that is, messages that are emitted by network devices. This capability is generally associated with fault management because it clearly relates to alarms. However, it can also support other FCAPS management function categories as follows:

■ Performance management, such as when the crossing of a certain threshold is reported, perhaps when utilization reaches a certain level

■ Configuration management, such as when events indicate certain changes in the network's configuration

■ Security management, such as in conjunction with security-related events, perhaps unsuccessful logon attempts into network devices or activities that smack of fraud

The following sections examine some other ways to organize management functionality.

OAM&P: The Other FCAPS

The previous section described at length the various functions that are provided by management organized along the FCAPS model. Although FCAPS is probably the best-known functional reference model, it is by no means the only one. Management functions can also be organized in other ways. Of course, the functions that ultimately need to be performed remain the same, independent of how they are categorized. What might change is the way in which those functions are grouped and organized, the way in which the functions need to interface with each other, the way in which information flows, and (if mapped to an actual network provider organization) the way in which responsibilities are assigned.

An alternative to the FCAPS categorization of management functions is known as *OAM&P*—Operations, Administration, Maintenance, and Provisioning. The OAM&P model is popular in particular with large telecommunications service providers, whose internal organization OAM&P often reflects much better than FCAPS, which is more popular with enterprises and data providers.

Without reiterating the individual management functions that we discussed earlier in the chapter, the OAM&P categories cover the management ground as follows:

- Operations involves the day-to-day running of the network—specifically, coordinating activities among administration, maintenance, and provisioning as required. It also includes monitoring the network to ensure that things run properly, although, in many cases, monitoring activities are also conducted as part of maintenance. This further illustrates the point that, in the end, any categorization is somewhat arbitrary, and different functional organizations might work best for different network providers.

- Administration covers the support functions that are required to manage the network and that do not involve performing changes (configuring, tuning) to the running network itself. Administration includes activities such as designing the network, tracking network usage, assigning addresses, planning upgrades to the network, taking service orders from end users and customers, keeping track of network inventory, collecting accounting data, and billing customers.

- Maintenance includes functionality that ensures that the network and communication services operate as they are supposed to. This involves diagnosing, troubleshooting, and repairing things that do not work as planned, to keep the network in a state in which it can be continuously used and provide proper service.

- Finally, provisioning is concerned with the proper setting of configuration parameters on the network so that the network functions as expected. Depending on what gets provisioned, different types of provisioning are distinguished. Equipment provisioning is concerned with updating equipment configuration parameters and installing and turning up equipment. Service provisioning is concerned with configuring the network end-to-end to provide or disable a service for end customers at the proper service level.

FAB and eTOM: Oh, Wait, There's More

Yet another functional management reference framework has been established by the Telemanagement Forum (TMF), a consortium of companies in the telecommunications space that includes service providers, equipment vendors, and system integrators. This framework is known as the Telecoms Operations Map (TOM) and has the concept of a management lifecycle at its center; in a sense, it competes with the older OAM&P model, and because it is newer, it is not yet as established. Fundamentally, TOM distinguishes among three lifecycle stages, each with its own unique set of management requirements: Fulfillment—Assurance—Billing (FAB). TOM applies these lifecycle stages at different layers that are clearly distinguished:

- **Network and systems management**—Roughly corresponding to the element and network management layers in TMN

- **Service development and operations**—Roughly corresponding to the service management layer

- **Customer care**—Roughly corresponding to the business management layer

For example, applied to the management of a particular service:

- Fulfillment ensures that a service order that was received from a customer is carried out properly. This involves turning up any newly required equipment (for example, customer premises equipment such as a cable modem), performing required equipment configurations, and reserving required resources in the network, such as bandwidth or ports.

- Assurance includes all activities required to ensure that a service runs smoothly after it has been fulfilled. Services need to be monitored to ensure that quality-of-service guarantees are met. Any faults that occur in the network need to be diagnosed and repaired to keep their impact on the service to a minimum.

- Billing involves making sure that the services provided and resources consumed are accounted for properly and can be billed to the user. This is a very important step because, without the ability to bill properly, any service provider would quickly go out of business.

More recently, TOM has been extended into eTOM, the enhanced Telecom Operations Map. eTOM widens TOM's scope and aims to include all aspects of business management, incorporating aspects as diverse as supply chain management, human resources management, financial asset management, and so forth. However, there are no additional aspects with respect to the FAB categorization of management functions.

There is much more to eTOM than can be reasonably described here. For example, specific functions at the various layers and lifecycle stages are called out, along with the interfaces and interactions between those functions, all of which eTOM specifies in great detail. eTOM thus goes beyond being a mere reference framework by defining a comprehensive set of standards that enables systems in an operational support environment to interact and interoperate with each other, and to collectively support a service provider's business processes.

How It All Relates and What It Means to You: Using Your Network Management ABCs

With so many functional reference models to choose from, which one is the best? Ultimately, it comes down to a matter of preference and to which model suits your network best. These reference models are, after all, virtual; the way in which you actually organize your management functions may look different altogether. You can cut things diagonally, horizontally, or vertically. The result in each case should be that you have partitioned the task of managing your network into smaller chunks that are much easier to tackle and digest than trying to conquer the entire task at once. The different models not only cut things differently, but they also apply a different number of cuts— yet each is perfectly valid and provides valuable orientation for how network management can be organized overall. In addition, they all provide a common terminology that can be used when discussing groups of management functions. However, someone well versed in the FCAPS model will have difficulty relating to someone who "grew up" in the OAM&P world, and vice versa. So how do the different models relate?

Table 5-1 provides a rough sketch of how FCAPS and OAM&P relate and effectively map to each other. An *X* in a cell indicates that the functions are closely related. An *(X)* indicates that the functions are still related, but to a lesser extent. An — indicates that the functions are only loosely related, if at all.

Table 5-1   *Relationship Between FCAPS and OAM&P*

	F	C	A	P	S
O	(X)	—	—	(X)	—
A	—	—	X	(X)	(X)
M	X	(X)	—	X	X
P	—	X	—	—	—

A word of caution: This mapping attempts to paint the big picture in broad strokes but is not entirely precise. For example, it should not be misinterpreted to mean that *configuration* is a synonym for *provisioning*. OAM&P provisioning is related to other FCAPS areas, such as security, in that it affects how security-related parameters will be provisioned. Likewise, FCAPS configuration plays a role in OAM&P administration because networks might need to be audited for their inventory, an aspect that, strictly speaking, is not part of provisioning.

With similar caveats, Table 5-2 provides a rough sketch of the relationship between FCAPS and FAB. Very roughly speaking, fulfillment encompasses configuration; assurance encompasses fault, performance, and security; and billing corresponds to accounting.

Table 5-2   *Relationship Between FCAPS and FAB*

	F	C	A	P	S
F	—	X	—	—	—
A	X	—	—	X	X
B	—	—	X	—	—

Chapter Summary

This chapter took a closer look at functional reference models. We took a tour of the most important management functions using the FCAPS model.

Fault management consists of functions to monitor the network to ensure that everything is working properly. Dealing with alarms and the large volume of events that are constantly being generated is one of the challenges that fault management addresses. However, it encompasses other functions as well, such as troubleshooting and diagnosis.

Configuration management is concerned with how the network is configured. This involves setting configuration parameters in such a way that the network can provide the services that it is supposed to. Configuration management also involves functions that enable users to audit a network and discover what's in it.

Accounting management deals with collecting and recording data about how the network is used and about the consumption of its services by end users. It is at the heart of being able to collect revenues and to be able to quantify the value that is derived from the network.

Performance management is all about collecting statistics from the network to assess performance and tune the network. The goal is to allow for proper allocation of resources in the network, such as removing bottlenecks, providing forecasts as input for network planning, and delivering the best possible quality of service with the given means.

Finally, security management is concerned with managing security-related aspects of the network. It is geared toward averting various kinds of security threats that a network and its management infrastructure are exposed to.

FCAPS is not the only way in which management functions can be categorized. Another model that is popular in particular with telecommunications service providers is Operations, Administration, Maintenance, and Provisioning (OAM&P), and more models exist. Each model reflects a different way in which the various functions that are required to manage a network can be grouped and organized. However, regardless of which model you prefer, at the end of the day, the functions that need to be performed when managing a network remain the same.

Chapter Review

1. What does FCAPS stand for?

2. What does OAM&P stand for?

3. What is the difference between alarm filtering and alarm correlation?

4. The management functions discussed in this chapter pertain not only to the element management layer that deals with individual pieces of equipment, but really to any management layer. Give an example of a fault at the element management layer, an example of a fault at the network management layer, and an example of a fault at the service management layer.

5. Give an example of a configuration operation at the element management layer, a configuration operation at the network management layer, and a configuration operation at the service management layer.

6. Give an example of an event sent by a network device that supports an accounting management function. Give an example of an event that supports a security management function.

7. Provide a technical reason, not a marketing reason, for why a service provider might choose to provide flat-rate billing.

8. Performance and accounting management are similar, in that both are interested in collecting usage data from the network. Describe an important way in which the use of this data and the requirements for its collection differ.

9. "I have no need for security management functions because I am using a dedicated and secure management network." Please comment on this statement.

10. Provide a rough sketch of how OAM&P and FAB relate.

Part III: Management Building Blocks

CHAPTER 6

Management Information: What Management Conversations Are All About

When a manager and an agent communicate, they ultimately "talk" about the device that is being managed. (Actually, this is not entirely correct—as you know by now, they could, for example, also talk about a service. For the purposes of the discussion here, however, we assume that the managed entity that is being represented by the agent is indeed a device.) For example, the manager might ask the agent how many packets have been sent over one of the device's interfaces, or the agent might send an alarm telling the manager that it has just detected a line error on one of the device's ports. Everything that managers need to know about the entity that is being managed constitutes *management information*. Management information, therefore, is ultimately what conversations between managers and agents are all about. This chapter picks up on and explores in greater detail the information viewpoint that was introduced in Chapter 4, "The Dimensions of Management."

Here are some of the things you will learn when reading this chapter:

- Understand what a Management Information Base is and what is contained in it

- Distinguish between management information, the specification of management information in management information models, and specification languages for management information that constitute metamodels

- Understand how an SNMP MIB module is defined

- Understand how design as a software engineering discipline can be applied to the modeling of management information

Establishing a Common Terminology Between Manager and Agent

Swiss author Peter Bichsel penned a great short story titled "A Table Is a Table." It goes roughly like this: A lonely man unaccustomed to social interactions is pondering why certain nouns are connected to certain objects. For example, why is a table called *table* and not, for example, *carpet*? He finds this thought intriguing and starts to reassign names, starting with the table, which he now indeed calls *carpet*. Of course, now the carpet needs a new name because otherwise the term *carpet* would become overloaded. So he calls it *closet*. The closet is renamed to *newspaper*, newspaper to *bed*, bed to *painting*, man to *foot*, and so on. While the foot lies in his painting, he forms many sentences with his new words that now sound funny and brighten up his mood. He starts renaming verbs, too. Many months go by and he eventually starts to lose track of the original names of objects. One day he goes on a trip to the city. First he laughs when he overhears people talk to each other. They speak the same language, but they use different terms in awkward combinations that don't make sense to him anymore—they call a carpet a table, a painting a bed, and so on. However, his amusement does not last long when he realizes that he actually can no longer understand them—and, perhaps even worse, that they cannot understand him. Although they speak fundamentally the same language, there is a complete communication breakdown because they use different terminology for the same objects. To his dismay, he ends up even lonelier and gloomier than before.

A central aspect of management information is that it establishes a common and mutually understood way by which agents and managers can refer to various aspects of the managed device. Without this mutual understanding, serious problems would arise that would render a network essentially unmanageable.

For example, think about what might happen if a manager were to monitor a counter that counts the volume of data traffic, thinking that it refers to the number of octets that are sent into the router over a port (incoming traffic), and the agent returns instead the number of octets that are received from the router over that port (outgoing traffic). If the router in question were an access router over which residential customers are connected, the manager might determine that the traffic pattern was suspicious because an unusual amount of traffic was sent from the customer to this port, which might be indicative of an ongoing attack. As a consequence, the manager might decide to switch off the port to cut off the suspected malicious customer. However, in reality, the customer might have simply been downloading a substantial amount of data and receiving it over that port, which is a common and perfectly permissible activity. Understandably, the customer would not be pleased if she were cut off.

Problems of a similar nature would arise if a manager wanted to retrieve the current count of octets received over what he thinks of as port 1 (the port that is on the far left when standing in front of the device), and the agent were to return instead the number of octets that were received over what the manager thinks of as port 8 (the one on the far right of the device). The manager, confusing those ports, would consequently also confuse what and who was connected on the other side of those ports. Again, serious problems would arise because subsequent management decisions would be based on the wrong facts.

In the first example, the manager and agent had a misunderstanding over the type of information being requested, confusing incoming with outgoing traffic. In the second example, the misunderstanding is not about the type of information (the counter in question refers to incoming traffic on a port alright) but about the particular instance of this information (how to refer to one of several such counters). In either case, the manager would not be able to manage the device because manager and agent have no way to refer to the same aspect of the managed device. In the worst case, the manager would be slow to realize that a miscommunication even existed and in the interim would base all management decisions on a misunderstanding. This misunderstanding would lead eventually to a degradation of networking services and all kinds of other problems.

For these reasons, it is important that manager and agent both assign the same terms (identifying the particular type of management information) and labels (identifying the particular instance of management information) to the real-world aspects of the device that is being managed. This way, port 1 is port 1 and not a port 8 to both manager and agent, and a sent packet is a sent packet, not a received packet. The pieces of management information that manager and agent refer to ultimately constitute the *managed objects* (*MOs*) that are part of the device's *Management Information Base (MIB)*. These concepts are of central importance in network management and are explained in the following sections.

MIBs

A device's management information is maintained by the management agent in the managed device's Management Information Base, or MIB (rhymes with *rib*). In the following section, we will take a look at what a MIB entails.

The Managed Device as a Conceptual Data Store

A MIB is best thought of as a conceptual data store. Managers can retrieve management information from the MIB by directing corresponding requests at the management agent—for example, using a "get" operation. In many cases, they can also manipulate and modify the information that is contained in the MIB—for example, using a "set," a "create," or a "delete" operation.

The MIB, of course, is not the same as a database. The MIB does not store information about the real world (the actual managed device) in a file system; instead, it is actually "connected" to the real world and simply offers a view of it. In other words, it offers an abstraction of the managed device that is used for management purposes.

When a manager retrieves a piece of information from a MIB, it represents an aspect of the device—for example, an internal register that has kept track of the number of packets that were received over a port, or a setting for a protocol timeout parameter. When a manager manipulates the information in a MIB, the actual settings of the device are modified, affecting the way that the device behaves in the real world. Management information hence provides the knobs that network managers can turn to control the device, and the displays that tell network managers everything they need to know to manage the device. MIBs are one of the central concepts in network management, and their importance cannot be overemphasized.

MIBs contain many individual pieces of management information about the managed entity—information about physical aspects such as ports and line cards, as well as about logical aspects such as protocol machines, software, and features of individual communication services. The pieces of management information in a MIB are commonly referred to as *managed objects* (*MOs*)—abstractions of individual aspects of the managed device that are not decomposed further for management purposes but are treated as one informational entity. In general, those aspects correspond to the "nouns" that are the subject of management conversations between managers and agents. Here are some examples:

- Retrieve statistical information about a *port* (that is used to connect a piece of equipment to a network)

- Create an *access control rule* (that specifies for a firewall which packets to filter)

- Configure the *connection endpoint* of an ATM connection

Each of the nouns in italics could be represented by its own MO.

Figure 6-1 shows a typical depiction of a MIB: a conceptual database that is associated with a management agent and that contains a number of MOs. MOs in MIBs are often shown arranged in conceptual tree structures. This is done because, in many cases, MOs have hierarchical containment relationships with each other. For example, an MO that represents an equipment chassis may contain other MOs that represent line cards, or an MO that represents a communications interface may contain other MOs that represent subinterfaces of that same interface. Similarly, in many cases, the names by which MOs are referred to are hierarchical in nature, not unlike the way in which postal addresses in the real world are hierarchical (a person's name *at the* number *of a* street *of a* city and zip code *of a* state). In the case of a MIB, MOs might have names such as "the number *of a* particular type of interface *on a* certain port *on a* certain line card" (as before, words printed in italics denote the different levels of the hierarchy). Details on how MOs are named depend on the metaschema—that is, the specification language that is used to model management information, a concept which is described later in this chapter, and on the management protocol that is used to access the management information. Management protocols are discussed in detail in Chapter 8, "Common Management Protocols: Languages of Management."

Figure 6-1 *MIB and MOs*

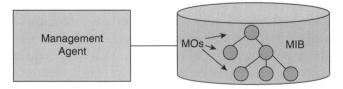

The actual real-world aspects of the entity being managed that MOs represent are referred to as *real resources* or *managed resources*, to distinguish them from their management abstraction, the managed objects. Just as the entirety of all real resources constitutes the managed real-world entity, the entirety of all MOs constitutes the managed device's MIB. In effect, the managed device consists of a "real resource plane" that exists independent of its need to be managed; the "management plane" provides the management infrastructure and views on it. Figure 6-2 depicts the relationship between the different terms.

Figure 6-2   *MIB and MOs, Managed Entity and Real Resources*

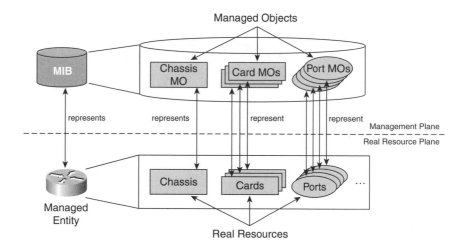

It should also be mentioned that, in addition to information about the real resources themselves, a MIB can contain information about how those resources relate, modeled as relationships between MOs. As mentioned earlier, the most common case is that of hierarchical relationships—for example, a chassis contains a card, a card contains a port, and a port contains a connection endpoint.

Categories of Management Information

The types of management information maintained in a MIB can be manifold (see Figure 6-3). The distinction of different categories of management information is important because, in general, management applications treat different categories differently and use them for different purposes.

- **State information**—This is information about the current state of physical and logical resources, along with any operational data. It includes information about whether the device is currently functioning properly, including what current alarm conditions there are and what the highest alarm severity is, or how long the system has been up and running since it was last rebooted. It also includes information about the current performance of the device and what it is currently doing, including packet and connection counts for various protocols, current CPU load, and utilization of bandwidth and memory.

State information is the management information that is most relevant for monitoring a network. Management applications cannot modify this information but can only retrieve it—state information is effectively "owned" by the device. In many cases, state information is subject to frequent and rapid change because it reflects the current activity of the device. For this reason, in many cases, management applications choose to not cache this information in a database, but retrieve it from the device whenever the current information is required.

Figure 6-3 *Management Information Categories*

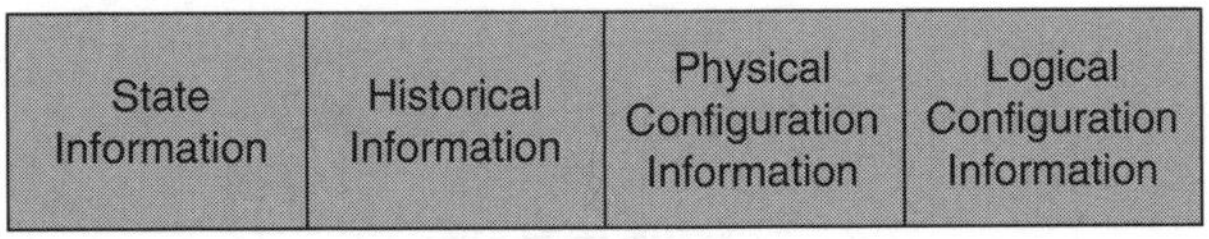

State Information	Historical Information	Physical Configuration Information	Logical Configuration Information

- **Physical configuration information**—This is information about how the managed device is physically configured. This includes information such as the device type, physical configuration in terms of cards and available ports, serial numbers, and MAC addresses.

  As with state information, physical configuration information is effectively "owned" by the device—management applications can retrieve it but cannot modify it. However, unlike state information, physical configuration information changes only rarely, if ever. For this reason, management applications in general choose to cache this information and store it in their database, for efficiency, instead of asking the agent repeatedly for it. Generally, it takes a physical action by a network technician to affect physical configuration information, for example by inserting a new line card into a piece of networking equipment for a capacity upgrade.

- **Logical configuration information**—This concerns various parameter settings and configured logical resources on the device, such as IP addresses, telephone numbers, or logical interfaces.

  Unlike other categories of management information, logical configuration information is typically controlled and can be changed by management applications and administrators with the required authorization, not by the device itself. It provides the "knobs" that network managers use to control the device. For this reason, in many cases, management applications choose to cache logical configuration information that is important to them in a database, knowing the information does not change unless they change it. Of course, an administrator or another application could change the information as well, thereby posing a potential risk for information stored in the management application's database and the actual logical configuration on the network element to run out of synch.

Logical configuration information can be further subdivided into startup configuration information and transient configuration information. Startup configuration information must be persisted by the device itself so that the device can survive reboots. Transient configuration information, on the other hand, is not persisted and can be lost or reverted to defaults if a device need to be restarted. The running configuration that is currently in effect at a router, and that might have changed since startup, typically represents transient configuration information.

■ **Historical information**—This includes historical snapshots of performance-related state information (such as the packet counts for each 15-minute interval over the past 24 hours), including logs of various types of events, such as a firewall log of recent remote connection attempts.

Historical information is different from other types of management information because it does not reflect actual managed resources. Strictly speaking, it should not be maintained in a MIB at all. Instead, it is simply "data" that is stored at the device. Typically, the purpose of this is to offload management applications, which can then simply retrieve this information in bulk from the device instead of having to incrementally collect it themselves in frequent itervals.

In some cases, management information that can be found in a MIB is not really management information at all. Instead, it represents parameters for certain actions that are to be performed on the device, such as a "ping" operation to be executed. Such instances normally constitute aberrations or special cases that most users and applications normally need not be concerned about.

The Difference Between a MIB and a Database

If a MIB is a conceptual data store, why not treat it the same way as a database, accessed through a database-query language such as Structured Query Language (SQL) using a database management system (DBMS)? Why bother with MIBs and management protocols? The answers to this question are manifold; they include the following:

■ **Footprint**—Regular DBMS mechanisms are heavier weight and require more processing resources than management interfaces. Keep in mind that many network devices have limited general-purpose processing capabilities. For a device, being managed constitutes overhead— its main function, after all, is something else, such as routing packets.

■ **Specific management requirements**—Although relations that are used in typical DBMSs to represent data are general purpose in nature and flexible, they are not well suited to capturing some of the constraints that are specific and common to management. For example, a lot of management information is hierarchical in nature—a device contains cards, which contain ports, which contain interfaces, and so on. Some management information is maintained by the agent (as with monitoring data), and other information is maintained by the manager (as with configuration settings). These types of requirements need to be captured, and a MIB should provide built-in support for them. At the same time, much of the general-purpose processing that DBMSs provide—for example, joins between tables—is not really needed in a management agent.

■ **Real effects**—A MIB is not a "passive" database, but a view on an "active" real-world system. Information in the MIB is accessed through and affected by not only management operations, but many other means as well—control protocols, the very functioning of the device, users logging on and reconfiguring the device through a command-line interface, and so on. Therefore, the MIB cannot truly be managed through a DBMS.

■ **Characteristics of the contained data**—A database typically contains large volumes of data that is largely of the same structure. That is, it contains few tables, with many entries each. A MIB, on the other hand, is much more heterogeneous regarding the type of information that it contains—it contains many different types of information, with relatively few instances of each.

Of course, none of this affects the fact that a management application—that is, the manager itself—generally stores information about the network that is being managed in a database and relies extensively on DBMS capabilities to provide its functions. However, a MIB is contained on the managed device—it is part of the agent, not the manager, and it represents one managed device, not a whole network with thousands of managed devices.

The Relationship Between MIBs and Management Protocols

You will find that the term *MIB* is often associated with SNMP, the Simple Network Management Protocol. SNMP defines a particular communication protocol that is often used between managers and agents; it is discussed in detail in Chapter 8. SNMP requires management information in a MIB to be represented according to the rules of a particular specification language, known as Structure of Management Information (SMI), introduced later in this chapter. This particular representation, not just the concept itself, is what SNMP refers to as MIB. However, to avoid any misconceptions, it should be noted here that, as a concept, a MIB does not depend on any particular management protocol, just as the general concept of a database is independent of the different ways in which its contents could be represented or exported—whether as comma-separated values as used in a spreadsheet, as a Hypertext Markup Language (HTML) document for rendering on a web page, or as a relation in response to an SQL query. In other words, if SNMP became obsolete and were no longer supported tomorrow, the concept of a MIB as a conceptual data store for management information would still remain valid.

This indicates that the general concept of a MIB as a conceptual management information store needs to be distinguished from the specific way in which MIBs are implemented as part of the management instrumentation of a device. Remember that a MIB is just a view of the underlying real device that is being managed, and the agent exposes this view. A management agent supports a particular management protocol to communicate with a manager, and that management protocol in general mandates a specific way of exposing a view of the managed device—a specific MIB "flavor." This flavor determines the specific syntactic rules of how management information is represented in the MIB, how MOs in the MIB are named and accessed by management applications, and how the MIB can be structured as a whole.

One such flavor consists of MIBs that are used in conjunction with SNMP—SNMP MIBs, so to speak. They provide one specific way in which management information is exposed. Other management protocols expose slightly different views, as Figure 6-4 illustrates. Although in theory MIBs could be defined to be truly independent of the management protocol, in practice, different management protocols require their own specific way of exposing a view of the underlying managed device, leading to their own specific MIB implementations. Sometimes the same real resource needs to be reflected in different views (that is, MIBs). In that case, redundant MIBs are implemented.

Figure 6-4 *Different Views of the Same Managed Entity*

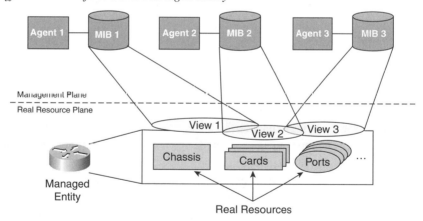

Some management protocols and interfaces have no specific notion of a MIB at all—that is, of a conceptual data store being accessed by a manager. They do not offer operations that specifically refer to a MIB—for example, there are no "get" requests that refer to MOs. Instead, management information is simply carried in the form of parameters of management operations. Case in point: command-line interface (CLI) commands that an administrator can enter at a console of a device. CLI is introduced in Chapter 8; however, to illustrate the point, here is a little preview of what CLI commands look like. Let us assume that a network administrator wants to configure a Border Gateway Protocol (BGP) neighbor on a router (never mind what a BGP neighbor is or what BGP does). The network administrator may type something like the following on the console (the command prompt is indicated in italics and is not typed by the network administrator—notice that the command prompt changes as a consequence of the command that was previously typed):

```
Router# configure terminal
Router(config)# router bgp 500
Router(config-router)# neighbor 192.168.1.1 remote-as 400
Router(config-router)# end
```

The first command causes the device to enter a special mode in which it can be configured. The second command tells the device that a specific routing process is to be configured—namely, the BGP process with the label 500. The third command sets up the BGP process so that it recognizes a system with the IP address 192.168.1.1 as a BGP neighbor that belongs to an autonomous system (never mind what that is, either) with the label 400. The fourth command returns to the original mode. Do not be concerned with the purpose and effects of these commands. The point is that, in those commands, there are no generic "configuration" or "set" operations that explicitly refer to MOs in a MIB. However, it should be clear that, even in this case, command parameters constitute an abstraction of the underlying device. They clearly refer to management information. For example, the BGP process labeled 500 constitutes, in effect, an MO in the device's MIB. The fact that it is referred to in the form of command parameters constitutes a particular view of the managed device that is specific to CLI. Although a MIB is not explicitly referred to in CLI, a MIB is implicitly still the target of the commands.

MIB Definitions

Now that you know what a MIB is and what it contains, let us take a look at how the information that goes into a MIB is defined.

The management information in a MIB in effect represents data. This data reflects the state of the device at the instant it is being managed. For example, if a manager requests information about the current use of a link and the request reaches the agent at 11:35:47 a.m., the information returned should reflect the use that the device is currently experiencing at 11:35:47 a.m. Of course, the manager needs to take into account the reality of communication delays; management information that the manager retrieves might not reach it exactly in real time, but generally close to it. Management information in a MIB is accordingly a snapshot of a particular device at a particular instant in time. When retrieving the same information from a different device, or from the same device at a different point in time, the value reflected in the information could be different. Of course, this comes as no surprise.

In data processing, data is based on underlying data definitions. Those definitions contain specifics such as the data type (for example, whether the data constitutes an integer, a string, or an array of other data) and an explanation of what the data represents (for example, a bank account number or a street address). The actual data is an instantiation of that definition—it contains, for example, one particular bank account number or one particular street address.

This is no different in the case of management information. The management information in the MIB instantiates a MIB definition. The contents of the MIB definition are also referred to as a *model*. It reflects the type of management information being represented and constitutes a management abstraction of the real world. For example, a model that underlies one MIB definition might contain management information that represents the endpoint of a TCP connection. In the model, this management information has certain properties associated with it. Those properties constitute individual data items and could include items such as the TCP port number, the IP address and port address of the remote endpoint of the connection, the number of packets that were sent over the TCP connection, and the number of packets that were received. Each property has its data type defined. Furthermore, the model defines other semantic constraints; that is, constraints that specify certain aspects having to do with the meaning of the model. One constraint might state that there can be several TCP connection endpoints at the same time, indicating that it is permissible for an instantiation of the MIB to contain several managed object instances that each represent a different TCP connection endpoint. Another constraint might define the conditions under which the information about a TPC connection endpoint is removed from the MIB (for example, after the connection terminates) and whether an event will be sent if that occurs. The MIB definition articulates the model and writes it down. For all practical purposes, the terms *model*, *MIB definition*, and *model definition* are used synonymously. In other words, the model establishes the terminology that will be used between manager and agent.

Equipment vendors publish the definitions of the MIBs that their devices implement. Management application vendors can then program their management applications to base their application logic on those definitions when dealing with a particular device. A MIB definition can thus in many ways be regarded as a contract between management application vendor and managed equipment vendor. Because of the investment management applications make in supporting a MIB definition and building application logic to it, MIB definitions that vendors publish must be stable and should not be subjected to change lightly.

In this section, we take a closer look at the models that MIBs are based on and how those models are defined.

Of Schema and Metaschema

As mentioned in the previous section, the model that underlies the management information in a MIB is specified in a MIB definition. Some people call the model the *schema*, reminiscent of a database schema that constitutes the definition of the database tables. The underlying "real world" that is being abstracted by the model is often called the *domain* because it constitutes the "subject domain" that the model is all about. In the example of the previous section, the domain of the model is that of TCP connections.

During runtime, the schema is instantiated in the device's MIB. For example, a specific MIB might contain at a certain point in time 18 TCP connection endpoints. Each of those TCP connection endpoints has particular values for the properties that are reflected in the MIB. For example, the MIB might contain the following management information about one of the TCP connection endpoints: TCP port number 189, the remote endpoint's IP address 247.168.3.17, the remote endpoint's port number 188, and the information that at this particular instance 452,895 packets have been sent and 38,657 packets have been received.

The schema that underlies the MIB remains constant over time. Regardless of when you ask the device, its MIB always represents information about TCP connections the same way, although, of course, the current values will vary. The information also is represented the same way in any other device, provided that it implements the same schema. In object-oriented parlance, the schema is the *class*, the MIB is the *instance*—ignoring for a moment that the schema need not be object-oriented. In fact, if the schema is object-oriented, it contains definitions of managed object classes, whereas the MIB contains managed objects that are instances of those managed object classes. The difference between the schema and its instantiation in a MIB is the same as the difference between a "BMW 3 series, 1996 model" and "the 3 series BMW with California license plate 3NAW875 and VIN# 1BAL44P4W9R355280, odometer reading 85667 and a dent on the left side of the rear bumper," or between "a penguin" and "my penguin, named Walter."

Confusingly, in network management, often both the schema and the particular instance on the device are called MIBs. In many cases, it is clear from the context what is meant, but sometimes it is not. As mentioned, a cleaner use of terms would be *MIB* (for the instance information) and *MIB definition* (for the model or schema).

Now we have established where the information in a MIB is defined, but an important part is still missing. The MIB definition itself needs to be specified using some specification language, sometimes also referred to as the *metaschema*. The term *metaschema* means "a schema of a schema," a definition of how to write and interpret model definitions. Figure 6-5 depicts the relationship between schema and metaschema, and model and domain.

Figure 6-5   *Schema, Metaschema, Model, Domain, and MIB*

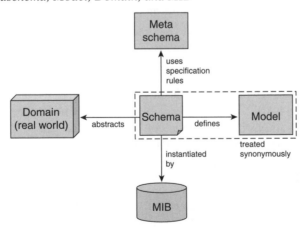

Quite a few MIB specification languages exist. Each of those languages is generally used to define MIBs that are to be used in conjunction with a particular management protocol; for example, the following:

- SMI and SMIv2 (Structure of Management Information versions 1 and 2), the MIB specification language that is used in conjunction with SNMP

- Managed Object Format (MOF), a specification language that is used in conjunction with a management technology called Common Information Model (CIM)

- Guidelines for the Definition of Managed Objects (GDMO), used in conjunction with the Common Management Information Protocol (CMIP), today of only limited commercial relevance

Perhaps surprisingly, given the popularity of the Web and web services, at this point in time, there is no well-established MIB specification language that is based on XML. However, there are quite a few proprietary management interfaces that are based on XML and have management information represented as XML documents. Some industry consortia—notably, the DSL Forum—have defined management information in XML for certain market segments. In addition, Netconf (discussed in Chapter 8) is an emerging management protocol standard that uses XML. Given these trends and the popularity of XML, it seems likely that standardized XML-based management metaschemata will emerge—for example, standard XML Schema Definitions (XSDs).

The Impact of the Metaschema on the Schema

In the fine arts, the media that an artist uses has a great influence over the type of artwork that results. For instance, the character of a painting is different if the artist uses water colors, oil colors, crayons, or a pencil. The difference is even more dramatic if clay is used, resulting in a sculpture instead of a drawing or a painting. Of course, each medium can be used to model the same aspect of the real world, such as a person. The resulting "model" is called a portrait.

In network management, the specification language constitutes the raw material out of which MIB definitions are molded by the MIB artist—that is, designer. Just as in the fine arts, many different media—in this case, specification languages—can be used to create a valid model of the device being managed. Just as a watercolor of a dog looks different than a drawing of the same dog, the character of the model that results looks different depending on what metaschema is used. Figure 6-6 illustrates this.

Figure 6-6 *Different Metaschemas, Different Characters of the Abstraction*

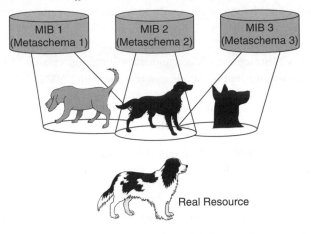

Real Resource

The following subsections discuss what impact the characteristics of a metaschema have on the resulting model, and what types of metaschema tend to be popular for different purposes.

Metaschema Modeling Paradigms

Without going into details of "real" metaschema, here are some examples of different types of specification means that different metaschemas offer.

One category of specification languages provides object-oriented constructs. This enables the designer of a schema to represent different aspects of the device as MO classes that can have attributes and that can emit notifications. Existing definitions can be reused and refined by allowing MO classes to be derived from other MO classes that are more general in nature. This corresponds to an object-oriented concept that is known as *inheritance*. The derived class is also called the *subclass*; the class that it is derived from is called the *superclass*. The subclass inherits the properties of the superclass and subsequently refines them. As an example, a Poodle class might be a subclass of a Dog class, which, in turn, would be a subclass of the Mammal class, and so on. Another example is an MO class that is used to represent ATM interfaces, which could inherit from a more general class to represent an interface generically—that is, any interface, not just ATM interfaces. Object orientation is the paradigm on which MOF and (in a different flavor) GDMO support are based.

A second category of specification languages enables users to specify MIB definitions in the form of tables and variables that can be grouped in certain ways. A table refers to one particular aspect of the device—a "class of MOs," so to speak, with the MO attributes represented by the table columns and instances by the table rows. Of course, tables are quite different from object classes— for example, they do not support inheritance. Their semantics are simpler and less powerful, but arguably more straightforward and simpler to implement on a device. This is the paradigm that SMI and SMIv2 provide. We examine SMI and SMIv2 more closely later in this chapter.

Other specification languages might simply model everything as commands and functions and their parameters without actually specifying much of an explicit model. This, of course, is the case for CLI, the command-line interface. Again, the way in which management information is represented is different from the object-oriented and table-based approaches. (As a side note, many people would not even consider CLI a management protocol, among other reasons precisely because it does not refer to a separate model and does not clearly distinguish between the management information and the functions used to access and manipulate it. CLI is discussed in greater detail in Chapter 8, "Common Management Protocols: Languages of Management.")

Matching Management Information and Metaschema

Each metaschema has its advantages and drawbacks; at this point, we do not get into these. It is important to note, however, that regardless of the metaschema chosen, the models that result can provide a management abstraction of the same underlying device. In practice, often several such models are provided simultaneously, each offering the capability to manage the device. In such a case, users can choose which type of model and associated management protocol works best for a particular purpose. For example, they could use SNMP for monitoring tasks that management applications perform, and use CLI with craft terminals that craft technicians operate.

In fact, just as artists prefer different media for different categories of subjects, such as using watercolors for landscapes instead of portraits, often different types of metaschema are used in conjunction with different categories of management information. Of course, this is a matter of not merely preference, but practicality: Some metaschemata lend themselves better than others to certain management tasks.

- Generally, management information that management agents on network equipment provide tends to be based on relatively simple metaschemata. This has to do with the fact that corresponding management agents tend to be easy to develop and do not require many processing resources, an aspect that is important for devices that, in many cases, are processing constrained.

  — State information is often modeled as tables and represented in SNMP MIBs because SNMP is the management protocol of choice for many monitoring applications.

  — Logical configuration information is often managed using CLI, meaning that often it is modeled only in the form of parameters of CLI functions instead of a more explicit management information model.

  — Historical information is often represented in proprietary formats, optimized for periodic retrieval in one large bulk file from a device.

■   When the management agent that provides the management information is not a network device, but a computer system, a managed application, or a management application itself (for example, in a management hierarchy in which one management application provides services for another management application at a higher management layer), support for object-oriented metaschemata and models such as MOF and CIM becomes a lot more common. In those cases, management agents are less constrained by computing resources, tilting the balance in favor of using metaschemas that might be more complex but also more powerful.

It is important to always remember that no matter what underlying metaschema is used, a MIB is always a view of a managed device. Accordingly, it is also possible to have multiple simultaneous views of the same device. For example, you could have the same management information accessible via an SNMP MIB and via a set of CLI functions. Each view, or each MIB, can be supported by its own management agent, each interacting with management applications through a different management protocol. The different management views that the various management agents provide can have a different scope—that is, they can cover different aspects of the same managed device. They can simply complement each other, they can overlap each other, or one can be a subset of another, as Figure 6-7 illustrates.

Figure 6-7   *MIB Scopes*

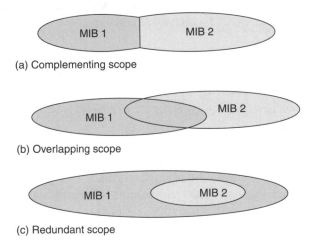

(a) Complementing scope

(b) Overlapping scope

(c) Redundant scope

A Simple Modeling Example

Let's take a look at an example. Imagine that you are tasked with defining a simple management information model for a device. All you are interested in managing is some basic system information about the device, such as the name of the device, where it is located, who the contact is, how long it has been running, and its TCP connections. The resulting models are graphically depicted in the following figures. All three represent the same underlying domain, but each is based on a different type of metaschema:

■ Figure 6-8 depicts an object-oriented model. In this example, a managed object class represents a managed system. It has three attributes to carry management information: SystemName, SystemContact, and SystemUptime, to carry the name used to refer to the managed system, the contact information of the group responsible for managing the system, and the time elapsed since the system was last started. The managed system is derived from a superclass (denoted by the line with the arrow), Physical Equipment, which has another attribute that Managed System inherits, SystemLocation. Objects of the class Managed System can contain objects of another class, TCP Connection (denoted by the line with the diamond). TCP Connection has more attributes: TCPConnectionState, PacketsSent, and PacketsReceived. TCP Connection maintains two different types of relationships to objects of another class: Endpoint (denoted by simple lines labeled with the relationship names). Those relationships indicate which endpoint is local to the connection and which endpoint is remote. Objects of the class Endpoint contain attributes with the address and port information of the respective endpoint.

Figure 6-8 *Example of an Object-Oriented Management Information Model*

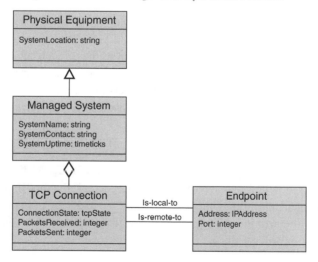

■ Figure 6-9 depicts a table-based model. In this case, the management information is maintained in two tables. The table named Managed System contains only one entry, including SystemName, SystemContact, SystemLocation, and SystemUptime as columns. The table named TCPConnections can contain many entries. It has columns for LocalIP, LocalPort, RemoteIp, RemotePort, ConnectionState, PacketsSent, and PacketsRecvd. The combination of the first four columns serves as a key for the table—that is, they are used to identify a particular table entry. The model here is a little more coarse-grained than the object-oriented one. For example, information about endpoints is not broken out separately.

Figure 6-9   *The Same Domain as in Figure 6-8, in a Table-Based Model*

ManagedSystem

SystemName	SystemContact	SystemLocation	SystemUptime

TCPConnections

LocalIP	LocalPort	RemoteIP	RemotePort	ConnectionState	PacketsSent	PacketsRecvd
...	...	...	...	...	...	...
...	...	...	...	...	...	...
...	...	...	...	...	...	...

■ Figure 6-10 depicts a "model" based on a set of dedicated functions. Here, the managed system is "modeled" by three functions: showSystemdata, showAllTcpConnections, and ShowTCPConnectionState. showSystemdata is used to retrieve information about the managed system. The function is defined so that it will return the name, system uptime, system contact, and system location when invoked. It is not necessary to define a parameter to identify the managed system because it is the system on which the function is invoked. Two other functions are introduced that allow a manager to modify the system name as well as system contact and system location information. TCP connections are "modeled" by the remaining two functions: showAllTcpConnections lists all current TCP connections on the device along with their local and remote IP address and port information, TCP connection state, and base statistics of the number of packets that were sent and received over this connection. ShowTCPConnectionState allows a manager to retrieve the TCP connection state of a particular TCP connection, identified by its local and remote IP address and port information.

Note that this model is specific about how the manager accesses the information. In the case of object-oriented and table-oriented metaschemas, the model did not define how to access management information. Instead, those functions are assumed to be provided by generic operations of the accompanying management protocol that is used to access the management information.

Figure 6-10   *The Same Domain as in Figure 6-8, as a Set of Functions*

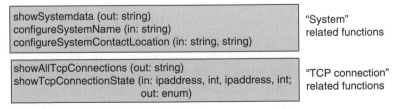

The models specified for each metaschema represent just one way in which the underlying domain can be modeled. Even with the same metaschema, the same domain can be modeled in many ways, just as you could draw different portraits of the same person that all look slightly different yet clearly resemble the same person. For example, in the table-based model, we might have decided to add a table just for endpoint information, in a manner similar to the way in which endpoints were modeled by their own object class in the object-oriented model. Likewise, we might decide to represent aspects of TCP connections that constitute statistical information in their own table, separate from those aspects that convey the more static configuration information and the TCP connection state. In the object-oriented model, we could have derived the TCP connection managed object class from a more general superclass that represents a generic connection. In the function-oriented model, we could have cut the functions and their parameters slightly differently. We might have introduced another function to retrieve TCP connection statistics, for example.

Which model is eventually defined is a matter of design. Design is a creative activity. There is no single "right" way to model the underlying domain. Instead, different models are possible, some of which might be more appropriate and some less appropriate than others in terms of how easy they make it to manage the device, how straightforward they are to implement, and how easily they can be extended and maintained.

Encoding Management Information

Finally, it should be mentioned that management information needs to also be encoded when it is sent over the wire as part of actual management communication. That is, all the managed object identifiers and values need to be "flattened" into a mutually understood representation that will fit into a management request or response that is exchanged between manager and agent. This aspect is closely related to the management protocol and is discussed further in Chapter 8.

Anatomy of a MIB

To get a taste of what a MIB looks like in practice, let's take a look at a specific MIB specification language and an actual MIB definition specified in it. Because of the ubiquity of SNMP, we use SNMP's Structure of Management Information (SMI) as our example, and for the MIB definition we take a look at an excerpt of MIB-2. MIB-2 was specified for use with devices that implement the TCP/IP protocol stack. It can hence be found on virtually any device that supports SNMP today and, in all likelihood, constitutes the widest implemented MIB in the world.

Our intent is not to go into every little detail of SMI and MIB-2—interested readers are referred to the literature and corresponding standards documents, which you will find listed in the bibliography given in Appendix B, "Further Reading." However, we do want to give some insight into the level of information that is specified and what a specification can look like.

SMI and MIB-2 are defined in standards documents by the Internet Engineering Task Force (IETF), the Internet's governing standards body. Documents published by the IETF are called

RFCs—Requests For Comments—and numbered sequentially. MIB-2 is defined in RFC 1213; SMI is defined in RFC 1155.

A newer version of SMI, called SMIv2 (SMI version 2), also is defined in a newer RFC, RFC 2578. SMIv2 is essentially a "superset" of SMI that contains a number of additional language artifacts that help make definitions more concise. However, SMI-defined MIBs, such as MIB-2, remain valid MIBs, and the differences between SMIv2 and SMI are immaterial for the introductory level of this overview; for all practical purposes, we can use SMI and SMIv2 synonymously here. Again, interested readers are encouraged to take a look at the ample amount of SNMP literature or at the RFCs themselves, listed in Appendix B.

Structure of Management Information—Overview

In SMI, MIB definitions are specified as MIB modules. A MIB module generally serves a particular purpose, such as to define management information related to a device's communication interfaces or to a voice-mail server feature that is embedded on a particular type of device. Accordingly, the MIB of any particular device instantiates multiple MIB modules, each of which represents one aspect of the managed device, as Figure 6-11 illustrates. Again, the term *MIB* is often used synonymously with *MIB module*; hence, you will often hear that a device supports "multiple MIBs," when really it has one MIB, the model of which is defined in multiple MIB modules.

Figure 6-11 *One MIB, Multiple MIB Modules*

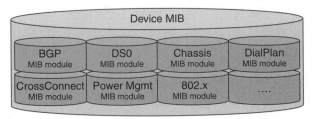

In essence, an SNMP MIB consists of a set of managed objects that instantiate object types that are part of a MIB module. Those managed objects are not objects in an object-oriented sense, but should better be thought of as MIB variables. However, for the discussion here, we stick with SMI parlance.

Actually, several kinds of information are defined in a MIB module:

- The object types themselves, the instances of which contain the actual management information—the "MIB variables." We explain object types in more detail later.

- Notifications, defining information that can be conveyed to managers as part of event messages (called traps in SNMP), sent unsolicitedly by the device.

- Nodes that represent nothing specific but that are introduced for grouping purposes. For example, a MIB module for the Border Gateway Protocol (BGP) might contain a node "BGP statistics," under which object types are grouped that represent different kinds of statistics about BGP.

Other types of information that are perhaps not as obvious at first include aspects such as the ones in the list that follows. There are more language artifacts, but a detailed understanding of them is not required for the big picture. The most important were actually introduced, or greatly enhanced, only with SMIv2:

- Textual conventions that define synonyms or "macros" for defining simple data types. Some common textual conventions that have been standardized include TimeTicks, to represent time in milliseconds that has elapsed since the last cold restart of the system, or IPAddress, to represent an IP address.

- Conformance statements (called "module compliance") that are to be filled out for particular agent implementations, used to identify which portions of a MIB module an agent actually supports.

MIB information is arranged into a conceptual tree. Every definition in a MIB module is represented by a node in that tree. Each node is named relative to a containing node; this name is also called the object identifier (OID). Accordingly, the tree is commonly referred to as an object identifier tree. The top node in a MIB module is the definition of the MIB module, which itself is registered as part of a larger, global, Internet object identifier tree. Figure 6-12 depicts an excerpt of the object identifier tree, containing the node for the MIB-2 module along with the first level of nodes contained below it. Other MIB modules are peers to the MIB-2 node in the tree and can subtend from either the mgmt, experimental, or private–enterprises nodes.

The mgmt node in the object identifier tree serves as the container for MIB modules that constitute official standards. As you can tell from the fact that MIB-2's identifier is 1, MIB-2 was the first such MIB module to be standardized. The enterprises node allows companies to add their own proprietary MIB modules into the object identifier tree. To do so, a company first obtains its own node underneath the enterprises node. For example, Cisco has its own node with the identifier 9. Below that, the company can maintain its own subtree. It is thus free to add its own MIB modules to the tree without needing to ask someone else for permission first.

Figure 6-12   *MIB-2 Object Identifier Tree (Excerpt)*

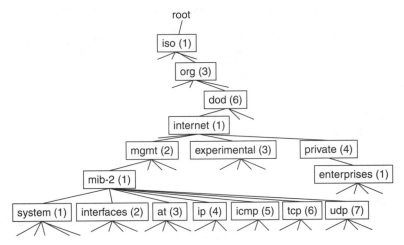

Underneath the node representing the MIB-2 module are a number of nodes that define the MIB module's structure—for example, a node called system, which is named relative to the containing MIB module, MIB-2. Underneath the system node, there will be other nodes (not depicted in the figure) representing object types for the system description, system contact, system location, and more. The object types that are defined as part of a MIB module—the ones that will be instantiated as managed objects in a MIB—are always leaf nodes of the tree; interior nodes mainly serve grouping and organization purposes.

As far as object types are concerned, two categories need to be distinguished:

- Object types that will be instantiated only once in an agent. This means that there will be always be exactly one instance of the object type in the MIB. Those are also called *scalars*. An example is an object type that contains the host name, or a serial number of a chassis, or some global settings for the device.

- Object types that can be instantiated multiple times. This means that multiple objects of that same object type can exist in a MIB. Those are also called *columnar objects* because they are thought of as a column in a conceptual table that can have multiple rows, one for each instance. An example is an object type that represents information about cards in a chassis, of which there could be multiple, or communication resources that are dynamically created and torn down during run time, such as connections. The conceptual table and rows are specified as nodes in their own right, as you shall see in the example in the following subsection.

Regardless of whether they are scalars or columnar objects, every managed object is of a simple data type, which comes as part of the SMI and SMIv2 specification language. Simple data types include strings and numerals such as integers, counters, and gauges, for the most part in 32- and

64-bit variants. As their name indicates, counters are used for counting something, such as the number of packets that are received. Counters are therefore always increasing. You can think of an odometer in a car as a counter. Gauges, on the other hand, are used to indicate a level or a current rate, such as the number of packets that were received in the past minute or the current use of bandwidth. Gauges can accordingly both increase and decrease. A speedometer in a car is a real-world example of a gauge.

There are no complex data types like the ones that are common in programming languages, such as arrays, lists, or structs. If someone wants to represent a piece of management information that would conceptually be better thought of as an object of a complex type, he must think of creative ways to represent that information as simple object types. For example, a struct that will be instantiated only once might be represented by defining several object types that are grouped under a common container. A struct with multiple instances could be represented as a table, with each row in the table containing one instance of the struct. An array might be represented by a table that includes an extra columnar object that represents the index of the array.

An Example: MIB-2

Let us now consider an excerpt from MIB-2. For brevity, portions of the definition are omitted. The symbol [...] is used to indicate where information is omitted within the definition excerpts. We start by taking a look at the "header" of the MIB module.

```
            RFC1213-MIB DEFINITIONS ::= BEGIN
[...]
            mib-2     OBJECT IDENTIFIER ::= { mgmt 1 }
```

This definition establishes mib-2 as a new node underneath a supernode called mgmt inside the Internet object identifier tree. (mgmt is imported from another standard; it identifies the subnode that is reserved for management information. Its complete OID is 1.3.6.1.2.) mib-2 is the human-readable form of the name; for machine-to-machine communication purposes, the equivalent numeric object identifier, 1, is used.

```
-- groups in MIB-II

system      OBJECT IDENTIFIER ::= { mib-2 1 }

interfaces  OBJECT IDENTIFIER ::= { mib-2 2 }

at          OBJECT IDENTIFIER ::= { mib-2 3 }

ip          OBJECT IDENTIFIER ::= { mib-2 4 }

icmp        OBJECT IDENTIFIER ::= { mib-2 5 }

tcp         OBJECT IDENTIFIER ::= { mib-2 6 }

udp         OBJECT IDENTIFIER ::= { mib-2 7 }

egp         OBJECT IDENTIFIER ::= { mib-2 8 }
```

What gets defined here are internal nodes that are used for structuring purposes. Each of those nodes will contain a submodule of the MIB module, also called a group. The groups are assigned numeral identifiers 1 through 8 underneath the mib-2 node. Figure 6-13 depicts another excerpt from the object identifier tree defined by MIB-2, reflecting the remainder of the excerpt of MIB-2 that is presented here.

Figure 6-13   *MIB-2 Naming Structure*

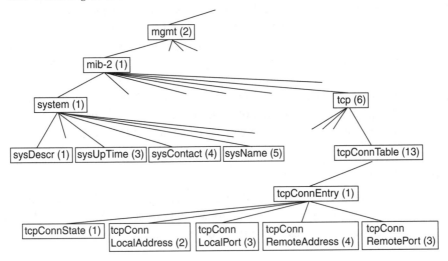

We now dive into the definition of one of the submodules, the system group. Note that the definition of MIB modules can be annotated with comments, which are lines prefixed with two dashes (--).

```
-- the System group

-- Implementation of the System group is mandatory for all
-- systems. If an agent is not configured to have a value
-- for any of these variables, a string of length 0 is
-- returned.

sysDescr OBJECT-TYPE
    SYNTAX  DisplayString (SIZE (0..255))
    ACCESS  read-only
    STATUS  mandatory
    DESCRIPTION
            "A textual description of the entity. This value
            should include the full name and version
            identification of the system's hardware type,
            software operating-system, and networking
            software. It is mandatory that this only contain
            printable ASCII characters."
    ::= { system 1 }

[...]

sysUpTime OBJECT-TYPE
```

```
        SYNTAX  TimeTicks
        ACCESS  read-only
        STATUS  mandatory
        DESCRIPTION
                "The time (in hundredths of a second) since the
                network management portion of the system was last
                re-initialized."
        ::= { system 3 }

    sysContact OBJECT-TYPE
        SYNTAX  DisplayString (SIZE (0..255))
        ACCESS  read-write
        STATUS  mandatory
        DESCRIPTION
                "The textual identification of the contact person
                for this managed node, together with information
                on how to contact this person."
        ::= { system 4 }
```

The system group contains a number of scalars—object types that will be instantiated exactly once. The definition of an object type consists of several elements:

- "Syntax" essentially defines the data type. sysDescr and sysContact are strings with a maximum length of 255 characters; sysUpTime is of a type TimeTicks. TimeTicks is a textual convention that is defined in an imported specification; it really refers to an unsigned 32-bit integer that represents an elapsed period of time in hundredths of a second, as reiterated in the description.

- "Access" specifies whether the object is a parameter that can be set by a manager (read-write) or whether it can only be read, such as when the object contains state information. In the example here, sysUpTime is read-only—the agent provides its value as it reflects state information. sysContact, on the other hand, is read-write—its value is provided by a management application to facilitate administration of the device.

- "Status" refers to the definition lifecycle. In the example, the status of every object is mandatory, meaning that every implementation of the MIB module must include it. The definition of the status is one of the aspects that has actually changed between SMI and SMIv2. In SMIv2, because of the introduction of module compliance statements, the distinction between object types whose implementation is mandatory versus those whose implementation is optional is no longer needed; both have been replaced by a new status, current. In general, every object type has a status of current. However, later revisions of MIB module may deprecate an object type. This means that new implementations do not have to support the object type but that it might be retained in existing implementations for backward compatibility reasons. In that case, the status would be deprecated. Finally, object types may also have a status of obsolete if they are no longer to be supported. Note that after it is defined, an object type never goes away even if it is obsoleted—this prevents accidental reuse of the same identifiers for another purpose because that reuse might lead to unintended confusion.

- "Description" contains an explanation of the intended purpose of the object type. In addition, it can contain specification of any behavioral aspects that cannot be captured otherwise. In that sense, a description is more than merely a comment; it can contain a specification of aspects that need to be implemented and complied with.

- Finally, each object type is assigned an object identifier, relative to a containing node.

We now turn our attention to another submodule, the TCP group. It contains definitions of management information for the TCP protocol. Among other things, it contains a definition of a table, as follows:

```
-- the TCP Connection table

-- The TCP connection table contains information about this
-- entity's existing TCP connections.

tcpConnTable OBJECT-TYPE
    SYNTAX  SEQUENCE OF TcpConnEntry
    ACCESS  not-accessible
    STATUS  mandatory
    DESCRIPTION
            "A table containing TCP connection-specific
            information."
    ::= { tcp 13 }
```

tcpConnTable contains the definition of the table. It looks similar to the definition of scalar object types, with two exceptions:

- Its syntax does not designate a simple data type, but a SEQUENCE OF objects of another type. Those objects are the table entries—the rows of the table.

- Its access clause indicates that it is not accessible—it can be neither read nor written to, so for management purposes, it carries no information on its own. It is the topmost container object for the columnar objects that make up the actual management information contained in this table.

```
tcpConnEntry OBJECT-TYPE
    SYNTAX  TcpConnEntry
    ACCESS  not-accessible
    STATUS  mandatory
    DESCRIPTION
            "Information about a particular current TCP
            connection. An object of this type is transient,
            in that it ceases to exist when (or soon after)
            the connection makes the transition to the CLOSED
            state."
    INDEX   { tcpConnLocalAddress,
              tcpConnLocalPort,
              tcpConnRemAddress,
              tcpConnRemPort }
    ::= { tcpConnTable 1 }
```

TcpConnEntry is the definition of the rows of the table. Its containing node is tcpConnTable. As with tcpConnTable, it is not accessible—it is a conceptual object. The accessible objects are the individual elements of the row—that is, the columnar objects. Two aspects make the definition of a table row unique:

■ The index clause is present only with object types that define a table entry. In database parlance, the index clause specifies the primary key of the table. It designates the columnar objects that are used to uniquely identify a row in the table. In this case, a row in the TCP connection table is identified by the combination of the local TCP connection address and port, and the remote TCP connection address and port.

■ The syntax clause does not designate a simple data type. It refers to a data type of TcpConnEntry that is specified separately and whose definition you will see in a moment. TcpConnEntry is a data type of type Sequence. A sequence essentially corresponds to the programming language of a struct. It references as elements the individual columnar objects that comprise a row in the table. The syntax of TcpConnEntry is defined as follows, right after the TcpConnEntry data type (do not confuse the data type and its syntax):

```
TcpConnEntry ::=
    SEQUENCE {
        tcpConnState
            INTEGER,
        tcpConnLocalAddress
            IpAddress,
        tcpConnLocalPort
            INTEGER (0..65535),
        tcpConnRemAddress
            IpAddress,
        tcpConnRemPort
            INTEGER (0..65535)
    }
```

Note that TcpConnEntry contains a definition of all columns of the table, including the columns that are collectively used as the index and any additional columns—in this case, tcpConnState. Each of the elements of the sequence designates its own object type that will be instantiated by the columnar objects that populate the respective column in the table. The only part that is now missing is the actual object type definitions, to resolve the elements identified in the TcpConnEntry sequence. Here are their definitions:

```
tcpConnState OBJECT-TYPE
    SYNTAX  INTEGER {
                closed(1),
                listen(2),
                synSent(3),
                synReceived(4),
                established(5),
                finWait1(6),
                finWait2(7),
```

```
                    closeWait(8),
                    lastAck(9),
                    closing(10),
                    timeWait(11),
                    deleteTCB(12)
              }
    ACCESS   read-write
    STATUS   mandatory
    DESCRIPTION
              "The state of this TCP connection.

              The only value which may be set by a management
              station is deleteTCB(12). Accordingly, it is
              appropriate for an agent to return a `badValue'
              response if a management station attempts to set
              this object to any other value.

              If a management station sets this object to the
              value deleteTCB(12), then this has the effect of
              deleting the TCB (as defined in RFC 793) of the
              corresponding connection on the managed node,
              resulting in immediate termination of the
              connection.

              As an implementation-specific option, a RST
              segment may be sent from the managed node to the
              other TCP endpoint (note however that RST segments
              are not sent reliably)."
    ::= { tcpConnEntry 1 }
```

tcpConnState is the first of the object types that comprise the table. It is worth noting that the definition of columnar object types does not differ from that of scalar object types. You cannot tell from the definition which is which. The one aspect that makes it a columnar object type is that the containing node is a table row (tcpConnEntry), and the name of the object type is referenced in the sequence that is defined as part of the syntax of the table row.

tcpConnState is also noteworthy as an example of an object type in which the description cause contains not only an explanation, but a specification of certain other aspects that would otherwise not be captured—in this case, restrictions with respect to the values that can be set, along with a description of the side effects that setting of this object will cause.

```
    tcpConnLocalAddress OBJECT-TYPE
        SYNTAX   IpAddress
        ACCESS   read-only
        STATUS   mandatory
        DESCRIPTION
                 "The local IP address for this TCP connection. In
                 the case of a connection in the listen state which
                 is willing to accept connections for any IP
                 interface associated with the node, the value
                 0.0.0.0 is used."
        ::= { tcpConnEntry 2 }

    tcpConnLocalPort OBJECT-TYPE
        SYNTAX   INTEGER (0..65535)
        ACCESS   read-only
        STATUS   mandatory
        DESCRIPTION
                 "The local port number for this TCP connection."
        ::= { tcpConnEntry 3 }
```

```
tcpConnRemAddress OBJECT-TYPE
    SYNTAX   IpAddress
    ACCESS   read-only
    STATUS   mandatory
    DESCRIPTION
            "The remote IP address for this TCP connection."
    ::= { tcpConnEntry 4 }

tcpConnRemPort OBJECT-TYPE
    SYNTAX   INTEGER (0..65535)
    ACCESS   read-only
    STATUS   mandatory
    DESCRIPTION
            "The remote port number for this TCP connection."
    ::= { tcpConnEntry 5 }
```

The example concludes with the definition of the remaining object types that are contained underneath a tcpConnEntry. Those object types are unremarkable in every way. The fact that they also serve as an index in the table is transparent in the definition of the object types themselves. Because they collectively serve as an index that needs to uniquely identify a table entry, the combination of the values tcpConnLocalAddress, tcpConnLocalPort, tcpConnRemAddress, and tcpConnRemPort must be unique as well—that is, it cannot occur more than once in the same MIB. This constraint cannot be inferred from the object type definitions themselves—only from the fact that they appear in the index clause of tcpConnEntry.

Instantiation in an Actual MIB

So far, we have described how a model to represent management information is defined in SMI and how different object types are identified through their OIDs. We have also mentioned that some of the object types can be instantiated once, others multiple times. But how are those instances identified during runtime in an actual MIB? This is one of the stranger aspects of SNMP and a little counterintuitive at first.

Object instances in a MIB are considered to be conceptually part of the same object identifier tree as the object type definitions themselves. This means that, from a naming perspective, the instances of an object type are subtending underneath the node that represents their object type. Quite conveniently, only leaf nodes in the tree of the MIB module definition can be instantiated. Those leaf nodes start growing new leaves underneath them, so to speak, that constitute the nodes of the object instances. Figure 6-14 illustrates this. The leaf nodes of the MIB module definition correspond to scalar object types, such as sysUpTime or sysName, which you encountered in the previous section, or to columnar object types, such as tcpConnState or tcpConnLocalPort, from the previous section. Below those nodes, the object identifier tree is extended with new nodes that correspond to the instances of the object types—the actual values that a manager can retrieve from the agent. This means that in the object identifier tree of the MIB, nodes that represent object types in the MIB module definition are no longer leaf nodes; the object instances are.

Figure 6-14 *Structure of SNMP MIB Object Identifier Tree*

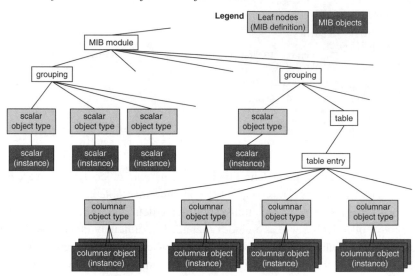

The object identifier of a MIB object consists of the object identifier of its object type, concatenated with a suffix to distinguish the actual object instance. As mentioned earlier, scalars need to be distinguished from columnar objects in how they are identified.

Scalars have only one instance in any particular MIB. They are designated a 0 identifier relative to their object type definition, which is appended to the object type's OID. The form of the object identifier is OID.0. So for the object type sysUpTime from MIB-2 with the OID 1.3.6.1.2.1.1.3, its instance in the MIB has the OID 1.3.6.1.2.1.1.3.0.

Columnar objects can have multiple instances that need to be distinguished from one another. Therefore, they need to be identified differently. Simply appending a 0 is not sufficient. You will recall that as part of the table definition, an index was defined that consisted of one or more columnar object types. This index is now used to identify the individual object instances. The object or objects that constitute the index are themselves part of the table entry that they help identify. To identify a given entry in the table, the values of each of the objects that are part of the index are concatenated and appended to the object type's OID to form the object instance OID. So the form of the object instance's identifier is "object type OID.*index*." Consider, for example (again, from MIB-2), object type tcpConnState, which has the OID 1.3.6.1.2.6.13.1.1. Assume that the row that the object type is part of has the following values for the columnar object types that are part of the index: 167.8.15.92 (local address), 227 (local port), 176.15.53.216 (remote address), 228 (remote port). Concatenating those values results in the index 167.8.15.92.227.176.15.53.216.228. Then the OID of the particular instance is 1.3.6.1.2.6.13.1.1.167.8.15.92.227.176.15.53.216.228. (Yup, OIDs can get pretty long.) Other columnar objects in the same table entry are identified by the same index, appended to their particular object type OIDs.

Figure 6-15 depicts how objects inside a table are identified as part of the object identifier tree.

Figure 6-15   *Object Identifier Tree for MIB Tables*

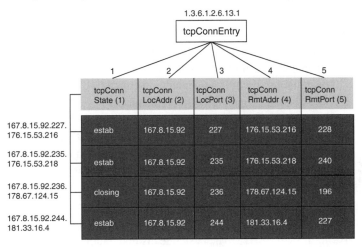

The way in which the object identifier for columnar objects is formed implies that the identifier of a columnar object that is part of the index contains its own value. Generally, therefore, changing this value is prohibited—doing so would basically invalidate the OID and lead to an implicit renaming of the object and of other objects that are part of the same table entry. To prevent this and other strange behavior, SMIv2 evolves SMI and requires module definitions to designate object types that are used as indexes to a table as *auxiliary objects*, mandating that they should no longer be directly accessible by management operations. They can be used only as part of an OID but cannot be read or written to directly. They really should never have been accessible in the first place—obviously, they should not be overwritten by managers because this would result in undefined behavior. And why would a management application want to address the index object directly? After all, if it knows the object's OID, by definition, it already knows its value.

We mentioned earlier that the OIDs of MIB definitions in the Internet object identifier tree are globally unique. Of course, this is no longer true for the OIDs of the object instances in a MIB. Those are unique only within their particular MIB. However, different managed devices have their own MIB that can instantiate the same MIB module definition. Each router that implements MIB-2, for example, has an object instance called 1.3.6.1.2.1.1.3.0 that designates the system uptime. Of course, the system uptime of router A is not the same as the system uptime of router B. Only the combination of a globally unique name of the managed device and the object's OID identifies a piece of management information that is truly globally unique.

Special MIB Considerations to Address SNMP Protocol Deficits

The way in which objects inside a table are identified points to some of the unique—some would say awkward—semantics in SNMP. Indeed, much of SNMP's complexity revolves around the treatment of tables. Another aspect of SNMP that is worth mentioning concerns the fact that at the time the SNMP protocol was conceived, the need for operations to create and delete entries in a table was not accounted for. However, there are many scenarios in which it is necessary for a management application to create and delete table entries. Consider, for example, an IP private branch exchange (PBX) system. A management application must be capable of adding (or removing) a phone, along with its phone number and the port number that it is connected to. In an SNMP MIB, the management information about the phones is likely to be contained in a phone table. Entries in the table represent management information for individual phones. Those entries must be created and deleted by management applications.

After SNMP was initially deployed, it became clear pretty soon that something needed to be done to overcome this deficiency. Interestingly, the solution consisted of defining special object types that would carry certain semantics to emulate the missing operations. This shows that, in some cases, the border between what constitutes management information and what constitutes an operation to act on management information becomes blurry. In this particular case, to emulate, create and delete operations, a special textual convention called row status was introduced with the newer version of SMI, SMIv2. The basic idea is that a table entry would include a special columnar object that would reflect a row status. Setting this object to a value of destroy would automatically delete the table entry. As a side effect, the entire entry would simply disappear from the MIB, along with its underlying real resource: in the IP PBX example, a particular phone extension. Creating an entry in the table is even stranger: The object in the table would be set to a value of create. (In fact, there are two versions of create—a create-and-go and a create-and-wait, depending on whether creation of the row needs to be staged, or occur in phases.) However, at the time the request is made, the table entry does not even exist, so how can a value of one of its (nonexisting) columnar objects be modified? The answer is that because of the special semantics of the row status object, the SNMP agent recognizes that a row status object is involved, so the object must be created as a side effect.

Modeling Management Information

We mentioned several times that the management information that an agent exposes across its management interface constitutes an abstraction of the managed device. This abstraction is based on a model of the real world, and information in the MIB is an instantiation of this model. Because it is used for management purposes, the model includes aspects that are relevant for management and omits aspects of the real world that are not—it abstracts them away.

For example, the software revision that is currently running on the device, the settings that are currently configured as timeout values for a particular protocol, and the device's serial number are all aspects that management applications might be interested in—for example, to schedule software updates, to tune network performance, or to take an inventory of what's in the network. Therefore, those aspects must be included in the device's management information that the agent exposes and must be a part of the model that represents the device. On the other hand, the color of the chassis that the device comes in, the number of chips that are contained on the main board, and the size of the packet that was last transmitted might not be of interest to any management application. Therefore, those aspects should be omitted from the model.

Finding the proper abstraction is not always easy because it is not obvious which pieces of information will really be needed. For example, is it important to include the time at which the last critical alarm occurred as part of the management information? Is it required to keep packet counter statistics on each different type of packet, or are summary statistics sufficient? Does a parameter for echo cancellation need to be configurable on a per-DS0 basis (that is, for each interface that terminates a voice connection), or is it sufficient and perhaps preferable to configure echo cancellation on a DS1 basis—that is, apply the same setting to all 24 or 30 DS0s that are grouped together into a DS1 and have them summarily configured?

If the model includes too little management information, the device will be more difficult to manage. As a consequence, in some cases, management decisions must be made without additional supporting information. Also, there will be fewer possibilities to fine-tune network performance because certain settings cannot be adjusted. In light of this, it is advisable to err on the side of caution—instead of risking providing too little management information and too few management knobs and displays, it can be a good idea to provide management instrumentation that goes a little beyond what seems to be the absolute minimum required.

However, including too much information as part of the model can also lead to problems. When there is too much management information, the management interface can be more complex than necessary. This requires users to learn and know how to interpret more pieces of management information than they would otherwise have to. Also, having to instrument the information on the device requires more effort and more time to develop, and could increase the memory footprint of the management agent in the device, resulting in higher cost. By the same token, management application development gets more expensive, too. To avoid adding too much management information and including too many management knobs and displays, model developers need to be clear about the purpose of the management information. They need to resist the temptation to include a real-world aspect of the managed device as part of the management information just because it is there. The model developer should have an idea of why a piece of management information might be useful for management purposes.

Finding a proper balance between what to include and what not to include in a model is important. Defining the proper abstraction to use when modeling a device for management purposes is not a trivial task. It is a matter of design, and design is a creative activity, requiring both expertise and intuition. Design is a discipline that requires a systemic approach as much as it requires intuition.

The lessons of object-oriented design can generally be applied here. Modeling techniques such as the Unified Modeling Language (UML) methodology can serve as a starting point for defining a model of a device for management purposes that is independent of any particular MIB definition language. The resulting model would then be a meta-metamodel, so to speak—a model of the managed entity that is independent of its actual specification as part of a MIB definition. This model then serves as the starting point to derive more specific MIB definitions that are specified according to a particular metaschema. Earlier in this chapter, you saw an example of how the same management information could be represented in different metaschemata.

When the same feature of a device is managed using different management interfaces, each with its own view of the device (that is, its own MIB), consistent terminology should be used to refer to the same underlying real-world entities. For example, an ATM connection endpoint should be referred to similarly in both a device's CLI and an SNMP MIB. In the earlier example, the term *TCP connection* was consistently used instead of calling it a TCP Connection in one schema and perhaps a TCP line or a TCP trail in another schema. Using consistent terms to refer to the same underlying managed resource makes it clearer to users that different management interfaces are indeed merely different views of the same aspect of the real world. When different and inconsistent terminology is used, simple facts such as this tend to be obscured, confusing users and application developers. One of the advantages of using an abstract model independent of a particular MIB definition language is that when this model is "translated" into different MIB definition languages, the resulting models tend to be consistent in their terminology and structure of managed objects they refer to.

It needs to be emphasized that no model is "right" or "wrong," per se, but different designs can be appropriate or less appropriate for the set of management tasks at hand. Different designs can also be more or less elegant. The structure of an elegant design is simple and straightforward to understand. It is efficient in the way that it allows users to access the management information they need for a given management purpose. In addition, it is easy to maintain and extend. This means that, in case a new feature needs to be incorporated into a model, it is possible to do so without requiring an overhaul of the model.

In summary, the following are some of the questions that need to be answered when defining a management model:

- Is the information that is contained in the model sufficient? Are any managed resources missing that should be included in the model? Is there enough management information in the model to support management decisions that network managers have to make? Are enough "knobs" provided to configure the device, to provision services over it, and to tune network performance? Are there enough displays that tell network managers what is going on at the managed device? Can the relevant management scenarios for the various management functions (such as troubleshooting, provisioning, and performance management) all be supported with the management information that is provided?

- Is the information that is contained in the model really necessary? For each piece of information, is its use clear? Is there at least one management scenario in need of that information? Would it have any impact on management if the information were **not** included?

- What is the proper granularity of the model? Is it too fine grained and will result in users not being able to see the forest,2 just a lot of individual trees? Are there too many little knobs that require turning but that would likely all be turned in the same way, so that just a few would do? Is the model too coarse grained? Does it aggregate information too much and not provide enough differentiation between individual underlying managed resources?

- What conceptual entities and managed resources are part of the model, independent of the particular model definition language? What terminology should be used for referring to what is being managed?

- Can the model be easily extended?

- Is it possible to reuse pieces of a model that already exist instead of redefining everything from scratch?

Chapter Summary

Management information is at the core of management communication that takes place between managers and agents. The model that underlies the management information provides the basis for the common understanding of the managed device between manager and agent. It includes information about the current state of physical and logical resources, historical information of past events and past state, physical configuration information, and logical configuration information. Management information is maintained by the management agent in the managed device's Management Information Base (MIB). The MIB can be considered a conceptual data store; it represents an abstraction and a view of the device being managed for management purposes. The managed resources of the device are represented by managed objects in the MIB.

A MIB is, first and foremost, a concept. However, specific management protocols require their own flavor of a MIB. This means that multiple MIBs might be supported concurrently by the same managed device, each by its own management agent, with each MIB constituting a different view of the same underlying real resources.

MIBs instantiate models of the various aspects, functions, and features of a managed device. Those models are defined using special definition languages. The definition languages for MIBs that are used in conjunction with the SNMP management protocol are SMI and its newer revision, SMIv2. Coming up with the proper design for a MIB module is as much an engineering activity as it is an art. It requires creativity and experience on the side of the designer and is facilitated by the use of systemic design methodologies.

Chapter Review

1. What does the acronym MIB stand for?

2. Name four categories of management information and tell what distinguishes them.

3. In what ways does a MIB differ from a database management system?

4. Name two of the different paradigms that can underlie a MIB definition language.

5. Can you think of a MIB object for which it would make sense to define a maximum access of write only?

6. What is the name of the language for the definition of management information used with SNMP?

7. In SMI, what is an important difference between an OID designating an object type and an OID designating an object instance?

8. Why are SNMP MIB objects not considered objects in an object-oriented sense?

9. SNMP MIBs use a hierarchical naming structure very similar to the structure many operating systems use to name files and folders. In which way is the object identifier tree of SNMP MIBs different from a naming tree for a file system?

10. What does the granularity of a model refer to?

CHAPTER 7

Management Communication Patterns: Rules of Conversation

Regardless of the particular management protocol that is used, interactions between managers and agents follow certain basic patterns. This chapter takes a look at those patterns—that is, how managers and agents interact. We discuss tradeoffs and the profound impact that the presence or absence of certain management interface capabilities has on aspects such as the efficiency of management communications, management application scale and performance, and the robustness of management against errors. The discussion of management patterns precedes the discussion of the actual management protocols themselves, which will occur in Chapter 8, "Common Management Protocols: Languages of Management."

When you have completed this chapter, you should be able to

- Explain the different layers that a management interface can be decomposed into

- Differentiate between polling-based and event-based management, and explain their impact on management applications and managed devices

- Assess the impact of the presence or absence of certain management interface capabilities on management applications

- Understand the difference between management and database transactions

- Distinguish different categories of management events and explain their specific relevance for network management

Layers of Management Interactions

In all networked systems, communications are structured into layers. This includes management communications. Before diving into the patterns of communication exchanges between managers and agents, let's talk briefly about how management communications are generally structured into layers—that is, the different roles and functions that you will find in layers of a management protocol stack.

The topmost layer of a communications stack is generally the application layer, which provides communication applications with services and communication primitives that they can use to directly communicate with each other. ("Primitives" refers to basic communication operations.) Examples of communication applications are e-mail (an associated protocol is the Simple Mail Transfer Protocol, SMTP) or file transfer (an example of a protocol is the File Transfer Protocol, FTP). Application-layer protocols are generally defined without concern for the physical characteristics of the underlying network (for example, wireless or Ethernet) or how to route the data across multiple intermediate hops. Lower layers in the communications stack address those aspects.

Network management is another example of a communication application. From the perspective of a communications stack, manager and agent are both considered applications. Accordingly, management protocols are fundamentally application-layer protocols as well. Therefore, the manager-agent interactions as described in the remainder of this chapter take place in the application layer.

Management communications can themselves be divided into several aspects. Some of them actually form management communication sublayers. For example, at one layer, manager and agents need to exchange management messages that represent management requests and responses; at another layer, they need to interpret the information payload that is carried as part of those management messages. In addition, managers and agents need to agree on a transport over which to carry the management messages. In other words, a management protocol by itself is not sufficient to establish interoperability between managers and agents, and describe the interactions that take place. A management protocol stack is needed.

Figure 7-1 depicts a reference model of the management communication layers of a management protocol stack. The layers of this stack are described in the following subsections, going from bottom to top. The bottom layer concerns the management transport and takes care of communication aspects that are management independent. The remaining three layers are in many cases addressed within the same management protocol. However, they do address separate concerns and are therefore distinguished.

Figure 7-1 *Management Communication Layers*

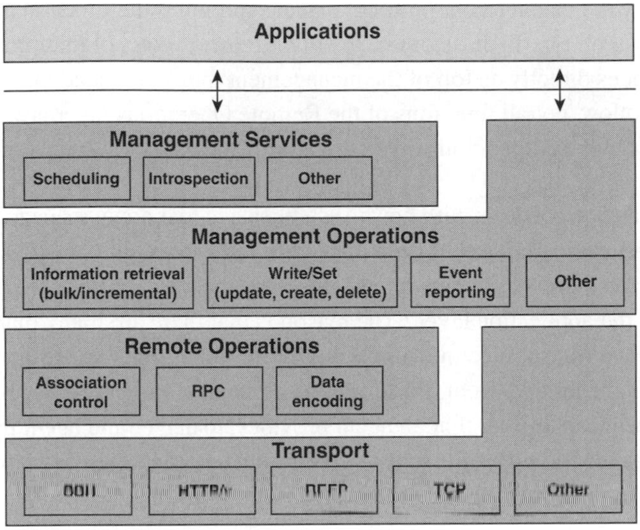

Transport

The transport layer is fundamentally agnostic and independent of the management protocol—it resides at Layer 4 of the OSI reference model and is the first layer that provides end-to-end communication services for the communicating systems. However, many management protocols make assumptions and impose restrictions on the protocols that they use as transport; hence, specification of a management interface always requires that the transport protocol being used also be specified. Examples of transport protocols that management protocols often use are the User Datagram Protocol (UDP), Transport Connection Protocol (TCP), Blocks Extensible Exchange Protocol (BEEP), Secure Shell (SSH), and Hypertext Transfer Protocol (HTTP). (The categorization of HTTP and SSH as transport protocols may be contentious because they are really application protocols in their own right that sit on top of another transport protocol. However, when used for management purposes and viewed from the management protocol perspective, they constitute just another transport.)

Remote Operations

The Remote Operations layer offers three distinct functions that complement and perform important services for the Management Operations layer on top: association control, remote operations support (in Figure 7-1, this is depicted a little simplified as RPC for remote-procedure call), and encoding of payload data. In many cases, those functions are provided not by a dedicated protocol, but by the management protocol that also provides the functionality of the Management Operations layer on top. In those cases, the management protocol that provides the management operations resides directly on top of the management transport. In addition, as is explained in the sections that follow, not all functions of the Remote Operations layer are always present; in this case, the Management Operations layer "bypasses" the Remote Operations layer.

■   Association control deals with how to establish and tear down management sessions—that is, management associations between managers and agents. Of course, the underlying transport layer already allows managers and agents to connect, so why is association control also needed at the application layer? The reason is that there are many management specific aspects that a transport connection is not aware of but that require a mutual understanding between manager and agent. For example, a manager might need to be aware of the management capabilities that an agent provides; manager and agent might want to negotiate a particular functional profile to use. In addition, an agent might want to determine in advance which management functions the manager will be allowed to invoke based on its user privileges.

In some cases, a management association is not based on an actual connection, but simply consists of a series of individual management transactions—the manager simply sends a management-related message to an agent, or vice versa. Accordingly, management associations could be short lived, although as a concept they are still valid.

■   Remote operations support involves the mechanism that is used to wrap and delineate management requests and responses in communication exchanges. Some readers might be familiar with remote procedure calls (RPCs). RPC is one example of such a mechanism and provides a useful model for the functionality that must be provided, although it is rarely used in management communications. The functions that need to be addressed include the following:

— Managing request/response IDs. These IDs are tags that allow applications to associate responses and requests. Management protocols are generally asynchronous, to allow a manager to issue several requests without needing to await responses from previous requests. This makes management communication more efficient than would be the case with a synchronous protocol. Figure 7-2 depicts the difference between the two. However, with asynchronous management communications, the order in which a manager receives management responses might not be the same order in which the manager issued the management requests. One reason for this is that some management requests trigger longer-running operations at the agent. If a second request does not depend on the outcome of the first request, the agent might decide to service the second request before the first one has finished executing and respond to the requests out of order. As a result, when a manager receives a management response, the manager needs to be able to tell which management request the response belongs to. For this to happen, the agent needs to include the ID of the original request in its response. Likewise, the manager needs to ensure that it uses a different ID for each management request that it sends.

Figure 7-2 *Synchronous Versus Asynchronous Management Operations*

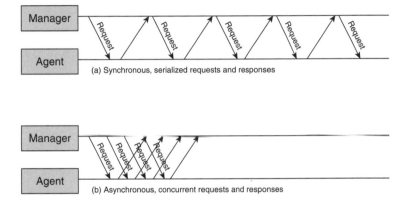

(a) Synchronous, serialized requests and responses

(b) Asynchronous, concurrent requests and responses

— Fragmentation and reassembly of management protocol data units (PDUs). A management PDU is a message of a management protocol. It contains a management payload, such as a management request and request parameters, along with some control information that is typically contained in a message header. In many cases, the underlying transport imposes a maximum on the PDU size that can be transferred in one shot. To shield the users of management operations from those limitations, a fragmentation/reassembly function can break up a management PDU into multiple pieces on the sender's end and reassemble those pieces at the receiver's end. Figure 7-3 depicts this concept.

Note that it is possible for a management request and the corresponding response to be of vastly different sizes. For example, the request by a manager to retrieve a subsystem's configuration can be very short, yet the response returned by the agent might contain substantial amounts of data and hence be very long. In addition, the size of the response often cannot be determined at the time the request is made. Without a fragmentation and reassembly function, some management requests may simply be answered with a "response too long" error, requiring the manager to break up the management request (for example, by requesting less information at a time) so that responses will be smaller.

Despite the fact that this is not an ideal situation, many management protocols do not support fragmentation and reassembly. Without such a capability, management applications must learn to live with limitations that are imposed by the transport and breakup requests when needed, as just described. Because of such limitations, in many cases, management protocols either require a particular transport that is known to meet certain requirements or articulate requirements that a transport must fulfill before it can be used in conjunction with the management protocol.

Figure 7-3 *Fragmentation of a Large Response*

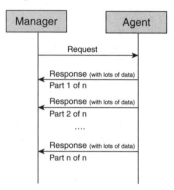

- Encoding, finally, entails how management information that constitutes the payload of management operations is "flattened" and encoded in a PDU. For example, when a value of an attribute of a managed object is included in a management request (for instance, 51), the value needs to be represented somehow (for example, as a string of the characters 5 and 1, or as an octet that contains a binary representation of 51). Of course, in addition to the values, the attributes that the values belong to, object identifiers, and parameter names of operations all need to be carried as part of the message. An encoding that is used in conjunction with SNMP is defined in the ASN.1 (Abstract Syntax Notation One) Basic Encoding Rules. Another encoding that is rapidly gaining popularity is Extensible Markup Language (XML). Other encodings are plain human-readable text (used in conjunction with syslog messages that agents use to convey events) and specialized binary encodings, which can be used in proprietary protocols for applications that are very performance sensitive.

Management Operations

The Management Operations layer is at the core of the management protocol stack. It provides the actual management primitives—that is, the base operations that are used to manage the network. Management primitives include different types of management requests, responses to those management requests, and events, all of which are explained in much more detail in the remaining sections of this chapter.

The specific primitives that are available depend on the specific management protocol. Management protocols are covered in detail in the next chapter. The overview here presents the basic categories of management operations that can be found in some form in most management protocols and that form the basis of the management communication patterns discussed in this chapter. The concept of those general operations and their use in management communication patterns needs to be distinguished from their specific instantiation as part of a particular management protocol.

Management primitives tend to be fairly generic in nature. More specifics about the particular operations are carried in the management information that accompanies them, as well as in additional parameters that are used to qualify the operation. Typical primitives include these:

■ Read primitives are used to retrieve management information. They are often referred to as get operations.

■ Write primitives are used to change or otherwise influence management information. They are often referred to as set operations.

  Write primitives are sometimes further subdivided into create, delete, and modify operations, depending on whether they result in the creation or deletion of logical entities (such as device subinterfaces or connection endpoints), or whether they change or update a logical entity that is already there.

■ Event-reporting primitives are used to communicate the occurrence of certain events by management agents.

■ Action primitives cause the managed device to "do" something, such as perform a self-test, load a software image, or reboot the device.

■ Less common primitives include acknowledgments for the receipt of management requests (not to be confused with a response—an acknowledgment merely indicates that a request was received and will be served and responded to in due time), and special-purpose primitives that are tied to very specific functions.

Management Services

Sometimes the management stack can include a fourth layer on top of the primitives that are offered by management protocols: the Management Services layer. Strictly speaking, higher-layer management services are not really a layer because management operations are still accessible to management applications on top and are not hidden underneath management services. Instead, they constitute an additional offering to management applications that builds itself on the Management Operations layer. Management services combine the management primitives provided at the Management Operations layer with additional capabilities. For example, they introduce special operation parameter values or special-purpose management information that provide a management service above and beyond the functionality that the management primitives provide. The following are examples of such management services:

■ A subscription service that allows management applications to subscribe to specific types of events based on certain filter criteria, such as all events pertaining to a specific port, or all events of a certain event type. (For example, this service might be provided by complementing management primitives with objects in a MIB that represent the filter criteria to be applied.)

■ An introspection service that allows management applications to retrieve information about what kinds of management information and management functions are supported on a managed device, as opposed to needing to rely on product documentation. This service might be provided by including the respective information (really, information about information— in other words, metainformation) in the MIB.

■ A remote scheduling service that allows management applications to set up a probe that periodically executes a management operation at certain times, without requiring the management application to issue a new request each time. (Again, the service could be provided by complementing management primitives with parameters or MIB variables that represent scheduling information, such as start time, end time, and frequency.

Manager-Initiated Interactions—Request and Response

Let us now turn to the way in which actual interactions between managers and agents, or management applications and managed devices, take place. Here we take a look at how management operations are used to conduct effective management communications. We start with interactions that are initiated by the manager. Interactions that are initiated by the agent are the subject of the next section. The patterns of interactions between managers and agents that are described are largely independent of any particular management protocol (although management protocols can include special provisions to cater to some of those patterns); instead, they are characteristic of management communications in general and help to understand how management protocols are used.

The most general interaction pattern between managers and agents consists of the exchange of requests and responses (see Figure 7-4). A manager makes a request—to retrieve a piece of management information, to change a configuration setting, or to cause it to perform an operation such as a self-test. The agent subsequently sends a response that includes a return code indicating whether the request could be successfully executed or whether an error occurred. The pattern of request and response is often also referred to as a *transactional* interaction.

Figure 7-4 *General Request and Response Interaction*

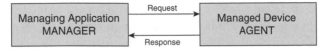

A typical request issued by a manager includes, at the minimum, parameters that specify the following:

■ The type of request being made

■ The management information that the request applies to or, alternatively, parameters that carry information needed to carry out the request

■ Additional housekeeping information—for example, an identifier for the request and security credentials such as authentication information to verify the identity of the requestor

Depending on the type of request, sometimes parameters with additional qualifiers can be included that specify additional behavior, such as what to do in case a request initially fails (keep retrying or return failure).

Upon receipt of the request, an agent first checks whether the request is valid. For example, it parses the request to see if it understands the request, it examines the manager's security credentials to verify that the manager is who he says he is, and it validates that the manager is indeed authorized for this type of request. If the request is not valid, the agent sends a response immediately to indicate failure. Otherwise, the agent services the request and, upon its completion, constructs a response with the results of the request.

At the minimum, a response includes the following:

■ A response code indicating whether the request was successful. In case the request was not successful, a reason should be given.

■ The result of the request—for example, the information that was requested.

■ Additional housekeeping information, such as the identifier of the original request, to help the manager match the response to the original request that it sent.

In the course of performing a particular management task, managers and agents often exchange multiple requests and responses. How this occurs determines to a great extent the efficiency of management communications. In general, the number and frequency of those exchanges for any one task should be kept as low as possible without sacrificing functionality and responsiveness of management applications. The following subsections examine different management tasks and how they are served with various communication patterns of requests and responses.

Information Retrieval—Polling and Polling-Based Management

Perhaps the most prevalent type of request/response management interactions involves requests for information by a manager, in which the manager interrogates the agent. This is also referred to as polling.

The basic pattern is very straightforward: The manager asks the agent for a particular piece, or pieces, of management information. The agent checks the validity of the request and retrieves the requested information. The agent then responds, providing the requested information in the response or an error-response code that indicates the reason the request could not be fulfilled. When the response is too large to be transmitted in one shot, it might need to be sent in multiple parts, as was shown earlier in Figure 7-3. An error message is sent in case the agent does not understand the request or does not know the type of management information that the manager is asking for.

The following subsections take a look at how this basic pattern is applied and varied, depending on the type of management information that is retrieved which is typically linked to different types of management tasks. As you shall see, different considerations for how to optimize the retrieval apply in each case, resulting in different interaction patterns.

Requests for Configuration Information

Configuration information that a manager requests can be information about the logical and physical configuration of the device. Compared with operational data and state information, configuration information changes only rarely and, when it does, generally only on behalf of a management application or a system administrator. Changes to configuration information are initiated not by the agent itself, but from the outside, whether it is a technician pulling a line card from a device or a management application configuring an interface. Because changes are so infrequent, this information is typically requested only rarely—not because management applications don't need it, but because the applications can cache this information in their own databases. In addition, often changes are effected through the management system itself, in which case it already knows about those changes. (Unfortunately, often there are other sources of changes than the management application itself, which can lead to problems. We discuss this in the section "Configuration Change Events.")

By maintaining a cache of a managed device's configuration information, when the management application needs to refer to this information, it does not have to send requests to the device. Requests for configuration information are thus minimized. There are several advantages to this:

- Management traffic over the network is reduced.

- Load that is imposed on the device to respond to such queries is reduced.

- Performance of the management application is improved. This is most noticeable when the agent is remote and needs to be reached over a wide-area network (WAN) link, thus introducing additional communication delays that do not apply when accessing the local database.

In general, configuration information is then requested only under the following circumstances:

- When a management application first takes management ownership of a device, to store the information in the management application's cache (that is, in its database) for the first time.

- When there is reason to believe that the cache is stale—that is, information in the database is out-of-date and needs to be reconciled. This is the case when operations unexpectedly fail that assume a certain configuration as a prerequisite. Another example is the receipt of event messages indicating that the configuration might have changed. (We discuss the latter in more detail in the section "Configuration Change Events.")

- In some cases, just before services are provisioned over the network, to ensure that the information about the devices that the service is provisioned over is indeed current and that everything goes smoothly. (Hiccups might still occur if the information changes in the time window between the configuration information request and the provisioning operations; we discuss this topic in the section "Management Transactions.")

Requests for Operational Data and State Information

Another type of management information that can be requested concerns operational data and state information. As discussed in the previous chapter, state information differs from configuration information in a number of important ways. For example, it is owned by the managed device itself and cannot be modified by management applications. Instead, it reflects the device independently of its need to be managed.

By its nature, operational data and state information can change frequently. In fact, some information changes extremely frequently—for example, a counter for octets on an outgoing link. Some counters can be incremented millions or even billions of times per hour, so a 32-bit integer to represent them is not enough; its value range might be exhausted in a matter of minutes. A 32-bit integer can hold only roughly four billion discrete values, after all! Other information will not change as frequently but might still change unexpectedly. For example, the operational state of a device that is highly available should be stable for months.

For these reasons, operational data and state information generally tend *not* to be represented in a management application's database. Management information is closely tied to monitoring the network and does not lend itself to being stored in a static cache. This leads to patterns in which operational data and state information are retrieved that are much different from the patterns that are used to interrogate managed devices for configuration information. Although on the surface both cases involve just requests for management information, the associated communication patterns and considerations for how to optimize them depend greatly on the type of information retrieved. Whenever an application is interested in a view of the state of a device, it must poll it for the current snapshot of operational data and device state, which is very different from configuration information that can generally simply be retrieved from a database.

Polling a managed device for operational data and state information is generally used in scenarios such as the following:

- **Device viewing**—A remote user wants to obtain a real-time view of a device, requiring a snapshot of the most current information.

- **Troubleshooting and diagnostics**—Erratic behavior has been observed in the network, and applications need to obtain current data from the device to determine the cause.

- **"Hot spot" polling**—A particular device is under scrutiny and specific observation; its state information therefore is polled repeatedly over an extended period of time. This is also referred to as periodic polling. In some cases, the polled data is used to plot a curve that updates every second or so, similar to plotting the chart of a stock over the trading day.

Although polling is a universal management communication technique, keep in mind that it is potentially an expensive operation. This makes polling inadequate for certain management tasks. When making a decision on polling, be sure to consider the load that it imposes on the managed device, specifically when polling needs to occur repeatedly and in shorter intervals. After all, the device's raison d'être is not to be managed, but to provide a communications function.

Therefore, a managed device should spend its processing cycles on, for example, routing packets, not responding to continuous management requests. Performing a function such as hot spot polling should therefore be the exception, not the rule. If it is indeed a requirement that a snapshot of certain state information be continuously monitored, other techniques should be used.

For example, if the purpose of continuously polling a state is to avoid missing a certain condition when it occurs, a shift from polling-based to event-based interaction patterns is advised. The idea behind event-based interaction patterns is to have the agent automatically notify the manager when certain conditions of interest occur, without requiring the manager to continuously poll. Polling is not just expensive, but it might be inadequate for other reasons:

- The condition might be missed despite continuous polling. After all, even if polling is frequent, it occurs at discrete time intervals. If the condition were to hold for only a brief period of time between two polling intervals, the polling application would not detect it, as shown in Figure 7-5.

Figure 7-5 *Polling-Based Monitoring That Misses an Important Condition*

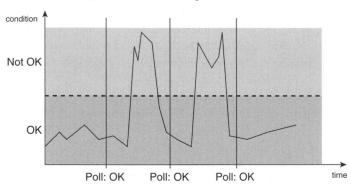

- In addition, the delay until the condition is recognized might be unacceptable. If the condition occurs and the previous polling cycle just missed it, the management application will have to wait until the next polling interval to detect it. Obviously, there is a tradeoff between an acceptable polling load and the acceptable delay and likelihood to detect the condition.

Figure 7-6 depicts the impact that the polling frequency has on the accuracy with which the polled condition or parameter can be approximated. In one case, the polling occurs only at times t_6, t_{12}, and t_{18}; in the other case, it occurs at every interval.

Figure 7-6 *Coarse and Fine Polling Samples*

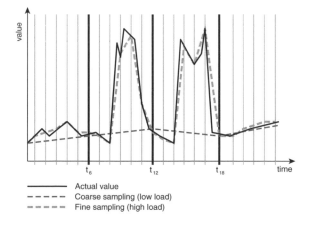

In real life, instead of constantly watching a pot while heating water for a cup of tea, you can use a tea pot that whistles to alert you when it boils. Similarly, many devices offer capabilities to alert a management application if a certain preprogrammed condition occurs, such as when a gauge crosses a certain threshold. Event-based management is discussed in detail in later sections.

If the purpose of continuous polling state is to observe trends over time, polling is effective but still expensive. Although sometimes it is the only option available, more effective interaction patterns exist that lighten the load on a managed device, management application, and management network. Specifically, instead of polling, it would be sufficient to instruct the device to take a snapshot at certain intervals without sending a request each time. Two variations exist:

■   The results of those snapshots are written by the agent into a local file, to be transferred in bulk at a later point in time. This solution is adequate when there is no need for the data to be provided in near–real time, as shown in Figure 7-7.

Figure 7-7   *Historical Data Collection on the Device as Opposed to Polling by a Manager*

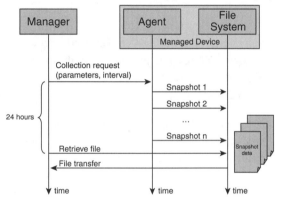

■   The snapshots are sent automatically when they are taken. What is sent in this case amounts to a special type of event. The computation overhead is higher than in the case of the first option—management communication takes place at every polling interval. However, snapshots are provided in near–real time, and there is no need for the agent to keep snapshots around in files—an important consideration if nonvolatile memory on the device is a scarce resource (see Figure 7-8).

Figure 7-8   *Automated Snapshot Collection*

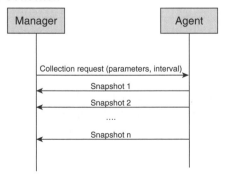

Of course, in both cases, the internal computational overhead to take the snapshot still remains. However, at a minimum, the redundant requests are taken out of the equation, which provides at least some relief.

We revisit this topic in the section "The Case for Event-Based Management."

Bulk Requests and Incremental Operations

Whether a request for management information concerns configuration or operational data and state information, there are two options for the granularity of the request. The first option (the default, in most cases) is to simply ask for a specific piece of management information. To get several pieces of management information, separate requests are sent. Management operations that concern one item at a time are also called *incremental operations* (respectively, incremental requests). In a variation, several items can be retrieved in the same request but still need to be called out explicitly.

Besides the incremental option, there is sometimes a second option that allows retrieval of information in bulk. In this case, not every piece of management information is separately named; instead, bulk retrieval asks for all information that meets a certain criteria, such as "all operational data of a line card" or "all configuration information." This is more efficient when it would otherwise be required to go through many iterations to retrieve the desired information, such as when every piece of operational data or all configuration information is to be retrieved. In some cases, incremental retrieval might not really be possible because the manager does not even know what management information exists on the agent to begin with. Either way, one information-retrieval request is followed by a response containing a large amount of information.

When management information is arranged into a conceptual management information tree, one way to retrieve information in bulk is to simply ask for an entire subtree. Operations that are directed not at any particular managed object but at any object under a certain parent node are called *scoped*. Scoping of operations is not restricted to requests for management information retrieval, but it is in this context that it is perhaps the most important. The scope of an operation is generally an entire subtree—for example, everything that is related to a particular communications feature, such as a routing protocol, or everything that is contained under a particular port or communications subsystem (see Figure 7-9). Fancy scope operations allow managers to additionally specify filters, for example, to apply only to managed objects in a subtree that are of a certain type, such as device ports.

Figure 7-9   *A Scope Applied to a Management Information Tree in a MIB*

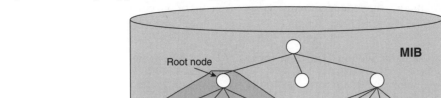

In practice, it turns out that the capability to scope operations is rarely supported on devices, mostly because this requires agent implementations that are fairly sophisticated. Nevertheless, it constitutes an important variation of the request/response management information-retrieval pattern that can significantly cut down the number of management interactions between managers and agents, and make life for management applications easier.

In the case of configuration information, another way to retrieve information in bulk that *is* widely supported and that does not require scoping is to retrieve the device's configuration file—a file that contains the complete configuration. This is an option that routers commonly support. We shall discuss configuration files in more detail in the section "Dealing with Configuration Files."

Historical Information

Historical information concerns snapshots of management information, typically performance data such as bandwidth utilization or packet drop rates that are taken at certain intervals in time. Collecting and analyzing these snapshots can reveal valuable information for network providers. For example, they may be able to determine how the use of the network varies over the time of day or the day of the week, or they might observe trends in the change of utilization of network resources. This helps network providers tune the network and eliminate network vulnerabilities, such as bottlenecks, and plan for how to evolve and upgrade the network. The collection intervals are most commonly 15 minutes, striking a balance between getting data with a sufficient degree of granularity and not drowning in the amount of data being collected.

The way in which management applications use historical data impacts the way in which applications from managed devices retrieve such data. This leads to communication patterns that are different from those that are used in conjunction with configuration information or operational data and state information. Although on the surface each case simply involves retrieval of management information, considerations for how to optimize this retrieval and the interaction patterns this results in depend greatly on the type of information retrieved.

One way historical information can be collected is to simply have a management application periodically poll the network—that is, emit regular requests for state information. This is a very straightforward approach. However, it has a number of drawbacks:

■ **Polling overload**—Having a management application poll devices across the entire network every 15 minutes can be a daunting task and requires a lot of horsepower. It can quite easily bring the application to the limits of how far it can scale. In addition, as was pointed out earlier, repeated polling adds a considerable load on the device, whose primary purpose in life after all is to provide communication functions over a network, not respond to management requests.

■ **Robustness**—A working management connection and management application are required for the polling approach to work. In case any hiccups occur (for example, because management connectivity is temporarily lost or because a management application is restarted), polling cycles are missed and gaps in the collected data can result.

■ **Calibration of interval lengths**—Perhaps most important, historical information that is collected through polling is not necessarily accurate because it is hard to guarantee that polling at the device actually occurs at the precise intervals. For example, a management application could be late in issuing a polling request, or the network could introduce a delay that varies over time, causing the request to reach the managed device at varying time intervals. Figure 7-10 depicts this problem. The result is that the polled data points only an approximate picture, not an accurate one, of the actual history.

Figure 7-10 *Skewing of Collection Intervals*

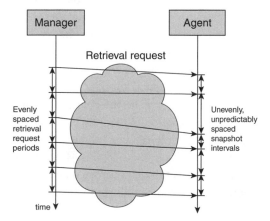

■ **Synchronization of interval start times**—Management applications typically want the time interval boundaries of the historical data to be the same across different devices. For example, the interval could always start at the top of the hour. This makes the data more comparable across the network than in the case of "rolling" boundaries (for example, device 1 at 12:00, 12:15, 12:30, and 12:45; device 2 at 12:02, 12:17, 12:32, and 12:47; device 3 at 12:06, 12:21, 12:36, and 12:51; and so on). Trying to achieve a synchronization of polling intervals across the network with a centralized management system is next to impossible.

A preferable approach is therefore to set up automatic collection at the device. This means that the management agent allows a management application or network administrator to configure which data will be recorded through snapshots, and at what intervals. The management agent then automatically takes the snapshot as requested and stores the snapshot data for later retrieval. This can be in a MIB that can be queried, or (the more common approach) it can simply be in a file in a known location, named according to a certain convention, that can later be retrieved from the device, such as through the File Transfer Protocol (FTP). Typically, one file is produced for every 24-hour period, containing 96 snapshots in the case of 15-minute snapshot intervals. In the case of performance counters, the snapshot data is generally already massaged to contain only the actual counts from that particular interval so that the application does not need to first compute the differences between the snapshots.

This way, the number and frequency of management requests and responses are reduced by orders of magnitude. No polling cycles are missed. Interval lengths are well calibrated, and interval synchronization becomes essentially a nonissue (assuming that time is synchronized across the network). The only drawback is that, in practice, not all devices are instrumented accordingly. In some cases, this forces applications to fall back to the periodic polling approach.

Configuration Operations

In the previous section, we discussed the communication patterns that are associated with management operations to retrieve management information from the network. Let us now turn to the second major category of management operations: configuration operations. Configuration operations aim to change configuration information—specifically, parameter settings that in some way affect the managed device's behavior. Where information-retrieval operations essentially involve nonintrusive reading of a conceptual "display," configuration operations involve turning conceptual "knobs." This can include, for example, configuring an interface, enabling or disabling a routing feature, changing access control lists that define firewall rules, or configuring where to send alarm messages. As with polling operations for management information, configuration operations generally follow a request-response pattern. However, there can be differences in how requests and responses are applied, resulting in certain management communication patterns that are specific to configuration operations, as outlined in the following sections.

Failure Recovery

One obvious difference between information retrieval and configuration operations concerns the possibility for failure. Because something on the device is to be changed, many more things can go wrong in the course of servicing a request than in the case when management information is retrieved. Here are some examples: The device might not support a particular configuration option that is requested, it might currently not have the required system resources to fulfill the request, or the request might conflict with some other settings. For those reasons, a management application that performs configuration operations needs to be sure to accompany them with corresponding error-handling procedures.

For example, what does the management application do if no response is received within a certain timeframe? This is a typical scenario and illustrates what needs to be considered. If the management application was retrieving management information, it could simply send another request and no harm would be done. With a configuration request, however, it might well make a difference whether the same operation is performed once or if it is performed twice. In this case, the application needs to tread carefully to deal with the different possible scenarios, as Figure 7-11 illustrates.

- Did the device never receive the request in the first place? In this case, the manager should resend the request.

- Did it serve the request a long time ago, but the response was lost? In this case, the manager should not resend the request, but should find out whether the earlier request was successful.

- Is it still busy executing the request? In this case, it might not be a good idea to resend the request. The manager should still wait.

Figure 7-11 *Missing Response Scenarios*

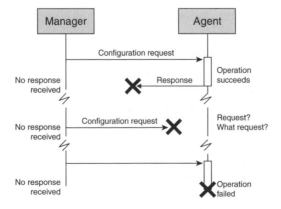

One way in which a manager can distinguish between those scenarios is when the agent offers a management function that allows the manager to inquire about the status of a management request, given the request ID. However, such a capability is the exception, not the rule. Another way for a manager to handle such a situation is to first retrieve management information that should reflect whether the parameter change took effect before deciding to resubmit a configuration request. Also, if the operation was part of provisioning a service, it is a good idea to simply test whether the service is actually working. Although such heuristics do not provide absolute certainty, they allow managers to distinguish with reasonable confidence cases in which a request was successful and should not be resent from other cases and to react accordingly.

Response Size and Request Scoping

A second difference between information retrieval and configuration operations concerns the size of a response. As was described earlier, in the case of scoped management information retrieval, one small request can result in the return of a substantial amount of information. On the other hand, in the case of configuration operations, the size of the response is typically similar to the size of the request. The response includes a return code that indicates whether the request was successful and perhaps the new setting that is in effect as a result, but not much more.

It is not common for configuration requests to return vast amounts of data. Although scoped configuration operations are conceivable in principle, they are rarely found. Of course, in some cases, bulk configuration is still desirable, such as when there are many instances of a particular type of managed resource on a device that are all to be configured in the same way. One example is voice gateways that have a large number of DS0 ports that terminate voice connections. Certain parameter settings are uniformly applied across the device, such as the echo-cancellation setting that is used to suppress unwanted echo on a line. A scoped configuration operation could be applied to change the echo-cancellation setting for every DS0 port.

In the example, an alternative obviates the need for scoped configuration altogether. Instead of modeling the echo-cancellation setting on a per-DS0 basis, it is also possible to build a larger scope into the parameter itself. For example, a single global parameter could be introduced that establishes an echo-cancellation setting that will take effect across a device. This way, there is no longer a need for a large number of individual configuration requests; they can all be replaced by a single request. Some fine-grained degree of control over parameter settings is given up in exchange for more efficient management. The situation is similar to catering for a banquet: Do you allow everybody to order separately for a maximum of flexibility? Or do you simply arrange for the same menu for everyone, to reduce overhead? The example also shows how design choices on how to model management information affect the management interactions that take place between managers and agents.

Dealing with Configuration Files

A third difference between management interactions for information retrieval and interactions for configuration operations is rooted in the way in which configuration information is maintained in the device. In some cases, configuration information is represented as managed objects in a MIB that can simply be set. In many cases, however, the "MIB" really consists of a *configuration file*—that is, a text file containing line items with the settings that are in effect. These line items are sometimes represented simply as a series of CLI commands that achieve the desired configuration. Instead of simply changing a setting, applying a configuration operation might involve explicit handling of the configuration files. (There could also be multiple files with subconfigurations that can be applied individually and that collectively provide the overall configuration. This makes the overall configuration easier to handle.) For example, the request for a configuration operation then involves this:

- Preparing a configuration file that contains the configuration that is to take effect

- Downloading this configuration file on the device

- Explicitly telling the device to switch over from the current configuration to the new configuration in the new file

In effect, the request for a configuration operation needs to be split into multiple steps that with a different approach could be avoided. Although this might seem awkward and inconvenient, it is not all bad and offers a number of advantages. For example, the need to deal with configuration files explicitly allows for a very straightforward implementation of configuration backup-and-restore functionality. Configuration files also make it simple to maintain different configuration versions—simply copy configuration files back and forth. By the same token, the configuration file approach is well suited to many similar configurations across the network—the same configuration file can essentially be applied to different devices of the same type across the network, with only minimal processing required to customize the file (for example, to account for different device IP addresses). This way, configuration of devices can be easily managed by using proven configurations as cookie-cutter templates applied across the network.

In many cases, such as with Cisco IOS routers, a hybrid approach is applied. Requests to change a router's current configuration do not require explicit handling of configuration files. The management agent instead simply applies the change to the current configuration, which is maintained in the router's memory. This configuration is also referred to as the *running config*. However, the configuration that is in memory is not automatically persisted, which means that if the router reboots, the change disappears. The router reboots not from the last configuration that it had in volatile memory, but from a configuration stored in a file—that is, in nonvolatile memory, the *startup config*. Users have to make a special request to transfer the running config to nonvolatile memory, to make the config that is currently running indeed the startup config.

Again, although it appears somewhat awkward that users and management applications need to worry about such things, there are some good reasons for it. For example, imagine that a configuration request is executed that causes a router effectively to crash or inadvertently bring down a communication service that had been working just fine. In this case, it will be a big advantage if upon reboot the device does not apply the most recent configuration parameter settings, which caused the corruption of communication services, but if it instead starts with a proven startup configuration that represents a device configuration that is known to be more stable.

A startup configuration file can perhaps be likened to a shopping list of the staples you typically use. When you go to the store (the device boots up), what is on the shopping list (your startup config) is what you intend to put in your shopping cart (your running config). As you keep roaming around the store, you might find some new items that catch your interest that you put in the cart at the spur of the moment, sometimes perhaps exchanging it for an item already in the cart. How about buying a roasted chicken for dinner instead of pizza? So over time, what you have on your shopping list and in your cart might diverge. However, if you go shopping again next week, you start again with the same shopping list that has withstood the test of time. Of course, in some cases, some of the new items that you have in your cart may have been so successful at home (your family loved the chicken and grew tired of pizza) that you adopt them for your shopping list permanently.

Finally, you might have different shopping lists prepared, akin to different configuration files to switch back and forth between for different occasions—one everyday shopping list for your whole family, another one for when you also have your in-laws, who are vegetarians, staying at your house, and a third when it's just you home alone and you can fall back to eating all the ice cream that you want because no one is watching.

Actions

Finally, some interactions cause the device to perform a certain action. Examples are a request for the device to reboot itself, a request to perform a self-test, or a request to "ping" another device to see if it can be reached. Those interactions are very straightforward: A request is sent to perform the action, and a response is sent that indicates the outcome of the action or any errors that were encountered.

One special case occurs when performing the action might take some time. This could lead to problems—what should the manager do if no response is received, as shown in Figure 7-12? If there has been some kind of fatal error, the manager might have to wait in vain indefinitely, so perhaps it should reissue the request. However, this could be problematic in itself if the agent is still working on the original request, causing it (worst case) to repeat the same action even though it is not needed.

Figure 7-12 *A Long-Running Request*

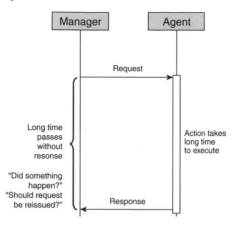

In such cases, it is useful if the management agent provides the means to modify the request/ response interaction and effectively split it into multiple parts, as Figure 7-13 illustrates. The initial response merely indicates that the request has been accepted by the device, without indicating the outcome of the action. A second request is then necessary to inquire about the status of the execution of the request and to retrieve the results. The original request can simply be referenced by its original request ID, providing another way in which this housekeeping information that we introduced earlier proves useful. (The possibility of long-running requests also provides yet another use of the request ID: the capability to refer to the earlier request in an effort to cancel it, where an agent offers such a capability.)

Figure 7-13 *Splitting Request/Response Interaction*

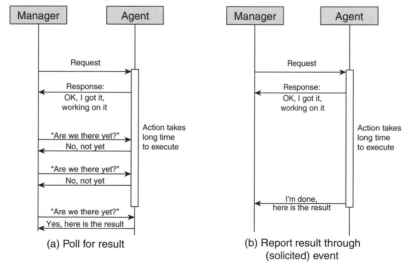

Of course, the price to pay is the overhead of the additional interaction. As an alternative to having the manager issue a second request, in a further variation of the interaction pattern, the result can be reported through an event that is sent automatically by the device when it is done.

Management Transactions

Sometimes management applications would like not having to issue a request/response pair for each configuration operation or management action, but instead be able to group several commands together and have them execute together as one unit. This is often the case when services need to be provisioned over a network.

Consider the simplified example of a service provider that wants to provision a digital subscriber line (DSL) service, as Figure 7-14 illustrates.

Figure 7-14 *Provisioning a DSL Subscriber Service*

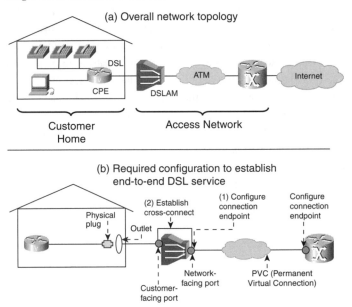

The customer connects his equipment—that is, his DSL modem, to a wall outlet that on the service provider's end leads to the port of a DSL access multiplexer (DSLAM). This port is referred to as the customer-facing port. The DSLAM, in turn, uses another port, the network-facing port, to connect through an Asynchronous Transfer Mode (ATM) network to an aggregation router. This aggregation router actually connects the customer to the IP network. The access portion of the network that includes the DSLAM is invisible to the IP network and, in effect, is treated like a wire (a pretty sophisticated wire, of course). So for the DSL service to work, the following is required:

- A connection needs to be set up (that is, provisioned) between the DSLAM and the aggregation router—more precisely, between the network-facing port of the DSLAM and a DSLAM-facing port of the aggregation router.

- Also on the DSLAM, the customer-facing port needs to be cross-connected with the network-facing port with the connection to the aggregation router.

The provisioning application needs to first check the DSLAM to see whether a network-facing port is available. If this is the case, it proceeds with the following two configuration requests directed at the DSLAM:

- **Configuration request #1**: Cross-connect the available network-facing port with the customer-facing port.

- **Configuration request #2**: Configure the network-facing port as the endpoint of a connection that points to the aggregation router at the other end.

In addition, the provisioning application needs to provision a connection endpoint at the aggregation router, which we will ignore for the moment. At this point, we are interested only in the configuration operations on the DSLAM. None of the configuration operations by themselves provides any value; either both or neither is needed. Therefore, if one of them fails, so should the other. Likewise, it would be a problem if between the check on whether the network-facing port is available and its cross-connection with the customer-facing port, another application would configure the same port for a different purpose. The corresponding requests should therefore ideally all be executed as if they were a single operation—they constitute a management *transaction*. In effect, the transaction defines a "new" operation, indivisible at the device, as follows:

```
Begin transaction {
    Operation 1
    Operation 2
    Operation 3
    }
End transaction;
```

The concept of a transaction is well known in the context of database management systems (DBMSs). Transactions are at the foundation of many applications that we take for granted. A classical example is that of a banking application that supports ATMs—in this case, not ATM networks, but automated teller machines. When a customer wants to withdraw money from the ATM, it involves several steps:

1. The bank checks whether there is enough money in the account.

2. If not, the request is rejected.

3. If so, the bank pays out the money requested and subtracts the amount from the original amount in the account.

Now, if it were not for database transactions, in a distributed scenario, it would be possible that the same amount is paid twice by the bank but subtracted only once from the account. For example, if two persons were to withdraw money at the same time, in both cases the bank would first check how much money is in the account, and then not only pay both and but also calculate the new account balance by subtracting the disbursed amount from the original account balance. Because in both cases the identical steps are performed, the bank would end up disbursing the amount twice, but it would be reflected only once in the updated account balance. Clearly, the bank does not want that to happen. Therefore, checking for the available amount and then subtracting the requested amount from the available amount is grouped into the same transaction and executed as one unit, without the possibility of someone else interfering.

Unfortunately, in network management, supporting true transactions (in the database sense) for management operations is very difficult. This is true not only for transactions that span multiple devices, but even when only a single device, or management agent, is involved. Fundamentally, the reason for this has to do with the fact that a management agent provides only a view of the real device, without actually having the real device under full control. Management applications need to account for the possibility of interference. For example, this could be a network administrator who simply logs on to a device and effects changes manually, using the CLI and circumventing the management application. Likewise, between the query for a state (for example, use of a port) and the action based on the response, the state might have already changed. Management communication exchanges involve time delays, and the world does not stand still in the meantime: Network-control protocols might interfere, physical components might fail; there are myriad possibilities why things can unexpectedly change.

Accordingly, there is generally a certain "fuzziness" associated with management transactions. Management applications need to take this into account, adapt to those limitations, and be prepared to handle exceptions. This is one of the reasons management applications can be quite complex. For example, application logic of provisioning applications typically involves the following steps in addition to the provisioning operations themselves:

■ Verification steps before configuration operations are applied to the network, including syntax as well as semantics checks, to increase the likelihood that the intended operation will succeed

■ Validation steps after configuration operations have been applied, to check whether the operations had the intended effect

Rollback of operations is required when part of a management transaction fails. *Rollback* refers to the undoing of the effects of operations that have succeeded but that need to be taken back because other operations in the same transaction have failed. Rollback is rarely supported by management agents and is instead generally the responsibility of management applications. In many cases, management applications are arguably better off this way. After all, rollback attempts might themselves fail. Also, some operations cannot be truly "rolled back" because they have already had an effect. For example, if an existing service were disconnected because a port was reconfigured, or if the device were rebooted as part of an action, those effects could not be undone. The best that can be done in such a scenario is actually a "roll forward," bringing the network into a configuration state that is well defined. Instead of having the network effectively left in an undefined state, in most cases, it is preferable to have management applications deal explicitly with such scenarios.

The transactional properties of management agents can be enhanced in several ways. A discussion of those techniques is beyond the scope of this book, but it is best to remember that management transactions are an important and nontrivial category of interactions between managers and agents, requiring careful design on the side of management applications. If someone claims to support a "management transaction," be sure to ask what is actually meant by this. For example, it might involve a facility that allows for grouping a set of commands and providing syntax checks for all commands up front before the first command is actually executed (this way, some transaction failures can be anticipated). It might also involve attempting some limited form of error recovery when things do go wrong, as Figure 7-15 illustrates. This can be extremely useful, but is still not quite the same as the types of guarantees and well-defined properties that are known from database transactions.

We should not conclude this section without briefly picking up on the part of the DSL provisioning scenario that we did not discuss. It concerns the need of the provisioning application to also provision a connection endpoint at the aggregation router, in addition to the configuration steps required at the DSLAM. This scenario is typical of service provisioning applications that in many cases need to successfully configure several managed devices to provision a service, with the possibility of any of the steps failing along the way. It means that the topic of management transactions applies not only to operations that are directed at a single management agent, but to management applications operating across devices as well. A detailed discussion goes beyond the scope of this chapter; suffice it to say that similar considerations must be made.

Figure 7-15 *A Management Transaction on a Management Agent*

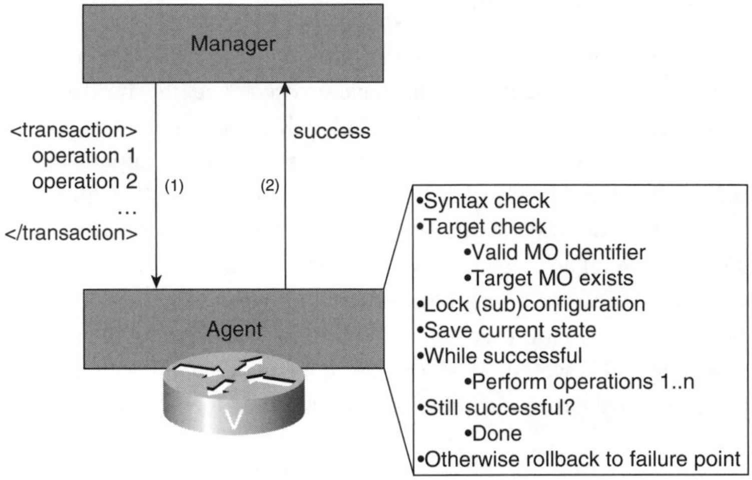

Agent-Initiated Interactions: Events and Event-Based Management

The second big category of interactions between managers and agents concerns events. Here, the agent initiates communication and sends the manager an event message to bring something to the manager's attention, usually about some type of occurrence or event that has occurred. For example, the event message could be an alarm that indicates that the device is overheating or that it has been experiencing a failure. It could indicate that a new configuration setting has just gone into effect. Or the event message could bring to a manager's attention that someone has tried to unsuccessfully log on to the device several times in a row, a possible indication of a suspicious activity. Basically, event messages correspond to interrupts that help managers do their jobs better. Event messages are sometimes also referred to as traps, specifically in the context of SNMP.

A quick note on terminology: Strictly speaking, the actual event that occurs in the real world needs to be distinguished from the message that is used to communicate the event. In practice, the term *event* is used for both the event and the message, thereby blurring the distinction between them. When it is necessary to explicitly distinguish between them, we refer to *event occurrence* and *event notification* (or, synonymously, *event message*), respectively.

Contrary to a response that is sent following a request, the agent determines on its own when it needs to send an event message, without waiting to be asked first. For this reason, event messages are often also referred to as unsolicited communications. Of course, "unsolicited" is not the same as entirely unexpected. In general, the device is configured to send event notifications to a specific manager. Alternatively, management applications can ask themselves to have event notifications sent to them—they *subscribe* to events.

Event Taxonomy

Events are used for many different purposes, notifying managers of many different types of event occurrences. Accordingly, they can be classified into a number of categories. The most common ones are as follows:

- **Alarms**—Unexpected events indicating a condition that typically requires management attention.

- **Configuration-change events**—Events that inform of a configuration change that has taken effect at the device.

- **Threshold-crossing alerts**—Events that inform that a performance-related state variable has exceeded a certain value, pointing to conditions that might require management attention to prevent network and service degradation.

- **Logging events**—Events that occur regularly and that are expected to occur during the operation of a network, that indicate what is currently going on in the network. In general, those events do not require an operator's attention but need to be logged (that is, written to a file or stored in a database) so that they are available for further analysis when needed. Logging events can be related to the following:

  - **Operator activity**—These events might be relevant for security purposes and provide trails of any commands that had earlier been directed at network devices.

  - **System activity**—These events provide for detailed execution traces. They can be useful in debugging a network but in general are simply turned off.

  - **Activity on the network and services**—These events record the occurrence of service-related events, such as the fact that a call was initiated, and can provide data used for accounting.

- **Informational events**—Any other kind of event.

To be useful, any event includes at least the following information:

- The system from which the event originated.

- A time stamp of when the event occurred. (In some cases, applications receiving the event add a second time stamp to indicate when the event was actually received.)

- The type of event that has occurred.

- Event detail information.

Beyond this, events might contain additional information, such as a sequence number of the event. In addition, each event category is typically associated with some very specific information that pertains only to this category. For example, a security event that reports operator activity also identifies the operator session, the command that was attempted, and possibly the response result (successful or not).

The following sections describe alarms, configuration-change events, and threshold-crossing alerts in more detail.

Alarms

Alarms communicate that some unexpected event has occurred that likely requires management attention. For example:

- A card on a router might have failed, requiring the card to be physically replaced.

- The temperature might be too high and there is a risk of physical damage to equipment.

- A port might have detected an unexpected loss of connectivity with the other side of the line.

Every alarm is an indication of an underlying condition. An alarm really is an event that reports the onset of the condition or the remission of the condition, in which case the associated alarm is really a clear event. You can picture a standing alarm condition as an LED that has gone on. The alarm then corresponds to a sound that is played when the LED first goes on, whereas the alarm clear corresponds to a different sound that is played when the LED goes off.

This means that an event that indicates that a device had to reboot unexpectedly is *not* an alarm— the fact that it rebooted might have occurred unexpectedly, but it is not some kind of condition that persists over a period of time. That would be an informational event that is sometimes referred to as a *transient* alarm.

Alarms must include the following additional information:

- **The type of the alarm**—This is the type of event that happened.

- **Alarm severity**—The alarm severity indicates the impact of the alarm—for example, whether it is affecting service. (Note that this is not necessarily the same as the priority of dealing with the alarm, which is determined by the management application that receives the alarm, not the agent that sends it. In some cases, dealing with a lower-severity alarm can be a high priority for a network manager, such as when it affects an important customer.) The following severities are fairly common and have been defined as part of a standard called X.733, which is issued by the ITU-T standards organization. (X.733 defines a list of standard information that is commonly associated with alarms.)

— Critical

— Major

— Minor

— Warning

— Indeterminate

— Cleared

■ **Possibly, a broader category for the alarm**—X.733 distinguishes between communications alarms (for example, unexpected loss of connectivity with a controller), quality-of-service alarms (for example, degradation of voice services), processing-error alarms (software process failures and the like), equipment alarms (for example, failed ports), and environmental alarms (such as a temperature that is too high).

More information exists that can be useful, but it is often not provided by network devices today:

■ A proposed repair action.

■ A list of other alarms that might be related to the same problem.

■ Additional information that might help in troubleshooting what caused the alarm, such as the settings of certain configuration parameters at the time of the alarm. This saves applications from needing to retrieve that information through additional requests.

Configuration-Change Events

Maintaining an accurate database of current device and network configuration is critical to many applications. As explained in the previous chapter, many applications cache configuration information of devices for efficiency. Configuration-change events communicate the fact that a configuration change has taken effect at the device. Processing configuration-change events is an important and efficient technique to prevent the cache from going stale. Of course, the application that initiated the configuration change will not be particularly surprised at the event; after all, the configuration change will have been confirmed in the device's response to the configuration request. However, other sources for configuration changes exist, such as other management systems or administrators who circumvent management applications altogether and simply log on to the device.

Configuration-change events are a major factor in enabling event-based management, as opposed to polling-based management. Without configuration-change events, applications must go periodically to every device and check whether the configuration has changed, typically by retrieving the relevant configuration information. This is the case even if no configuration information has changed, which generally is the vast majority of cases. Therefore, this is an extremely wasteful approach, impeding the scale of management applications, burning management communication bandwidth, and wasting CPU cycles on the managed devices that could be spent routing packets (which is why such bulk synchronization operations typically take place only during off-hours in the middle of the night, to minimize any service interference). In addition, when changes do occur, management applications have a stale database until the next polling cycle, which could be hours later. The problem is further compounded by the fact that provisioning applications need to make sure that they operate on configuration information that is current. This requires additional information-retrieval requests to be issued before sending the configuration request itself, to increase the chance that the configuration operation will indeed have its desired effect. This means that the device and management application must process even more requests and responses than they would otherwise have to.

Ideally, configuration-change events include the following additional information:

- **The configuration change that was applied**—The configuration parameter(s) and managed objects affected and their new settings

- **The originator of the change request**—For example, the identifier of the management session that initiated the configuration change

- **The request identifier**—In case any issues come up later and the precise steps that led to the configuration change need to be retraced

Unfortunately, comprehensive configuration-change events are in many cases not available or do not include the entire information about the configuration change. For example, configuration-change events might simply notify the manager that a change has taken place, without indicating what the change actually was. This is a big step over having no configuration change because the management application now knows exactly when the information in the database is stale and when it is accurate. However, the manager subsequently still must send extra requests to the device to retrieve the information that it needs to synchronize the database.

Figure 7-16 depicts the difference between a polling-based approach and a configuration-change event–based approach to keep a management application's database in synch with a device.

Figure 7-16 *The Impact of Configuration-Change Events*

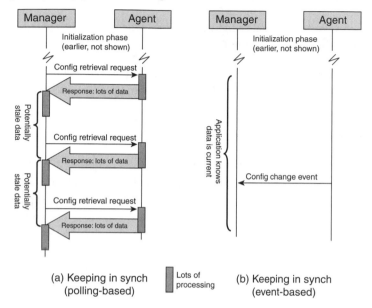

(a) Keeping in synch
(polling-based)

Lots of processing

(b) Keeping in synch
(event-based)

Threshold-Crossing Alerts

Threshold-crossing alerts (TCAs) indicate to a management system that some monitored MIB object or management variable has crossed a certain preconfigured value—a *threshold*. It enables network management to be proactive rather than just reactive (see Figure 7-17).

Figure 7-17 *Threshold-Crossing Alerts*

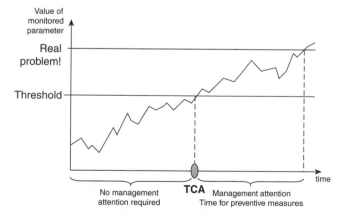

Consider the following examples of TCAs:

- **Your car's low-fuel indicator light comes on**—The remaining gas fell below a threshold of a 2-gallon reserve. Time to look for a gas station before you run out of gas.

- **Your son gets a warning slip from school**—The threshold that he crossed was being late to class three times in a row. Time to intervene to avoid problems with performance.

- **Utilization on a critical link exceeds 80 percent**—Time to look at ways to increase capacity before it runs out.

TCAs enable you to build management applications for monitoring that are driven by events, rather than having to rely on centralized polling to monitor network health. Again, this results in management applications that can scale orders of magnitude better than applications that rely on polling. In addition, event-driven applications are more responsive because they do not have to incur the delay that is associated with polling cycles. TCAs are useful in many situations, such as in proactive fault management, where the crossing of certain thresholds could be indicative of impending problems. Instead of waiting until the problem actually occurs and impedes services and users, the operator can take preventive measures.

TCAs share certain properties with alarms, most importantly, the fact that the crossing of a threshold corresponds to the onset of a certain condition. Accordingly, as with alarms, TCAs can clear. This means that a TCA should also be sent when the condition of a crossed threshold no longer exists and the value of the management variable has dropped back to an acceptable level. Basically, the cleared TCA tells the operator "Never mind" or lets the operator know that whatever measures were taken in response to the original TCA had the desired effect.

TCAs should include the following information:

- The name of the threshold or MIB variable being monitored for threshold crossing (there might be several)—for example, utilization of link X

- The value of the threshold—for example, 80 percent

- Whether the threshold has been crossed or cleared

To further complicate matters, the monitored variable could oscillate around the threshold value. This would result in excessive numbers of TCAs and TCA clears being sent. To avoid this situation, the clearing of a threshold is typically triggered only when the value drops not just below the original threshold, but below a second, lower threshold. That threshold is called the *hysteresis* threshold, as Figure 7-18 illustrates. The hysteresis threshold must be crossed to clear the TCA and to allow a new TCA to be triggered when the threshold is crossed again.

Figure 7-18 *Hysteresis Threshold and Clearing of TCAs*

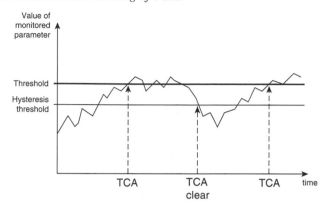

The Case for Event-Based Management

By now, you know that two fundamental communication patterns exist in the monitoring of networks:

- **Polling based**—The manager relies on periodic requests and responses to monitor the state of the network.

- **Event based**—The manager relies on event messages that the agent sends automatically.

Theoretically, it is possible to use either pattern to get the job done. However, the difference between theory and practice is that, in theory, they are the same, but in practice, they are different. The significance of the event-based pattern is that, in general, it is a lot more efficient, less wasteful, and more scalable, and it allows applications to be much more responsive than is the case with periodic polling. Therefore, wherever possible, event-based management should be the pattern of choice. Remember the analogy of needing to watch a pot with water until it boils versus using a teapot that will whistle when ready.

The following list summarizes some of the aspects that are affected by the choice of management pattern. Although its purpose here is to make the case for event-based management, the aspects that are listed are characteristic of the considerations that influence the use of management interaction patterns and that ultimately impact management interface design.

- **Number of required communication exchanges for a given task**—Each exchange results in interrupts at both the management application and the device, encoding and decoding of payload, possibilities of errors requiring special handling, in addition to the consumed management bandwidth and computation resources that are needed to fulfill a request. In general, it is a good idea to design interfaces to minimize the number of interactions required for typical tasks. Event-based management tends to be more efficient than management that relies on periodic polling.

- **Timeliness**—Is management information required in real time or near–real time within seconds, or is it sufficient for managers to obtain it in non–real time for processing during nightly batch operations? In the latter case, polling-based management might be just fine, but if it is important for management application to stay current with management information from the network at all times, event-based management is generally required.

- **Request-processing capacity on the managed device**—How many polling requests can a managed device handle without impeding its other functions? Being capable of sending proper events can shield the device from being polled with high frequency.

- **Wastefulness**—Management interfaces and communication patterns should be defined so that little waste occurs, avoiding the exchange of data that is effectively thrown away. For example, retrieving a large amount of management information just to identify a small fraction that has changed constitutes waste. Compared to event-based management-interaction patterns, periodic polling is extremely wasteful in many cases.

- **Available management bandwidth**—The amount of management bandwidth required is directly related to the number of communication exchanges and the amount of management information exchanged. In many cases, event-based management is more resourceful regarding management bandwidth because management information is communicated only when something of interest to the application has occurred; unnecessary management requests thus are avoided.

- **Management application scale**—How much processing is required by the manager to obtain the information that it really needs? With management that is based on periodic polling, the management application often has to do much more work than with event-based management.

Reliable Events

To allow management applications to be truly event driven without needing to rely on polling when events are available, those events need to be reliable. This means that a management application must be confident that all event occurrences are indeed reported through event messages and that no events are missed.

In practice, many event mechanisms that are used in network management are not truly reliable, as you shall see in our discussion of management protocols in the next chapter. This is unfortunate because management applications that could otherwise be entirely event based might still need to also rely on polling, at least occasionally, to make sure that nothing important has been missed. In these cases, we say that management applications are *event directed* but still polling based.

The following techniques are used to make management events reliable:

- Use a reliable transport protocol over which management events are communicated. This approach is the most straightforward and is very effective. Its only limitation is that if the transport connection is down or the management application suffers a failure, until a new transport connection is established or the application recovers, events can still be lost. This is comparable to when you are participating in a phone conference. The conference connection might carry perfectly everything that is spoken. Nevertheless, if one party temporarily walks away from the phone or accidentally disconnects from the call and has to redial into the conference, he will have missed anything that was said in the interim.

- Add sequence numbers to the event information and provide the capability to replay or retrieve events upon request. If events are numbered consecutively, a gap in event numbers allows applications to detect that messages have been lost and recover them using the replay capability. Of course, this requires that the device not simply forget about the event upon sending, but retain a memory. Even without a replay capability, it is useful to know whether something was missed.

- Require events to be acknowledged. This means that the agent needs to retain events until it receives an acknowledgment that they have been received. If an acknowledgment is not received within a certain period of time, it should resend the same event messages. Again, this is not unlike a phone call, in which the speaking party expects the listening party to say "mm-hmm" once in a while. To be more efficient, the application might acknowledge several events with one acknowledgment message, as long as the acknowledgment is not delayed to the point that it would trigger resends by the agent. The main drawback of the approach to acknowledge events is that, although it is effective, it places a significant burden on the agent. Not only does the agent need to retain a memory of event messages that were sent, but it needs to keep track of which messages are safe to discard because they were acknowledged and of when to retransmit events.

We stated earlier that events are fundamentally one-way communications from the agent to the manager that do not require a response. So is an acknowledgment scheme for events a violation of this principle? No, because the event still does not involve a request in any way. An acknowledgment is hence fundamentally different from a response, which communicates some kind of "answer" to a "question."

On the Difference Between "Management" and "Control"

Unlike manager-initiated communications, events do not involve a request. The agent simply sends the event without asking anything in response from the manager. Remember that the network needs to be capable of providing its function independent of its need to be managed. If it were to ask for something back from the manager—if the agent was making a request, in effect—this fundamental principle would be violated.

Of course, there are cases in which a device needs to make requests to another system, without which a communication service the device provides would not properly function. For example, a device might have to request another system to translate a phone number into an IP address so that it can direct a call to the proper recipient, or it might request to be assigned an IP address so that it is able to send and receive data traffic. However, in those cases, the "other system" is not considered a management system, but a controller that itself constitutes a part of the network. The corresponding communication exchanges involve not management traffic, but control traffic, usually involving dedicated control protocols, not management protocols. Put simply, managed devices generally do not make requests, whereas controlled devices often do.

As a side note while we are on the topic, another difference between management and control is that control typically involves much more stringent performance requirements than management. Network control requires responses typically in the subsecond range. For example, a phone call that is being dialed must cause the phone on the other end to ring pretty much immediately. Management applications, on the other hand, have more relaxed requirements and can typically afford to take at least a few seconds to carry out a task.

Chapter Summary

Management exchanges between managers and agents follow certain patterns. Those patterns pertain specifically to when managers and agents are management applications and managed devices, but similar considerations apply for interactions between management applications. The considerations are independent of any particular management protocol and, in fact, point to the different ways in which management protocols are used.

Transactional patterns are based on requests that are initiated by the manager and responded to by the agent. Most management tasks require multiple exchanges to fulfill a particular purpose; the efficiency of management communications depends in part on the number and frequency of those exchanges. Depending on the type of request, certain variations and optimizations can be applied to the way in which requests and responses are exchanged. Important categories of interaction patterns include the following:

- Retrieval of configuration and status information, which is facilitated if the agent supports functions that allow it to retrieve information in bulk (scoping)

- Provisioning of device parameters, which is facilitated if the agent offers functionality that supports transactional properties that will reduce the need for validation, verification, and the undoing of effects of unintended or only partially successful operations

- Collection of performance snapshots, which is facilitated by collection capabilities that can be set up inside the managed device itself

Event-based patterns involve messages that are sent from agents to managers whenever an event occurs that might be relevant to management applications, without needing to first be solicited. Where event-based management is supported, it results in much greater management efficiency and better real-time characteristics than management that needs to rely exclusively on polling. Different categories of events serve different purposes and carry different information. Important categories are alarms (for monitoring and fault management), configuration-change events (to keep management applications' databases synchronized with the network), and threshold-crossing alerts (for proactive and preventive management). However, true event-based management requires that events be reliable and guaranteed to not be lost.

Chapter Review

1. What are the fundamental interaction patterns between the management agents?

2. Assume that you have a network with 1000 devices and 1500 links. Assume that a performance management application is interested in 18 performance parameters per link and 7 performance parameters per device. Assume that with incremental information-retrieval requests, you can retrieve five parameters at a time. Someone asks you to build an application that will keep a database of historical information of those parameters, using 15-minute intervals. What rate of management requests and responses must your application support per second? Furthermore, if it takes an average of 5 seconds to receive a response from a device, how many requests must the application be capable of handling in parallel?

3. What do you call the capability to apply the same management operation to multiple managed objects simultaneously, using only one management request?

4. One important technique that could be supported by devices to facilitate management transactions involves locking the device—that is, allowing a single management session to take management "ownership" of the device and allow no one else to modify the configuration during that time. Such a capability is very powerful, but in what ways does it still fall short of true management transaction support? For bonus points, can you think of new management issues that it introduces?

5. One technique that can be used to roll back management transactions involves reverting to an earlier configuration file. Discuss advantages and drawbacks of this technique.

6. Why can management actions never be subjected to management transactions?

7. In network management, what is an alarm?

8. Does a TCA have more in common with a configuration-change event or an alarm? Why?

9. Is it possible to support polling-based alarm management? If so, why is alarm management generally event based?

10. Name three techniques that can be used to make events reliable.

Common Management Protocols: Languages of Management

In the previous chapter, we provided an overview of management communication patterns and how management protocols are effectively applied in practice. In this chapter, we finally take a closer look at the management protocols themselves—the specific languages that managers and agents use to communicate with each other and exchange requests, responses, and event messages. The presented protocols constitute a sampling of what are arguably the most important and widely deployed network management protocols today, but it should be mentioned that they are by no means the only ones that exist.

When you have finished this chapter, you will be able to:

- Name the most common management protocols

- Understand how they are positioned and what their most important distinguishing characteristics are

- Explain management primitives and protocol message structure used with SNMP

- Grasp the reasons for the enormous popularity of the command-line interface (CLI), while appreciating some of the challenges faced by management applications that use it

- Understand how syslog works

- Explain the use of Netflow and IP Flow Information Export (IPFIX)

- Describe the latest trend in management protocols, Netconf

SNMP: Classic and Perennial Favorite

The Simple Network Management Protocol (SNMP) is probably the best-known management protocol. It is widely used particularly in the data-networking world and for monitoring applications. We keep the following discussion short and somewhat simplified, to focus on the big picture. For readers who are interested in further detail, plenty of excellent literature exists that is dedicated to just this subject. See Appendix B, "Further Reading," for a bibliography.

SNMP is defined in a series of Internet Engineering Task Force (IETF) standards that date back to the late 1980s. They cover not only the protocol itself, but also the MIB specification language, SMI, and its successor, SMIv2; a series of standard MIB definitions; and even the architecture of agent implementations. As far as the protocol itself is concerned, there are actually three versions: the original SNMP, often referred to also as SNMPv1, and SNMPv2c and SNMPv3. The versions build on each other, and even with the availability of SNMPv3, many SNMPv1 implementations still exist. Therefore, we describe each of them in the following subsections.

SNMP "Classic," a.k.a. SNMPv1

The original SNMP protocol is today often referred to as SNMP version 1, or simply SNMPv1. It continues to be widely used. As the name suggests, it was devised first and foremost to be simple— that is, simple to implement for agents on managed devices, which might have constrained processing and memory resources. However, it is not necessarily simple for management applications to use. In some cases, its simplicity also means that managers must work around certain limitations. In addition, the functionality offered by SNMP management agents is not always as powerful or as elegant as management applications would like it to be.

As is so often the case in engineering, it is all about tradeoffs. The original designers of SNMP decided that it was important to keep SNMP agent implementations simple and, as a consequence, push a little more complexity into management application logic itself. First, there would be fewer management applications (perhaps a few dozen) than agent implementations (perhaps hundreds, if not thousands). Also, management applications would not be subjected to the same type of computation resource constraints as network devices. Therefore, managers would find it easier than agents to accommodate complexity. This decision led to SNMP agent implementations becoming rapidly available and quickly gaining widespread acceptance, with management applications following suit.

Interestingly, at the time it was designed, it was widely believed that SNMP would eventually be replaced by a different and much more powerful protocol that would make the job of management applications easier. The other protocol was the Common Management Information Protocol (CMIP). However, because of its power (and, arguably, because it was in many ways ahead of its time), CMIP turned out to be much more complex to implement and, therefore, never gained widespread commercial relevance, validating the design decision to keep SNMP simple.

SNMP Operations

Chapter 6, "Management Information: What Management Conversations Are All About," described how MIBs for use with SNMP are defined using SMI or SMIv2, and how objects in those MIBs are identified using their object identifiers, or OIDs. The chapter also explained how OIDs are formed and how SNMP MIBs are structured using the object identifier tree. This section finally puts this knowledge to use. The SNMP protocol provides the operations that are used to access a MIB and interact with it. The operations all use OIDs to refer to objects in the MIB, so a basic understanding of the concept of OIDs is an important prerequisite for understanding SNMP.

SNMP defines a set of five management operations, which are the primitives on which all SNMP management is based. Get and get-next requests are used to retrieve management information from a MIB. Set requests are used to write to a MIB. Get responses are used by agents to respond to get, get-next, and set requests. Finally, traps are used to send event messages. We discuss those operations in the following sections.

All SNMP operations commonly include a parameter that is used to carry management information. The parameter contains a list of variable bindings. A variable binding is a name/value pair that consists of an OID that identifies a MIB object, and a value of that object.

Get Request

A manager uses a get request to retrieve management information—that is, MIB objects—from an agent. In addition to an identifier for the request, a get request includes as a parameter a list of variable bindings that specify which objects are requested. A variable binding is a name/value pair of MIB objects. In this case, for the object value, a null value is given. After all, the manager is interested in the object values but does not know them; if it knew what they were, it wouldn't have issued a get request in the first place.

Although more than one MIB object can be retrieved at a time, with SNMP, delivery of messages only up to a certain size (possibly as small as 484 octets, or bytes) is assured. If messages become larger than that, implementations might run into interoperability issues. In practice, this limits the amount of information that can effectively be retrieved per request.

Get-Next Request

A manager uses a get-next request to retrieve management information from an agent, just as with a get request. However, contrary to an ordinary get request, the OIDs in the variable bindings do not specify the objects that are to be retrieved directly. Instead, for each OID specified in the request, the agent is requested to return the object with the OID that comes in lexicographical order right *after* that OID. An OID supplied with a get-next request can be but does not have to be an OID of an actual object.

For example, assume that an agent has a MIB with objects as depicted in Figure 8-1. If the manager issues a get-next request with an OID of 0, it is equivalent to the manager having issued a get request for the object with the lowest lexicographical OID in the MIB—in this case, the instance of countA with an OID of 1.3.6.1.387.5.1.1.0. This is the object that will be returned. The manager could also have issued a get-next request for the OID 1.2, or 1.3, or 1.3.6.1.350, or 1.3.6.1.387.5.1—they would all have resulted in the same object to be returned.

Figure 8-1 *Navigation of a MIB with Get-Next*

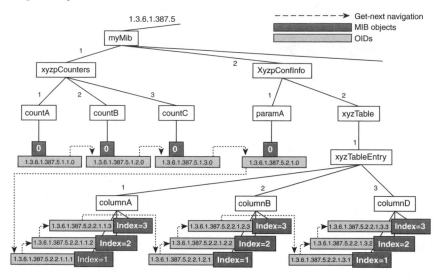

To abbreviate the OIDs a bit, let us in the following substitute the prefix 1.3.6.1.387.5 with the word myMib. With this notation, the OID of the countA object is myMib.1.1.0. If the manager subsequently issues a get-next request with the OID of the countA instance that was returned with the response to the previous get-next request, the object instance with the first subsequent OID will be returned—namely, myMib.1.2.0; that is, not countA, but countB. In other words, a get-next request directed at countA has the same effect as a get request directed at the object *after* it, countB.

By the same token, a get-next request that specifies the OID of an object type is equivalent to the get request of the OID of the first object instance of that object type—the object with the lowest index in case of a columnar object, or the only object instance in case of a scalar. In this example, a get-next of myMib.1.2 (the countB object type) is equivalent to a get of myMib.1.2.0 (the countB object instance). A get-next of myMib.2.2.1.2.2 is equivalent to a get of myMib.2.2.1.2.3 (column B in the third row—in other words, the row with index 3—of xyzTable). And so on. The dashed arrows in the figure indicate the way the MIB is traversed with the get-next if each subsequent get-next operation contains the OID of the object that was returned in response to the previous get-next operation.

So why would anyone need an operation like this, when a manager could use a get request and simply specify the desired object's OID directly? The reason is that in quite a few situations, the manager actually might not know what objects are in a MIB and hence what OIDs to ask for. Using get-next requests, a manager can effectively discover an agent's MIB. The manager can simply start with an OID of 0 to retrieve the first object, use that object's OID to retrieve the next one, and so forth. This pattern of iterative get-next requests is also called *walking a MIB*.

Being able to walk a MIB is especially useful in the case of MIB tables. In many cases, entries in a table are dynamically created and deleted by the agent—the contents of the table change over time, and with it do the indexes of the objects in the table. An example is a MIB table that represents a routing table because routing table entries are subject to occasional change through routing protocols. To traverse a table, for example, you can simply start with the OID of the table—not an instance of a columnar object within the table, but the OID given to the table definition in the MIB specification. The agent then returns the object with the first OID lexicographically behind it—that is, the first columnar object of the first row in the table. With the OID of that object, you continue on until you get to an object that, per its OID, is no longer part of the table. At that point, you know you have reached the end.

Interestingly, the way the get-next operation works means that a table is traversed by column, not by row. Remember that the OIDs of the columnar objects in the MIB are formed by concatenating the object type definition with the table index. This means that for any columnar object in the table, every index needs to be traversed before get-next finally moves on to the next columnar object type, or the next column in the table. Consider again the example from Figure 8-1. When issuing a get-next operation for OID myMib.2.2.1.2.2, the next OID will be myMib.2.2.1.2.3 (the object in the next row of the same column), not myMib.2.2.1.3.2 (the next column in the same row).

So what if you want to retrieve a table row by row? This is still possible, of course. Just as with the get operation, a manager can specify several variable bindings with several OIDs to retrieve in the same get-next request (the same message-length limitations apply). The agent returns the object with the next lexicographical OID for each of the OIDs specified. Therefore, one way in which a manager can retrieve a table row by row is by specifying several OIDs in the same get-next request at the same time. Each OID designates a different columnar object type, but with the same index. This way, get-next iterations proceed along multiple objects in multiple columns at the same time. Figure 8-2 illustrates this. For xyzTable/Entry, you can substitute your favorite MIB table, such as a table with operational data for your device's interfaces; for colA, colB, and colC, you can substitute the columnar objects of its table entries that you are interested in, such as the number of packets that were sent over the interfaces, the number that were received, and the number that were received but discarded.

Figure 8-2   *Row-by-Row Navigation of a MIB with Get-Next*

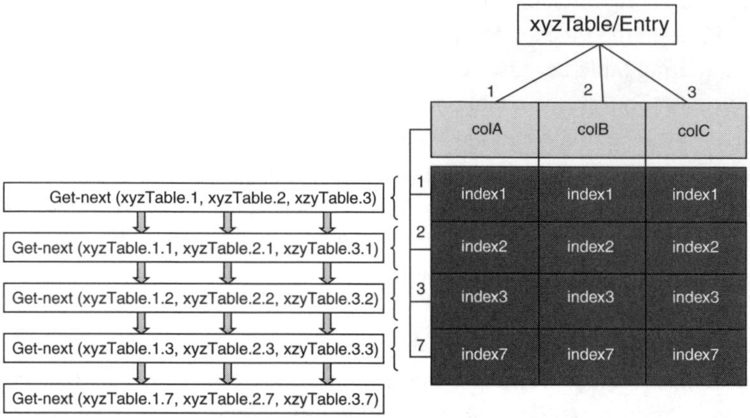

Set Request

A manager uses a set request to write to a MIB—that is, to set a MIB object to a particular value. The structure of the set request is exactly the same as with get and get-next, except that, in this case, the object values in the variable bindings are not set to null, but contain the values to set the respective objects to. The same restrictions related to message size apply as before.

Set requests are used in several ways. The first, most obvious, and most common use of set requests is to change the way a device is configured by adjusting certain parameter settings. However, although this is the use that was originally intended, it turns out that it is not the only one.

A second use is to cause the creation and deletion of logical entities in a MIB. An example is the creation of phone extensions for users connected to an IP PBX. Assume for a moment that a phone extension is represented as a row in a MIB table, with columns for the extension phone number, the username, and the identifier of the port to which the phone for this extension is connected. How do you add a row to this table to create a new phone extension, or delete one? There are no dedicated SNMP protocol operations for this purpose. Hence, set requests are used. As was explained in Chapter 6, the definition of the table can include an additional special-purpose columnar object, called a row status. Requesting that the row status of an existing table entry be set to destroy deletes the logical entity represented by the table entry. Likewise, requesting that the row status of a table entry to be set to create then creates a corresponding logical entity.

In the case of the phone extension, the table would accordingly include a fourth columnar object to indicate this row status. The strange part is that this concept allows the manager to issue a set request for an object that does not (yet) exist, as in the example for a phone extension. So it is really stretching the semantics of SNMP a bit. Normally, if a variable binding provided as part of a set request contained the OID of an object that does not exist, the agent would return an error.

However, in this case, the agent can tell from the type of object that is involved that a logical entity represented by a table entry should actually be created as a side effect of the set request.

A third use, stretching the set semantics even further, is to cause the device to perform an action. A typical example that illustrates this use is the "Ping MIB" defined in RFC 2925, where the setting of certain MIB variables causes a device to ping another IP address (see Figure 8-3). This means that the managed device sends an Internet Control Message Protocol (ICMP) echo request to the other IP address to see how long it takes to get a response. This capability can be used to troubleshoot connectivity problems because it allows a manager to check whether device A is reachable from device B.

Figure 8-3 *The Ping Operation*

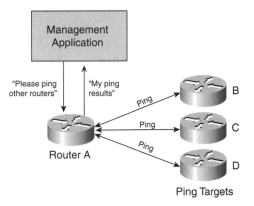

Figure 8-4 shows an excerpt of the MIB. It shows two tables, pingControlTable and pingResultsTable. A request to conduct a ping is achieved by setting a corresponding table entry in the pingControlTable. You would never want to actually retrieve the MIB objects in the ping control table—those are the parameters used to control the ping operations. There is one table entry for each system that ping requests are directed toward. Some columnar objects contain the parameters needed for pinging, such as the IP address of the system to ping and how often to conduct a ping (the MIB does allow you to set up pings to be performed periodically). In addition, two columnar objects serve as the ping trigger—setting them to certain values causes pings to be executed. The second table, pingResultsTable, is used to record the results. The manager can find out the results of the ping operations by retrieving the corresponding objects.

Figure 8-4   *Pinging Using a MIB*

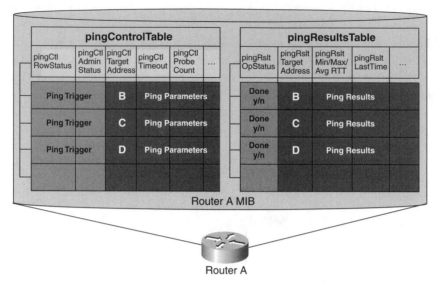

Get-Response

An agent sends a get-response to a manager in response to a request. Contrary to what the name suggests, the responses are not restricted to get requests—there are no separate responses defined for get-next and set requests. Instead, the agent sends a get-response for these as well. A get-response includes the following parameters:

■ The identifier of the request that it contains the response to.

■ An error status that amounts to a response code that indicates whether the request was successful or resulted in an error.

■ An error index that carries further information, in case an error did occur.

■ A list of variable bindings. The variable bindings contain management information that is returned as part of the response. In case of a response to a get request, each variable binding contains the OID and value of a MIB object that was retrieved. The same is true in case of a response to a get-next request—note that the OID in the get-response therefore does not correspond to the OID in the variable binding of the get-next request, which contained an OID that lexicographically preceded the retrieved object's OID. In the case of a response to a set operation, the variable bindings contain the OIDs of the objects that were set and the values they were set to, basically repeating the information of the set request itself.

Trap

A trap is used to convey an event by an agent to a manager. It is unconfirmed—that is, the manager is not expected to send a response back to the agent. The trap includes the following information:

■ **Who is emitting the trap**—Parameters that specify the address of the agent and the type of system that is emitting the trap.

■ **What occurred**—Parameters that identify the type of event.

■ **When it occurred**—A time stamp of when the trap was generated by the emitting system, measured not in absolute time, but in terms of system uptime, or time since the last booting of the system.

■ **Additional information, conveyed in a set of variable bindings**—Those variable bindings contain objects with their OIDs and values that could be of interest to the receiving manager in conjunction with the event that occurred. For example, a trap that indicates that a printer has jammed might include also the location of the printer (if configured in a corresponding MIB object), the identifier of the print job during which the jam occurred, and the user to which the print job belongs. If this information is included with the trap, it saves the manager from needing to issue subsequent get requests. This not only increases management communication efficiency, but it can also improve reaction time.

SNMP Messages and Message Structure

SNMP operations are communicated between managers and agents using SNMP messages. An SNMP message in essence consists of three parts (see Figure 8-5):

■ The SNMP version number.

■ A community string. This string must match a corresponding string that is configured at the device with the SNMP agent for the request to be accepted. In effect, it amounts to a password. Because this password is not encoded but sent in the clear, and because no other form of authentication of the sender takes place, SNMPv1 is considered to have very weak security—an issue discussed in the next section.

■ The SNMP protocol data unit (PDU). This is the encoded SNMP operation itself, including a field that identifies the type of operation along with the operation parameters, as outlined in the previous subsection.

Figure 8-5 *SNMP Message Structure*

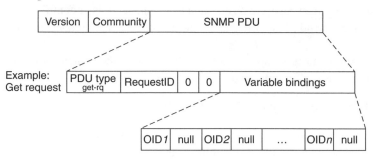

The format of the PDU as well as of the message itself is formally specified in a syntax called ASN.1 (Abstract Syntax Notation 1). ASN.1 is encoded into the string that is sent using a set of basic encoding rules, called BER. ASN.1 and BER are irrelevant to understanding the concept of SNMP, but in case you happen to come across those acronyms, this is where they fit in.

In terms of parlance, the distinction between *SNMP message* and *SNMP PDU* is a bit confusing. In most protocols, the term *PDU* refers to the entire message that is being exchanged. With SNMP, the term *PDU* really refers only to the operation payload that is the most important but not the only part of the overall message.

As mentioned in conjunction with the discussion of the get operation, with SNMP, delivery of messages is ensured only up to a certain size, which is 484 octets, or bytes. Although many implementations support larger messages, not all of them do. Therefore, use of such larger messages poses a risk that implementations will run into interoperability issues. In practice, this limits the amount of information that can be exchanged with each request.

SNMPv2/ SNMPv2c

As SNMPv1 gained widespread support, it turned out that certain aspects about it were perhaps a little too simple. SNMPv1 is notoriously inefficient at retrieving large amounts of management information, knowing no concept of scoping or bulk requests. It offers only minimal security, making it vulnerable to security threats, which effectively prevents SNMPv1 from being used to change the configuration of managed devices—in many cases, the risk of compromising the integrity of the network is simply too great. This has resulted in SNMPv1 being used mainly for monitoring, but not for provisioning applications, even though it originally was intended as a generic protocol to cover the entire breadth of management functions. Other shortcomings involve the expressiveness of the specification language, SMI, and the lack of capabilities such as the creation and deletion of logical entities by management applications in a more straightforward manner.

For those reasons, a second version of SNMP was introduced to address the most pressing limitations: SNMPv2. The most important aspect of SNMPv2 as a protocol was the introduction of two new management operations in addition to those already known from SNMPv1: a get-bulk request and an inform request.

With get-next, the object whose OID immediately follows the OID supplied in the variable binding is returned. But what about the case in which the manager wants not just the next object, but also the ones after that? The get-bulk request addresses this. The get-bulk request operation enables managers to retrieve larger chunks of management information with one request. It works in a way that is similar to a get-next request. However, with a get-bulk request, in addition to a list of variable bindings, the manager provides an additional parameter—the max repetitions parameter. This parameter specifies how many successors should be returned for a given OID. This might not just be 1 (as is implicitly the case with a get-next request), but a number that is greater than that—say, 5. This relieves the manager from needing to separately iterate for each subsequent object.

Consider the earlier table from Figure 8-2. A get-bulk request that includes the OIDs of columns A, B, and C of xyzTable with max-repetitions of 4 results in the entire depicted table to be returned in the get response. As a minor optimization, get-bulk request also introduces a second parameter called non repeaters. This parameter enables the user to exclude the first n objects in the variable bindings from the rule that several successors to those objects, per max-repetitions, will be returned. This means that to those objects, only get-next request semantics are applied.

Note that the same length limitations to SNMP messages still apply, including SNMP messages that carry response PDUs. This means that, for example, it is still not possible to retrieve a MIB or a larger table in one shot because the message size for the resulting response would be easily exceeded. Nevertheless, the fact that iterations are saved in many cases still leads to a significant efficiency improvement.

The second new operation with SNMPv2 is the inform request. This operation amounts to a notification that the recipient needs to confirm—that is, acknowledge. Whereas the trap operation allows the sending of notifications unidirectionally (and unreliably), the inform request provides a mechanism that allows an SNMP agent to send reliable events. Acknowledgment occurs through the same response PDU that is sent in response to any other request.

The implementation of confirmed notifications involves a lot more complexity than with unconfirmed ones. The reason is that now the agent needs to retain a memory of notifications that were emitted and manage what to do in case an acknowledgment is not received—for example, when to retransmit. Simply sending and forgetting notifications is a lot simpler. Accordingly, the inform request is not primarily intended for use between device-based agents and management applications, but rather for communication between management applications when one application temporarily plays the role of an agent.

Of the two operations, the availability of the get-bulk request has had significantly more impact than the inform request. One reason is that although SNMP remains popular as a management protocol supported by network devices, its use as a communication mechanism between management applications—the intended scenario that inform requests were supposed to address—has not caught on.

SNMPv2 brings improvements over SNMPv1 beyond those two operations. It redefines PDU formats so that the same PDU structure can be used for any SNMP operation, including requests and responses. This facilitates the processing of SNMP messages. To take into account that get-response is in no way restricted to responses to get requests, SNMPv2 also renames the get-response operation simply as response. In addition to the protocol improvements, with SNMPv2, SMIv2 was introduced as a MIB specification language, as discussed in Chapter 6.

The architecture of SNMP was devised in a manner that is modular enough that SNMPv2 (and v3) continue to also support SMI-specified MIBs. Even the reverse is (almost) true, so SNMP can be used to manage MIBs that were specified in SMIv2. (The only exceptions involve objects that have a 64-bit representation of an integer or counter, but certain workarounds exist even for these cases.)

SNMPv2 was also supposed to address SNMPv1's security deficits. This aspect, however, is where SNMPv2 ran into significant roadblocks during standardization and falls short. Making a long story short, this led to SNMPv2, for all practical purposes, still being based on community strings, hence also termed SNMPv2c (*c* for "community"). There are also other variations of SNMPv2 than SNMPv2c, but not until SNMPv3 were the security aspects finally addressed for good.

SNMPv3

SNMPv3 is the newest version of SNMP. It can essentially be thought of as SNMPv2c plus security. This means that it retains the same management operations as SNMPv2c, but it introduces alignments to SNMP messages to carry proper security parameters that finally make SNMP a secure protocol. This allows for the encryption of management messages and strong authentication of senders. Thus, SNMPv3 is much less vulnerable to security attacks. Now for the first time, when an agent receives an SNMP request, it can determine with confidence that an authorized manager issued the request and that the message was not tampered with.

In addition to the protocol itself, SNMPv3 has significantly enhanced the scope of what it covers. For example, it now includes a standardized and modularized architecture for SNMP agent implementations. However, these aspects are less relevant for interoperability between SNMP agents and managers and are therefore not discussed here. SNMPv3 does not introduce a new specification language. There is no SMIv3; SMIv2 is still in effect.

So with SNMPv3, finally it becomes feasible to use SNMP for applications that have greater security needs than monitoring, such as provisioning applications. In the meantime, however, management applications have learned to work around SNMP for those purposes and rely on other technologies, such as CLI (see the next section). Whether SNMPv3 will become more widely adopted for purposes other than monitoring remains to be seen.

SNMPv3 has become much more powerful yet also more complex than the original SNMP specification that appeared almost a decade earlier. In part, this reflects greater maturity and also increased agent processing capabilities and availability of more powerful implementation tools. SNMP is a picture-book success of the approach to start with an offering that is initially as simple as possible, to enable widespread adoption, and then to expand carefully later to overcome the most important limitations associated with that simplicity, thus increasing its value further.

CLI: Management Protocol of Broken Dreams

Although SNMP is the best known management protocol, many other interfaces are used as well to manage devices. In the data-networking world, probably none is more important than CLI, which is supported by the vast majority of deployed routers and switches. If you administer a very small network, there is even a chance that this is the only management interface that you will ever use.

CLI Overview

Command-line interface (CLI) was conceived to make it easy for human operators and administrators to interact with networking equipment—in particular, data-networking devices. It is reminiscent of the character-based command-line interfaces used with computer operating systems such as UNIX. This is actually not surprising—at the end of the day, a router is nothing more than a special-purpose computer with a set of networking interfaces and a special-purpose operating system. In fact, the first routers *were* servers running the UNIX operating system. That is how the company Sun Microsystems first started—SUN, after all, is the acronym for Stanford University Network.

Many books on data networking contain sections that tell you how an administrator can configure the discussed features in practice. For example, a book on Multiprotocol Label Switching (MPLS) might feature a section that tells you all about setting up virtual routing functions, MPLS tunnels, and other good stuff, providing you with a set of associated commands that you can simply type into the device through a device console. At the same time, the commands are an excellent way to explain the operability and functionality of different features. These commands—that, for example, a Cisco Certified Internetworking Expert must master—are all examples of CLI commands.

There is no single, standardized CLI. Instead, there are different flavors, which generally differ between vendors and even different operating systems of the same vendor. For example, the CLI on Juniper's operating system, JunOS, is not the same as the CLI on Cisco's Internet Operating

System (IOS). Nevertheless, they all share the same underlying principles that are discussed here. For the examples in this book, we draw on the Cisco IOS CLI.

Because the CLI is intended for human interaction, it offers many features to make such interactions easier:

■ Help functions (typing a ? behind a command to display the list of available command options)

■ Autocompletion (needing to type only the first few characters of a command or option that make it unique, and using the Tab key to tell the system to fill in the rest)

■ Prompts (enabling you to enter different command modes, and reminding you of that mode by the form that the prompt takes)

Example 8-1 shows a typical sequence of commands used to configure an IP address on a Fast Ethernet interface. The part that is displayed to the user is depicted in normal font; the portion that is typed by the user is in bold.

Example 8-1 *Configuration of a Fast Ethernet Interface Using CLI*

```
Router# configure terminal
Enter configuration commands, one per line. End with CNTL/Z.
Router(config)# interface fastethernet 5/4
Router(config-if)# ip address 172.20.52.106 255.255.255.248
Router(config-if)# no shutdown
Router(config-if)# end
Router#
```

A few aspects in the example are worth noting because they are characteristic of the way in which CLI works:

■ After entering the initial command, **configure terminal**, the device displays a small help text. Also, the prompt changes from **Router#** to **Router (config)#**, indicating that the router is now in a different command mode, where it expects a configuration command to be entered.

■ After entering the **interface** command, the prompt changes again, to **Router (config-if)#**. This indicates that it has entered a command submode, where it expects not just any configuration command to be entered, but a configuration for an interface.

■ When all is said and done, the router exits the configuration mode and displays the original prompt. Note that the prompt matters; if the user were now to type **interface fastethernet 5/4** again, the router would most likely not understand the command because it is no longer in configuration submode.

The concept of modes and submodes is an interesting property of CLI. It allows devices to offer a concept of security levels that administrators can easily understand and accept. For example, to change a configuration, the administrator needs to first enter configuration mode, which requires special authorization. The same level of authorization is not required to simply display information. Also, administrators have to type less—once in configuration mode, they don't need to type **configure** again, for example. This makes administrators much more productive.

Let's take a look at another example. Assume that the administrator wants to display the management information (configuration information as well as operational data) for the interface that was configured earlier. For this purpose, the administrator needs to enter a **show** command. In response, the device displays a report with the requested information. Example 8-2 illustrates this.

Example 8-2 *show Management Information for a Fast Ethernet Interface*

```
Router# show interfaces fastethernet 5/4
FastEthernet5/4 is up, line protocol is up
Hardware is CatGK 100Mb Ethernet, address is 0050.f0ac.3058 (bia 0050.f0ac.3058)
Internet address is 172.20.52.106/29
MTU 1500 bytes, BW 100000 Kbit, DLY 100 usec,
reliability 255/255, txload 1/255, rxload 1/255
Encapsulation ARPA, loopback not set
Keepalive set (10 sec)
Full-duplex, 100Mb/s
ARP type: ARPA, ARP Timeout 04:00:00
Last input 00:00:01, output never, output hang never
Last clearing of "show interface" counters never
Queueing strategy: fifo
Output queue 0/40, 0 drops; input queue 0/75, 0 drops
5 minute input rate 0 bits/sec, 0 packets/sec
5 minute output rate 0 bits/sec, 0 packets/sec
7 packets input, 871 bytes, 0 no buffer
Received 0 broadcasts, 0 runts, 0 giants, 0 throttles
0 input errors, 0 CRC, 0 frame, 0 overrun, 0 ignored
0 input packets with dribble condition detected
8 packets output, 1658 bytes, 0 underruns
0 output errors, 0 collisions, 4 interface resets
0 babbles, 0 late collision, 0 deferred
0 lost carrier, 0 no carrier
0 output buffer failures, 0 output buffers swapped out
Router#
```

Again, several aspects are worth noting:

■ Configuration information is referred to in a slightly different form than when it was configured. In the **config** command, the user entered ip address 172.20.52.106; the output here displays "Internet address is 172.20.52.106". Similar, but not the same.

■ The information content on different lines differs: Some lines contain what amounts to one MIB variable (Queuing strategy: fifo); others contain several (Received 0 broadcasts, 0 runts, 0 giants, 0 throttles).

■ Different delimiters are used (a colon [:] for the value of the queuing strategy, nothing in the case of "7 packets input").

An administrator can make perfect sense of the information that is presented. However, the use of different delimiters and text that surrounds the values that are being returned make CLI relatively difficult for scripts and applications to use. The reason is that those applications need to develop custom processing for the responses before they can interpret the results. This is also referred to as screen scraping. We revisit this particular aspect in the next section, "Use of CLI as a Management Protocol."

CLI commands are organized in a hierarchical manner. Commands that perform a similar function are grouped under the same level and same name. For example, this name could be a verb that denotes the type of function, or it could be a noun denoting the subsystem that the command is applied to. You have already encountered this in the examples: The **show** command is really part of a group of commands that display information about different aspects of the device. You could request to **show interfaces** as we did previously, to **show bgp** to display information related to the BGP routing protocol, or to show any of myriad other possibilities. Likewise, **interfaces** is a noun common to many commands. You encountered the **fastethernet** variant, but there are many others—VLAN interfaces, ATM interfaces, ISDN interfaces, and so on.

The hierarchy can be several levels deep. For example, consider another noun, **ip**, for the Internet Protocol. A whole group of commands begins with **show ip**, each dealing with different aspects related to the IP protocol, as in **show ip policy-list**, **show ip ospf**, **show ip rip** (the latter two with further options below them), and so on. Figure 8-6 shows an excerpt of a hierarchy for the **show** command as used on Cisco routers.

Figure 8-6 *CLI **show** Command Hierarchy*

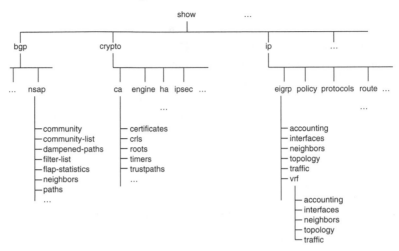

This structure is one of the aspects that makes CLI so easy to use for humans—in essence, it provides for a common syntax structure and enables features such as autocompletion. Having said that, there is no fixed set of CLI commands; it is always possible for a new feature to introduce its own new command and parameters. This is different from a protocol such as SNMP, which has a fixed set of primitives, although, of course, what is represented in MIBs can be arbitrarily extended.

Use of CLI as a Management Protocol

Strictly speaking, CLI is not a management protocol at all. It is a command-line interface, intended for human users who interact with the device directly, not through a management application that abstracts away the details of how the communication with the device takes place. Therefore, it is perhaps a bit unfair to point out some challenges that are associated with CLI related to uses that it was not designed to support. However, management applications are faced with the problem of how to access certain management functionality at the device. In many cases, not all features are covered through SNMP or other management interfaces. This requires applications (as well as operator-defined management scripts, subsumed in our discussion under management applications) to fall back on what is available, which is generally CLI. Therefore, we need to discuss CLI in this context as well.

As mentioned, the main challenge for applications in using CLI is not issuing the CLI commands, but properly interpreting the results that are returned. Humans and electronic applications are wired very differently in the way in which they perceive information. In short, unlike with a traditional management protocol, CLI commands have no common response syntax and no straightforward common grammar that would allow applications to easily process and parse what the device returns. This is particularly true for **show** commands. Different CLI commands introduce their own formats and grammar, resulting in different "screens" that are presented back in response. The application needs to know how to "scrape" the relevant information from that response. There is no common way across all CLI commands, for example, to easily distinguish success and reasons for failure, although obtaining a clear return code is quite important for applications to know whether they need to do any kind of exception handling as a result. In general, there is also no way to derive from a **config** statement what the response to a corresponding **show** command will be; they are not necessarily symmetric, as get and set operations would be in SNMP.

To illustrate the challenges with screen scraping a little further, Example 8-3 presents another **show** command and its output.

Example 8-3   *show Management Information Displayed in Table Format*

```
Router# show cdp neighbors
Capability Codes: R - Router, T - Trans Bridge, B - Source Route Bridge
S - Switch, H - Host, I - IGMP, r - Repeater

Device ID        Local Intrfce   Holdtme   Capability   Platform    Port ID
JAB023807H1      Fas 5/3         127        T S          WS-C2948    2/46
JAB023807H1      Fas 5/2         127        T S          WS-C2948    2/45
JAB023807H1      Fas 5/1         127        T S          WS-C2948    2/44
JAB023807H1      Gig 1/2         122        T S          WS-C2948    2/50
JAB023807H1      Gig 1/1         122        T S          WS-C2948    2/49
JAB03130104      Fas 5/8         167        T S          WS-C4003    2/47
JAB03130104      Fas 5/9         152        T S          WS-C4003    2/48

Router#
```

The format of the information that is returned is completely different from the output of the earlier **show** command! The format essentially resembles a table, complete with column headers and a legend. Thus, individual values or entries in lines within the table do not repeat what they represent—their meaning will be clear to an operator who is visually looking at this as a table. Table entries are delimited not by commas or colons, but merely by blank spaces. The presentation is nicely organized and quite compact and easy for humans to make sense of. It is also an example of the beauty of having **show** commands be flexible in the way in which they present information to humans: In Example 8-3, display of management information as a table works very well; in Example 8-2, that was not the case, and a different display format was chosen.

An application, on the other hand, needs to know in advance that the format in which the information will be presented is different from that of another **show** command, and has to develop custom code to process it. The application sees the information presented in the table of Example 8-3 as a one-dimensional sequence of characters, whereas humans see it in two dimensions. In essence, to an application, the output from the **show response** from Example 8-3 reads as follows (line breaks have been replaced with the <CR> character, tabs with the <TAB> character):

```
Capability Codes: R - Router, T - Trans Bridge, B - Source Route Bridge <CR> S - Switch,
H - Host, I - IGMP, r - Repeater <CR> <CR>Device ID <TAB>Local Intrfce <TAB>Holdtme
<TAB>Capability <TAB>Platform <TAB>Port ID <CR>JAB023807H1 <TAB>Fas 5/3 <TAB>127
<TAB><TAB>T S <TAB><TAB>WS-C2948 <TAB>2/46 <CR>JAB023807H1 <TAB>Fas 5/2 <TAB>127
<TAB><TAB>T S <TAB><TAB>WS-C2948 <TAB>2/45 <CR>JAB023807H1 <TAB>Fas 5/1 <TAB>127
<TAB><TAB>T S <TAB><TAB>WS-C2948 <TAB>2/44 <CR>JAB023807H1 <TAB>Gig 1/2 <TAB>122
<TAB><TAB>T S <TAB><TAB>WS-C2948 <TAB>2/50 <CR>JAB023807H1 <TAB>Gig 1/1 <TAB>122
<TAB><TAB>T S <TAB><TAB>WS-C2948 <TAB>2/49 <CR>JAB03130104 <TAB>Fas 5/8 <TAB>167
<TAB><TAB>T S <TAB><TAB>WS-C4003 <TAB>2/47 <CR>JAB03130104 <TAB>Fas 5/9 <TAB>152
<TAB><TAB>T S <TAB><TAB>WS-C4003 <TAB>2/48 <CR><CR>Router#
```

Different lines contain very different contents. Sometimes what is contained after a <CR> or between <TAB> characters is a value for some parameter; sometimes it is not. Different text elements are not self-explanatory.

If only a few commands need to be supported, it is not a major challenge for developers of management applications to develop custom code for them. On the other hand, there may be hundreds of commands and different response formats, in which case supporting all of them becomes a more significant challenge. And of course, if the format of the output changes in a subsequent release, the application needs to be adapted accordingly. Equipment vendors try to avoid this, but, unfortunately, in reality there are cases where this does happen. For example, someone might decide to introduce an additional line in the column headers, to change the sequence in which two columns are displayed, or perhaps even to introduce a new parameter to display. In this case, the processing of the output has to change, and the affected application logic needs to be at least partly redone. Management applications possibly even need to be able to accept and distinguish between different variations of output for the same command, depending on which device the command is directed at. This is necessary when different devices or even different versions of the same device each introduce slight variations in the format.

Finally, as the name indicates, CLI is all about commands—in other words, management interaction patterns that involve requests and responses. There is another aspect of management communication that CLI does not address and was never intended to, but that is covered in certain management protocols such as SNMP. This aspect, of course, concerns events. Even if operators or management applications wanted to rely solely on CL, they would need to revert to other mechanisms for events if such a capability is needed. One such mechanism is the subject of the next section.

syslog: The CLI Notification Sidekick

syslog (by convention, written in lowercase) originated in the server world—for example, with UNIX hosts. It has become extremely popular as a simple mechanism for managed devices to emit event messages and is today provided by most data communications equipment—routers, switches, and the like.

syslog Overview

As the name indicates, the purpose of syslog is to write system messages to a log—that is, to a file where a system administrator can analyze them as needed. Each syslog message is essentially intended to result in an entry in that log. However, by posing as a logging host, management applications can often receive messages directly as they occur, without needing to take the detour of retrieving log entries from a log file.

Many network devices are extremely chatty when it comes to syslog and constantly generate syslog messages for all kinds of stuff. syslog messages can include everything from critical alarm conditions that are encountered to mundane debugging statements that are issued when processing passes a certain line in the code. Basically, while operating, a router constantly mumbles statements such as, "I think I may have just dropped the tenth packet in a row," "I'm experiencing good utilization on my link," "Look, I'm currently in this new branch of code," or "Strange— someone just tried to log into me a hundred different times, trying a different password each time." It is not unlike a person at work speaking to himself all day, uttering all kinds of statements that range from the mundane to the important, whether the coworkers are interested or not: "Nice weather today," "The statement sent from accounting looks off by $10,000," "I think I need to go to the bathroom," "Hmm, seems like the building is on fire."

The resulting log entries provide a general trail of the activity of the device. As such, many syslog messages that are generated might never be of any practical use. However, under certain circumstances, the capability to retrace much of the device's activity trail using those logs can be invaluable. Usually this is the case when there is some kind of trouble, such as services degrading severely, suspected network break-ins, or unexplainable erratic network behavior, but also when particular network deployments need to be debugged or fine-tuned. In the end, any particular application needs to decide for itself which messages it is interested in and which it can afford to ignore.

As with CLI, syslog messages are designed to be human readable. And as with CLI, syslog was never intended as a management protocol. However, as with CLI, people eventually started using it as one. syslog is essentially the ideal natural complement to CLI. It provides the capability for the device to emit event messages without solicitation, which complements the request/response pattern of CLI. And just as CLI often offers the only way to make certain management requests, syslog is often the only way available to obtain messages about certain events.

In many cases, syslog messages constitute little more than a "print" statement in the code, which is intended to be used and interpreted by an administrator looking at the messages in a log file. This means that syslog shares some of the same weaknesses as CLI when it comes to automatic processing by applications. These weaknesses involve the difficulty to parse messages that lack structure and are originally intended primarily for humans, not applications.

syslog messages have two parts, a message header and the message body. The message body contains the content of the message itself. It is the "informal" part of a syslog message, not subjected to any inherent constraints. In many cases, it simply contains plain English text. The message body is prefixed with a message header. The message header contains minimal but essential information about the message itself in a very structured manner. This information includes the time when the message was emitted, the name of the host that emitted the message, the severity of the message (anything from alert to debug), the subsystem that emitted the message (often referred to as facility), and a so-called mnemonic (that is, a name for the type of message). These information fields constitute the least common denominator of information that should be present in every event message. This information might not be much, but it is enough to make syslog messages fairly accessible to applications in addition to humans.

Here is an example of a syslog message:

```
172.19.209.130  000024: *Apr 12 18:01:55.643: % ENV_MON-1-SHUTDOWN: Environmental
Monitor initiated shutdown
```

This message indicates that a shutdown of the device was initiated by an environmental sensor (perhaps the device was getting too hot). The originator is a device with IP address 172.19.209.130. 000024 is a sequence number. The message was generated on April 12, 18:01:55.643 local time. The facility emitting the alarm is ENV_MON, the severity is 1, and the mnemonic is SHUTDOWN. The message components up to the colon after ENV MON-1-SHUTDOWN are all part of the message header. The rest of the message is part of the message body.

Here is another example:

```
01:14:11: %IPPHONE 6 REG_ALARM: 25: Name=SEP003094C38724 Load-3.2(2.9)
Last=Initialized
```

The second syslog message has a slightly different format than the first one. This illustrates the fact that syslog messages do not adhere to one common and standardized format. For example, the message in the example here does not include the originator's IP address. Including this IP address as part of the message is not required in many cases and provides nothing more than an added convenience: For one, many managed devices log syslog messages in a log file at the device itself. In that case, the application that retrieves the log file knows what device it retrieves the file from. The application therefore does not require the IP address, which identifies the device, to be also included in the syslog messages themselves. In addition, even if the receiver of syslog messages is a remote management application, the receiver will be capable of inferring where the syslog message originated. This is done by exploiting the fact that syslog messages are generally transported over the User Datagram Protocol (UDP), and UDP datagrams already contain the originator's IP address. Some cases require special consideration, such as when Network Address Translation occurs. In that case, one IP address is effectively substituted for another in transit, but this is a rare scenario that we do not concern ourselves with here.

There are other ways in which the format of the syslog message in the second example differs from the one in the first. For example, the second message contains a sequence number (25 in the example) in a different position than the first message. There is also a variation in the format that is used to represent time. Finally, the message body text in the second example appears a little cryptic for human users and is probably intended for an application that knows how to interpret syslog messages that originate from facility IPPHONE and have a mnemonic of REG_ALARM.

The fact that there is not one fixed format of syslog messages has triggered standardization in this area, as discussed in the following subsection.

syslog Protocol

For a long time, there was no true standard that syslog messages had to follow. As mentioned, syslog originated from messages that were logged by the UNIX operating system. However, syslog has been treated just as a loose recommendation and was never rigorously specified as a standard. Consequently, over time, different variations of syslog message formats proliferated across different vendors and device types. For example, they differed on details such as the precise format that is used to represent time—mm-dd-yyyy, or dd:mm:yyyy, or yyyymmdd. Also, in some cases, messages contain additional extensions that are present in some formats but not in others; a popular example involves numbering of messages.

In light of this situation, the IETF is in the process of passing a particular version of syslog as a standard, which is simply called the syslog protocol. It might seem odd that one of the oldest management message formats around is also one of the most recent to get standardized. In some ways, it feels like hearing that a couple that you have known for many years and that has been living together for all this time without being married seemingly out of the blue decides to finally tie the knot. The IETF syslog protocol is just one of many syslog variations, but because this particular one has a good chance of becoming a dominant syslog format going forward, we use the current draft as an example to explore the different fields that a syslog message can contain.

According to this IETF syslog protocol, a syslog message consists of a header part, an optional structured data part, and a message part (see Figure 8-7).

Figure 8-7   *syslog Message Structure According to IETF*

Header							Structured Data			Message
Priority (facility*3+ severity)	Version	Time stamp	Host name	App name	ProcId	Message ID	SDE1	...	SDEn	Message

ID	param name	value

The header part includes the following fields:

- The priority is a combination of a facility and a severity. The facility allows categorization of a message according to some criteria (for example, kernel message) and is given a numeric code. The severity is a number from 0 to 7, with 0 being the most severe and 7 being the least severe. The priority is formed by multiplying the numeric code of the facility by 8 and adding the severity to it. For example, a syslog message with facility 7 and severity 3 has a priority of 59 ($7 \times 8 + 3$). The reason for this apparently strange scheme has to do with backward compatibility of the syslog protocol with existing implementations.

- The version number of the syslog protocol.

- The time stamp, according to a well-defined format.

- The host name, identifying the system from which the syslog message originates. The identifier should be the so-called fully qualified domain name, but other identifiers, such as the static IP address of the host, also can be used.

- The application name and the process ID, which identify the subsystem and process that are responsible for emitting the message.

- Finally, the message ID, an identifier of the type of syslog message.

The structured data part is optional but is perhaps the most interesting part of the protocol. It allows the syslog message format to be extensible to a certain degree and to carry additional parameters that are formally defined. This obviates the need to put the corresponding information into the body part of the message, which is still free format—anything goes.

Structured data is contained in a set of fields, called structured data elements (SDEs). SDEs are optional; there can be none, one, or several of them. Each SDE contains a label that identifies the SDE, followed by a set of name-value pairs (again, none, one, or several of them), each containing the name of a parameter and its corresponding value. The meaning of those parameters is specific to the structured data element.

By introducing proprietary structured data elements, anyone can define their own syslog protocol extensions. For example, a vendor might introduce an SDE that identifies the configuration version currently on the device at the time the syslog message is generated. If a recipient is familiar with the data element as defined by the label, it can interpret the data that it carries and take advantage of it. If not, the recipient can ignore it and should still be able to make sense of the rest of the message—it cannot take advantage of the added value provided by the SDE, but otherwise no harm is done.

Compare this with the scenario in which a product has a bar code printed on the box. The bar code contains certain information that makes perfect sense for its intended application but probably not to you, the consumer. However, you will still be able to understand the rest of what the package says.

Finally, the message part consists of the message itself. It is still free format and does not require, for example, an underlying formally defined management information model. Of course, vendors can follow their own proprietary conventions of what to put in the message, but basically, anything goes.

Here is an example of a syslog message that is IETF syslog protocol compliant:

```
<35>1 2006-06-11T22:14:15.003Z mymachine.example.com su - ID58 - 'su root' failed
for wbuchhau on /dev/pts/8
```

The facility of the message has a value of 4; the severity is 3 (because $35 = 4 \times 8 + 3$). The version of the syslog protocol is 1. The message was created on 11 June 2006 at 10:14:15pm UTC (in essence, Greenwich Mean Time), 3 milliseconds into the next second. The message originated from a host that identifies itself as mymachine.example.com, from an application or subsystem named su. The process ID is unknown; the identifier of the type of message is ID58. There is no structured data, as indicated by the - in the Structured Data field. Finally, the message itself is "'su root' failed for wbuchhau...".

The final example is taken from the specification and includes some structured data. The structured data element is called exampleSDID@0, and it includes three parameters, called iut, eventSource, and eventID.

```
<165>1 2003-10-11T22:14:15.003Z mymachine.example.com evntslog - ID47
[exampleSDID@0 iut="3" eventSource="Application" eventID="1011"] An application
event log entry...
```

syslog Deployment

Two roles are distinguished with respect to the systems that are involved in the exchange of syslog messages: The syslog *sender* sends the syslog messages. The syslog *receiver* is the recipient of syslog messages. Generally, syslog sender and receiver correspond to management agent and manager, respectively. However, syslog receivers often have no role in actively managing a device. In fact, in many cases, the receiver resides in the device itself. The syslog receiver is simply the receiving end of a syslog message that is generally responsible for logging the message to a file on a disk.

A syslog receiver can accordingly be

■ The device itself, writing the messages that it generates to a local log file. This log file can be viewed by system administrators or, for example, transferred as a file via the File Transfer Protocol to an external management application when desired.

In most cases, devices have limited storage. To avoid overflowing the local file system, devices often put mechanisms such as the following in place:

— A log file has a certain maximum size. When the end of the file is reached, logging of subsequent messages starts again from the beginning, overwriting the oldest previous messages. The file can be accompanied with a pointer that points to the line with the most current entry. This mechanism is also called a *circular log file* (see Figure 8-8).

Figure 8-8 *Circular Log File*

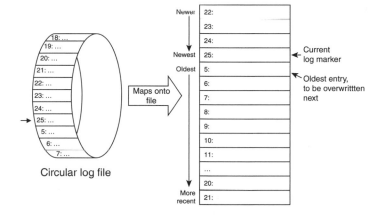

— Log files are created with a certain capacity—for example, one file per day, named according to the calendar date, or one file per 1000 entries, numbered sequentially. When the allocated log file capacity is reached, the oldest file is purged from the system.

■ A centralized logging host, receiving messages from several devices and logging those messages for them. Applications access this logging host instead of individual devices to access the log records (see Figure 8-9). This can reduce load on the network devices. An external host typically also has greater storage space and can be centrally backed up, facilitating the overall management task. Applications and system administrators turn to the logging host instead of the devices themselves to retrieve any particular logs.

Figure 8-9 *Logging Host*

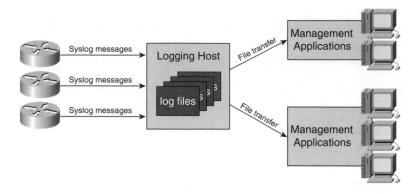

A centralized logging host often also functions as a syslog *relay*. A syslog relay receives syslog messages on one end and sends them to another receiver on the other end—it is a proxy. This means that, in addition to logging syslog messages, it forwards those messages on to various applications. In doing so, it possibly applies a filter so that they each receive only messages that are of interest to them (see Figure 8-10). We discuss management proxies and other ways to organize management deployments in Chapter 9, "Management Organization: Dividing the Labor."

Figure 8-10 *syslog Relay*

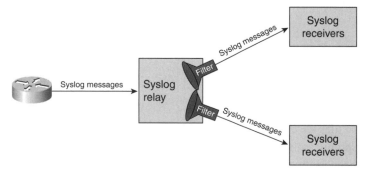

- A management application, receiving syslog messages for processing. Here, the receiver is finally truly a manager, which treats syslog as a management communications channel for events. In many cases, the manager does not just log the messages, but processes and acts on them as they occur. In many cases, management applications are deployed so that they receive syslog messages through a relay, not from the device directly. This is specifically the case when multiple applications should receive messages so that no additional load is put on the managed devices to send multiple copies of the same message to different recipients.

Netconf: A Management Protocol for a New Generation

The management protocols that we have discussed so far have all been around for more than a decade, predating the rise of the World Wide Web and web technologies such as the Extensible Markup Language (XML). A decade, in the Internet age, is considered a very, very long time—so long, in fact, that those management protocols are sometimes considered legacy technologies. This means that they are proven and have withstood the test of time, yet they might be showing signs of age because they do not take advantage of technology that was invented later.

With this in mind, we turn to some newer management protocols that promise to be more than just new fads that will fade as quickly as they appeared (and there have been plenty of those); they seem destined to make their mark.

Netconf is one such management protocol. It is geared specifically toward managing the configuration of data-networking devices. Currently, at least, it is not targeted at monitoring functions and managing state information—the assumption is that another protocol such as SNMP will be around to handle those aspects. This means that the scope is a little more limited and focused, compared to more general-purpose protocols. As explained in Chapter 6, there are significant differences among different types of management information and how they are used. Netconf, currently under standardization by the IETF, takes this into account.

The fact that Netconf is designed for device configuration does not mean that it could not be used or expanded for other purposes. In fact, it already allows for the retrieval of state information, although this does not constitute a central capability. Support for events is another area that has long been under discussion. For now, however, Netconf is best positioned in the configuration management space, where it can fill the void left by SNMP, as explained earlier, and by CLI, which is geared more to human users but is not easily accessible to management applications.

Netconf Datastores

Netconf picks up on the notion that the configuration information of devices can be thought of and handled as being contained in a datastore (one word, per the Netconf spelling) that can be handled like a file. In essence, a configuration datastore corresponds to a device's config file—the set of configuration statements that need to be executed to bring the device into its desired configuration state.

As a protocol, Netconf provides the operations that are necessary to manage those datastores. For example, Netconf offers operations that allow a manager to change the contents of what a particular datastore contains (that is, edit the configuration). It can also retrieve the contents of a datastore from or deliver them to the device. The datastore, of course, resembles a MIB. However, in contrast to SNMP, which offers management operations that target the individual managed objects inside the MIB, the management operations of Netconf essentially target the MIB as a whole, or portions thereof.

Netconf allows management data inside a configuration datastore to be organized in a hierarchical, treelike fashion that defines different scopes, as the example in Figure 8-11 illustrates. Management information that logically belongs together can be grouped into a "container within the container." This makes it more easily accessible to applications. The handling of datastores is facilitated because they do not always have to be manipulated in their entirety; they can be dealt with one part at a time. For example, the overall configuration of a device can be divided into multiple subconfigurations, for different cards, subsystems, and so on. The device configuration contains the configuration for a card, which partly contains the configuration for a port, which, in turn, contains the configuration for an interface. Logical subsystems such as BGP and voice gateway capabilities also can be contained in their own separate subconfigurations within the overall configuration. Hence, the overall configuration is organized in a hierarchical, treelike manner.

Figure 8-11 *A Hierarchical Datastore in Netconf*

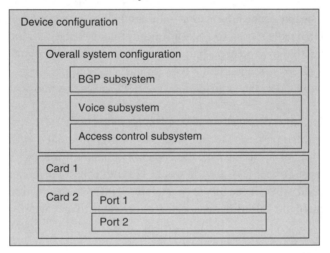

With this organization, management operations can be applied to individual subtrees, corresponding to the different subconfigurations, instead of the configuration information in its entirety. For example, a user can apply a Netconf operation to the overall device configuration, or can specify that it should be applied only to the configuration of a particular card or subsystem, assuming that the configuration information is organized accordingly. This capability is part of a feature that is referred to as *subtree filtering*.

What is precisely contained in the datastores is outside the current scope of the Netconf specification. For example, Netconf does not have a notion of which parameter settings or configuration statements are valid for a particular type of device, or even the specification language in which they need to be specified. Netconf does not have a specific notion of a MIB specification language—an important difference, for example, to SNMP. All that Netconf provides are the wrappers for this management information. In fact, to be exact, it does not even provide the wrappers, but it does provide the facilities to navigate a datastore in which such wrappers are defined using an XML structure, as explained in the next section. Inside those wrappers can be whatever models the device supports. This could be the device's CLI, a proprietary model, or perhaps be a model that will be standardized later. If your management information can be organized in a hierarchical fashion, Netconf enables you to wrap the different pieces individually and manage them separately, not unlike a cookie jar containing individually wrapped cookies.

Netconf and XML

One of the distinctive features of Netconf is the fact that it uses XML as encoding for its management operations. XML is a cornerstone of web technology; it is a language that allows for the representation of information in a structured way. Obviously, a discussion of XML goes way beyond the scope of this book; there is a rich set of literature for the interested reader. We just briefly discuss some of the most fundamental aspects as far as they are relevant for the remainder of the discussion.

XML documents contain so-called *tags* that are used to delimit different pieces of information within the document. Tags are defined by users, who can associate different tags with different semantics. For example, the information of an administrator's e-mail address could be captured in an e-mail tag. In an XML document, the e-mail address could then be represented something like this:

```
<email>alex@cisco.com</email>
```

<email> and </email> are the opening and closing brackets that contain the data element associated with the email tag. An XML document consists of many lines of such tagged information. The tags themselves and the semantics associated with them are not part of XML; they are defined by users or by protocols such as Netconf.

XML provides the means to specify such tags. It also provides the means for users to define what amounts to templates for XML documents, and defines how documents that supposedly follow such a template need to be processed. Those templates specify the structure for an XML document and which XML tags a particular type of XML document must or may contain. One particular type of template definition mechanism (itself also defined in XML) is called XML Schema Definition, or XSD.

The information that goes into an XML document can be pretty much anything: a page that is to be rendered on a web browser, a record with customer information used by a business application, or, as in this case, information about management operations. When information is encoded in XML, it results in an XML document. This means that in Netconf, every management operation—every request and every response—is encoded as an XML document that is passed between manager and agent. This document contains the information on what operation is requested, what the operation parameters are, and the contents of the datastore that is carried as part of the request. Netconf defines the needed tags along with the templates for the documents that correspond to the various operations or messages.

In addition, the configuration information inside a datastore is itself encoded in XML. Netconf assumes that the datastore will contain tags that divide the configuration information into different portions that should ideally be arranged in a hierarchical, treelike structure. Netconf does not define the tags themselves, but provides support in its operations to navigate the configuration information structure that results—this is exactly what subtree filtering is about.

We take a look at what an XML document in Netconf looks like at the end of the next section. To be able to better comprehend what the document contains, we first turn to the Netconf architecture.

Netconf Architecture

Netconf is built around an architecture that acknowledges the fact that management communication involves multiple layers. It distinguishes between the following layers that are also depicted in Figure 8-12 and that largely reflect what we discussed in the previous chapter.

Figure 8-12 *Netconf Architecture*

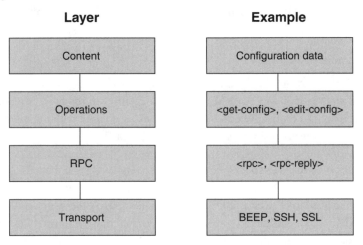

- The transport protocol layer provides for the underlying communication transport. Different transports are possible and can be used—for example, Secure Shell (SSH) and Block Extensible Exchange Protocol (BEEP). Those protocols are specified elsewhere and are not specific to management. What Netconf does is specify the requirements that a protocol must meet so that it can be used. (It also specifies bindings for a few transports, including the ones mentioned.)

For example, the transport must provide support for authentication. This allows manager and agent to ascertain that the other side is indeed who it claims to be. Obviously, this is an important security property—if your device is asked to change its configuration, you want it to be sure that the request came from the authorized manager, not from an intruder. Upper Netconf layers do not provide this function. Therefore, for this and some other functions, Netconf relies on the protocol that Netconf messages are transported over.

- The RPC layer provides primitives that enable managers to invoke functions on agents, using a request-response pattern. The primitives that Netconf provides are, accordingly, RPC and RPC reply. RPC alludes to a remote-procedure call—that is, a management request. RPC reply is the response to that call. The response can include an indication of success and be accompanied with additional information, or it can be an error response. The operations of the operations layer are wrapped into those RPC elements.

- The operations layer contains the guts of the Netconf protocol—that is, the management operations themselves. This includes everything from managing the management association itself to operations to manipulate and push around configuration files. We discuss the details of the operations layer in the next section.

- The content layer deals with the management payload—specifically, the configuration data that is contained in the configuration files that are subjected to the Netconf operations. What this data is and how it is represented is actually outside the scope of the Netconf specification; Netconf stipulates only that some such content needs to be provided.

Eventually, a dedicated management information specification language and data models might be standardized for use with Netconf, but this is not the case today. Having said that, Netconf does make the assumption that management information can be transported as part of an XML document. After all, Netconf operations are encoded as XML documents and require management information to be exchanged between managers and agents. Management information must therefore be "XML-ized."

Of course, XML-ized data can take many different forms. It can be represented in a sophisticated XML document in which every parameter and attribute is represented through its own standardized tag. On the other hand, it can simply consist of a set of XML tags that are used to delimit a configuration file in its entirety. Although this conforms in letter, it violates the spirit of Netconf. In some ways, it is reminiscent of the old joke of the man (perhaps one of the blind men from the earlier story) who wanted to take an elephant across the border (see Figure 8-13). Of course, Customs did not allow it and sent him back. Undeterred, the man decided to get two pieces of toast, spread butter on them, and stick one on the elephant's belly, the other on the elephant's backside. When he came back to the border, Customs tried to send him back again, but he objected: "Of course, I wouldn't try to take an elephant with me, but a sandwich can't be forbidden!"

Figure 8-13 *The CLI Blob Elephant and the XML Sandwich*

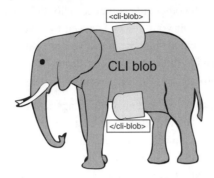

In most typical implementations, the Netconf payload data at the minimum takes a form in which individual CLI statements are delimited by XML tags. In addition, CLI statements that belong to different subsystems are grouped to delimit different configuration subtrees. This particular aspect is revisited in the next section, "Netconf Operations."

Figure 8-14 depicts the structure of a Netconf message. You can see how management content in the message is encapsulated by Netconf operations and their parameters, which, in turn, are encapsulated in an RPC wrapper, which, in turn, is put on a transport in the application protocol layer.

Figure 8-14 *Netconf Message Structure*

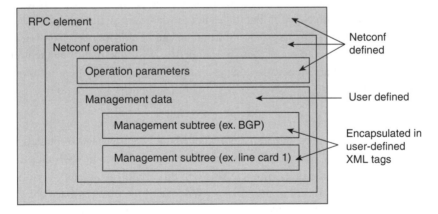

Example 8-4 provides a taste of what an XML document representing a Netconf request looks like.

Example 8-4 *A Netconf Request*

```
<rpc message-id="101"
      xmlns="urn:ietf:params:xml:ns:netconf:base:1.0">
   <get-config>
     <source>
       <running/>
     </source>
     <filter type="subtree">
       <top xmlns="http://example.com/schema/1.2/config">
         <bgp/>
       </top>
     </filter>
   </get-config>
 </rpc>
```

The RPC tags (<rpc message-id = "101" ..> and </rpc>) provide the RPC opening and closing brackets that frame the overall message. The Netconf operation here is **get-config**, again enclosing the rest of the message in the corresponding tags (<get-config> being the opening, "</get-config>" the closing bracket). Two parameters are provided with the request: the **<source>** specifies the config being requested (in this case, the running config), whereas the **<filter>** specifies the subtree within the config being requested (everything in the config belonging to bgp).

Example 8-5 shows a reply to the request.

Example 8-5 *A Netconf Reply*

```
<rpc-reply message-id="101"
     xmlns="urn:ietf:params:xml:ns:netconf:base:1.0">
  <data>
    <top xmlns="http://example.com/schema/1.2/config">
      <bgp>
        chunk of BGP data
      </bgp>
    </top>
  </data>
</rpc-reply>
```

Netconf Operations

At this point, we can finally turn toward the guts of Netconf, the operations layer. As mentioned, Netconf is built around the notion that management information in general, and specifically configuration information, can be thought of as being contained in a conceptual datastore. In the case of configuration information, this datastore is a configuration file, in short referred to as "config." Not coincidentally, this resembles how things are handled using CLI on a router.

Different examples of config datastores exist (not all are supported on all devices): The running config contains the configuration that is currently in effect at the device. Strictly speaking, it might not even be persisted as a file; it is just the collection of configuration settings that are in effect at the device, some of which might have been caused by an administrator entering commands through the CLI. The startup config, on the other hand, is persisted. It contains the configuration settings that will take effect if the managed device must be rebooted. In addition, other files might contain a configuration as well. For example, a given configuration might be saved as a backup that a device can revert to if needed. Another example is a configuration file that is constructed by a provisioning application and that contains the configuration for a particular service. The provisioning will want to upload this "canned" configuration to the device when the service needs to be turned on. Closely related to this is the concept of a candidate config, a file that a management application uses to prepare a new configuration that is intended to replace another configuration when ready.

Netconf offers the following management operations:

- **get-config** is used to retrieve a config file from the device. It takes as a parameter the source of the config—that is, the config file to be retrieved. The default is the running config. Other configurations can be targeted as well, such as the startup config or a file with a different version of a configuration, if such a capability is supported by the device. A second parameter allows specification if the entire config, or merely a subtree, is to be retrieved. It provides a corresponding filter expression that is applied to the XML document in which the configuration information is represented.

- **get** is a generalization of **get-config**. It is the only Netconf operation that goes beyond configuration information and allows the retrieval of state information as well; this is basically any information that would be returned by a CLI **show** command.

- **edit-config** is used to modify and change a configuration—that is, the contents of a configuration datastore. Again, the parameters are the config that is to be changed, an indication of whether the entire config or a specific subtree is affected, and the new configuration data that is to be added. In addition, a qualifier provides a choice of several editing variations: For example, an existing configuration (or portion thereof, as specified by the subtree) simply is replaced by a new chunk of configuration. Alternatively, the existing contents must be merged with some additional configuration statements.

    Note that in case the running config is targeted, editing the config also implies that the changes are actually applied to the device—they result in management commands being executed. This raises questions such as what to do when one of the commands is syntactically invalid or if it fails for some other reasons. Should the Netconf agent stop at the first invalid command it encounters, should it attempt to execute the rest of the commands, or should it attempt to "roll back" and undo the effects of the first commands that were successful? Can the agent be asked to validate a configuration before applying it? Therefore, Netconf provides additional options that enable the manager to specify the desired behavior when the operation is invoked.

Some options involve functionality that all devices might not support. One example is the capability to perform a syntax check before accepting a config datastore. Another example involves the capability to perform a rollback on a partial failure. Netconf therefore permits such capabilities to be optional. At the beginning of a Netconf session, a system advertises which of those capabilities it supports and allows the other system to invoke.

- **copy-config** is also used to change a configuration. It is thus similar to **edit-config**. However, unlike with **edit-config**, the change is not made within a configuration; the configuration target is replaced in its entirety. The parameters are the source configuration that contains the new configuration, the target configuration that is to be replaced, the specification of a subtree filter (if applicable), and any options that qualify the behavior that is expected during execution of the new commands in case the target config is the running config, as described under **edit-config**.

- **delete-config** does just that—it removes a configuration from a device. Of course, the running config cannot be deleted.

- **Lock** and **unlock** enable a manager to request exclusive access to a configuration. While a manager holds a lock, other users are not allowed to change the configuration. This includes other Netconf sessions, as well as CLI sessions or any other management interface. This capability is important to support transactions on the device and avoid scenarios in which another user or an application inadvertently interferes with a set of changes that are in progress.

In addition to those management operations, Netconf offers two operations to terminate a Netconf session: **close session** is the graceful variant that allows operations that are already in progress to end before the session is torn down, whereas **kill-session** aborts the session abruptly.

So how is a Netconf session opened? The Netconf manager (the client, in Netconf parlance) and the Netconf agent (the server, in Netconf parlance) do what most people do when they first meet: They say hello. At the beginning of a Netconf session, each system sends a "hello" message. While they are at it, they use the opportunity to introduce themselves, specifically to tell the other side about any of the additional capabilities that they support and that go beyond the minimum capabilities that are required by the protocol. This is called the capabilities exchange. In essence, it sets the expectation of to what functionality and options the peer can leverage in management exchanges. Quite a few optional capabilities are defined, including the previously mentioned capability to perform a validation on a configuration and to perform a rollback on error.

Netflow and IPFIX: "Check, Please," or, All the Data, All the Time

Finally, we turn to a management protocol that is specialized and optimized for one very particular purpose. The protocol in question is Netflow. A very similar protocol, called IPFIX (IP Flow Information Export, pronounced "I.P.fix") has the same technical goals and is currently under development by the IETF standards organization. We focus our discussion on Netflow because it has a wide deployed base today, but you will find that the discussion carries directly over to IPFIX.

Netflow was first introduced by Cisco and is geared toward collecting data about networking traffic from a device. You can use this data to answer questions such as the following:

- Who are the top "talkers" in the network?

- How much traffic is being exchanged between two destinations?

- How are links in the network being used?

- Where are the traffic bottlenecks in the network?

In theory, the collection of such data could also be attempted through a more general-purpose management protocol. However, a big challenge is posed by the fact that large volumes of information need to be collected and transferred. Because Netflow and IPFIX are specialized for this particular application, they incur less overhead and are more efficient than other management protocols that have to serve other purposes as well.

IP Flows

Netflow communicates statistical information about IP-based data traffic that "flows" over a router. The statistics are provided on a per-flow basis. A flow consists of all traffic that belongs to the same communication context, basically IP data packets that belong to the same "connection." Of course, IP is completely packet based and has no notion of a connection—that is its whole point. However, chances are, applications that communicate with each other using IP will exchange in general more than one packet when they start communicating, as Figure 8-15 illustrates.

Figure 8-15 *IP Traffic Flowing over a Router*

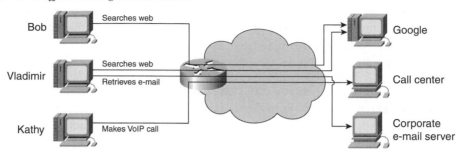

For example, a file-transfer application breaks up the file that is to be transferred into many individual packets. All the packets belong to the same transfer and need to be delivered over the network, and all might "flow" over the same router. The same is true for an image that is transferred for viewing a web page, or for a Voice over IP conversation carried out between two users. Therefore, if a router sees one packet coming from and going to a certain direction, chances are, there will be others. This is what is meant by a flow. Of course, in some cases a flow will indeed consist of only a single packet, but typically there is more than one packet to a flow.

A flow is uniquely identified by the following pieces of information (in database parlance, they would be considered keys):

- Source address

- Source port

- Destination address

- Destination port

- Protocol type (for example, whether the IP packet carries TCP or UDP)

- Type of Service (TOS) byte (a byte in IP that identifies the type of service, used to differentiate different categories of traffic)

- Input logical interface (identified by the same index that is used for the interface in SNMP MIBs; this is needed because, in addition to the source address and port, in the case of private networks with private IP address spaces, the other pieces of information might not be unique to one flow).

Data that is collected for each flow constitutes a flow record. It includes the keys that identify the flow, as well as the time when the flow started, when it stopped, and how many packets were transported as part of the flow. This data is extremely useful for management applications that offer accounting and performance management functionality in several ways:

- Knowing how much traffic of what type was sent at what time from where to where allows network managers to account for detailed network use by individual users. This is important if a network provider wants to charge based on actual traffic consumption instead of charging simply a flat access fee.

  Of course, as traffic flows across multiple routers, the network provider must be sure to avoid double-counting the same traffic on multiple counters. This can be ensured by correlating flow records that are collected on multiple routers, or by taking into account only the flow records generated by the access router through which a particular user is known to connect to the rest of the network.

- It provides a wealth of data for traffic analysis, bottleneck, and network planning.

- It can provide an invaluable tool to spot and defend against attacks on a network that carry certain characteristics in terms of the traffic patterns they generate.

Netflow Protocol

On an individual router, with traffic coming from and going to all kinds of different directions, at any point in time there may be tens of thousands of flows in progress, depending on the router's capacity. This obviously leads to a huge volume of flow data that needs to be collected and transferred. At the same time, the data is extremely uniform—basically, it is the same data that is of interest for each flow. Hence, there is only one type of "record" to be transferred. This observation is what motivated the introduction of a dedicated special-purpose protocol rather than attempting to use a more general mechanism such as SNMP or syslog. This protocol simply consists of putting flow records into Netflow packets and exporting those packets to a recipient. The recipient of Netflow packets is commonly referred to as a *Netflow collector*. Similar to a logging host for syslog, the task of the Netflow collector is to store the data that is spewed out by the routers at a very high rate and make that data available to the number-crunching applications.

Figure 8-16 roughly illustrates how a Netflow packet is structured. It consists of the following elements:

Figure 8-16 *Netflow Packet Structure*

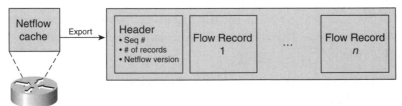

- A header contains bookkeeping information:

  — The sequence number of the packet, for storing packets that are received in the proper order and determining whether any data is missing

  — The number of flow records contained in the Netflow packet

  — The version number of the Netflow protocol itself

- The header is followed by a sequence of flow records. Each flow record includes the keys that identify the flow, as well as the statistical data collected for it.

Now, how is a flow managed inside the router? When a packet with a new combination of the seven keys (source and destination IP addresses and ports, TOS byte, protocol type, and input logical interface) is detected, a new flow is entered into a special store on the device, called the Netflow cache. In this cache, data about the flow is maintained. For example, a packet counter is incremented as packets belonging to that flow go by. Incidentally, the data in the cache is used for other purposes. Specifically, it facilitates the routing decision for packets on the flow: Simplistically, the router sends subsequent packets that belong to the same flow in the same direction as the earlier ones, without needing to make more complex individual routing decisions for each packet.

When the router determines that the flow has ended, the corresponding entry in the Netflow cache expires. This means that the information about the flow is flushed from the cache and a flow record is prepared for transmission using the Netflow protocol. A flow is considered ended in these circumstances:

- No traffic has been detected on a flow for a certain time interval (typically 15 seconds, but ideally configurable).

- A packet is detected at the application-protocol level that indicates that the data transfer supported by the flow has completed (for example, in case of a TCP connection, this is indicated through TCP FIN or RST packets, two special kinds of packets that are part of the TCP protocol).

- If a flow has been going on for a long time (typically 30 minutes, but, again, ideally configurable), eventually the router simply declares the flow ended and starts a new one. Otherwise, it would be impossible for the Netflow collector to be informed of the flow, even though it might represent a significant amount of traffic over the network. Using a telephone analogy, this would be like talking to someone overseas for months without ever putting the phone back on the hook and, therefore, if an accounting record were generated only upon completion of the call, never receiving a bill for it!

Finally, it needs to be mentioned that, as with SNMP, several versions of Netflow exist:

- Netflow v5 is the version most commonly used today. It has all the capabilities that were discussed here.

- Netflow v7 is geared to switches, not routers.

- Netflow v8 offers an aggregation capability. This allows it to be configured on a router so that it combines the data from several flows into one record—for example, summing up all traffic from one source, regardless of the destination. This reduces the volume of Netflow data being exported and makes collection easier.

- Netflow v9 is the newest version. It allows the records that are exported to be customized using a greater selection of different statistics that can be collected. The record format that is being exported from the device is defined using a special template. The protocol is enhanced to allow for transmission of that template in addition to the flow records themselves, so that Netflow sender and receiver are always in synch on what the data that is being exported actually represents.

Finally, as mentioned in the beginning, the IETF standards organization is in the process of standardizing a protocol with the same goal as Netflow, called IPFIX. In fact, the possibility exists that IPFIX will end up looking remarkably similar to Netflow v9. From a technical perspective, the goal and general principles are virtually the same. The more important difference is political, in that IPFIX will be endorsed by an open-standards organization, whereas Netflow constitutes a de-facto standard with a large installed base but whose specification is owned by a company.

Chapter Summary

In this chapter, we took a closer look at some of the most important management protocols. Management protocols are languages that are spoken between managers and agents.

SNMP, the Simple Network Management Protocol, is perhaps the best-known management protocol. It is today widely deployed and the management protocol of choice, particularly for monitoring applications. SNMP is based on the notion that management information is organized into MIBs, with individual management variables, or managed objects, addressed using object identifiers (OIDs). SNMP provides a small set of primitives that enable a manager to read from and write to a MIB, and an agent to send events. SNMP comes in three versions, all of which are in use today. The original SNMP, now often referred to as SNMPv1, is the simplest version and, for agents, the easiest to implement. SNMPv2c adds several capabilities—most important, a more efficient means to retrieve larger amounts of management information. SNMPv3 addresses the lack of security that prevented earlier SNMP versions from being used for applications that are sensitive to security needs, such as provisioning. It is much more complete, yet also more complex and less simple than the original SNMPv1 protocol.

CLI, the command-line interface, provided with most data-networking equipment, is not really a management protocol at all, but an interface devised for human interaction with a device. It offers many convenience features that are designed to make administrators extremely productive. Because it offers comprehensive functional coverage, sometimes it is also used by management applications, specifically in the provisioning space. However, the need to perform screen scraping that is associated with the lack of a common presentation for CLI responses presents significant challenges to build and maintain those applications.

syslog is used to log messages for all kinds of events from network devices. Being little more than a glorified "print" statement, it offers a good way for administrators to figure out what has been going on with a device, although, as with CLI, syslog is often also consumed by management applications. More recently, some features have been added to an IETF-defined version of syslog that allow the definition of extensions that make it a more general-purpose protocol for management events.

Netconf is a new management protocol that is based on XML technology and geared specifically to configuration management. It picks up on some of the deficiencies of CLI with respect to its use by management applications. It is based on the concept of hierarchically structured datastores that, for example, can contain CLI statements and that can be manipulated in a manner similar to files. Netconf offers the corresponding management operations to edit, copy, change, or delete those configs, or datastores. Netconf also enables managers to specify some of the behavior to apply when executing the commands inside a configuration datastore—for example, how to react when one of the commands fails (continue? stop? roll back?)—and to lock a configuration to avoid unintended interference by other users and applications.

Netflow is a special-purpose management protocol that is used to collect large volumes of statistical data about networking traffic, defined as flows. It is the basis for many performance and accounting management applications. Several versions of Netflow exist—version 5 is the most commonly used, and version 9 has the widest functionality. IPFIX is a sibling protocol to Netflow that is defined by the IETF; it has the same goals and very similar capabilities.

Other management protocols exist, and not every management protocol is supported by every device. Sometimes the same management task can be accomplished through different management protocols. For example, SNMP, CLI, and Netconf can all be used to alter the configuration of a device, and SNMP and syslog can both be used to communicate a management event. However, the presented protocols complement each other in more ways than they compete. To conclude the chapter, Figure 8-17 roughly illustrates how the presented protocols are positioned.

Figure 8-17 *Management Protocol Positioning*

User / Application	Humans	Applications
Monitoring	CLI, syslog	SNMP, syslog
Configuration	CLI	Netconf
Data Collection	n.a.	Netflow/IPFIX

- SNMP, Netconf, and Netflow/IPFIX are all targeted at management applications. SNMP is primarily used for monitoring and retrieving state information and operational data from devices. Netconf is primarily intended to provision devices and manage configurations. Netflow and IPFIX are specialized to collect statistical information about IP-based network traffic from data-networking equipment.

- CLI is targeted at human users. Applications also use it to provision devices when necessary.

- syslog is used by humans (such as administrators needing to inspect logs) and management applications alike. As far as human users are concerned, it complements CLI. Sometimes event coverage of syslog and SNMP overlaps. syslog provides generally wider coverage than SNMP, but when available, SNMP is often preferred by applications because of its rigid formal structure and semantics.

Finally, it should be mentioned that the protocols discussed in this chapter are predominantly found in network management scenarios in which the agent is a managed device. They are not as common when the agent is a management system itself and management systems communicate with each other. At those upper management layers, communication occurs in many cases through interfaces such as web services, middleware that is used to tie software applications together, or proprietary application programming interfaces. We pick up on the related and more general topic of management integration in Chapter 10, "Management Integration: Putting the Pieces Together." However, before we do, we turn our attention to how management functionality is divided among different systems.

Chapter Review

1. Why is SNMPv1 not considered secure? How could a hacker exploit its security holes?

2. One of the advantages of SNMPv1 lies in the simplicity of its agent implementations. Does this simplicity also have drawbacks?

3. Explain the difference between an SNMP trap and a syslog message.

4. What is the most important reason CLI is hard to use for management applications?

5. In what way do CLI and syslog complement each other?

6. SNMP has a specific concept of MIBs. Where is the MIB in Netconf?

7. One criticism in conjunction with SNMP concerns reliability because SNMP in general uses UDP as a transport, in which packets (and, hence, SNMP management requests or responses) can be dropped. Describe an obvious way of handling reliability in Netconf.

8. File transfer protocols allow the transfer of files between two locations. Netconf operations have some resemblance to file transfer protocols, in that they allow the copying, transfer, and deletion of config files. Name three ways in which Netconf differs from a simple file transfer protocol for configuration files.

9. What is a flow in Netflow?

10. We stated that Netflow can help you identify the top talkers in your network. How? (You may assume that each talker connects to your network using a static IP address—that is, an IP address that does not change.)

Management Organization: Dividing the Labor

You learned earlier in this book that management tasks are typically split up and jointly accomplished by systems that play different roles. The managing system, in a manager role, communicates with a managed system in an agent role. This suggests that management is typically organized in what amounts to a client/server model, in which a management application (one client) manages the various systems and devices on the network (many servers). However, this is not the only way in which management can be organized; different variations are possible.

We presented a number of examples of such variations earlier in this book: The TMN reference architecture that we discussed in Chapter 5, "Management Functions and Reference Models: Getting Organized," divides the overall management task into multiple layers. Requests from higher layers trickle down layer by layer until they finally hit the device. This suggests that not a single, centralized management system, but different systems could be involved, to share in the overall management task. For example, a service provisioning application might break up a provisioning request into several network provisioning tasks. These tasks are then passed down to a network management or element management system, which, in turn, translates these into management requests for the managed devices.

Another example was given in Chapter 8, "Common Management Protocols: Languages of Management," in which we discussed the fact that with both syslog and Netflow, intermediaries are often introduced between managed devices and management applications—namely, logging hosts (for syslog) and Netflow collectors (for Netflow). The purpose of these intermediaries is to perform certain auxiliary functions, such as collecting and organizing management data. This offloads the actual applications from the stringent real-time processing and scaling requirements for those tasks that they would otherwise be exposed to.

In this chapter, we take a closer look at different ways in which management can be organized and how management functionality can be divided between different systems. We do not consider how different tasks would be organized in a network provider's organization; we discussed some considerations related to those aspects in Chapters 3, "The Basic Ingredients of Network Management," and 4, "The Dimensions of Management." Instead, we take a purely technical perspective. We look in particular at the "vertical" division of management tasks, with different systems needing to collaborate to ultimately achieve a common purpose.

At this point, we are not concerned with the "horizontal" division of labor into different tasks, such as using one system to perform fault monitoring and another one to provision the network, because it does not require the same degree of cooperation between them as does the "vertical" division of tasks. This is an aspect that we touch on when we discuss management integration in Chapter 10, "Management Integration: Putting the Pieces Together."

These are some of the subjects discussed in this chapter:

- How management hierarchies can be used to scale management of your network

- Different philosophies for the distribution of management tasks, such as management by delegation, management by objectives and policy-based management, and management by exception

- Techniques for implementing different styles of management

- Techniques for mediating different management interfaces and the challenges that are involved

Scaling Network Management

Applying the manager-agent paradigm directly is the classical way to organize management of your network: A centralized management application is responsible for managing a certain aspect of your network. The management application contains all required application logic and communicates with the managed devices, sending requests and receiving responses and events.

This organization is time proven and works extremely well in many scenarios. It has simple semantics that are easy to understand. The responsibilities are clear. However, the managing application/managed device approach has inherent limitations in its ability to scale—that is, to keep up with growing size and complexity of the networks to manage. Overcoming these limitations requires dividing and distributing the management task in various ways, which generally leads to a management hierarchy. Furthermore, there are different ways in which the resulting distributed components can cooperate to accomplish the overall tasks, reflecting different network management styles or philosophies. In the following sections, we take a closer look at those aspects.

Management Complexity

There are two distinct aspects to management complexity that affect scale and must be dealt with when developing and deploying management systems and designing operations-support environments. First, there is complexity that is associated with developing, deploying, maintaining, and extending management applications and operations-support systems. It involves the challenge of how to scale the capability to develop systems that keep up with growing network and service complexity. In addition, there is the issue of how the systems themselves can scale to keep pace with the rapid growth and sheer size of the networks that they need to manage. We refer to these complexities as build complexity and runtime complexity, respectively.

Build Complexity

We first explore the aspect of build complexity—that is, the complexity of scaling management application development. Imagine for a moment that you were tasked to build a simple service provisioning application—for example, to provision digital subscriber line (DSL) service as explained in Chapter 7, "Management Communication Patterns: Rules of Conversation." We assume that you have a single type of DSL access multiplexer (DSLAM) to deal with and a single type of aggregation router. Provisioning a DSL service involves sending certain configuration commands to the DSLAM and to the aggregation router. Because you know how to map the way the service needs to be set up to those configuration commands, you can code these commands right into your core application logic. A single application module can handle everything fine.

At some point, new types of equipment likely are introduced into the network. Perhaps there is a need for additional and different network equipment that can serve a larger capacity, perhaps there is a new model with more features available, or perhaps you want to add equipment from a different vendor to avoid being dependent on a single supplier. This means that the provisioning system needs to be updated to deal with different types of devices, each with some variation in management interface. The application logic must be extended to take those differences into account—for example, to send different configuration commands, depending on the particular equipment type that is involved.

Next, if you incur the situation that you need to not only support a new device, but also incorporate an entirely different access network technology. Some of your customers do not want DSL, but prefer cable. You decide that you are not in the DSL service business, but really in the residential Internet access business and should be agnostic to the particular access network technology used. The provisioning logic again needs to be extended accordingly.

Of course, things don't stop there. Eventually, you might have to add support for additional services. Perhaps it becomes a requirement to provision value-added services, such as voice, in addition to Internet access. This means that new types of equipment need to be introduced, such as Session Initiation Protocol (SIP) proxies and voice-mail servers.

At some point, the growing complexity of the network threatens to overwhelm your capacity to maintain and extend your management application. The number of combinations of different equipment types, access network types, and service types that are possible and that need to be supported grows exponentially. Simultaneously, the build complexity of your application increases and puts to the test your ability to scale your development to keep up with the changes and new requirements that you are confronted with. If your application consists of a single piece of application logic, this can be a formidable challenge. For example, if every change in a management interface causes ripple effects throughout the entire application, you are in big trouble.

To support all those requirements in a single, centralized system without turning it into an expensive, inflexible monolith is a tall order. It is a big challenge to keep the complexity of management applications under control in light of the multitude of different services, managed devices, and management interfaces that need to be supported. To be able to keep up, it becomes quickly clear that a modular management application architecture is required.

Modularizing the application means that the overall management task is partitioned and distributed within the system. For example, one module might hide the specifics of how to access different types of DSLAMs. Modularizing provides a single application programming interface that allows other application modules to configure ports and cross-connects on a DSLAM, while hiding any differences in configuration commands between different types of DSLAMs. As new types of DSLAMs are introduced, only this device access module needs to be updated. Other parts of the application, such as the core provisioning logic, are unaffected. Other modules handle other device categories, such as voice servers.

Other modules can be introduced that contain the logic to set up connectivity between devices for different access network technologies. One such module might handle DSL, another one cable, and a third one fixed wireless. Each of those modules leverages the functionality of the device access modules to interact with devices in the network. Finally, the core provisioning logic becomes a module itself.

The point is that, to get a handle on build complexity, it is necessary to move beyond organizing the management task in a way that has a single module or application responsible for managing the entire network. As mentioned earlier, the key to managing a network without letting its complexity overwhelm you is to divide and conquer the task at hand and introduce layers of abstractions. This is true also for the development of management systems. Breaking up the management application into separate modules makes the overall system much easier to build and maintain.

The management application logic still resides within the same system, but if the modules are decoupled enough, you might even run them on separate hosts, as separate, specialized systems. This implies that there is a duality between how a management application can be organized into separate modules and how the overall management task can be organized into separate, cooperating management systems. Figure 9-1 depicts one possible way of breaking up the functionality of provisioning Voice over IP over DSL services that originates from application modules, per the earlier example. The result is a set of multiple cooperating management systems, each of which can run on a separate host.

Figure 9-1 *A Scenario for Managing Residential Voice over IP over DSL Services*

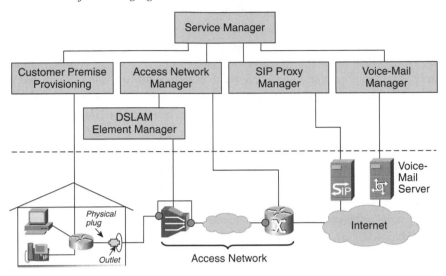

Without being fully aware of it, you have effectively introduced a truly distributed system that has much more horsepower than an application running on a single host. So not only have you addressed the issue of build complexity and how to effectively maintain and extend your operations support environment in a way that scales, but you have also taken a step toward scaling the management of your network itself. This brings us straight to the next topic, runtime complexity.

Runtime Complexity

As with any centralized architecture, when a centralized manager constitutes the single point where it all comes together, it is cause for a number of concerns.

The most fundamental concern has to do with scaling. A single point might have trouble scaling when the domain that it manages (the number of instances of services, the number of network devices, the number of end systems) grows beyond a certain size. As you saw in Chapter 1, "Setting the Stage," we cannot necessarily expect relief from Moore's law. Moore's law states that, over time, processing power increases exponentially, which might suggest that scaling limitations that have to do with processing power will take care of themselves over time. However, the complexity of what we need to manage grows as well, sometimes even faster than the processing power itself. So scale is not a concern that is easily dismissed.

Of course, if the need arises, normal software-engineering techniques to better scale a management system can be applied—for example, by allowing the system to be distributed across multiple servers. Ideally, a management system will scale linearly—if a second server is added, it will double management horsepower, and if ten are added, management horsepower will increase tenfold. In many cases, scaling management systems this way is completely sufficient. Nevertheless, if the size of the management task grows exponentially, it still might be difficult to keep up with.

A second concern with runtime complexity involves vulnerability against failure. As in other application domains, high-availability application and server architectures can provide relief, at a price. In addition, it needs to be taken into account that, in addition to protecting against system failure, you also must guard against loss of connectivity. If you have a highly available system but a construction crew outside your network operations center takes out your wide-area network (WAN) connection, you do not want to be stopped dead in your tracks. Also, high availability can be addressed by hardware only to a certain degree. For example, if the building that hosts your management system floods or bursts into flames, highly available hardware alone won't save you. You need to have software capabilities that enable you to distribute—and redistribute—your system geographically, across multiple locations.

The key to dealing with runtime complexity, as in dealing with build complexity, lies in the way the management task is organized. The most common way of doing this is to introduce management hierarchies, which is the topic of the next section. Of course, it needs to be realized that even a management hierarchy is at some level still fundamentally centralized. However, if enough tasks are performed by subordinate systems, introduction of a management hierarchy nevertheless alleviates scaling concerns. In combination with software-engineering techniques to build robust and distributed systems for the components and applications that are part of the management hierarchy, it can be successfully applied to virtually any management scenario today.

Management Hierarchies

As indicated earlier, a single system is generally not sufficient to manage a network. Instead, the work needs to be distributed. Let's look at a real-life analogy. Consider a person who owns and runs a small business. As the business grows, the business owner might no longer be able to manage the business single-handedly. So she gets help. She still wants to be in charge of running the overall business, but she distributes certain tasks across her people. Eventually, she starts building an organizational hierarchy.

In essence, we need to do the same with network management. This results in the building of a management hierarchy (see Figure 9-2).

Figure 9-2   *A Management Hierarchy*

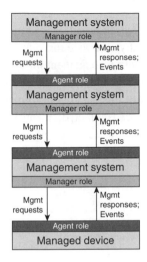

Subcontracting Management Tasks

In a management hierarchy, certain management tasks are subcontracted to different systems. In effect, the subcontracted systems constitute management *proxies*: To the subordinate system, it appears that the proxy is the manager. However, the manager proxy is really only a conduit, acting on behalf of another management system that is invisible to the managed system in the agent role.

You've already seen one example of management hierarchies—the specialization of applications along the different layers in the TMN hierarchy. In this case, the different systems are each management systems in their own right, each operating at its own layer of abstraction. A management system in an intermediate layer is a manager for the systems below it. At the same time, it functions as an agent for management systems above it.

We discussed the TMN hierarchy extensively in Chapter 4 and do not need to repeat this discussion here. However, hierarchies do not always need to follow the TMN layers. Management hierarchies can be formed in other ways. They can involve subcontracting pretty much any management task. It is particularly attractive to offload an application of simple yet communication- and computation-intensive tasks. This can greatly aid in making applications scale better. Here are some simple examples:

- Polling a link for its utilization on another application's behalf

- Sending a threshold-crossing alert when utilization exceeds a certain level

- Computing the average link-utilization information across a set of access routers at a particular enterprise site so that the upper-level application does not need to do it itself

You will see many more examples in the sections that follow.

Generally, management hierarchies also result in information hierarchies, as shown in Figure 9-3. For example, in the TMN hierarchy, a service management system might translate management information from the network about management information of relevance to a service—for example, "The network is experiencing a lot of packet drops on a particular link." The service management application translates this data into information about how this affects service, identifying which particular service is affected, quantifying the impact it has on the service, and identifying the customers who are affected—for example, "Customer Maggie experiences a crappy picture for her Video on Demand (VoD) service."

Figure 9-3   *Management and Information Hierarchies*

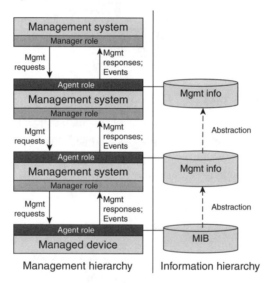

In many cases, intermediate systems in a management hierarchy do not form a complete layer that abstracts all management functionality from below. Instead, intermediate systems perform a specific helper function and are bypassed for other functions (see Figure 9-4). For example, one such function might involve sifting through large amounts of "raw" management data and distilling it into more meaningful and more compact information. In the preceding example of computing the average link-utilization information across a set of access routers, only one piece of preprocessed information—the average—should be sent back to the NOC, as opposed to the pile of raw link-utilization data that is aggregated and abstracted by the average link-utilization information. Again, we present more examples in a later section.

Figure 9-4 *A Management Hierarchy Involving Helper Functions*

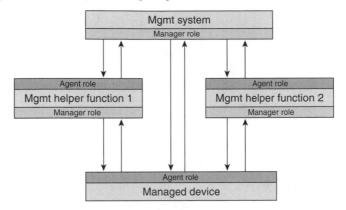

Deployment Aspects

In addition to distributing the processing task, management hierarchies can reduce requirements for management communication bandwidth. With a management hierarchy, it might no longer be necessary to deploy all management functionality centrally in a NOC. Instead, it is possible to deploy subordinate management systems geographically close to the equipment that they are supposed to help manage—for example, a particular branch location of an enterprise. This can help make more efficient use of management communication bandwidth, which is of particular importance when the management network has only slow wide-area network (WAN) connections to the NOC and when network bandwidth is prohibitively expense.

The information hierarchy implied by the management hierarchy typically means that the large volumes of data that are communicated at the lowest layer are gradually replaced by less and more compact data that is communicated as we go up the hierarchy. High-frequency, high-bandwidth management operations can now be handled by systems that are geographically very close to the managed equipment, perhaps connected over a local-area network (LAN). The communication back to the NOC in many cases then is less frequent and less voluminous because it involves a higher layer of the information hierarchy. Figure 9-5 shows an example. Note that although this example shows only one subordinate system per branch location, there might easily be several, each serving a particular purpose and providing a particular helper function. At the same time, for some management functions, the application in the NOC still needs to talk to the devices directly.

Figure 9-5 *Distributed Deployment of a Management Hierarchy*

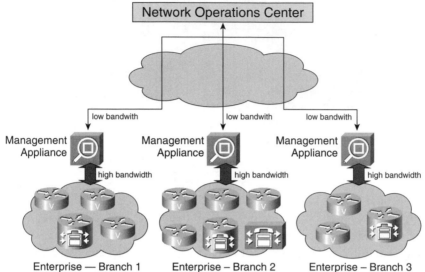

The management systems across which management tasks are distributed can be software applications in the traditional sense, each running on its own hosts and offering a user interface. One needs to be aware that, despite all its benefits, this introduces a secondary management problem, and care needs to be taken to keep it from getting out of hand. After all, if additional UNIX or Windows server hosts and database management systems are required, they will require, at a minimum, system administration as well. To use an analogy, now that you've brought in cats to check the mouse population, how will you herd the cats?

Another possibility is to deploy management functionality in the form of management *appliances*. This does not mean that they are refrigerators or microwave ovens. It simply means that management functionality is packaged as one component that includes both hardware and software that can be deployed very much like a piece of network equipment with the rest of the network. A management appliance can be thought of as something similar to a router, which itself is nothing other than a special-purpose computer with embedded routing software, except that in this case certain management functions are embedded. The functionality provided by management appliances is typically less sophisticated and more focused on a special purpose than a full-fledged management application. Also, it is limited to management functionality related to the element management layer—that is, functionality close to the network. The advantage of an appliance is that it is much simpler to administer and manage than a traditional management system. However, it does not eliminate the need to be managed completely; it does need to be hooked up to the management network and takes up physical space.

Regardless of whether management appliances or more traditional management systems running on general-purpose computing hosts are used, as the network grows, chances are that more of them need to be added over time just to keep up. But there is another, plentiful resource whose processing power will always keep up with the size of your network, regardless of how large and how fast the network grows. That resource is the network itself, or, to be more precise, the equipment in the network. Network devices, after all, are computers—admittedly, special-purpose computers—that are supposed to focus on their communication function, but nonetheless they may have a few extra cycles to spare for management purposes. Tapping this resource might be hard unless you are an equipment vendor, but sometimes devices do provide additional functions that allow them to be programmed. Where such a capability is provided, it can be used to take care of the scaling problem in a significant way. The processing power keeps up with the size of the network—when your network grows exponentially, so does the computing power at your disposal.

Of course, strictly speaking, the result might no longer be a true management hierarchy because the lowest layer of management functionality is collapsed into the device. However, from a functional viewpoint, the same hierarchy is still in effect—except that the lowest managing layer now happens to be implemented on the managed system itself. This is depicted in Figure 9-6, which shows how the functionality of one of the helper functions from Figure 9-4 can be implemented on the device itself.

Figure 9-6 *Deploying Management Functionality on Managed Devices*

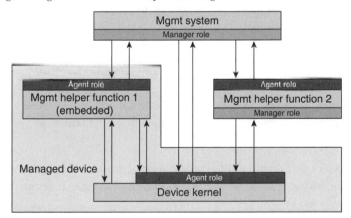

Of course, there are limiting factors to how much management functionality can be realized on network equipment, most importantly the amount of horsepower (both CPU and memory) that each device has available. After all, a router's main task is to route packets, not to serve as a general-purpose computing platform. But for tasks that are computationally simple and can cut down on the amount of data or the number of required management exchanges, their realization on the device is a very attractive option. The capability to include additional management functionality on the device is often advertised under grandiose names—"embedded management intelligence" or "self-managing" ("self-healing," "self-tuning," "self-protecting," and so on) or "autonomic." The fundamental idea in each case is to include management functionality on the managed systems themselves that would otherwise need to be provided by outside management applications.

Management Styles

We have now seen that management tasks can be distributed across many systems and that distributed management functionality can be deployed in different ways. The remaining question is how to best make use of these capabilities.

A lot of business administration literature discusses different business management approaches. Actually, scaling the task to manage networks is not all that different from scaling the task to manage other business functions, such as managing people in an organization. Therefore, let us for a moment take a look at how organizations are managed in real life. Going back to the example of the small business owner, after she has received help, what does she ask the help to do? How does she manage her subordinates? Maybe she is not really willing to relinquish control and becomes a micromanager. Eventually, this is likely to create problems. For one thing, it might cause job dissatisfaction with her subordinates, although in the case of management systems this is admittedly not a problem. However, it might simply not be a very efficient way to do things. Ultimately, the subordinates need to be leveraged better by adjusting the approach to management—the style or philosophy according to which management takes place. Typical management styles include these:

- **Management by delegation**—You delegate tasks to your subordinates. You clearly establish what you want them to do and let them do it.

- **Management by objectives**—You establish goals with your subordinates and leave it up to them how to achieve them. You don't tell them how to do the work, just what the outcome should be.

- **Management by exception**—In this variation of the other management styles, you normally put the subordinates in charge but become involved in case something unusual happens and escalation is required.

It turns out that the same principles apply to network management as well and can significantly help in scaling. So how are these principles applied? We explore this in the following subsections.

Management by Delegation

Management by delegation involves an upper-layer management system delegating certain tasks to lower-layer systems—in some cases, the managed systems themselves. This is a very common theme that can be found across the various management functional areas. In many cases, tasks suitable for delegating are routine tasks that do not require interaction with a management operator or administrator. They involve a relatively low level of intelligence but often require sifting through a large amount of management data. Therefore, delegation of such tasks significantly offloads upper-layer systems. Here are some examples:

Fault management:

- **Logging of events**—Two tasks are delegated to subordinate systems: the task of persisting events and the task of filtering out events that are of no interest to the application. The latter can take the shape of the subordinate system offering an event-subscription service. This service allows upper-layer systems to subscribe only to those events that they are interested in as defined by a set of criteria. Examples include events of a certain type, alarms of a certain severity, events affecting a certain system, and events that meet some combination of those criteria. The subordinate system inspects incoming events and forwards only those events that meet the criteria.

- **Deduplication of events**—The task of identifying event messages that are being sent redundantly and suppressing the duplicates is delegated to the subordinate system. This can be particularly useful if events are deduplicated across multiple systems. Compare this to an accident on a highway, which could trigger many people to make 911 calls, putting additional load on the system. Deduplication ensures that only one 911 call is put through, which, in turn, ensures maximum responsiveness and dedication of resources to that one call.

- **Correlation of events**—Beyond deduplication, this involves delegating the task of correlating events in general, to reduce as much as possible the amount of "noise" that the upper-layer system needs to deal with.

Performance management:

- **Netflow collection and aggregation**—The task of collecting and logging Netflow records is typically delegated to a system known as a Netflow collector. This is a special-purpose system designed for this particular task. In addition, it might be useful to delegate additional tasks to the collector, such as aggregating data across Netflow records.

- **Polling of devices for statistics**—A management application might be interested in receiving snapshots of current statistical parameters at certain points in time, such as the current CPU utilization, to plot performance graphs and perform offline trend analysis. Polling imposes a substantial load on management applications, particularly if they have to poll many devices across the network. This is a task that can be easily delegated.

■ **Preprocessing of statistical information**—Converting counters that aggregate data over a long period of time into discrete values to indicate the current rate is another example of a simple task that can easily be delegated and performed in conjunction with polling devices for statistics. For example, a counter that counts the packets received on an interface since the system was first started up can be converted into values that indicate how many packets were received in each time interval. The number of packets is determined by subtracting the value at the beginning of the interval from the value at the end of the interval to record by how much the counter was incremented during the time interval. Note that this provides a rough estimate only because the points in time at which a sample is taken might not always be evenly spaced. This is because of fluctuations in the time that it takes a request for statistical information to be processed by the device, as was explained earlier.

Accounting management:

■ Correlation of call detail records across the network—This is an example taken from telephony. Phone calls made across the network result in so-called call detail records (CDRs) that are generated during the call. A CDR includes information such as when the call was started, when it ended, how much data was transmitted, and so on—much like flow data in Netflow or IPFIX. This data is the basis for billing users. Because several systems that are involved in a call can generate a CDR, CDRs that relate to the same call need to be eliminated to avoid double counting. This occurs by matching CDRs that contain the same call identifier, meaning that they relate to the same call that was made. This is another task that is simple enough yet requires a good deal of number crunching—a prime candidate for delegation to a subordinate system.

Configuration management:

■ **Autoconfiguration backups**—A subordinate system might be tasked with taking periodic snapshots of device configurations and backing them up, in case corruption occurs and they need to be restored.

■ **Value-added configuration management functions**—These could include scoping configuration retrieval across the network. Here, a superior system would really like to be provided with a convenience function that allows it (for example) to retrieve configuration information across a group of devices or an entire network domain through a single request. The task of dividing this into individual requests and collecting the responses is delegated to the subordinate system.

■ **Distribution of software patches across the network**—In this example, an image upgrade might need to be distributed across the network. This task can be delegated to a subordinate server to which devices inside the network are pointed to retrieve their new image. Alternatively to this "pull" model of devices pulling their own images, the server might also realize a "push" model, uploading the new images to the devices.

Some tasks that can be delegated to a subordinate system are not suited for delegation to the network elements themselves. This concerns particularly tasks that involve coordinating multiple devices, such as the CDR correlation across the network or the scoped configuration retrieval. However, many tasks can be delegated either to a dedicated subordinate system or to a network element. In some cases, some network elements offer a function, whereas others do not. In those cases, subordinate systems can act as "equalizers," providing external "intelligent" agents for devices that are otherwise more limited in their functionality, as shown in Figure 9-7. In those cases, the subordinate system acts de facto as a *management gateway*, offering a set of higher-level functionality at the interface that it exposes in its agent role and mapping this to more primitive capabilities offered by the managed system below. We get back to the subject of management gateways in the next section.

Figure 9-7   *A Subordinate Management Helper System as Equalizer*

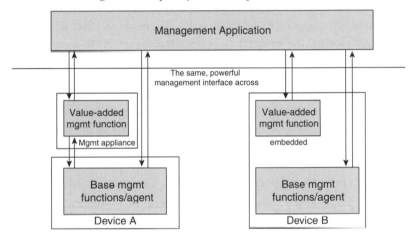

Functions such as those just described are offered in many forms. Sometimes they come as their own full-fledged products. Sometimes they simply come as a feature or embedded capability of the managed device. One well-known technology that implements management by delegation is called RMON, for remote monitoring MIB. RMON is basically a special SNMP MIB that enables managers to delegate certain management tasks to so-called RMON *probes*. The probe can be a system in its own right, such as a management appliance, or it can simply reside on the device (see Figure 9-8).

The types of tasks that can be delegated to an RMON probe include collecting statistics (taking snapshots of MIB variables at certain intervals in time), subscribing to certain types of notifications, and generating threshold-crossing alerts. (This last capability is also a prime example of a function to enable management by exception, explained later in this section.) Tasks are delegated by configuring the MIB accordingly. Over time, several MIBs related to RMON have been introduced to expand the functionality that was originally defined.

Figure 9-8   *Management Using RMON Probes*

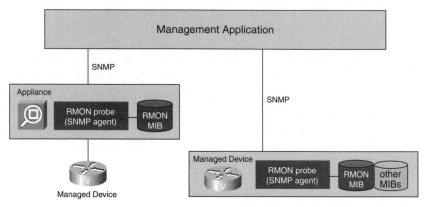

Finally, it should be mentioned that ultimately it might be desirable to have management by delegation occur by allowing an upper-layer management system to delegate tasks "on the fly"—for example, to generate management scripts for execution by lower-layer applications when needed. Although this is potentially very powerful, such concepts have not really moved past the research stage. The concept is promising, but it raises many issues that need to be addressed. For example, from a security standpoint, it needs to be ensured that the delegated task indeed originates from an authorized system. Also, because the behavior of the network with regard to management can be altered on the fly, extra care needs to be taken that the delegated tasks have the intended effect and don't spin out of control and wreak havoc on the network. Debugging and troubleshooting a network can become significantly more complicated.

Management by Objectives and Policy-Based Management

The idea behind management by objectives is that a management system establishes certain goals for a subordinate system, and the subordinate system translates these goals into the required lower-level actions to ensure that those goals are met. This way, the upper-layer management system can focus simply on setting overall "policy" for management of the network that establishes the management objectives. The subordinate system handles translating the policy into actions. The subordinate system offers a management interface at a relatively high layer of abstraction that allows upper-layer management systems to configure policies on the system, and possesses the necessary intelligence to translate those policies into the necessary actions and behavior.

In network management, the principle of management by objectives is accordingly closely linked to what is commonly referred to as *policy-based management*. In fact, the term *policy* is certainly one of the more popular buzzwords in network management because, to many people, it suggests that, by some magic, you get something (desired results per management policy) for nothing, or at least without needing to think through what needs to be precisely done to achieve those objectives. Of course, there is no magic, and anyone expecting magic is bound to be disappointed.

Nevertheless, policy-based management plays an important role in network management today, so we investigate it a little more closely.

First, what is a "policy" in management? Two types of policies can be distinguished:

- *Policy goals* establish an objective. An example is, "Do not let voice services for end users that are already provisioned on the network be negatively impacted by voice services for end users who are provisioned later."

- *Policy rules* define conditions and actions, intended to establish how certain situations (that occur when the conditions in the policy rule are met) should be dealt with (the action part in the policy rule). An example is, "If there are already 80 voice users connected to the network through a particular T1 port (which allows 24 users to make a call at any one time), then reject any attempt to provision additional voice users (because the possibility of users blocking each other when trying to make calls would become too high)."

Policy goals and policy rules are closely related. Indeed, both are different ways to express policy. Specifically, policy goals can generally be rephrased and expressed as policy rules. In the preceding example, a policy rule that is equivalent to the policy goal would be the following: "*If* there are so many voice services for end users already provisioned that any attempt to accommodate additional users could result in negative impact for existing services, *and* there is a request to add a new user (the policy condition), *then* the request to add a new user should be denied (the policy action)." The distinguishing factor, if any, is hence the level of refinement at which the policy is specified. In the preceding example, the policy rule that we encountered is more concrete than what was stated as part of the policy goal. The rule stated specifically that if there are 80 users already, additional users should not be accepted. The goal, on the other hand, did not state specifically how many users would be acceptable.

The fact that it is possible to refine policies indicates that, just as with management information and management systems, there can be policy hierarchies, in which abstract and higher-level policies are transformed and implemented by lower-level policies. Policies can be established at a very high level, such as a business policy ("Maximize the installed base of voice users while keeping customer satisfaction above a certain level") and be broken down successively. For instance, the business policy that was just mentioned could be broken down into the policies mentioned earlier, realizing that customer satisfaction might have something to do with the likelihood that the attempt to place a voice call will be blocked and that, therefore, policies should be put in place to avoid excessive oversubscription of voice services.

The preceding example, in which the policy specified when to accept or reject a provisioning request, is an example of a policy that influences management behavior. In some cases, however, policies go beyond management and are used to directly influence how the network behaves. The boundary between the two is somewhat fleeting. Here are some additional examples of policies:

- "If a new voice call were to deteriorate the quality of ongoing voice calls, then do not accept it." This example is similar to the earlier one, but it applies only after voice services have already been provisioned. It refers to the situation in which more users want to simultaneously place calls than the system can realistically handle. In a VoIP environment, for example, accepting too many calls might result in dropped packets or increased delay or delay jitter (differences in interpacket arrival times), which would negatively impact voice quality for everybody. Therefore, it is best to simply accept no new calls beyond a certain point—better to disappoint one user than to have all of them complain. Of course, for a network element, it might be hard to assess at what point voice quality would indeed deteriorate from the acceptance of an additional call. The policy therefore needs to be broken down further, into a policy at a lower level (next bullet).

- "If there are more than 24 calls in progress and a new call request arrives, deny it." This refines the preceding policy and provides a condition that is very easy to validate. The number of acceptable calls in progress is an example of a policy parameter that could well be configurable on a network element directly. This particular parameter would be termed a Call Admission Control (CAC) feature that allows the specification of a criteria on a network device of when to accept call requests and when to deny them.

- "If the utilization on a link that is protecting another link goes above 50 percent, use a different route for excess traffic until utilization drops below 50 percent." In this example, you might have this policy configured for two links that back each other up so that if one of them fails, the other carries all the traffic. Clearly, this can work only if jointly they do not carry more than 100 percent of what either one of them could carry alone. Hence you want to keep the utilization of both below 50 percent. (Of course, you could also go for an 80/20 or 70/30 split, but this type of behavior might be more complex to control.)

- "If your management link experiences congestion, suspend reporting of all alarms with a severity of less than 'major', and suspend all periodic upload of collected statistical data, and send an event to the user indicating that this suspension has gone into effect." The purpose of this management policy is to ensure that network elements remain manageable even in times of high congestion. In fact, during times of high congestion, it may be most critical that important management traffic gets through, so you don't want it to be stuck in a "management traffic jam" with things that are less critical.

In essence, policy-based management is most commonly used to simplify management by establishing policies on how certain situations should be dealt with when they occur. Typical applications for policies are to establish criteria for how some kind of resource should be allocated when there is resource contention—that is, when not enough resources are available for everybody, as indicated by several of the previous examples.

Policies provide guidelines and encode certain behavior that is expected under certain conditions, without requiring intervention by upper-layer management. This is very similar to reflexes that the human nervous system is capable of: When dust gets in your eye, you blink as a reflex, without needing to first think about it. The brain deals with this type of situation at the level of the subconscious, without requiring conscious decisions to be made. One difference in network management is, of course, the fact that policies can be programmed into the network and thus the "reflex" behavior can be altered. Of course, this means that when that happens, those policies need to be managed.

Finally, it should be mentioned that policy-based management is generally built around a standardized conceptual architecture that involves several distinct roles, as Figure 9-9 shows.

Figure 9-9   *Policy-Based Management*

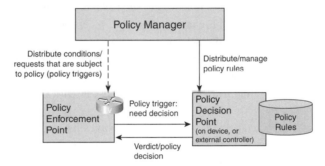

- A Policy Enforcement Point (PEP) is the point at which policy is enforced—that is, conditions that are subjected to policy are recognized, and policy actions are executed.

- A Policy Decision Point (PDP) is the point at which a decision on what to do in a current situation is made. Based on the conditions reported to it by the PEP, the PDP makes an inference based on policy rules on which action, if any, should be performed, and communicates the resulting verdict back to the PEP, which executes it.

  In some cases, the PDP resides on the same system (perhaps an intelligent network device) as the PEP. But this is not always necessarily so, and the architecture allows for maximum flexibility in this regard. Separating the PDP and PEP allows policies to be enforced at points in the network that are relatively simple, without much intelligence or processing capacity, because they are essentially "remotely controlled" by more intelligent systems. In this sense, policy-based management very much resembles a controller-based architecture, in which a smart controller (the PDP) controls and makes the decision for dumb endpoints (the PEPs).

- Finally, a policy manager is responsible for managing (specifically, distributing) and fine-tuning the policies. For example, should the CAC limit indeed be set to 24 calls, or can it be less restrictively set to 30? Under what precise load conditions on the management network should the reporting of events with a lower severity be suspended? These rules need to be established and distributed to the PDPs. Likewise, unless they are already built into the PEPs, the conditions that can trigger a policy rule need to be distributed to the PEPs so that the PEPs know about the types of events and actions that are subjected to policy. As mentioned earlier, management of policies (to enable policy-based management—the two should not be confused) is clearly a management task in its own right.

Management by Exception

Management by exception aims to relieve management applications of management tasks while things are going smoothly but involve them when something unusual occurs. This is akin to a sales clerk in a store who is allowed to ring up the register but needs to call a supervisor when an unusual scenario or unforeseen problem is encountered, such as handling a customer return, dealing with a stuck register, or completing a purchase that exceeds a certain amount. Management by exception often involves delegating tasks that concern the monitoring of the network or managed domain to a subordinate. The subordinate monitors whether everything is operating normally and alerts the application when something unusual is spotted. This allows the management application to focus only on scenarios that truly require management attention.

The prime example for management by exception involves threshold-crossing alerts. The subordinate system monitors certain parameters and sends an alert when a certain threshold is crossed—for example, when utilization exceeds a certain level. Of course, many refinements of the basic TCA mechanism are possible to make it smarter and more sophisticated, such as automatically adjusting thresholds depending on a context. To use an analogy from healthcare, you might deploy a heart rate monitor that automatically dials (alerts) a doctor whenever the pulse rate exceeds 120 (a threshold). This works perfectly fine in a setting inside a hospital. However, outside the hospital, this simple threshold setting might no longer be appropriate and you would need to refine it. For example, if the pulse rate is exceeded but the person monitored just returned from jogging, you might want to hold back on that emergency phone call.

Management Mediation

In management hierarchies, the management interface that is exposed at different levels of the hierarchy is generally not the same. Instead, it changes in a number of important ways:

- **Information**—For starters, the information that is exposed over interfaces at different levels of a management hierarchy is not identical. You saw many examples of this a little earlier. For example, performance-related management data that is provided by managed devices can be aggregated at the intermediate level. The system at the intermediate level then offers the aggregated information over its interface to the managers on top, not the raw management data that was collected from the devices.

- **Services**—In addition, the services offered by the agents at different levels of the management hierarchy might not be the same. Again, you saw many examples of this, such as the intermediate system for event management that offers a subscription service for events, whereas the management interface at the device might offer no such service.

- **Protocols**—Finally, not even the protocols might be the same. Again, drawing on the earlier examples, it is perfectly conceivable for a polling service for statistical information to provide this statistical information through SNMP and an SNMP MIB, while itself having to use CLI **show** commands to retrieve some of the needed information from the devices. Likewise, an intermediate system that performs automatic configuration archival services might expose a Netconf interface to systems on top of it but might have to rely on CLI when talking to the devices below it.

This means that between the agent at the bottom of the hierarchy and the manager at the top, some kind of management translation is needed. Of course, when different layers of management are involved, such as element and service management, nothing else is expected. But sometimes even translation at the same management layer is required, as evidenced by some of the preceding examples. In some cases, a manager might simply not support the same management protocol as an agent. Again, translation services are needed, much as there can be a need for interpreters when two persons who do not speak each other's language need to communicate.

Translation between managing and managed systems is also termed *management mediation*. Management mediation is an important topic and a recurring theme in network management; it involves protocols as well as services and management information. Therefore, we take a closer look at management mediation in this section.

The introduction of management hierarchies is one of the reasons management mediation is needed. As a side note, the reverse can be true as well: Management hierarchies might be introduced because management mediation is required. This can be the case when managers do not support the interfaces that management agents offer—given the proliferation of different management architectures and interfaces that exist, not an uncommon scenario. In this case, intermediate systems might be introduced to perform the required mediation, which, of course, leads to a management hierarchy. Therefore, the need for mediation could well be a motivation for management hierarchies, not just scaling concerns.

In most networks of significant size and complexity, sooner or later, multiple management interfaces and protocols have to be supported. This situation could be avoided only if all subordinate systems offer the same management interface, meaning that they all have to agree on one common standard. However, this is a circumstance that is extremely unlikely. For one thing, despite all intentions to be standards based, some vendors will always perceive the need for some competitive differentiation. Standards tend to be trailing-edge, common denominators, and they don't tend to address leading-edge capabilities. For this reason, standards might not be available for every new feature that needs to be instrumented, and even if a standard is planned, vendors and network providers might not always be willing to wait until one becomes available. In addition, the useful thing about standards is that often there are many to choose from. So which one should be supported? Many agents—specifically, those implemented on network equipment—have limited computing resources to work with and cannot afford to implement multiple interfaces.

Building multilingual management applications that support a variety of management architectures, interfaces, and protocols might be feasible, in some cases, as shown in Figure 9-10. The problem is that often this is prohibitively expensive and possibly results in bloated software. Application vendors are interested in focusing their development resources on the development of new application features, not merely on the support for new interfaces for additional devices; this increases application coverage but not application functionality.

Figure 9-10 *Multilingual Managers*

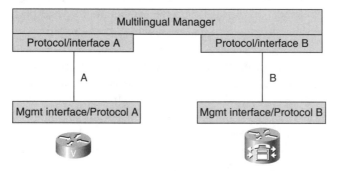

The alternative, then, is to introduce a component in the middle that offers one interface in an agent role that superior systems can use, while using a different interface—or several interfaces—to talk to the systems below. In human terms, the component performs the role of an interpreter, translating, for example, to and from Russian, Chinese, or German for an English-speaking client. In management terms, such interpreters are referred to as management gateways; the translation function they perform is referred to as management mediation. Management gateways are designed to obviate the need for a manager to be multilingual, even if it does not support the management interface of some of the devices that it manages, as Figure 9-11 shows.

A management gateway is positioned between a manager and an agent. We need to distinguish between the interface that is provided by the agent and that the management gateway needs to work with, and the interface that the management gateway emulates and provides to the manager on top. There is no established terminology for this, so for the purposes of this book, we refer to them as *target interface* and *source interface*, respectively. The target is the interface that the management gateway emulates, and the source is the one that is provided by the agent below, as Figure 9-12 shows.

Figure 9-11 *Management Gateways as a Technique to Manage Networks with Heterogeneous Management Interfaces*

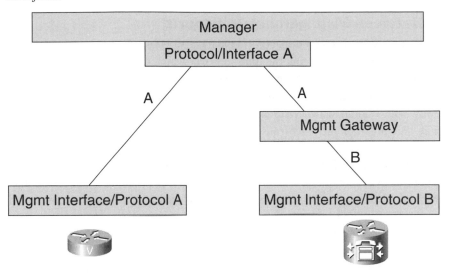

Figure 9-12 *A Management Gateway*

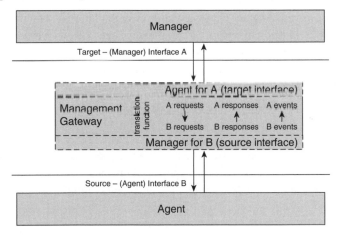

Management mediation can take place at several levels:

■   Mediation at the transport level

■   Mediation of the management protocol itself, including remote operations, management operations, and management services

■   Mediation of management information

We take a look at each one in the following subsections.

Mediation Between Management Transports

Mediation between different transports is the most straightforward aspect of management mediation. It concerns changing the transport over which management messages are carried midstream. For example, a management agent might support UDP as transport protocol, but a management application wants to use an SSH or BEEP transport. This requires a transport gateway in the middle, which terminates one transport connection, strips the management message from it, and puts it on the other transport connection.

Strictly speaking, this is not really management mediation at all—it is the functionality of a transport gateway that does not involve any translation between the management messages being exchanged. Identical transport gateways can also be used for applications other than management.

The reason this is mentioned here at all is that, in some cases, management protocols rely on the management transport for certain functionality. It is important that when transport gateways are used, the functionality that is expected of the transport is still supported end to end. Otherwise, issues might arise. One example is the Netconf protocol, which requires the transport to offer certain security functions. If the transport gateway simply puts messages on a different transport for some leg of the management connection, the function that is expected from the transport might no longer be preserved. Another example that is easy to picture is a management protocol that assumes a reliable transport to ensure that no messages get lost, with the transport protocol taking care of automatically retransmitting messages as required. If a transport gateway somewhere in the middle simply puts messages on a different transport that does not offer this capability without making up for this deficiency in another way, management messages could still be lost. All that it takes is one part of the connection to be compromised to lose the capability for the end-to-end connection.

The implication is that in some cases, the use of a transport gateway is not as transparent to the applications above as might perhaps be expected. This must always be taken into account when transport gateways are used, to ensure that management communications will not be negatively affected.

Mediation Between Management Protocols

Mediation at the management protocol level involves translating management messages of one protocol into management messages of another one—specifically, mapping between the management primitives.

From a naive point of view, this should be relatively straightforward if the capabilities between the protocols that are involved are equivalent. In this case, it should be sufficient to essentially perform a syntactic transformation that can occur during runtime. For example, for mediation from SNMP (manager) to CLI (agent), an SNMP "get" request might be translated into a CLI **show** command, or for mediation from syslog (agent) to SNMP (manager), a syslog message might be mapped to an SNMP trap. In mediation that takes place purely at the protocol level, it might be assumed that there is no need to understand the management information that constitutes the payload of the message. In the end, all you want to do is move the management information payload from one container to another.

It turns out that this assumption generally does not hold. Management protocol and the way in which management information is represented are sufficiently tied together that some mediation of management information also is required. In other words, mediation between management protocols is generally not possible without mediation between management information at least at the syntactic level.

For example, consider the example of a syslog (agent)–to–SNMP (manager) gateway, which you expect to convert syslog messages to SNMP traps. As simple as syslog messages are, they contain a set of parameters, such as facility, severity, and mnemonic. This information must be converted into SNMP trap parameters, but which ones? There are no equivalent parameters in an SNMP trap message. Of course, other parameters, such as the variable bindings, exist, but to use those requires at least some amount of information translation.

The mapping between management protocols can be performed using several techniques. For example, you can specify a set of translation rules. The prerequisite for this is having a common grammar of both protocols. Individual rules define how different artifacts from the two grammars relate and should be translated.

Alternatively, you can simply use templates. You check whether a message matches a certain pattern—the template. If it does, you simply substitute the template with another one. Any payload within the template is carried over or substituted using a set of rules. As an analogy, imagine that you travel to Germany. You don't speak German, but you try to get around using a dictionary that contains certain phrases. You want to ask a local "What's the time?" You find the phrase and point to its translation: "Wie spät ist es?" The answer comes back: "Es ist 10 Uhr 30." The dictionary shows that "Es ist *hh* Uhr *mm*" translates to "It is *hh*:*mm*." You substitute *hh* for 10 and *mm* for 30, and, voilà, you have made a successful translation. The phrases in the dictionary are your templates, some of which can contain certain parameters.

Templates are essentially a degenerated form of rules, defining one rule for each type of message that can occur instead of analyzing messages in terms of their grammar. It is a brute-force approach based on pattern matching and text substitution. Its advantage is that it is simple and well suited to translate management messages that lack a rigorous grammar. Templates are hence well suited for mediation that involves responses to CLI commands (remember the difficulties associated with screen scraping) or the body part of syslog messages (this really involves payload, not the protocol itself; we discuss this example in more detail in the next section). The disadvantage of the template approach is that potentially a large number of templates must be defined, and templates break easily if the underlying messages change between different versions of network equipment. If in the preceding example the local had answered "Es ist halb 11" ("halb 11" also means 10:30), you would have been at a loss to understand the response because this would not fit the template or phrase given in the dictionary.

Mediation of Management Information at the Syntactic Level

As mentioned, mediation between management protocols involves some degree of mediation between management information. In its simple form, such a mediation is syntactical in nature, meaning that conversion can occur without understanding the deeper "meaning" of individual pieces of management information that are conveyed.

Example: A Syslog-to-SNMP Management Gateway

We return to the example of a management gateway that is supposed to convert syslog messages from a syslog agent into SNMP traps for an SNMP manager. One way this could be accomplished is as follows:

A simple "syslog mediation MIB" is defined, as shown in Figure 9-13. The basic idea behind this MIB is that it provides a notification type that is used to carry a syslog message. The different fields of the syslog message are conveyed through corresponding variable bindings in the SNMP trap message; the objects that are to be included in those variable bindings are defined as part of the syslog notification type. Accordingly, the MIB consists of a set of scalars, one for each of the various parameters that occur in a syslog message—for example, scalars for facility, severity, mnemonic, message body part, and so on. In addition, a single notification type is defined for notifications that are caused by a syslog message. The objects in the MIB will never be retrieved by an application; they only serve as placeholders to hold information in the traps.

Figure 9-13 *A Syslog Mediation MIB*

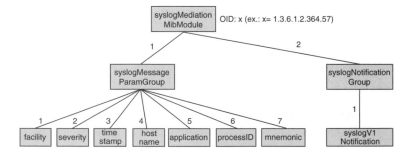

Now, when a syslog message arrives, the gateway strips off the different parameter fields—the facility, the severity, the mnemonic of the message, its message body, and so on. It then creates an SNMP trap message, creating a list of variable bindings that include each of the scalars from the syslog mediation MIB. The value of the facility object is set to the value of the facility field in the syslog message. The values of severity object, mnemonic object, and message body object are likewise set to the values of the corresponding fields in the syslog message. Then the resulting SNMP trap, containing the same information as the original syslog message, is forwarded on to the receiving management application. Figure 9-14 shows an example.

Figure 9-14 *Syslog Message to SNMP Trap Mediation per Fictitious Syslog Mediation MIB*

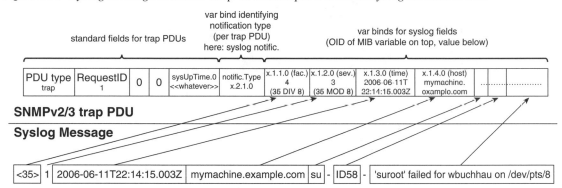

Example: An SNMP-to-OO Management Gateway

A second, more complicated example involves mediating between SNMP on the agent side and a management interface with an object-oriented (OO, for short) information model on the manager side.

Object-oriented information models model the managed domain in terms of objects—for example, a port, a connection, and a card on a device might all constitute objects, each representing a corresponding real-world counterpart. The definition of the information model specifies each kind of object that can occur in terms of an object class. Object classes are defined in terms of attributes that they contain, notifications that they can emit, behavior they exhibit, and methods that an outside application can use to interact with instances of the object class. During runtime, the object classes are instantiated into object instances. Of course, there is a lot more to object orientation, but this short description should convey the general idea and suffice for our purposes.

None of the management protocols that we introduced earlier used an object-oriented information model, but such protocols and management interfaces do exist. Also, many management applications follow a layered architecture in which application logic operates on an object-oriented information model, and a lower layer inside the application translates this object-oriented model into the management interfaces that are used for interacting with the subordinate management agents. This means that this specific mediation scenario is applicable to many applications.

An algorithm converting an SNMP MIB into an OO model could work roughly as follows, as is also illustrated in Figure 9-15.

Figure 9-15 *SNMP MIB–to–OO Mediation*

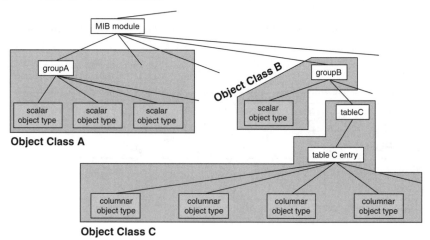

- Tables

    — Each table translates into an object class. The object class is identified by the object identifier (OID) of the object type defining the SNMP table. Instead of the OID, the human-readable name (stripped of the Table suffix that is used by convention at the end) could be used, but the OID is assumed here.

    — Each column within the table translates into an attribute of the object class. As an attribute name, the OID of the table column is chosen. More precisely, it is the relative OID of the columnar object type. The relative OID is simply the suffix of the columnar object type's OID that is appended to the OID of the corresponding table entry object.

    — Methods for the object include get methods for readable attributes and set methods for writeable attributes.

    — Table entries translate into object instances. Object instances are named using the table index.

    — If a table includes a row status allowing deletion and creation of rows, the corresponding object class offers so-called constructors and destructors—that is, methods that allow a management application to create or delete object instances.

■   Scalars

    — Scalars that are grouped under the same containing OID are grouped into another object class, containing one object instance, named by the group's OID in the SNMP MIB.

    — Each scalar represents one object attribute.

    — Again, methods for the object are get and set for the readable and writeable scalars, respectively.

■   Notifications are conceptually emitted by a dedicated notification object.

In Chapter 6, we discussed an excerpt of MIB-2 as an example of a MIB definition. Applying the algorithm to the MIB-2 excerpt that was depicted in Figure 6-13 would yield two object classes (for readability purposes, we use human-readable names instead of their OID counterparts): the object class named system has the attributes sysDescr, sysUpTime, sysContact, and sysName, whereas the object class tcpConn has the attributes tcpConnState, tcpConnLocalAddress, tcpConnLocalPort, tcpConnRemoteAddress, and tcpConnRemotePort. The MIB depicted in Figure 6-15 is translated into four instances of objects of the class tcpConn—objects that are named 167.8.15.92.227.176.15.53.216, 167.8.15.92.235.176.15.53.218, 167.8.15.92.236.178.67.124.15, and 167.8.15.92.244.181.33.16.4, each corresponding to an entry in tcpConnTable.

Now, when a management application makes a get request for a particular object and attribute, it specifies the name and class of the object that is requested, as well as the name of the attribute. Because the names were algorithmically derived from the MIB, the mediation gateway can convert them automatically to an OID used for the SNMP get request.

Similarly, when a management application makes a create request, this is automatically translated into a corresponding SNMP set request, including variable bindings for each of the parameters in the create request, the OIDs of which are constructed using the corresponding attribute names.

Limitations of Syntactic Information Mediation

As simple as the previous examples were, they show the limitations of syntactic mediation.

We turn first to the syslog-to-SNMP gateway. Of course, the gateway does allow an SNMP manager to receive syslog messages without needing to understand and parse syslog. However, the traps produced by the mediator likely look a little different than what would have been emitted by a native SNMP agent at the device. To distinguish those traps, we use the terms *mediated traps* and *native traps*, respectively. Perhaps most tellingly, the mediated traps do not relate to any objects in actual SNMP MIBs other than the syslog mediation MIB.

Consider the example of a message indicating a problem with an interface. A native trap likely would include the OID of the affected interface as part of the trap's variable bindings, making it easier to follow up on the trap, such as to retrieve additional information about the interface to facilitate troubleshooting. Not so in the case of the mediated trap. Of course, it still includes information about the affected interface; however, this information is buried in unstructured manner somewhere in the object that represents the body part of the syslog message. The contents of the message's body part are still conveyed as a "blob," even though it is transported as part of a trap.

This points to a second problem: Although the management application is relieved from needing to understand and parse syslog message formats, much of the mediated trap's payload information still requires additional parsing and interpretation that with a "native" trap would not be required. Specifically, the additional parsing and interpretation involves the message body, which, in many cases, includes essential additional information, but not in a way that relates to information in an SNMP MIB. It is not any easier to understand as part of an SNMP trap than it is as part of a syslog message.

Similar issues apply in the case of the OO-to-SNMP gateway. The resulting interface exposes an object-oriented model. However, the model reflects the structure of the MIB that it was derived from, which, in many cases, is not the same as the structure that would have been chosen for a "native" OO model designed from the ground up. For example, object orientation offers facilities to express inheritance—an "is a kind of" relationship between object classes that gives much of the power to object-oriented approaches. The mediated model does not include this notion and, hence, does not provide the corresponding benefits. (Having said that, refinements to the algorithm are possible that in certain cases make it possible to emulate inheritance, but only to a limited degree.) Likewise, object-oriented models can include a notion of containment, again an aspect that is not captured in the mediated model.

The results in each case are the following two most important limitations to syntactic mediation of management information:

- Generally, syntactic mediation does not leverage the full power and expressiveness of the information-modeling language that is being mediated to. The mediated model is therefore less rich than a native model would be.

- Certain artifacts of the information model being mediated from are not fully hidden. A management application still needs to deal with those artifacts at the semantic level, although not at the syntactic level.

Mediation of Management Information at the Semantic Level

Mediating management information without the limitations of the syntactic transformation approaches requires a semantic understanding of the management information involved. This means that custom translation rules need to be crafted, mapping the mediated management information to the target information model.

For example, in the case of mediation from syslog (agent) to SNMP (manager), it would be necessary to determine which specific syslog messages should trigger which specific SNMP traps, along with rules for the translation of the message body part into specific SNMP notification parameters. Those rules would consist of templates, one per syslog message, that specify how different parts of the message body translate into variable bindings of the SNMP trap message.

In the case of mediation from SNMP (agent) to OO (manager), it would be necessary to specify for each method, attribute, and object class of the target OO model how they map into MIB objects and SNMP management operations. The reverse direction (how to map SNMP MIB objects into object attributes of the OO model) must be specified as well, to be able to process responses properly.

This type of mediation overcomes the limitations of syntactic mediation. The price, obviously, is that much more up-front development effort is required, along with much more intelligence in the management gateway. This makes the approach substantially more expensive. It is no longer sufficient to perform one-size-fits-all mediation during runtime. Instead, conversion rules need to be developed beforehand and deployed on the gateway before mediation can successfully take place.

Stateful Mediation

Ideally, management mediation follows a simple pattern: The management gateway receives a request message from a manager and translates it into an equivalent request message for the agent. When a response or event message is received, the gateway translates it into an equivalent response or event message that it sends back to the manager. The pattern is very straightforward and clean; management mediation involves not much more than transforming a message that the gateway can forget about after it is sent. What to do with those messages—for example, how to react when things go wrong—is of no interest to the gateway; this is the responsibility of manager and agent. The gateway is merely a conduit, a messenger. It does not care what the messages really mean. After it has done its part—that is, after it has translated the message that it received and passed on the translated message—it does not need to keep a memory (or "state") around about the fact that the translation ever occurred. This is referred to as *stateless* mediation.

So much for the ideal case. Unfortunately, in real life, things are often less than ideal, and for management gateways, the situation is no different. For management gateways, this means that stateless mediation is subject to certain limitations. Those limitations surface whenever the target interface (the one the gateway exposes to the manager) has capabilities that cannot be translated in a one-to-one manner to the source interface (the one that the agent exposes, that the gateway has to work with). This can occur in the following scenarios:

- The target interface supports management functions that are not offered by the source interface. For example, the target interface supports an event-subscription service that the manager expects to use but that the underlying agent does not provide.

- The target interface supports certain options for management functions that the source interface does not support. For example, the target interface might include an option to apply a get operation to all objects in a MIB subtree that meet a certain criteria, whereas the source interface offers no such capability.

- The target interface exposes management information that is not available in the same form at the source interface. For example, the target interface might provide a managed object with the sum of all packets that were routed over ports on that card, whereas the source interface might provide the same information only for the individual ports.

- There are even simpler scenarios, such as the target interface requiring the request identifier to be included as part of the matching response message, whereas the source interface might have no notion of request identifiers.

Despite such "semantic mismatches," which are also schematically depicted in Figure 9-16, in most cases, mediation is still possible.

Figure 9-16 *Semantic Matches and Mismatches in Management Mediation*

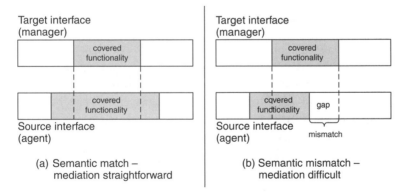

In the first example, the management gateway can emulate the event-subscription service by remembering which subscriptions the manager requested and then filtering the events that are received as required. The management gateway needs to understand what the subscription requests entail, intercept those requests, and, instead of translating them into management requests for the agent, provide the needed functionality itself. The agent being managed does not even have to realize that any of this is taking place.

■ In the second example, the management gateway needs the capability to resolve the identifiers of objects that might fall in the requested scope and then break up the request into a series of requests directed at the individual managed objects at the agent, collect the responses from the agent, check for each response if the filter criteria is being met, and then aggregate them into a response message to the manager.

■ In the third example, the management gateway needs to understand how the piece of management information being requested relates to other management information that can be retrieved from the device. In this case, it needs to understand that the requested information constitutes an aggregate of other management information available at the device. As with the second example, the gateway needs to retrieve that information possibly in multiple requests and aggregate the information for the response being sent back to the manager.

■ In the last example, the management gateway needs to retain a memory of the request identifier until the response from the agent is received so that it can include the identifier in the response to the manager.

In each case, the gateway needs to do much more than just translate messages. It might need to do the following:

■ Break a single operation into multiple steps

■ Deal with exceptions and be capable of providing transactional semantics—in other words, know what to do when an operation fails that is one in a series of steps

■ Provide additional management logic, as in the event subscription example

■ Cache management information from the underlying agents, for example, so that it can resolve a management operation's scope

Above all, it needs to retain *state*—a memory of what subscriptions it needs to serve, of intermediate results that need to be collected and aggregated to prepare a response, or of the identifier of a request that it received earlier. Therefore, this type of mediation is called *stateful* mediation.

Stateful gateways are much more powerful than stateless gateways. As the examples show, many functions could simply not be offered with gateways that are stateless. In addition, stateless gateways expose the limitations of the interface of the underlying agent, whereas stateful gateways can smooth out those limitations, to a great extent. The price for this added power is, of course, added complexity in the gateway. The heavier the management gateway becomes, the more it will start to resemble a full-fledged management application in its own right.

In the end, there is no magic: a simpler interface is simpler to implement by an agent, and a more powerful interface offloads management applications, but in the end, the work needs to be done somewhere. Hence, if you want to mediate from an agent with a simple interface to a more powerful interface that can be used by a manager (by far the most common scenario), the difference in power must be made up somewhere—and where else if not the management gateway?

Chapter Summary

Management is a task that is inherently distributed and that might have to be distributed beyond basic manager-agent management topologies to keep up with the exponential growth of networks that need to be managed. This distribution almost inevitably leads to management hierarchies, with management tasks cascading across multiple systems, with intermediate systems playing the role of both agent (to their superiors) and manager (to their subordinates).

Management hierarchies imply information hierarchies, leading to management information that gets increasingly condensed, aggregated, and abstracted. This is a key to making management scale. It also allows for efficient deployment of management when the links between the network operations center and remote locations are bandwidth constrained.

Management tasks can be distributed according to different management philosophies— management by delegation, by objectives, and by exception. Policy-based management and RMON are examples of specific technologies that are geared toward distributing management tasks as close to the edges of the management network as possible. Ideally, management tasks could be pushed all the way to the managed devices, tapping into a computation resource that, by definition, grows just as fast as the network itself. Although this is feasible in some cases, this approach has some limitations, not the least of which is the need for the managed devices to spend their computing resources on their primary task instead of additional management functionality.

We also took a look at management gateways that mediate between different management interfaces. The need for mediation arises as the variety of management interfaces and protocols proliferates. Management mediation leads to a special variation of management hierarchies, where the system in the middle is tasked with bridging the gap between the manager at the top and the agent that it manages at the bottom. Far from simple message translation, management mediation is a complex topic that in many cases involves significant application complexity. The most simple form is syntactic, stateless mediation, but more often stateful and possibly semantic mediation is required.

Chapter Review

1. Assume that you have to manage an enterprise network with several remote branch locations. You are told that you need to collect performance data from each remote location to assess the total traffic that goes to headquarters, that is directed to other enterprise locations, and that goes to destinations outside the enterprise. Your low-bandwidth WAN connection that leads back to your network operations center doesn't seem to have enough bandwidth to allow for the export of all the Netflow data from the remote locations. What other options do you have?

2. What is RMON?

3. Give an example of a management task that a management appliance could provide.

4. If management by delegation is such a great idea, why don't we simply delegate all management tasks to the network?

5. What do the acronyms PDP and PEP stand for?

6. How can policy-based management help scale management?

7. What are the main limitations of syntactical management mediation?

8. Why is stateful mediation more complex than stateless mediation?

9. Assume for a moment that you have two fictitious management protocols, SIMP and COMP. SIMP is a very simple protocol, providing only a small set of the most basic management primitives. COMP is much more powerful; it offers all the capabilities that SIMP offers, plus additional functionality. For example, COMP enables you to apply the same management operation to a group of managed objects that meet a certain criteria, and it offers a threshold-crossing alerting capability, whereas SIMP does not. Now assume that you are asked to build two management gateways, one for SIMP managers to manage COMP agents, the other for COMP managers to manage SIMP agents. Which of the two do you expect to be simpler? Why?

10. Would you expect semantic mediation of management information that involves CLI as the source (agent) interface to be simple or hard? Why?

Part IV: Applied Network Management

Management Integration: Putting the Pieces Together

As we saw in earlier chapters, managing a network involves a great variety of functions—from monitoring devices in the network to provisioning services, from diagnosing networking problems to planning for optimum network performance, from detecting security breaches to assessing the impact of planned network maintenance on existing services and customers.

One of the challenges in network management—indeed, some would argue, the "holy grail" in network management—lies in providing operational support infrastructure and management systems that are integrated. This means that all management functionality that is required for everything that needs to be managed is provided in one holistic solution, as opposed to providing the functionality in multiple, separate parts that essentially form separate islands. Having multiple management islands can cause many problems that could be avoided with an integrated solution: Data needs to be maintained redundantly and can run out of synch, training cost increases for operational staff that needs to be familiar with a multitude of systems, and management tasks fall through the cracks.

In this chapter, we take a closer look at the challenges that are associated with integrated management. Recognizing what those challenges are is the first step in confronting them successfully. The chapter also discusses some techniques that can be used to tackle those challenges and some of the trade-offs that they involve. In the course of the discussion, we start putting together many of the pieces from the earlier chapters.

Here are some of the things that you will learn by reading this chapter:

- Get to know many of the factors that make management integration a challenge, which is a prerequisite for being able to deal with them successfully

- Understand how the different management dimensions encountered in earlier chapters can be used to approach management integration

- Recognize trade-offs between platform- and component-based integration approaches, and between tight and loose management integration

- Learn about approaches that can help you reduce the complexity of management tasks you might face

The Need for Management Integration

In practice, the diversity of things to be managed and the diversity of functions needed for management easily lead to a diverse set of management applications that are used to manage a network. Management integration aims to provide an operations support environment in which management functionality is seamlessly integrated and holistic, end-to-end management support is provided.

Before we get into what the challenges of management integration are and how those challenges can be successfully approached, let us start by taking a look at the various reasons why management integration is of such importance. To that end, let us set the stage by discussing the benefits that are to be gained from management that is integrated compared to management that is not. We also explain why management integration is not just a technical problem. As the saying goes, "Beauty lies in the eye of the beholder." Similarly, what constitutes management integration lies in the eye of the beholder—or, rather, the issues that need to be addressed as part of integrated management depend in part on the perspective of the party involved.

Benefits of Integrated Management

Having management that is integrated—as opposed to management that is based on a piecemeal approach that consists of multiple management "islands"—is important for many reasons that include the following:

- It helps ensure that management tasks do not fall through the cracks. Management tasks that are supported by a holistic, integrated operational support environment do not need to rely as much on manual procedures and leave little to chance, compared to management tasks that are not supported by such an environment.

- Integrated management systems and holistic operational support environments (from here on, simply referred to as integrated management infrastructure) reduce the need for training and increase the pool of available personnel that can carry out operational tasks. With integrated management systems, operators need to be well versed in fewer systems and machine interfaces.

- Integrated management infrastructure facilitates management of the management itself—that is, of the management systems and management network that need to be managed in addition to the production network itself. Management environments that are not integrated require much more manual administration, supervision, and intervention to keep network operations running smoothly.

- Integrated management infrastructure eliminates (or at least reduces) the need for operators and network administrators to enter redundant data. For example, in a nonintegrated management environment, information about which network elements need to be managed and how to reach them (IP addresses, user credentials) frequently has to be entered multiple times, potentially into every management application that needs to know about the network elements. The result is lower operations efficiency: After all, entering this information takes time and effort. Even worse, it is error prone.

■ In the same vein as the previous point, integrated management infrastructure reduces or eliminates the need to keep the same data redundantly in multiple locations, such as in separate management applications. Maintaining redundant data can be an issue, even when it does not have to be entered redundantly, because that data can potentially run out of synch. When it does run out of synch, cleanup can be a mess.

■ Integrated management infrastructure helps reduce the management load on the managed network. In nonintegrated management environments, different applications might all need to query a managed device for the same management information. This not only wastes bandwidth on the management network, but it also causes avoidable CPU cycles spent by the device responding to management queries instead of passing network traffic. This additional load can be quite significant, particularly when applications rely on frequent polling.

■ Integrated management infrastructure makes it easier to have management information available whenever and wherever it is needed, sometimes in conjunction with applications where it might not be expected at first. For example, the same data about existing network inventory might need to be accessed for the following very different purposes:

— Network planning (determine additional needs based on what is already available in the network)

— Network monitoring (know what to monitor)

— Service provisioning (determine network equipment that needs to be configured to carry an instance of a service)

— Help desk (be able to trace a problem with the level of service that a user is experiencing to possible culprits in terms of network equipment that might cause the problem)

■ Integration can help feed itself, in the sense that management infrastructure that is already integrated will be easier to integrate with other parts of the business if the need arises, fostering further integration. There will be only one system with (hopefully) one well-defined interface to interact with instead of a hodgepodge of different components with all kinds of interdependencies.

In other words, management that is integrated results in management that is also much more efficient than it would otherwise be. Compare the situation depicted in Figures 10-1 and 10-2. In Figure 10-1, the operator has to deal with a multitude of different systems, each with its own user interface and database. Clearly, this situation is intimidating, if not overwhelming. In addition, the devices in the network will be hit with requests from multiple directions. In Figure 10-2, this situation has been replaced by one that is much simpler. The complexity has been absorbed by a single integrated management system—elusive perhaps, but the subject of the management integration quest.

Figure 10-1 *Nonintegrated Management, All Too Often Management's Reality*

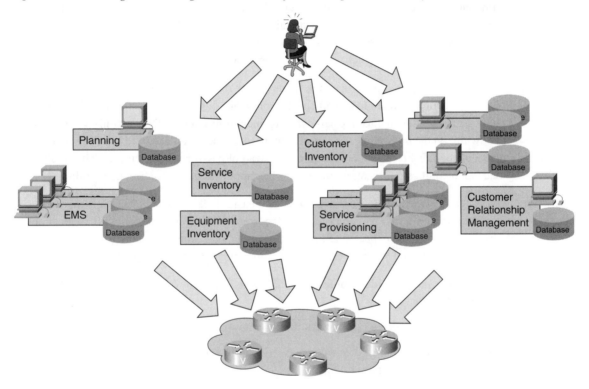

Nontechnical Considerations for Management Integration

This book deals mainly with management technology, so our discussion of management integration focuses on its technical aspects. However, it should be mentioned that management integration is not only a technical problem involving management systems and applications. There is also significant organizational dimension that involves the structure of the network provider organization that manages the network. In fact, the issues with management integration at the technical level mirror in many ways the issues that can occur at the organizational level, and the approaches to dealing with those issues need to take similar aspects into considerations, as illustrated in Figure 10-3.

Figure 10-2   *Integrated Management, Management's "Holy Grail"*

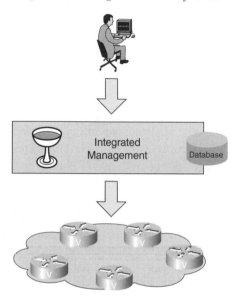

Figure 10-3   *Duality of Management Integration Problem: Organization vs. Operational Support Infrastructure*

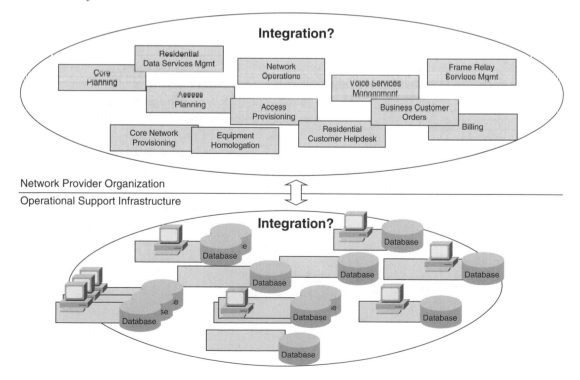

For example, imagine a situation in which the responsibility for network operations is distributed across several groups and none of them feels responsible for a particular problem that comes up during the running of the network. This spells trouble for the provider of the network. The same is true if different groups want to use the same piece of equipment for different purposes but fail to communicate with each other, resulting in the groups breaking each other's network configuration.

These might be drastic examples. However, tasks falling between the cracks and mutual finger pointing between groups are problems that are not unheard of in network provider organizations. Integrated management implies that there is also a need for the different organizations that are running the network to be "integrated" and complement each other to function efficiently.

Different Perspectives on Management Integration Needs

Let us now take a look at who has an interest in integrated management and why—in other words, the different perspectives from which integrated management can be approached. The main difference between the perspectives is the scope of what management integration entails. We start with the perspective of the equipment vendor for whom integrated management has the most constrained scope. After that, we proceed to enterprises and service providers for whom the scope of what management integration entails becomes increasingly larger.

The Equipment Vendor Perspective

The question of what to provide for integrated management is typically answered in a fairly straightforward manner by equipment vendors, particularly if they are concerned with shipping only a few types of devices. In general, the vendor's customers expect to be offered what amounts to an element management system, integrating various element management functions for a device, as Figure 10-4 shows. For better or worse, the vendor's management offering is essentially considered an extended equipment feature. (This is actually a two-way street because the equipment vendor's customers generally expect and demand just that. In too many cases, the people who make purchasing decisions are separate from the people who later need to run the network.) Of course, significant differences exist between different customers and market segments, but, in the end, this is what things boil down to in many cases.

Figure 10-4 *Typical Management Integration Scope—Equipment Vendor*

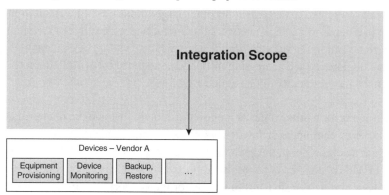

As a result, for the equipment vendor, integrated management means the need to provide an integrated management application that will allow that vendor's devices to be remotely configured, audited, and monitored; their configurations to be backed up and restored; and device images to be upgraded. The embedding of those applications into a larger operational context is generally left to the vendor's customers and to independent software vendors and system integrators.

There are exceptions, of course. Some equipment vendors view themselves as end-to-end solution providers, not point product providers. In that case, they could be treating management as a business in its own right and essentially play the dual role of an equipment vendor and of a systems integrator and application vendor. They realize that the ability to efficiently operate and manage the network is a significant factor in the economic equation for their customers. But for equipment vendors who treat management de facto as an extended feature of the equipment that they sell, this is as far as integrated management goes. And who is to blame them? From their perspective, this makes perfect business sense and allows them to focus on their core business and competence.

Of course, even with a relatively limited integration scope, equipment vendors do need to realize that in some scenarios, their management offering needs to be embedded into a larger operational context that might require integration with other systems. We get to these scenarios in the next subsections. An important aspect, often at least as important as the functionality of the management applications themselves, is therefore that the equipment vendor provides open and well-documented interfaces as part of the management applications that will facilitate such an integration to take place.

The Enterprise Perspective

The scope of integrated management becomes larger in the case of a small to medium-size enterprise that needs to manage a network that includes a wide range of different types of devices from different vendors. In such environments, typically a variety of element management systems (EMSs) are deployed, each addressing the management needs for equipment of different vendors and each used independently of one another.

This might work for a little while, as long as the domain that is to be managed and the number of different types of equipment in the network remain limited and are still easily overseen. However, inevitably, at a certain point, the need for further integration arises. The individual vendor-dependent EMSs need to be either replaced by a vendor-independent system or complemented by systems that integrate certain EMS functions for the network. Figure 10-5 depicts this increased integration scope. For example, it might become necessary to introduce an application to monitor the overall health of the network from a single place, which provides a view of the health of all the devices in the network and of all alarms that are occurring. The alternative to having to keep an eye on different vendor-specific applications becomes simply unacceptable at a certain point. In essence, this would require an operator to sit on a swivel chair to be able to easily switch among multiple terminals that each run a different application. This type of integration—or lack thereof—is generally referred to as "swivel chair integration"; you already encountered this in Chapter 1, "Setting the Stage." Even if the operator were able to access the applications from one terminal that runs multiple clients, it would not improve the situation by much—and not just because of the limited real estate that is available to display information on a computer screen.

Figure 10-5   *Typical Management Integration Scope—Medium-Size Enterprise*

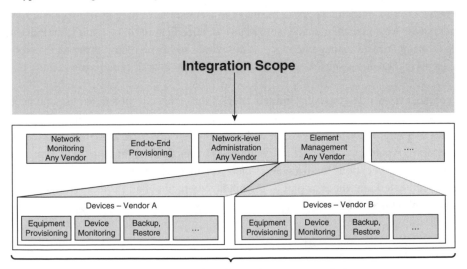

As the enterprise gets larger, the need for further integration arises. For example, requirements such as the need for a central inventory of networking equipment might enter the picture, or the need for an integration of employee databases and network user accounts so that user accounts are automatically established or revoked when employees join or leave the company. In addition, requirements might arise for network management capabilities that go beyond individual network elements but that concern the network as a whole —for example, this could be the capability to manage and monitor end-to-end connectivity between enterprise locations.

The Service Provider Perspective

Management integration takes on a whole new level of complexity for a telecommunications service provider that has to manage literally thousands of different types of systems, devices, and applications supplied by dozens of vendors, used to provide not just one type, but a great variety of different services.

In such an environment, many different tools have to be integrated that are provided by different suppliers and equipment vendors—each of which might be "fully integrated" from their limited perspective. However, how to integrate element management is only one of many considerations because it will be impossible to manage the network one device at a time. Management at the network management layer to manage end-to-end connectivity is no longer an option, but becomes instead indispensable.

In addition, entirely new management functions that did not occur at the level of the enterprise have to be dealt with, each needing to be integrated with the rest of management. Here are some examples, along with a description of specific requirements they impose on integration:

- **Billing for services**—Of course, some IT departments in enterprises might also "bill" departments internally for communication services. However, the significance of billing for a service provider puts this function in the spotlight. Billing typically requires the capability to relate information about service orders, customers, and the network itself (such as information on network addresses and ports) to be able to attribute accounting records to the right customers. Accordingly, billing imposes significant requirements on management integration because much of this information is also related to management functions other than billing and is potentially maintained by different management applications.

- **Monitoring of service level agreements provided to customers**—(Service level agreements are contractual obligations regarding the quality of the service being delivered—more on that in Chapter 11, "Service Level Management: Knowing What You Pay For.") The association of observed network outages with services and end users that will be affected by them needs to be facilitated. This requires integration between applications for the management of services and service level agreements with applications for network monitoring.

■ **Management of service orders and integration of management of the network with the management of the service provider's supply chain**—For example, in fulfilling a service order, the service provider must ensure that the necessary network equipment is already deployed or, if it has not, that it is on back order and scheduled to be delivered and deployed by the time the service order becomes due. This requires integration among inventory, service order management, and provisioning systems.

■ **Integration of network operations with other business functions**—For example, this might include customer care so that help-desk personnel has access to current network status when responding to customer inquiries.

The list goes on. In summary, service management and business management functionality becomes a critical component of integrated management for service providers. This means that the scope of management integration is no longer just "horizontal," calling for the same management functionality for increasing numbers of managed devices and device types to be integrated. Instead, the need for integration becomes "vertical" as well, having to integrate entirely new categories and layers of management functions, as Figure 10-6 shows.

Figure 10-6   *Typical Management Integration Scope—Service Provider*

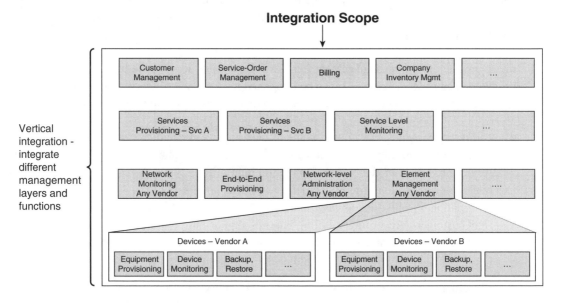

Integration Scope and Complexity

As you have just seen, the scope of what needs to be integrated as part of management depends on the perspective. It can be observed that as the scope of integration grows, its complexity grows in two dimensions simultaneously: horizontally and vertically. Horizontally, the number of devices and network technologies that need to be integrated increases. However, with growing network size and complexity, it is no longer sufficient to merely integrate and add more systems while still providing essentially the same functionality. Instead, complexity also grows vertically at the same time and makes it necessary to deal with functions of the upper layers in the TMN hierarchy. New phenomena emerge that require new management functionality to be dealt with, phenomena that are not really an issue in operations of a more limited scope. Just as it becomes more important to address management integration, it becomes more difficult to do so, as Figure 10-7 shows.

Figure 10-7 *Correlation Between Integration Importance and Difficulty*

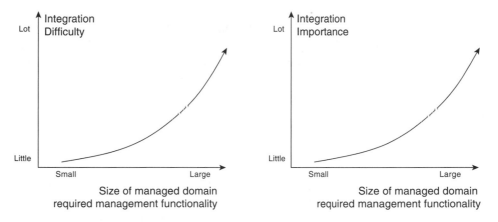

As a network provider, when you are looking for an integrated management solution, you might find that there is nothing available on the market that can do it all. At this point, you need to ask yourself whether you indeed need all the systems and tools in your management infrastructure to be fully integrated, or whether you can afford to break up your management tasks into several distinct areas, each of which can be integrated on its own.

If you are a small to medium-size business, you will most likely rely on commercial off-the-shelf management software to manage your network, perhaps augmented by some home-grown management scripts. However, as an alternative, you might decide to outsource some of your management and buy many of your communication services as a "managed service" from an outside managed service provider instead of providing those services yourself by managing your own network. Of course, any service provided by a service provider is "managed." What is different about "managed services" is that they constitute services that are provided by networking equipment on your own premises; you could choose to entirely manage those services yourself, unlike other services where this choice does not exist, such as perhaps global long-distance telephone calling that does require relying on not just your own but a service provider network.

If you are a large service provider, the option to completely outsource your management goes away. Otherwise, it would imply repositioning yourself to effectively become a reseller, not a provider of communication services. (Having said that, even a service provider typically outsources some aspects of management, such as the processing of billing information, and relies for some service aspects on other service providers, such as for additional international transmission capacity.) However, custom development to achieve management integration becomes a feasible option because you are able to achieve economies of scale that a small network provider cannot attain. You might not do all the custom development yourself, of course, but you can contract a systems integrator for that purpose.

Even so, attaining complete integration of all management functionality for your entire network still presents a formidable challenge, and an expensive one. If instead you decide to break up your overall management task into a number of more loosely coupled pieces and focus on integrating each one of them individually, you can better attain a solution and significantly reduce the total cost. In effect, instead of multiplying complexities of integrating individual subtasks with each other, you are merely adding them up and can deal with one problem at a time. (See also the section entitled "Quantifying Management Integration Complexity.") This leaves you with a significantly lower price tag overall than trying to develop the all-integrated solution.

Of course, you need to tread carefully either way: If you break up your management task too much, you are left with a scattering of different tools and a fragmented, piecemeal approach to network management in which things are run inefficiently, important tasks fall through the cracks, and, in the worst case, the functioning of your communications infrastructure is severely compromised, putting your business at risk. This is the very situation that you need to avoid. The challenge accordingly lies in finding the "sweet spot." That would be the point at which the sum of the cost of providing an integrated management infrastructure and the cost of operating the network using that infrastructure is at its minimum, as Figure 10-8 shows. Note in the figure that the sweet spot does not have to coincide with the point where operational cost and integration cost are equal.

Management Integration Challenges

Several factors make management integration a challenge. They have to do with the different dimensions along which integration occurs: On one hand, management functions need to be integrated across the managed domain—the different devices, networking technologies, and services that need to be managed and to which the same management function applies. On the other hand, different management functions have to be integrated as well. This leads to interesting challenges from a software-engineering perspective.

Figure 10-8 *Sweet Spot of Management Integration Benefit and Cost*

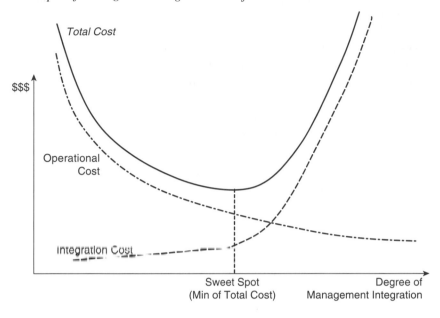

In the subsections that follow, both integration dimensions are discussed, in an attempt to capture what causes the complexity that makes management integration a challenge. We also discuss how management integration complexity can be characterized and quantified according to a set of equations. Understanding the factors in those equations and how they can be influenced is an important prerequisite for making smart choices that simplify management integration.

Managed Domain

As mentioned earlier, the challenge of providing integrated management is compounded by the fact that, just as the importance of integrated management grows, the complexity of what needs to be managed—that is, of the managed network or the "managed domain"—is also increasing. For one, this phenomenon is related to scale—that is, to the number of network devices. More important, it is related to their heterogeneity.

Heterogeneity refers to the fact that different types of devices need to be managed—different device models, devices of different vendors, devices for different networking technologies, and so on. Compare this to homogeneous environments in which all devices to be managed are alike, which obviously simplifies the management task. Increasing heterogeneity implies that network management needs to be capable of dealing with a greater variety of management interfaces. The same device and network features might have to be managed in different ways. For example, one device might offer Simple Network Management Protocol (SNMP) support and a special SNMP MIB to manage certain features, whereas a second device might also support SNMP but provide a different MIB for the same purpose; a third might offer only a set of command-line interface (CLI) commands.

Also, in general, different types of devices differ in the features that they offer, even if the devices play a similar role in the network. Of course, different features each impose their own requirements for management. For example, one device might offer a feature that allows a manager to configure a policy for connection admission control. The feature allows network managers to specify how many connections may be in progress until the device should deny additional connection requests. This avoids connections cannibalizing each other in their competition for resources, such as processing power or bandwidth. Another device might offer no such feature. Integrated management infrastructure needs to accommodate management for all the different feature variations that could be encountered.

As a second example, even when two devices offer the same networking feature, they might need to be managed differently. For example, the level of granularity at which the feature needs to be managed could differ. Consider the case of a network device that supports voice services in the role of a so-called voice gateway. One parameter that can often be configured concerns which voice codec should be applied. (The voice codec determines how the audio is encoded as binary data when sent over the network; different codecs make different trade-offs between required bandwidth and sound quality.) Whereas one device might allow the codec to be configured on a per-port basis, another device might allow it to be configured only for the entire device or for a group of ports instead of each individual port. Again, all these differences need to be accounted for by a solution for integrated management.

Another aspect of heterogeneity concerns the number of different services that are provided over the network and need to be managed. In the past, a network was often dedicated to a single service, such as phone service or Internet dial-up service. Today networks are increasingly converged, which means they support a wide variety of services that all use the same network infrastructure. For example, the same network might support data services and telephone (Voice over IP) service.

On one hand, this is excellent news as far as network management is concerned: Where formerly several networks needed to be managed, now there is only one. In fact, reducing management cost is one of the main motivations for network convergence. However, the fact that multiple services need to be supported simultaneously can lead to some management challenges of its own. Converging of services also requires a certain degree of integration in the management of those services, whereas previously they could be managed completely independently of one another. The reason for this is that, in a converged network, different services compete for the same networking resources—something that management needs to address properly.

Consider the example of two services that both want to use the same port. Managing both services separately in a nonintegrated manner using separate management applications could lead to the same port first being assigned to one service by one service management application, then reassigned to another service by another service management application, breaking the other service. Both applications keep track of their use of networking resources but are unaware that they could conflict with one another because each is competing for resources with another service—this aspect was not an issue in a nonconverged network.

A second example involves competition for Digital Signal Processing (DSP) resources. Imagine a device with DSP resources that are limited so that they allow the device to provide one service with traffic encryption and another service with data compression, but not both at the same time. Again, if both services are managed independently and are unaware of one another, conflicts between them can arise.

Software Architecture

As mentioned earlier, business realities often dictate that network providers deal with different management systems and tools that they then try to fit under one umbrella. However, let us briefly assume that we could start with a clean slate. Could we simply build an integrated management application that does it all? Intuitively, this would be the first approach to take. Let us pursue this possibility for a moment to see what it would entail and what difficulties we might encounter. This will give us insights about the challenges that need to be dealt with from a software-engineering perspective. There are other and more effective approaches to management integration; nevertheless, the lessons learned here should prove helpful.

Challenges from Application Requirements

For starters, our integrated management system needs to be capable of providing all management functionality that is required. Of course, as we have seen in earlier chapters, so many functions are involved in managing a network that being able to provide them all through a single system seems unlikely. Even if it were possible to do so for one particular environment, different network providers have different needs, making the task of building something where one size fits all (and that would be customizable enough to make it work in different settings) daunting indeed.

Our integrated management system also needs to be highly scalable, to support very large network deployments. After all, if multiple separate systems had to be deployed because of lack of scale, with each system managing a different part of the network, the resulting management infrastructure could hardly be called "integrated." Of course, at a certain point it might be necessary to add processing horsepower, perhaps in the form of additional server hosts, but this should not affect the users of the management system, the network operators; in fact, it should be transparent (that is, unnoticeable) to them. However, another aspect of scalability is easily overlooked: Scalability also applies to the other direction. Management systems often need to be capable of also supporting very *small* network deployments in a way that is not cost prohibitive. This way, as the network grows, the need to change or migrate operational support infrastructure in midstream can be avoided.

Then there are the obvious challenges from needing to deal with the complexity of the network itself that we just discussed. This implies that a management system's software architecture needs to be capable of supporting myriad different underlying entities that need to be managed, each with its own unique characteristics and variations in management interfaces.

Hence, the integrated management system must be very easy to extend and maintain regarding the systems that it manages. Importantly, it should be capable of decoupling the release cycle of the application software itself from the release cycle of the entities that it manages—that is, the managed devices. In other words, every time a new type of equipment is added to the network and needs to be supported by the management system, a new management software release should not be required.

Of course, this type of requirement is well known in other areas, such as computer operating systems. Consider, for example, the need to add support for new printers. This is generally accomplished through printer drivers that contain instructions on how to translate between a generic application programming interface (API) that applications use to print and a device-specific command set. In general, new drivers can be dynamically added without requiring a new release of the operating system, or even a restart. Our integrated management system should support an analogous capability. Of course, a management driver in general turns out to be significantly more complex than a printer driver.

Challenges from Conflicting Software Architecture Goals

Another difficulty arises from the fact that different management functions can impose conflicting requirements on the software architecture that the integrated management system is to be based on. At times, those requirements could be difficult, if not impossible, to reconcile in a single system. This point is a little more subtle than the previous ones yet is just as important, so let us elaborate further on it.

In Chapter 1, we mentioned that one of the challenges in building management applications lies in the wide range of architectural properties that they require. For example, for a provisioning application, reliability is of utmost importance. The application needs to make sure that provisioning commands indeed had the desired effect and must go to extra lengths to ensure that. After all, if services do not work as anticipated, customer satisfaction will plummet, revenue will be lost, and additional cost will be incurred to diagnose and fix things. At the same time, how quickly the management transaction executes is of lesser concern—a customer generally does not perceive a difference of a few minutes in the time that it takes to turn up a new phone service to be critical.

On the other hand, for an alarm monitoring application tasked with monitoring the network for alarms, the biggest concern is to minimize the amount of time that passes between the instant a problem occurs and the instant the network manager is alerted. Time is money, and in some cases, network outages can cost thousands of dollars every second. Consider, for example, the consequences when a flight-booking system or a network that connects bank tellers goes down. Information that is related to the alarm, such as which users might be affected, has to be very quickly identified, and state changes need to be quickly propagated through the system. Delayed delivery of alarms may be unacceptable because the state of the network changes rapidly, and receiving updates that are late can be almost as bad as receiving no updates at all.

None of these applications is trivial to build, per se. Try to combine all of them into one integrated system, and you are faced with a problem that can be quite difficult to solve. Application properties such as minimized latency and optimized reliability can have different implications on the underlying software architecture and need to be addressed in different ways. At a minimum, they differ on where architectural emphasis should be placed. Excellent judgment is required on how to make the necessary architectural trade-offs to arrive at a system that is well balanced overall. The example of a provisioning application and of an alarm monitoring application that we just encountered should illustrate this point, which Figure 10-9 also depicts.

Figure 10-9 *Conflicting Architecture Goals*

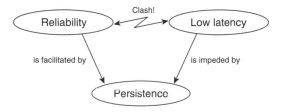

In the case of the alarm monitoring application, special consideration needs to be given to rapid state propagation and event delivery, which might have to be traded off with reliability. For example, for the sake of performance, it might be undesirable to persist into a database every event or equipment state change that is observed because this could slow things down. On rare occasions it is of course possible that an application module fails and some transient information about the network device is lost. However, with some effort, it is generally still possible to recover all important information through special exception-handling procedures, such as by auditing the device for its current state. Although this is not ideal, it is still much more acceptable than the alternative of more sluggish application responsiveness.

The provisioning application, on the other hand, could well make the trade-off the other way: Precedence needs to be given to reliability and persisting what is being done every step along the way. This ensures that services are reliably turned up, even in the case of failures along the way. For example, it might be unacceptable to accidentally issue the same provisioning command for a second time, which might accidentally occur in a scenario in which an application has to be unexpectedly restarted and it is not clear how far a sequence of previous provisioning steps had progressed—an ill-defined network state might otherwise result. Taking the necessary precautions and logging things into a database every step along the way takes priority over trying to send commands to network elements and processing their responses in the fastest possible manner.

Hence, important calls have to be made for the software architecture of our integrated management system. For example, how often should management information be persisted in the database—every time a change occurs, for maximum robustness, or only periodically, for improved performance? Should state changes be propagated to interested applications using callback functions in synchronous fashion, interrupting them in what they are doing, or is it better to follow a more asynchronous model in which applications are expected to actively retrieve them?

Eierlegende Wollmilchsaun and One-Size-Fits-All Management Systems

To summarize the gist of the discussion to this point, trying to address the needs of multiple management applications in a single system inevitably leads to situations in which the best that can be accomplished might be a compromise—hopefully acceptable, but not the best that could be achieved for each function individually.

For all practical purposes, the likelihood of being able to build a truly comprehensive integrated application that fits everybody's needs is, well, slim. The German language has a term for it: *eierlegende Wollmilchsaun,* referring to an egg-laying, wool-giving, milk-giving pig—a farmer's dream, except for the fact that, unfortunately, it doesn't exist.

So what should be done? In the case of the eggwoolmilkpig, farmers generally revert to the second-most-desirable option: They get some chickens, a sheep, a cow, and a pig instead. Of course, this conglomeration of animals takes a little more effort to tend and uses up a little more space than a single animal. However, at the end of the day, they accomplish the same purpose.

In the case of management systems, why not build multiple applications that each serve a particular purpose and simply make sure that they can work well together? Or if applications have already been built, just use existing applications and perhaps provide some "glue" and additional auxiliary functions that allow them to work together. This is indeed what needs to be done, and we investigate corresponding approaches in the next section. But before we do, let us summarize what we have discussed so far and get a handle on how we can express the complexity of management integration a little more formally.

Quantifying Management Integration Complexity

One could state in a simplified manner that the inherent complexity of providing integrated management for a given managed domain is the product of several factors. This can be expressed as follows:

Management integration complexity = scale complexity * heterogeneity complexity * function complexity

We take a closer look at each of those factors in the following subsections.

Note that the factors that contribute to management integration complexity are multiplied by one another, not merely added. For them to be added, the factors that contribute to the overall complexity would have to be independent of one another. This would be the case only if it were sufficient for the management infrastructure to consist of a number of systems that simply exist side by side. In that case, the complexity of providing the management infrastructure would be much lower—it would be merely the sum of its parts. On the other hand, to truly integrate the parts, a multitude of interdependencies need to be addressed, the complexity of which is more appropriately expressed as a product, not a sum.

Scale Complexity

Scale complexity results from the size of the domain that needs to be managed—in other words, the sheer number of devices in the network. The management task is a lot simpler for a small business that has a handful of equipment to manage than for a telecommunications service provider with hundreds of devices in the core of the network and tens of thousands of access devices. Scale does matter. Nevertheless, it is perhaps the least of the factors that determine overall management complexity. Scale complexity could be simply defined as a function of the order of magnitude of the number of managed pieces of equipment or, to account for the different scale and complexity of the equipment itself, of the number of ports in the network that needs to be managed. This is expressed in the following equation:

Scale complexity = f(#ports, #devices)

Heterogeneity Complexity

Heterogeneity complexity defines the degree of uniformity, or lack thereof, of what is to be managed in an integrated fashion. Clearly, if only a single type of router that is deployed across the network needs to be managed, the task is a little simpler than in the case of 10 different equipment types from five different vendors. Accordingly, the heterogeneity complexity of a network can be roughly defined as the product of several factors that are functions of the following:

- The number of vendors whose equipment is deployed in the network

- The number of networking technologies that are converged in the same network (for example, DSL, cable, and fixed wireless for a set of access networks, or MPLS and ATM for a backbone network)

- The average number of different types of devices that are used for each networking technology

- The average number of different versions of each device type (for example, different software images reflecting different revisions in the equipment's operating system)

Expressed as an equation, this yields the following:

*Heterogeneity complexity = f(#vendors) * f(#technologies) * f(#device types) * f(avg # of device versions)*

The factors that contribute to heterogeneity complexity are once again multiplied, not added, for reasons analogous to those that were outlined for management integration complexity as a whole.

Function Complexity

Function complexity results from the variety of different management functions that are to be integrated. Two factors determine function complexity: the number of distinct functions that need to be integrated, and the depth with which you want integration to occur. This is characterized in the following equation—again, a product, not a sum, for analogous reasons as for the previous equations:

*Function complexity = f(#management functions) * f(integration depth)*

The fact that the number of functions that are to be integrated is a factor in determining integration complexity should intuitively be clear. A system that integrates functionality from multiple applications tends to be significantly more complex than the sum of the complexities of each application being realized in its own respective system. The number of management layers that need to be addressed in integrated fashion can also be factored in here. Addressing application management, service management, and network management each through their own respective system is significantly simpler than trying to have them all seamlessly integrated.

The depth of integration is a little harder to capture. It has to do with the extent to which functions are really integrated. It is possible for integration between management functions to be very shallow, reflecting the fact that they are internally realized through separate and largely independent applications. For example, two management functions that are only shallowly integrated might share their user administration and be launchable from the same screen but have little else in common. The look and feel of their graphical user interfaces (GUIs) might still differ, data and internal databases might not be shared, interfaces that are exposed to other applications might be entirely disjointed, and access to managed devices might not be coordinated. Deep integration, on the other hand, might make it virtually impossible for users to distinguish where one application ends and another begins, or even whether multiple applications are involved at all. Obviously, deep integration is much harder to achieve than shallow integration.

Approaches to Management Integration

The integration problem is generally too large to be tackled all at once. Often there is a trade-off to make: Does management infrastructure have to be integrated all the way, thereby making management more efficient but more expensive? Or is it acceptable not to integrate certain aspects, to lower management integration complexity and cost, at the expense of operations that might be a little less efficient as a consequence? If a decision is made to settle for less than full integration, the decision of where to make the cut should be carefully evaluated. The cut should be made in a place where a high reduction in management integration complexity and cost results, yet operations efficiency is minimally impacted.

This needs to be approached in systemic fashion, one aspect at a time. At this point, it helps to remember that there are different dimensions in network management, which we discussed earlier in Chapter 4, "The Dimensions of Management." One possibility for integration is to take a look at these dimensions and decide which dimension is the most crucial for integration. This provides the starting point from which to tackle integration.

For example, in one particular case, it might be decided that integration is most important along the lines of management functions (integrated alarm management for the entire network, for example). At the same time, integration of different functions with each other (alarm management and inventory management, for example) might be of lesser importance. This integration approach could be a good fit in case of a network provider organization that is primarily grouped along functional responsibilities instead of different network technologies, for example. This way, the management infrastructure is integrated for the function that each group is primarily interested in. In the example, the fact that other management functions are not as well integrated is deemed less critical because an individual group will not be concerned with those other management functions and, hence, will not be affected as much by a lack of integration. (Having said this, some coordination between the groups may still have to occur and should be supported by the management infrastructure.)

Integration might also start with any of the other management dimensions, for example:

- The network technology being managed—for example, addressing management integration separately for the core router network, for the DSL access network, and for the mobile wireless network

- The layer of the network being managed, separating management of the physical transmission network from the switching and routing networks

- The management layer, integrating service management on one side and element management on the other

The choice of which dimension to use as you begin integration is significant for management integration. When you are finished integrating along the first dimension, you can start taking on the second dimension that reflects your second priority. You might never get to the last dimension and your least priority, but you will end up with management that is integrated to a degree that should suit you well.

Adapting Integration Approach and Network Provider Organization

One aspect that will likely influence a network provider's approach to management integration is how its operations organization is set up. The larger the network that needs to be managed, the more important it becomes how the organization that is responsible for managing the network is structured. After all, the management organization itself is an important part of how networks are managed; hence, integrated management does not stop at the technical infrastructure but needs to take the organizational dimension into account as well. In addition, because the management infrastructure is supposed to support the organization in the most effective manner possible, the way the organization is set up profoundly impacts the integration that needs to occur for the systems and applications that make up the management infrastructure.

The questions that need to be answered when setting up a management organization to run a network are very similar to the questions that concern technical issues. For example, should management be organized primarily along function, with one group responsible for equipment deployment and provisioning, another for network planning, and a third for monitoring and maintaining the network? Or would an alternative organization be preferable that revolves around network technologies, with one group responsible for the time-division multiplexing (TDM) voice network, a second for access networks, and a third for the IP and Multiprotocol Label Switching (MPLS) core? Figure 10-10 depicts a matrix of functions that have to be supported for a fictitious network provider organization.

Figure 10-10   *A Roles and Responsibilities Matrix for a Fictitious Network Provider*

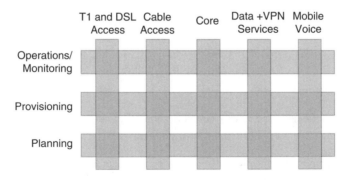

Different network providers might answer these questions differently. Regardless of what particular organization results, a couple rules should be observed:

■ It needs to be clear who is responsible for what. Accountability must be as clear as possible; otherwise, the ability to react appropriately during times of crises will be jeopardized. Situations must be avoided in which different groups point fingers at each other, each claiming that it is not responsible for problems that have arisen.

■ The number of interactions and interdependencies between groups should be minimized. When trying to divide the overall task of running a network, the division that results in the greatest independence among the resulting pieces generally is preferable. The fewer interdependencies exist, the more robust the overall organization will be against failures in particular functions, and the more efficient it will turn out to be.

Figure 10-11 depicts this principle in a simplified manner as a graph optimization problem: Assume a network provider organization with different functions and interdependencies, depicted as a graph on the left side of the diagram. The organization decides to split network operations across two groups, each of which is to be responsible for roughly the same number of functions. Two possibilities to organize are depicted as organizational cuts A and B, respectively. Cut A is clearly preferable over cut B because it involves fewer interdependencies.

Figure 10-11 *Approaching Reduction of Organizational Interdependencies from Graph Theory*

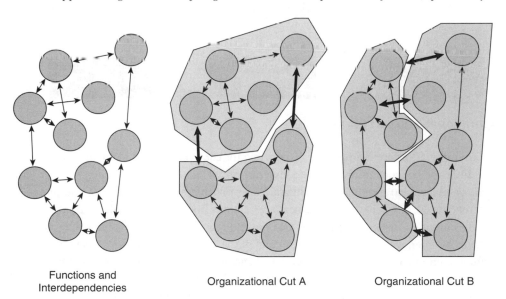

Functions and
Interdependencies

Organizational Cut A

Organizational Cut B

■ Where dependencies between different groups exist, processes need to be clearly defined that define the "rules of engagement" between the groups. Those processes need to be accompanied by clear communication paths. As in the case of establishing who is responsible for what, this increases accountability and reduces the chance of finger pointing.

Regardless of the particular way in which the network provider organization is structured, integration of the technical management infrastructure should go hand in hand with it. The management infrastructure needs to support the network provider organization in the best way possible and, to a certain degree, reflects its structure. To this end, Figures 10-12 and 10-13 depict two alternative organizations to support the roles and responsibilities matrix from Figure 10-10; one is organized along support function, the other along supported services and technology. Note in each case the differences in terms of operational support infrastructure.

Figure 10-12 *Organization and Operations Support Infrastructure Along Functional Lines*

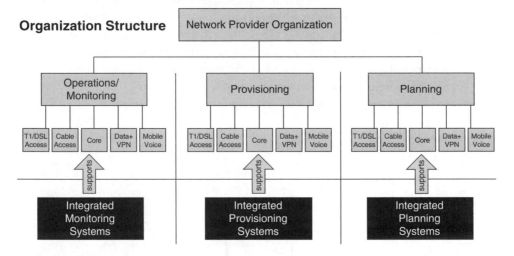

For example, if different groups are responsible for equipment provisioning and for monitoring, very little can be gained from trying to integrate provisioning and monitoring systems. However, much can be gained from trying to integrate the provisioning applications for equipment from different vendors, and alarm management applications from different vendors. By the same token, if different groups are responsible for the core and access portions of the network, management systems do not have to integrate management of the entire network, which also relaxes some scaling requirements. In that case, more is to be gained by the integration of different management functions, limited to just this particular portion of the network. Likewise, the interfaces and dependencies among the different systems of the operational support infrastructure tend to reflect the interfaces and dependencies between the organizations that own them.

Figure 10-13 *Organization and Operations Support Infrastructure Along Technology and Service Lines*

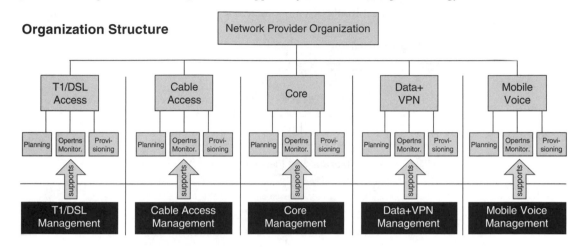

Platform Approach

A common approach to management integration is to integrate management applications using a *management platform*. A management platform is a software system that provides common infrastructure services for management applications, along with a base set of management functions that are typically intended for monitoring a network. Management platforms are often accompanied by software development kits that facilitate the development of additional functionality. Additional management applications are available, sometimes offered by independent third parties, that "plug into" and integrate with the management platform. There are several popular management platforms and accompanying product suites on the market today.

At its core, a management platform constitutes a piece of management middleware that resides on top of a computer operating system and below management applications that build on top it, as shown in Figure 10-14. The management platform provides the "integration glue" for the management applications. In this sense, it can be thought of as a "management system operating system." The idea is that every management application and every management tool that the network provider needs should be capable of running on the same management platform. The management platform, along with the applications that run on top of it, therefore becomes the only system the network provider will ever need. The management platform effectively becomes a "Jack of all trades" that is integrated by design—integrated at least to a similar degree as applications running on a desktop PC, which use the same GUI widgets, the same file system, the same device drivers, the same internal communication mechanisms. By adopting the principles of an operating system that allows multiple applications to be provided and run semi-independently on top of it, the platform approach avoids the pitfalls of a monolithic one-size-fits-all management system.

Figure 10-14 *Management Platform Concept*

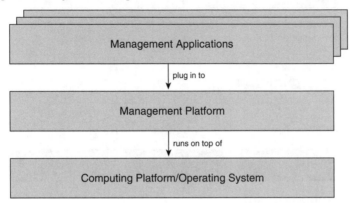

For readers who are interested in the software-engineering aspects of management platforms, the following subsection dives briefly into the common management application infrastructure that a management platform typically provides. Subsequently, we discuss application functionality that a management platform typically provides out of the box.

Common Platform Infrastructure

Like a computer operating system, a management platform provides a set of infrastructure that management applications commonly need and that developers of applications for the platform consequently do not have to build themselves. This infrastructure goes beyond building blocks that are incorporated into application code in the form of software libraries. Instead, it involves common services that live in their own process space during runtime. Applications that need to use those services interact and exchange information with the platform components that provide those services. Platform infrastructure includes also mechanisms that applications can use to coordinate, communicate, and exchange data with one another—think of Object Linking and Embedding (OLE) in operating systems.

Infrastructure in management platforms typically includes (but is not limited to) the following:

- A common database for storing information.

- Common system-administration facilities, including user administration, error logging, and database backup and restore.

- Device communication services, typically provided through some kinds of device communication handlers that allow applications to exchange requests and responses with the managed devices in a way that is easy to use and program against, and that will encapsulate any required communication protocol stack.

- Internal directory and name-resolution services, allowing applications to (for example) resolve the names of network elements and managed objects to the network addresses and identifiers used to communicate with them.

- Network-discovery services, identifying devices in the managed network domain.

- Management information caching and network inventory, storing and maintaining information about managed devices in the database, from device credentials that are needed to "log on to" a device and maintain a management session with it, to information about the physical and logical configuration of a device as well as the software image and operating system version running on it.

- As an extension of the management information cache, services to keep track of the current alarm state of managed devices, including the highest severity level of any alarm condition that has not cleared, or the reachability state of the device (which indicates whether the device is responsive to management requests).

- Event-distribution and -registration facilities, allowing different application modules that are interested in events from the network to subscribe to them, without requiring managed devices to send events to each application separately.

- Application component registries, allowing application modules to announce themselves to the system and possibly to exchange information with each other.

- A common help system.

- A GUI framework to facilitate development of applications with a common look and feel, possibly including facilities that enable drag-and-drop between different application functions.

- Application programming interfaces (APIs) and possibly a software development kit (SDK). The APIs and SDKs provide common software building blocks, such as GUI widgets, which allow the management platform to be extended and new applications to be developed for it while leveraging its existing infrastructure.

Also, as in the case of a computer operating system, the infrastructure includes facilities that allow applications to make use of new peripheral devices, which, in this case, means to manage new equipment. It is generally a requirement to be capable of adding support for a new piece of equipment dynamically, without requiring a new management platform software release (and, in some cases, without even needing to stop and restart the platform). Typically, this is achieved by management software that is data driven. This means that device-specific application logic is not hard-coded into the algorithms of the management platform. Instead, where device specifics come into play, the management platform is provided with a set of device-specific driver data in a separate file or data store that can be loaded during runtime. The driver data includes information about how to communicate with the device—for example, what management interfaces and MIBs it supports, the syntax of commonly used CLI commands, perhaps even a graphical icon that tells the platform how to represent the device on a GUI. The management platform contains software that can interpret the data as needed to derive what it needs to do to perform its functions—for example, how to communicate with the device and audit it, how to interpret event messages sent from the device, and how to render a graphical depiction of the device on a screen. With operating systems, such capabilities are known as device drivers or plug-and-play. Figure 10-15 depicts the analogous concept for a management platform.

Figure 10-15 *Device Driver Concept*

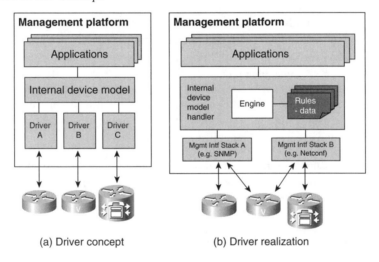

(a) Driver concept   (b) Driver realization

In Figure 10-15, part (a) depicts device drivers as a concept—applications can operate on an internal model of the device, with device specifics mapped to this model through means of drivers. (Note that in the context of management applications and platforms, other terms are generally used, such as device adapters or model handlers—the underlying idea, however, is the same.) Part (b) of the diagram depicts how such drivers might be realized. The component realizing the internal model contains a software engine that interprets driver data that contains rules for how to map the internal device model onto operations on the device. Actual communication with the devices occurs through a set of management protocol stacks such as SNMP, Netconf, or CLI over which the operations are carried as specified in the driver rules.

There are some inherent limitations that govern how far such capabilities go in management platforms. Support provided by the platform generally extends to providing basic discovery of the device—for example, understanding how to audit its basic hardware and networking configuration, as well as monitoring its alarm state. It might also allow users to browse the device's management information. The platform might not be capable of understanding what the information means, but it is still a useful capability because an end user can make sense of it. However, more comprehensive management support requires capabilities beyond that: For example, new devices might have new features with very specific management requirements that require additional management application logic and very specific knowledge about the device. Also, services might have to be mapped in a very specific way to the new device's configuration, which again requires a deeper understanding of the device.

Typical Platform Application Functionality

Like most computer operating systems, a management platform comes with a set of applications that are built in and ready for use by network managers. As with computer operating systems, the boundary between which applications are part of the platform itself and which are separate applications that build on top of it can be fleeting. As mentioned, separate applications can be offered by the same vendor that supplies the management platform, or they can be offered by independent third parties.

Examples of base applications that come with a management platform include the following—as before, this is a noninclusive list, and specifics vary with each product:

- Network topology views, along with capabilities to underlay the view with maps and to animate icons to indicate the state of managed devices, to provide network managers with an overview of the network

- MIB browsers and CLI terminals, enabling network managers to interact with devices and explore their management information

- Alarm viewers, enabling network managers to view the current list of alarms in the network

- Basic alarm correlation and filtering functions

These basic capabilities can be accompanied by a wide array of additional functions that cover a vast spectrum, from network-performance analyzers to functions that allow distribution of new software images to managed devices, from expert systems for network diagnostics to workflow engines, from special-purpose applications for the management of storage-area networks to special-purpose applications that assist with the planning of physical wireless access point topologies.

Custom Integration Approach

Another approach to management integration is to avoid relying on a management platform, but to instead custom-integrate multiple systems and applications that are otherwise independent. The resulting operations support infrastructure is often also called a "solution." (One might wonder, a solution for what? The answer to this question is, of course, a solution for the problem of how to provide an integrated management infrastructure.) Hence, a solution consists of multiple management systems and applications that are integrated to work together and collectively form the operations support infrastructure that is used to manage the network.

The following subsections discuss the challenges that are associated with this approach, and considerations and techniques that can be used to address those challenges.

Solution Philosophy and Challenges

Contrary to applications that run on a management platform and rely on the management platform's infrastructure, each of the systems and applications that is integrated in a solution incorporates sufficient infrastructure to be capable of running on its own. They constitute a set of loosely coupled solution components, which coordinate with each other as required to exchange data and provide an integrated management experience. Where a management platform provides off-the-shelf integration, custom integration is pursued in the case of a solution.

The promise of the custom integration approach is that it might better fit the particular needs of an operations support organization than would be possible with a one-size-fits-all management platform. Importantly, it allows the use of best-of-breed components for different management functions without restricting the users to those components that happen to be available on a particular management platform. Where a management platform might resemble a shark, a solution resembles a school of tuna that can take on the silhouette of a shark when needed but that is more nimble and flexible otherwise.

Ideally, the components in a solution should fit together and complement each other like Lego blocks. For this to occur, each component must have a well-defined scope of functionality. A component generally also needs to offer a northbound interface, allowing other applications and components on top of it to "flow through" operations to the network. (The term *northbound* interface originates from the fact that the interface is generally driven by applications that reside at a higher layer in a management hierarchy and that in diagrams are therefore drawn on top [or, if the diagrams were a map, to the north] of the application that provides the interface.) Likewise, a solution component can interface southbound with components of lower management layers and can collaborate with other systems and applications to the east and west as needed.

The trouble is that, in reality, different applications that need to be converted into components of a solution rarely fit so easily. Multiple issues must be overcome—for example:

■   Most of the time, components are not metaphorically shaped like Lego blocks, but they resemble shapes that are closer to potatoes or horse radishes that, while wholesome, are hard to fit together. Figure 10-16 depicts this situation. The fact that collectively they might have functional gaps that need to be filled is only the most obvious of the issues. Just as important, the functionality of different components might overlap, which can also be a problem: In a management solution, just as in an organizational structure, it is important to have clear responsibilities and accountability. If the same function can be performed from multiple places, certain complications could arise: It requires synchronization between the parties involved, the same tasks may have to be tracked across different components, and in case things go wrong, the responsible component might be hard to identify.

Figure 10-16   *Custom Integration—Theory and Practice*

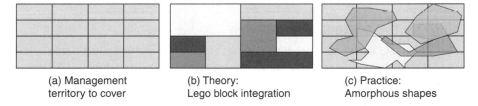

(a) Management
territory to cover

(b) Theory:
Lego block integration

(c) Practice:
Amorphous shapes

In addition to issues of functional coverage, components might not fit together easily. In general, even if components offer comprehensive interfaces, making them work together requires significant effort up front and is a far cry from plug and play.

■   Components are likely to require duplicated infrastructure, which makes solutions harder to deploy. Because most of the applications and systems that are used as components also can function independently of any other particular system, they might require different computer operating systems or database management systems. When this is the case, they need to be deployed on separate hosts, which can significantly increase the footprint of the management infrastructure versus what would otherwise be required. Hosts cost money and take up space. Just as important, this increases the effort that is required to administer and maintain the management infrastructure itself.

■   It is harder to create a seamlessly integrated user experience than with a platform approach because, in many cases, components come with their own screens and look-and-feel. This is one reason why custom-integrated, component-based solutions are often not an ideal fit in environments where human users are expected to interact with (multiple) applications. Solutions are better suited for scenarios in which humans do not need to interact with most components of the solution components directly (except, perhaps, under special circumstances), but where instead applications interact with other applications through their electronic interfaces and APIs. Another good fit for solutions is environments in which organization boundaries match component boundaries—that is, environments in which each distinct group or network manager would be using only one of the applications directly anyway. Integration in such scenarios can focus on the exchange of data between the applications using their electronic interfaces and APIs, without concern for human user experience.

■   The solution as a whole is harder to sustain and keep updated. Changes in server host infrastructure impact potentially many applications, unless components are not integrated with regard to their use of infrastructure, which leads to other issues, as described earlier. For example, if an organization wants to upgrade to a new revision of an operating system or a database, all applications need to support the new revision before a migration can occur. Likewise, if new devices or networking services need to be supported, support needs to be potentially added in multiple places simultaneously. This can significantly compromise the nimbleness that is supposed to be achieved through the solution.

Considerations for Top-Down Solution Design

Let us investigate a few aspects that should be considered when designing a solution architecture for an integrated operations support environment that is made from different collaborating components. The first aspect concerns ownership of different pieces of management information and the establishment of which component in the solution is in charge of what function. The second aspect concerns how the solution interacts with the managed devices and the establishment of clear chains of command and escalation chains. The third concerns the use of "umbrella" components such as workflow engines to facilitate collaboration in a top-down fashion.

Who Owns What

We mentioned earlier the importance of establishing clear roles and responsibilities in network management. This is true for groups in a network provider organization as well as for applications and systems that are to interact as part of a holistic operational support infrastructure.

Establishing roles and responsibilities in an integrated management solution entails defining which component owns what piece of data or management information and is responsible for maintaining it. As a general rule, there should be exactly one owner for each piece of data.

It might be worth keeping all data in a common repository so that applications always know where to find the data they need. The repository would be conceptually centralized, although, of course, it might (and, indeed, should) internally be realized in distributed fashion, with appropriate replication and mutual backup mechanisms in place to achieve scaling and reliability objectives. Any component can retrieve data in the repository as needed. However, the responsibility to maintain the data could be distributed across different components. For example, one element management system could maintain information about network equipment of a particular vendor or equipment type, a service order system could maintain information about services that customers ordered, and a network management system could maintain data about the provisioned connections in the network. Separate repositories also could exist for different types of information, such as a network inventory and a service inventory. In some cases, information in the inventory can be seeded (that is, initially be populated) by human administrators who define what equipment needs to be managed.

Individual systems and applications that are part of a solution can still cache data as needed. However, the location of the authoritative copy of information and who maintains it must never be in doubt; this must be one of the first things to be clarified in any solution architecture. This appears to be self-evident, but it must be mentioned because it truly helps to avoid issues regarding synchronizing replicated information; this can be among the most difficult problems to solve in integration between otherwise independent systems, and it simplifies getting to the root cause of problems if things ever go wrong.

Chains of Command

Another related issue concerns how components in the solution interact with the managed devices in the network. When following a TMN-like hierarchy, upper-layer systems that need to interact with the network, such as to provision a service, instruct lower-layer systems to carry out requests, such as to configure a port on a device, until finally requests reach the network element. The responses are propagated back up accordingly.

A major advantage of this architecture is that a clear hierarchy makes it easy to keep things in synch. The element management system at the lowest management layer can coordinate the requests that are intended for the device. If the element management system is responsible for keeping the solution's network inventory updated about the device, it will be capable of doing so very easily because all requests lead through it.

A disadvantage of this architecture is that it can lead to inefficiencies because requests have to trickle down multiple layers. This can negatively impact performance. In addition, in many cases, there is no real advantage in having these layers for purposes of information aggregation and abstraction. This can be the case, for example, when a service provisioning system already has a very precise notion of a device-specific parameter that needs to be touched to manage a service, such as the echo cancellation and codec settings for a voice port. From the perspective of the systems on top, the added value that the lower-layer management systems provide (for example, in terms of hiding intricacies of the management interfaces of different types of devices) is at least partly offset by aspects that make the job of provisioning more difficult. For one, more "rainy day" scenarios need to be accounted for—more possibilities exist for things to go wrong because multiple components requiring multiple interactions are involved. In addition, a dependency is introduced on the lower-layer component—let us not forget that this component could be a full-fledged management system in its own right. For example, if it is late to market and does not support the required device type and interface in time, the service provisioning system will not be capable of performing its job in the meantime.

For these reasons, there will always be a temptation to have components in a solution bypass other components to interact with the network directly, as shown in Figure 10-17. In those cases, care needs to be taken to not violate the earlier principle of needing clear owners for certain responsibilities. If a component is bypassed, it can no longer coordinate access to the underlying systems and network devices, which can lead to resource-contention issues. It could also be harder for the component to maintain the management data that it is responsible for. Of course, in the case of the provisioning example, it can be argued that an element management system might still be capable of maintaining the inventory information of "its" devices even if bypassed by provisioning applications. The reason is that the element management system will have synchronization mechanisms with the network elements in place that will inform it of any changes to the configuration that are made. Still, bypassing components is an issue that should not be done lightly. Careful consideration needs to be given to the benefits of having a clear chain of command versus taking some pragmatic shortcuts that might or might not be necessary. After all, the cost of synchronizing different applications after the fact could offset the presumed efficiency gains.

Figure 10-17 *The Temptation of Bypassing Management Chains of Command*

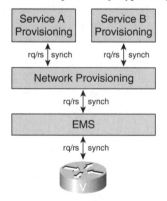

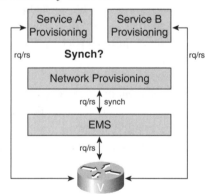

(a) Clear chain of command, straightforward synchronization, inefficient "waterfall" command propagation

(b) No clear chain of command, efficient command issuance, synchronization between systems lost

Umbrella Coordination

Finally, if there are many activities that involve interactions among multiple components, introducing an umbrella system should be considered—a system that can act as a central coordinator. This is called an "umbrella" because it acts as a common front end to users, shielding network managers and external systems from needing to individually interface with the various components underneath the umbrella. An example of umbrella systems is a workflow system that takes care of interactions with users or external systems at the front end, while accessing and coordinating different components at the back end, as needed.

The main advantage of having a central coordinator is that it focuses integration activities on one system. It tends to result in simpler solution topologies when compared to solutions in which components are effectively treated as equals. Such solutions involve a larger number of mutual dependencies that resemble a mesh, which consequently also involve a greater number of integration steps. The simplification in integration steps in many cases justifies the cost associated with introducing the additional umbrella component. Figure 10-18 depicts the difference between umbrella and mesh integration.

Figure 10-18 *Integration Topologies—Umbrella vs. Mesh Integration*

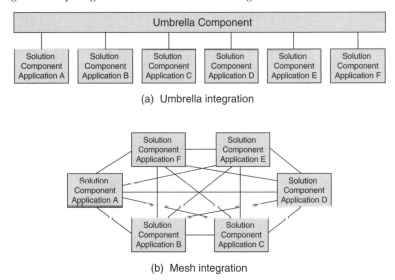

(a) Umbrella integration

(b) Mesh integration

Component Integration Levels and Bottom-Up Solution Design

As mentioned earlier, integration between components is not something that is binary—something is either integrated or it is not. Instead, integration occurs at different levels—integration can be shallow or deep. This is good news: It means that it is often possible to start with very simple steps to begin integrating different applications and systems, and successively deepen the integration later.

Integration touches on different technical aspects of the systems to be integrated. Many of these aspects can be approached independently of one another. For example, integration of databases has little effect on the integration of user interfaces (or lack thereof), and vice versa. Here are some ways in which integration between different systems can be successively deepened along several lines in a "bottom-up" fashion:

■ User interfaces are the most obvious area of integration. At the most shallow integration level, two applications' user interfaces can run on the same client, viewable on the same computer monitor. As a next step, each application makes functions of the other application accessible from its own user interface. For example, an alarm management application might enable a user to invoke a device view that an element manager provides. As an initial step, it might simply be possible to invoke the device-viewing function from a drop-down menu in the alarm management application, which invokes a screen from the element management application, from which the user can navigate to the desired device. With increasing integration, the user should be able to invoke the view for a particular device from the displayed alarm information itself, without needing to navigate to the device first. Ultimately, it might get to the point that both applications share the same look and feel. Deep integration is achieved when the user can no longer distinguish which function belongs to which application.

■ Databases are a key to deep integration. The databases of applications that are to be integrated need to become successively more aligned with increasing levels of integration. As a first step, different management functions should use the same database management system infrastructure and backup/restore utilities without actually sharing schemata (that define what data is to be stored and how) or the data itself. As integration progresses, applications should start aligning their schemata, up to the point that they can actually start sharing each other's data. Deep integration is achieved when the applications share all data and no longer keep individual copies of data just for their own use.

■ Communication with the managed devices should become increasingly coordinated between applications as integration deepens. Without integration, each application will communicate and synch up with the managed devices individually. They discover and audit the devices separately and on their own. They may also subscribe to the same events, requiring managed devices to send events redundantly even if the management functions reside on the same host. As integration starts to occur, applications first start converging on using the same communications stack, then successively coordinate their communication needs; for example, they share events that are received from the device and discover each device only once for all the integrated applications. Deep integration is reached when managed devices are never hit twice for the same purpose.

■ Other areas affect the depth of integration, including the electronic interfaces that are exposed to other applications, user administration, help functions, and even less technical aspects such as product documentation and installation and upgrade procedures.

Integration can hence be considered an n-dimensional integration space, with database, GUI, northbound interfaces, and so on each constituting different and independent integration dimensions. To characterize the degree of integration, an integration profile can be formed by indicating the degree of integration on an axis for each integration dimension and then connecting the resulting coordinates. Figure 10-19 depicts this. Full integration between different systems can be characterized in terms of a shape that approaches a circle, whereas integration that is less than perfect leads to differently shaped integration profiles.

Figure 10-19   *Integration Dimensions and Integration Profiles*

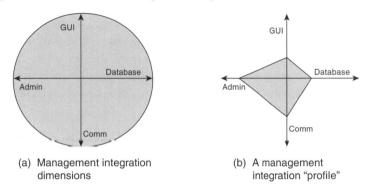

(a) Management integration
     dimensions

(b) A management
     integration "profile"

The Role of Standardization and Information Models

In Chapter 4, we discussed the role of standards in network management. It should be mentioned that standardization also plays a big role in integration among different components. After all, the intent of network management standards is to facilitate interoperability between different systems, which facilitates their integration. Standardization concerns not only interfaces between managing and managed devices, but also interfaces between different management systems. We discussed this in conjunction with the TMN hierarchy, in which you can have systems acting as managers and as agents at different layers of the hierarchy. Organizations such as the TeleManagement Forum (TMF) aim specifically to standardize interfaces between the different systems that are involved in the management of large networks. The fundamental idea is always the same: By building toward a standardized interface, different systems can achieve at least a basic level of interoperability right out of the box, without requiring additional custom development effort. At a minimum, this makes integration easier than it would be otherwise.

Beyond communication protocols and services that are provided across interfaces, a significant consideration for integration concerns management information. If different applications are based on the same abstraction of the underlying managed domain, there is no need to translate between different information models, which is where a good deal of the integration effort lies. Having a common semantic understanding among all involved parties of the managed domain provides a powerful model to achieve deep, "true" integration. Therefore, modeling is often at the heart of integration efforts.

In practice, it turns out to be quite difficult to achieve standardization of management information. The following are some of the obstacles that need to be overcome:

- A model needs to be reasonably rich and complete for its defined scope to be useful. It is difficult to formulate a model in a manner that is at the same time generic enough that it does not break easily when applied to different situations, many of which might not be foreseen at the time the model is first defined, and specific enough that the model is still efficient to use.

  Often it is most pragmatic to settle on a well-defined least common denominator, which compromises between seeking consistency on one hand and keeping the model easy to use and not bogging down applications on the other hand. In other words, it focuses on the 20 percent of the information that is required for 80 percent of interactions between systems that need to be integrated. It is also helpful if a model has a well-defined scope and focuses on a very specific and clearly bounded problem.

- It can be a challenge to maintain standardized models and keep them up-to-date. Managed technology evolves quickly, while standardization traditionally moves slowly.

- To be successful, a standardized information model must be defined in a way that makes it is very easy to understand, use, and implement. If the model becomes too complex, there is a risk of it becoming hard to learn and use. In addition, the information model must provide an obvious benefit not just for integrators who want to use the interface, but for the interface developers as well, to achieve the necessary degree of acceptance.

Of course, as with all things that get standardized, in many cases there are different standards to choose from, which runs somewhat counter to the purpose of standardization. Here, as in networking itself, Metcalfe's law applies, which states that the value of a standard increases with the square of the number of systems that support it.

Containing Complexity of the Managed Domain

Management integration is a key factor in simplifying the management task for network provider organizations. However, management can be simplified in other ways. These involve containing and avoiding management complexity in the first place instead of dealing with it once it occurs. To keep management complexity low, it helps to take a look at the factors that contribute to management complexity, discussed earlier in this chapter.

One major factor is heterogeneity complexity—dealing with the complexity caused by heterogeneity in the network. Incidentally, this factor is, to a certain extent, in the control of the network provider himself. One way to reduce heterogeneity complexity lies in minimizing the number of device types and equipment vendors deployed in the network. Each additional vendor and equipment type means new interfaces, new operational procedures and deployment rules, and possibly additional element management systems.

Of course, a network provider might come to the conclusion that it is still necessary to deploy equipment of multiple vendors and types, sometimes for nontechnical reasons. For example, competition might be a good way to keep suppliers on the edge to offer the best possible deal. However, this advantage needs to be carefully weighed because it can easily be offset by a higher total cost of ownership (which factors into the cost of running the network) that is incurred because of the added heterogeneity complexity. If a network provider uses a variety of equipment models from multiple vendors that perform similar functions, one way to contain complexity is to separate them in the topology of the network as much as possible. For example, if network operations are divided into different regions or subnetworks, it is generally a good idea to deploy equipment of one type and vendor in region A and equipment of a different type and vendor in region B instead of mixing them. This way, there is significant homogeneity at the level of network regions, which might be run by different groups that are then each exposed to only low heterogeneity complexity. At the same time, this retains the advantages of multiple suppliers.

By the same token, it helps to introduce "cookie-cutter" topologies and configurations across the network wherever feasible. For example, the deployment structure of each remote site of an enterprise should follow exactly the same pattern, or at least one of a very small number of different patterns (small, medium, large). This way, when a new type of service is provisioned, the same proven configuration that was tested once and is known to work can be reused across the entire network. When faults occur in some part of the network and troubleshooting becomes necessary, chances are, the same symptoms have been observed and the same problem has been resolved somewhere else in the network before, so the same resolution can be applied. The use of cookie-cutter topologies and configuration enables network managers to build up and reuse a large knowledge base of operational experience across the network instead of needing to custom-interpret each scenario they are confronted with.

Of course, this requires significant deployment discipline. For this to work, a network provider needs to resist the temptation to introduce variations across the network unless they are absolutely required. The benefits from standardizing deployment are well known across industries, and networking is no exception. A well-known example from which important lessons for network management can be learned is Southwest Airlines, which managed to remain profitable in an industry at a time when it was difficult to do so. One of the reasons attributed to this is that the company has managed to keep heterogeneity complexity low—which, in this case, means operating only one kind of aircraft and, unlike most other air carriers, resisting the temptation to diversify the fleet. As a result, there is only one type of aircraft to maintain, flying personnel can be deployed on any flight, and economies of scale can be realized that otherwise would not be possible.

Chapter Summary

Having an operational support environment that consists of multiple disconnected islands can lead to many problems when running a network. For example, it introduces the need to maintain (and keep consistent) multiple sets of data that might overlap, it leads to the risk of management tasks that fall through the cracks and are not resolved properly, and to operational inefficiencies that might result from the friction that arises between separate groups and systems that are isolated from one another yet need to work together to run the network smoothly. Most of these issues can be avoided with management that is integrated. At the same time, achieving truly integrated management is a major challenge and hence constitutes in many ways network management's "holy grail."

Management integration represents not only the technical problem of integrating multiple functions, applications, and systems into one integrated operational support environment. It has an organizational dimension as well, involving how different groups can best work together and complement each other in running a network. Integration of operations support infrastructure can follow along the different management dimensions that were introduced in earlier chapters. It often follows the way in which operations are organized, integrating those functions first that are of importance to a particular group, while defining interfaces to the parts of the infrastructure that primarily serve other management functions and parts of the organization that the group needs to interact with.

Several factors influence the complexity of management integration, in addition to systems and software architecture challenges at the heart of the task of integration itself. These include scale (the sheer number of things that need to be managed), heterogeneity (the diversity of what needs to be managed), and the number of management functions that need to be integrated. To address management integration successfully, it can be helpful to devise ways in which the complexity of the management task itself can be reduced. For example, when possible, cookie-cutter configurations should be applied, and unnecessary variations in subtopologies (for example, across different sites of an enterprise) should be avoided.

Several approaches exist for integrating functionality of management applications. Management platforms represent one such approach, providing commonly used management functionality out of the box and complementing that with infrastructure that other applications can build on top of and plug into. The solution approach, on the other hand, is to combine best-of-breed applications and systems that can each also stand on their own. They are integrated into one common operations support environment, often requiring significant custom integration effort in the process. It is also possible to combine both integration approaches by integrating a management platform with additional systems and applications in an operations support environment. In that case, the result basically constitutes a special case of a solution in which one component simply happens to be a management platform.

The trade-offs between platform-based integration and solution-based integration commonly involve lower cost and a smaller footprint that favor of the platform approach vs. the capability to custom-tailor and optimize the operational support infrastructure to the very specific needs that favor the solution approach.

Chapter Review

1. Imagine that you are a service provider. An equipment vendor offers you an integrated management system. Which aspects of management integration will such a system be unlikely to address, even if the equipment vendor's claims are, from his perspective, entirely correct?

2. Which factor has perhaps the most significant impact on management complexity?

3. Provide an example of how management integration as a technical issue mirrors management integration as an organizational issue.

4. Give three examples of management application infrastructure that is commonly provided by management platforms.

5. Why can functional overlap between management applications in an operational support environment be a problem?

6. Provide two examples of technical obstacles that can increase a management solution's footprint.

7. Which industry consortium concerns itself with the standardization of interfaces between management systems in operations support environments?

8. Contrast shallow with deep integration of applications at the user interface level.

9. Name three ways in which complexity that is caused by heterogeneity can be reduced.

10. How do cookie-cutter deployments make network management easier? Are there any downsides?

CHAPTER 11

Service Level Management: Knowing What You Pay For

In general, providers and beneficiaries of networking services maintain a business relationship with each other: The network provider provides a product to a customer. In this case, the product happens to be a networking service (or perhaps a data center service—but without loss of generality, we simply refer to networking services here). In return, the customer (who is also the user of the service) is expected to pay the service provider for the networking services provided. This is not unlike other business transactions: Customers pay for a product. In return, they expect to receive the product in good quality and performing to its specifications.

Unlike many other products, networking services are often highly customized to meet individual customer needs. In addition to its function, an intrinsic part of a service includes its technical properties, such as performance, capacity, and availability. Those properties are collectively referred to as the *service level*. The specification of the service level that is expected to be delivered for a service constitutes an important part of the definition of the service itself. The specification of a service regarding a service level typically occurs in the form of a *service level agreement (SLA)*. An SLA defines the technical terms of the service that is being provided—the targeted service level. In addition, it includes business terms, such as precise terms of what will happen if the agreed-to service level is not met. SLAs are hence at the core of the business relationship between the user and the provider of a networking service.

The topic of service level management is therefore of fundamental importance, both to the providers of networking services, who need to ensure that they are meeting service levels they have agreed to, and to the customers, who want to validate that they are indeed getting what they pay for. Service level management uses many of the techniques that were introduced in earlier chapters. Therefore, the discussion of service level management serves also illustrates some of the ways in which management technology can be applied in practice.

Here are some of the things that you will learn after reading this chapter:

- Understand the components of a service level agreement and how SLAs are defined

- Get to know examples of service level parameters

- Discover what business considerations need to be factored into defining service level agreements

- Learn how to plan and manage a network for a given service level

- Understand how management techniques are applied to monitor and validate service levels

The Motivation for Service Level Agreements

In the context of this chapter, we often refer to the providers of networking services as service providers. However, as in previous chapters we do not mean this term to be restricted to traditional service providers; it can include also enterprise IT departments or even organizations running a data center.

Service providers run networks or data centers not just for the heck of it, but so that benefits can be derived from the services that run over it. In the case of an enterprise's IT department, the beneficiaries are the various groups and employees of the enterprise that require data and voice services as part of their technical infrastructure. In case of a traditional service provider, the beneficiaries might be residential customers who want Internet connectivity, telephone service, or perhaps digital television services. The beneficiaries might also be enterprises who want the service provider to provide data connectivity between their different sites. The beneficiaries might even be other service providers who want to lease additional transmission capacity to cover a spike in bandwidth demand, or who want to lease a portion of the access network to gain access to residential end customers in cases where they do not own the lines themselves.

This means that the relationship between the providers and the beneficiaries of networking services are typically business relationships that are accompanied by business arrangements. The network provider delivers a product (in this case, a communications service), and the customer is expected to pay for it. (Payment can take different forms. For example, the payment for an enterprise's IT department consists of its funding.) In return, the customer demands a product (a communications service) that works as advertised.

Now, products are generally defined not just by their functionality, but by other characteristics as well. For example, when you buy a car, you expect that the car will provide the functionality that enables you to drive from point A to point B. However, there are many distinguishing characteristics beyond that. Some characteristics relate to performance: How fast does it accelerate? What mileage do you get? Other characteristics relate to capacity: How many does the car seat? How large is the trunk? Characteristics can also relate to availability: How often will you need to bring it in for maintenance?

The characteristics of a product determine to a great extent the value you will be able to derive from it, how much you will be willing to pay for it, and whether you even want to buy it in the first place. Clearly, if a car is advertised to accelerate from 0 to 60 mph in 5 seconds, you will accept having to pay more for it than for a car that is in all other ways identical but takes 50 seconds. By the same token, if you buy a car expecting 5 seconds 0–60 acceleration because that is what was advertised, and you later find out that the real number is somewhere around 15 seconds, you will likely be annoyed and perhaps even demand a refund. The same is true when you buy a car because of its advertised 15,000-mile service intervals, and later you find out you that you need to bring it in twice as often because all kinds of problems occur in between.

The same is true for communication services. In addition to the pure functionality, each service is defined by a multitude of characteristics, which can be expressed as parameters. Those parameters can relate to performance: How much bandwidth is available—are we talking about 10 Mbps or 1 Gbps? How long is the delay from the time when you pick up a phone to when you hear a dial tone—will you always get the tone within half a second, or are there times when you will have to wait for half a minute? Other parameters can relate to capacity: How many transactions per second does your web-hosting provider support? Parameters can also relate to availability: Is the service guaranteed to always be available, or are there times when it can be "down"? If so, how long will it be down, and how often do such outages occur—is it once a year only, or can it occur more often than that? Are outages announced beforehand so that you can plan around them, or do they happen unexpectedly?

Such parameters define the level of service that is provided. Therefore, they are also referred to as *service level parameters*. The set of service level parameters that collectively defines the characteristics of a service that are important to a user is collectively referred to as *service level*. Generally, customers have to pay more for a higher level than for a lower level of service. In turn, they expect the agreed-upon service level to be met or exceeded; otherwise, they will be justifiably upset.

In many cases, communication services are highly customized because the precise needs and circumstances of different customers differ, particularly regarding the service levels they require. This is not so much the case for residential customers, whose telephone and Internet service follows boilerplate specifications. However, it is the case when the customers are enterprises or other service providers.

Consider a Virtual Private Network (VPN) service, by which a service provider offers to interconnect the various sites and remote office branches of enterprise networks. Depending on the particular scenario, the sites and remote office branches can vary greatly in number, size, and geographical distribution. Clearly, those differences, along with the differences in traffic characteristics that they imply, need to be factored in when ordering the service. Similarly, when an Internet data center provider hosts a company website, it makes a big difference whether the site to be hosted is the platform of an e-commerce vendor, the online presence of a financial services provider, or the site of a regional pizza restaurant chain that offers driving directions to its stores and coupons for printing. The requirements on the service in terms of capacity, availability, and performance vary greatly.

This means that, in practice, not only can the same service functionality be realized in many different ways, but it can also be offered with greatly varying characteristics. Some of those characteristics can be just as important to a customer as the functionality of the service itself. For example, what good is having cheap long-distance voice service if most of the time you do not successfully get dial tone for a free outside line? To an e-commerce provider, what good is a hosting provider that cannot keep up with the required volume of transaction, leading to lost business?

This is the why service level agreements (SLAs) are introduced. SLAs are contracts between the provider and the user of a communications service that stipulate the service level that is expected for the service—characteristics of the service that relate to aspects such as its performance, capacity, and availability properties. Because communication needs vary greatly between customers, SLAs are often customized and negotiated on a case-by-case basis instead of being part of a boilerplate product offering.

In an SLA, the desired service level is defined by a set of *service level objectives*. A service level objective consists of a service level parameter and a target value for that parameter that must be met or exceeded. For example, a service level objective might stipulate that the capacity on a link that connects two enterprise sites is 100 Mbps. (The capacity of the link constitutes a service level parameter.) Another service level objective might state that on weekdays between 8 a.m. and 6 p.m., availability of the link must be 99.9 percent. (In this case, the service level objective is further qualified by a time interval during which it is in effect.)

The provider of the network service guarantees to the customer that the service level objectives will be met. For that guarantee to have "teeth," the SLA generally also contains nontechnical aspects. Those aspects spell out what is to happen in case the service level falls below the target and certain objectives are not met—ranging from remedial actions that will be taken to financial penalties that will be incurred. Hence, as was mentioned before, SLAs provide the basis for the business relationship between providers and users of communications services.

Identification of Service Level Parameters

An important decision about SLAs concerns what parameters to use to define the service level objectives. A parameter in an SLA must meet three criteria, discussed in the following subsections:

- **Significance**—It must be significant and meaningful for the service that is being defined.

- **Relevance**—It must be relevant to the context in which the service will be used.

- **Measurability**—It must be measurable and objectively verifiable.

Significance

Which service level parameters are candidates for inclusion in an SLA depends greatly on the type of service. They must "matter" for the service.

Many people think of service level parameters mainly in terms of the classical network performance and capacity parameters, such as bandwidth, delay, and jitter. A classical example concerns network jitter, which refers to the variations in the delay of packets that are experienced. Jitter is a parameter that is important to voice services because it can negatively affect voice quality. At the same time, network jitter is irrelevant for e-mail service.

However, network performance and capacity parameters alone do not tell the whole story. Although those parameters are meaningful for networking services that provide raw connectivity and have an impact on services running on top of them, in many cases, they do not paint an adequate picture. To refer back to the example, although jitter can certainly be a cause for poor voice quality, to the user, this does not adequately describe the quality of the voice service itself. Many readers will have experienced examples of poor quality of service in the context of mobile voice service. In general, complaints will not be of the nature, "It seems that network jitter is really bad today." Instead, users will complain about issues such as "The network dropped my call three times," "There is background noise on the line," or simply "My voice quality is crap."

Characteristics such as dropped calls, background noise, and perceived voice quality are much more meaningful to users of the voice service than jitter. Therefore, those characteristics are ultimately the ones that should be captured as service level parameters. This means that, in general, service level parameters should be articulated in terms of the particular service itself and should be applied at the same layer of the communications stack rather than a layer or two further down. Significant service level parameters relate directly to the service experience.

Of course, service level parameters of a lower layer can impact service level parameters of an upper layer. An understanding of those dependencies is important to the provider of the service, but it is not significant for the articulation of the SLA, as discussed next in a little detour.

A Brief Detour: Service Level Relationships Between Layered Communication Services

Services such as voice generally rely on services provided at lower layers, such as data-transmission services. Therefore, there are dependencies between the levels of service that are experienced at different layers.

For example, there could be a relationship between the quality of the voice service that is experienced and the link or routing capacity at a lower layer: If the capacity is too low, voice packets will be lost and the quality of the voice will suffer. However, to average users, it will be hard to ascertain a precise relationship between the parameters of the service that they are interested in and the service level of a networking layer below it. If your service provider tells you that you have a capacity of 512 kbps between two company sites to make voice calls, how do you know if this will be adequate for your purposes? Being told instead that you can carry up to 16 simultaneous voice calls (each compressed at a data rate of 32 kbps) is a lot more meaningful. It articulates the capacity in terms of the service of interest. (Of course, the relationships between service level parameters of services at different layers will not always be as simple as in the example. For example, voice might be compressed further, leading to variable bit rates, or the service might comprise both voice and data traffic that need to be carried simultaneously.)

At the same time, other aspects of the service level might not be related to a lower layer at all. For example, a user might experience echo during a call or clipping, with the other end cutting in and out. Those aspects will severely degrade the user experience but are likely completely unrelated to lower layers in the communications stack. Instead, the cause might be the codec that is used to digitize the voice and assemble the payload of the voice packets that are subsequently sent across the network.

Accordingly, the most significant parameters to use in an SLA are those that are related the actual service itself, independent of how the service might be realized and without assumptions about how the service might leverage underlying technology. It is important to not confuse the level of a lower-layer service with the level of the service that is actually the subject of the SLA.

Figure 11-1 illustrates an example of different service level parameters at different layers of communication services. Although the parameters in the example are related and poor service levels at lower layers impact service levels at upper layers, they are clearly different.

Figure 11-1 *Differences in Service Level Parameters, Depending on the Layer of the Service*

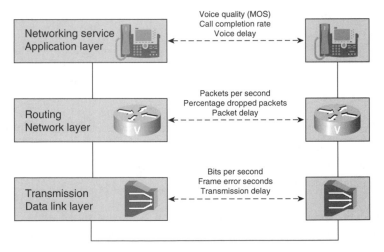

The example involves a network provider that provides telephone service using Voice over IP in an enterprise. The telephone service is an application that runs on top of an IP network. Of course, somewhere at the lower layers, packets that contain the packetized voice need to be routed and transmitted over network links. At that layer, the following constitute relevant service level parameters: raw transmission bandwidth (bits per second), the number of seconds during which frame errors occur, and transmission delay.

On top of that layer, IP packets are routed across the network. Here, relevant parameters include the number of IP packets that can be routed over the network per second, the percentage of packets that are dropped, and the delay with which packets are received. There is a relationship between the percentage of dropped packets and the frame error seconds at the layer below, but clearly they are different.

Finally, at the layer of the voice service itself, there will be service level parameters such as voice quality (measured using a metric known as mean opinion score, MOS), call completion rate, and voice delay. Of course, there is again a relationship with service level parameters of the layer below. For example, voice delay is impacted by packet delay. However, the two are not identical. The reason is that other factors can add to the end-to-end voice delay, such as dejitter buffers at the receiving end. Such buffers introduce a slight delay because they wait a few milliseconds after the packet is received before playing it out, to smooth out any differences in packet interarrival intervals, as shown in Figure 11-2. To the user, of course, what matters is the voice delay as a whole, not the delay of some component that factors into the voice delay.

Figure 11-2   *Dejitter Buffer to Smooth Out Packet Interarrival Intervals*

Variable packet interarrival rate	**Dejitter buffer**	Constant packet interarrival rate

Example: Voice Service Level Parameters

The following are examples of service level parameters that are significant for a voice service. The examples illustrate some of the considerations that go into defining such parameters and how user concerns translate into service level objectives.

- The time that it takes until a user hears a dial tone when picking up the phone. Several service level objectives might be associated with the same service level parameter: One objective would define the average time that should not be exceeded for this parameter. A second objective would define the maximum acceptable time beyond which the service would be considered unavailable.

- End-to-end voice delay. Service level objectives based on this parameter should specify the maximum end-to-end voice delay that is not to be exceeded.

■ Call completion rate—that is, the percentage of call attempts that are actually answered by the other side. Again, we need to be careful in defining the precise meaning of the parameter. "Answered," in this case, should mean that the call attempt leads to either a ring tone on the other side, so it can be picked up, or to a busy tone, if the other party is busy. In this case, even though the call does not actually go through, this scenario would count as a completed call attempt. Of course, a call is not considered completed when, for example, a "fast busy" is received, meaning that the other side cannot be reached because of network or signaling overload.

■ Busy hour call attempts (BHCA), the number of call attempts during the busiest period of the day. The number of BHCAs that can actually be served (that is, that get a dial tone within the time that is stated in the service level objective) is a service level parameter relating to a voice service's capacity, not performance or quality. It can be stated as a total and, if needed, can be broken down to different company sites.

Of course, this number is influenced by the calling pattern—that is, how the service is actually used. Most important, the duration of calls is a factor in how many networking resources will be tied up, which influences how many calls can be served. Likewise, the distribution of call has an impact—that is, the percentage of calls that take place between sites on the same network versus calls with the outside world. Accordingly, the number of BHCA that must be supported is an example of a service level objective that should be accompanied by clearly spelled-out assumptions about its context—the average call holding time (for example, average duration of 2 minutes) and the call distribution.

■ The length of time that it takes until a ring tone is received after a call is dialed. This is another example of a parameter that might be associated with multiple service level objectives: Average duration until ring tone would be an objective separate from the objective of a maximum time until ring tone that is never to be exceeded. If a ring tone is not heard within the maximum permissible time, the call will count as not completed.

■ Average mean opinion score (MOS). MOS is a metric used by persons to rate the (sound) quality of calls. It is also possible to synthetically generate a MOS.

■ Availability of the service during peak hours and during off-hours. Availability should be clearly defined. One way to define availability might be the percentage of time periods during which a user receives no dial tone or calls cannot be completed.

■ Time to provision a new user. This, like the next one, is an example of a parameter that relates to how the service is managed, not just the service itself.

■ Number of provisioning operations (add/delete/move users) per day.

One takeaway from these examples is the fact that service level parameters are closely related to actual end-user concerns of the provided service and involve much more than network-performance parameters such as network delay and jitter.

Relevance

As mentioned previously, a service level parameter that is to be included as part of a service level-objective in an SLA must meet three criteria. Significance is the first. Relevance is the second.

It is not sufficient for a service level parameter to be significant in terms of it defining a characteristic of a service. In addition, a service level parameter must also be relevant—that is, important enough to be included as part of a service level objective in the SLA. Not every parameter that can be defined and that relates to a service has to be included in an SLA. In fact, it can be counterproductive to include too many parameters because they need to be also monitored and enforced. If parameters are included that are not really relevant, they shift attention away from those parameters that truly matter and tie up resources that might better be spent otherwise. Which parameters to include is often highly dependent on the context in which the service will be used.

Consider the example of an SLA for data-connectivity service. If the connectivity will be mainly used for file transfers to perform payroll processing, it makes little sense to define service level objectives that relate to jitter (variations in the delay of subsequent packets delivered over the same connection) or end-to-end delay. On the other hand, if the same data-connectivity service is purchased by a video service provider that intends to stream live TV over the link, the same parameters could very well be of high importance and should be included.

A parameter might also not be relevant when it is simply not expected to be a factor. For example, when any realistic service level objective based on that parameter is highly likely to be met anyway, its inclusion in an SLA could be pointless. An example concerns the BHCA parameter that we just encountered for voice service. The number of supported busy-hour call attempts might very well be relevant to a large enterprise, in which lots of intraoffice calls are made and questions might arise about whether the underlying voice network will be capable of handling such volumes. However, chances are that it is not important for a voice service for a small business—there will simply never be an intraoffice call volume that is high enough for that parameter to be a factor.

Measurability

Service level parameters that service level objectives are based on also need to be measurable. It must be possible to determine whether a service level objective is being met or violated, and to do so in a manner that is practical. The whole purpose of the SLA is to define what constitutes an acceptable service level in a clear and verifiable manner. If the actual value of a service level parameter cannot be determined, defining corresponding service level objectives becomes pointless because it would be impossible to tell whether they are being met. By the same token, if a parameter can be measured but the cost of doing so is prohibitive—that is, higher than the benefit of making sure a corresponding service level objective is indeed met—for all practical purposes, it can be considered fairly useless.

Although this seems like stating the obvious, how to measure service level parameters is a problem that is often far from trivial. This particular aspect is discussed in further detail in the section on service level monitoring.

We already encountered an excellent example of a service level parameter that is both appropriate and relevant to include in an SLA in the context of voice services: the mean opinion score (MOS). MOS is a measure of voice quality that users experience during a call. As such, it involves human perception. Several possibilities exist for determining it: For example, users are asked during and after each call to judge the quality they experience. In general, this is unacceptable because it is disruptive to the service itself. Another possibility is for trained personnel to continuously make test calls. This might turn out to be cost-prohibitive, particularly because many calls need to be made to achieve adequate coverage—samples that are large enough to be statistically meaningful.

An alternative is to make automatic measurements using software that analyzes call samples. Such software can generate synthetic MOS scores that provide a good approximation of actual MOS scores. Although this is not the same as a human MOS score, both parties might agree to use such measurements as a valid substitute.

This points to another issue. In this and other cases, to avoid later disputes, it can be important to determine beforehand how a parameter will actually be measured. What if the user says that the voice quality sounds pretty bad, but the service provider respectfully disagrees? An SLA needs to anticipate potential ambiguities and, if appropriate, spell out how a particular service level parameter will be measured and what method will be used to determine whether the service level objective is being met.

Defining a Service Level Agreement

An SLA needs to answer a number of questions:

- What will the service provider deliver—what are the service level objectives?

- How will service level objectives be tracked and verified?

- What will happen if the service provider fails to deliver?

An SLA should specify other aspects as well, such as who the contacts are and the terms under which the SLA is allowed to be changed. However, the previous items constitute the most crucial aspects and are discussed in more detail in the following subsections.

Definition of Service Level Objectives

When deciding which service level objectives to include, you need to make a number of considerations:

■ Determine which service level parameters and which service level objectives are really critical to your needs. To identify candidate service level parameters, remember that they must meet the criteria that we just discussed in the previous section of being significant, relevant, and measurable. Furthermore, you need to think about what target levels are really required.

Of course, everybody wants to get the best service possible. However, it needs to be understood that a better level of service generally has its price, just like everything else. Therefore, the trade-off between cost and benefit must be considered, as shown in Figure 11-3. In general, the incremental benefit of a higher service level should outweigh the cost that is associated with it. For example, are five nines (99.999 percent) of availability really needed, or will three nines (99.9 percent) or even 98 percent do, in light of the fact that 99.999 percent could be 10 times as expensive as 98 percent? What will be the impact on the business if only 100 instead of 1000 transactions per minute can be handled—would it mean losing enough business to justify the extra cost of being able to support 1000 transactions, or would it not be noticeable?

Figure 11-3   *Trade-Off Between Cost and Benefit of Higher Service Levels*

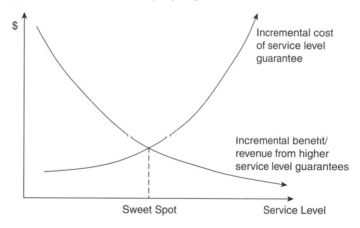

In some cases, it might also make sense to introduce further qualifications to service level objectives. For example, one target level might apply during core business hours when you really cannot afford to compromise your service level, but the same service level might not be required around the clock. In such cases, it might be entirely appropriate to make that distinction in the SLA.

Related to this, clarify whether any periods will be required for maintenance and upgrade activities, and make provisions for such activities as part of your service level objectives. Particularly with availability objectives, it is important that scheduled unavailability be clearly differentiated from unscheduled unavailability. For example, an SLA might state that there will be a scheduled maintenance window between 1 a.m. and 4 a.m. on the first Sunday of every month during which the service might not be available and service level objectives will not be in effect during that time.

■ Be as specific as you can be when defining service level parameters:

— Clearly define the terms that you use and what they refer to. Some examples of terms that might be ambiguous and might require clarification were given earlier in this chapter. One example concerned what constitutes a "completed" call. Another example concerned "delay" that could apply to the network level (delay of packets) as well as to the service level (delay of voice).

— State any assumptions about context, as appropriate. An example earlier in this chapter involved being specific about expected average call-holding times, which influences what guarantees can be made for service level parameters such as busy-hour call attempts. Clearly, whether calls last an average of 30 minutes or 30 seconds has an impact on the amount of networking resources that are consumed, which impacts service level parameters that rely on the same networking resources.

■ Finally, be realistic. As a service provider, you should enter into SLAs only with objectives that you fully expect to keep. SLAs are a fundamental cornerstone of a trusting relationship with a customer and express a confidence that the agreed-upon service levels can indeed be met. You should never enter an SLA expecting not to keep it, only because (for example) the defined penalties are deemed acceptable. Likewise, as a customer, you should be aware of the implications of service level objectives—asking for things that are obviously unreasonable is asking for trouble.

Tracking Service Level Objectives

In defining service level objectives, you need to also be clear about how those will be verified and how the underlying service level parameters will be measured. This is important not only to avoid disputes later; it can also help identify any misunderstandings about what the service level parameters entail. Here are considerations to take into account:

■ Be clear about where parameters are measured. For example, if you have a service level objective for an application hosting service by a data center that concerns response time, by stating where you are measuring, you are also clarifying what you are measuring. Consider the scenario depicted in Figure 11-4: As a data center provider, are you measuring the round trip-response time from the time a response enters the data center to the time that it exits (T5 + T6 + T7 + T8 + T9)? Or are you instead just measuring T5 and T9 because too many application dependencies in T7 are outside your control? Clarifying this up front also clarifies the meaning of the service level parameter itself. (Also bear in mind that, to the end user, the measure of real interest concerns the entire round-trip time—actually, the sum of T1 through T13.)

Obviously, if a service level objective depends on factors such as time of day, you also need to be clear about when you measure. Likewise, if a service level objective does not apply to times of scheduled maintenance intervals, you need to ensure that you will cease measurements during such intervals and not accidentally include them in service level parameters that aggregate measurements over time, such as averages.

Figure 11-4 *Different Points to Measure Service Level Parameters, Example Data Center*

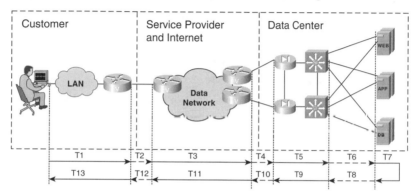

Overall response time: T1+T2+T3+T4+T5+T6+T7+T8+T9+T10+T11+T12+T13
SP can measure: T3, T11
DC can measure: T5+T6+T7+T+T9, or T5, T7, T9

- Be clear how parameters are measured—that is, what measurement techniques and methods are used. Will actual production traffic be measured, or will additional probes be used that inject test traffic? In some cases, there could be a question about how to calibrate measurements. For example, if you measure packet delay between two different points in the network, how do you make sure that you are adequately capturing the difference between the time the packet was sent and when it was received? If you use the local time at each end, questions about the accuracy of such measurements could arise.

- Make sure that measurements are statistically relevant. Whenever measurements have to rely on sampling, another question concerns the confidence that you have in the statistical relevance of the sample. Taking too many samples is often not feasible because of the additional load that measurements and test traffic impose. However, how do you make sure that what you observed in a measurement is not a freak aberration? Likewise, if service level objectives are being violated, how do you make sure that your samples will capture that? In general, a cost is associated with taking samples because of the additional load they impose, so no more samples than are truly necessary should be taken. Sometimes it is a good idea to work with confidence intervals—for example, to define samples that give you 95 percent confidence that your measurements are accurate within a 2 percent range of the target value.

■ Finally, it should be clear who measures and how your measurements can be verified. In the earlier example, an outside party will not have access to the incoming and outgoing firewalls ports and will not be able to actually measure T5 + T6 + T7 + T8 + T9; the best that it might do is to measure T4 + T5 + T6 + T7 + T8 + T9 + T10. The assumption is that T4 and T10 should be negligible and, hence, the two are the same, but what if they are not and what is depicted as a link between the Internet service provider and the data center turns out to be an access network in its own right, which introduces a non-negligible delay? In anticipation of this and similar situations, the service provider (in this case, the provider of the data center) sometimes includes access to service level statistics to the customer as part of the service itself. In some cases, an independent party might be called on to certify service levels.

Dealing with Service Level Violations

Despite all the best intentions of everyone involved, the possibility exists that service level objectives will be violated. To prepare for such cases, a good SLA needs to clearly spell out what will happen in such an event. Think of it as a prenuptial agreement between network provider and customer.

What happens in case of a service level violation involves several aspects, each of which should be addressed in the SLA:

■ Restoring the agreed-to service level. This is what needs to happen first, of course. Think of this as the emergency response plan. An SLA might spell out a committed plan of action for how to restore the agreed-to service level in case of violations. The plan of action should include commitments such as the following:

— Inform the customer when a service level violation is detected—usually, this needs to happen without undue delay and within a short time interval

— Provide the customer with regular updates on the current status of problem resolution at specified time intervals

— Take adequate action to respond to a service level violation within a certain time interval

— Restore service levels within a certain time interval

For example, an SLA could contain a statement such as the following: "During the core business hours (M–F 6 a.m. to 8 p.m.), the service provider will respond to incidents that affect five or more users within 10 minutes of detecting the incident. The user will get a status update every 30 minutes until the problem is resolved. Problems that relate to service availability will be resolved within 60 minutes, all other problems within 4 business hours."

Of course, it provides a certain sense of security to know that plans to safeguard the SLA are in place. However, because the SLA has already been violated, what difference does having a committed response plan really make—what prevents a service provider from violating it as well? Keeping commitments in how to respond to service level violations can significantly impact the business relationship between service provider and customer in the aftermath. For example, when a service level objective was violated but the service provider does everything committed to in the emergency response plan to restore service, the overall business relationship should remain intact. On the other hand, if the network provider breaks that commitment, it might give the customer the right to immediately terminate the contract and demand higher damages. This leads us to the next points.

■ Make up for service level that was not delivered. Of course, even the most responsive reaction to a service level violation and the quickest restoration of service levels do not change the fact that a violation of service level objectives did indeed occur. In essence, a part of the product was not delivered as promised. An SLA should therefore spell out any penalties to make up for that fact. Those penalties can range from a temporary reduction of service fees to much higher penalties, such as reimbursing the customer for the impact on the business. Typically, penalties are capped at a certain amount that is calculated to be in reasonable proportion to the price of the service. Penalties should be defined on a scale that takes the following into account:

   — The number of violations. If violations occur all the time, this is obviously more significant than if they happen once in a blue moon.

   — The severity of violations. If response time objectives are missed by a few percent for a few seconds, this is much less significant than response time objectives that are missed by a factor of 2 for half a day.

   — The particular service level objective that was violated. For example, a missed availability objective might be much more significant than an objective relating to response time.

For example, an SLA could contain a statement such as the following: "In the event of 1 to 5 incidents of service level objective violations, the fees will be reduced by 5 percent. In the case of 6 to 10 incidents, fees are reduced by 15 percent. In the case of more than 10 incidents, fees will be reduced by at least 30 percent and an action plan will be prepared to avoid reoccurrences. In the event of a violation of availability objectives, the following penalties apply: Availability between 99.5 and 99.9 percent: Reduction of fees by 20 percent. Availability between 99 percent and 99.5 percent: Reduction of fees by 50 percent." And so on. You get the idea.

- Reconsidering the future business relationship and possibilities for bail-out. If service levels are constantly not met or severely violated, it could be an indication that the service provider is simply not fit to live up to the terms of the SLA. For such cases, it can be important for the SLA to contain an escape clause that specifies the conditions under which the service contract can be terminated prematurely—better an end with horror than a horror without end. Clearly, a customer wants to avoid being caught in a business relationship that obviously does not live up to expectations. Even if the service provider offers penalties, ultimately, the customer is not after penalties, but being provided service at the level that is required to run the business.

Managing for a Service Level

Of course, we are not finished after an SLA has been defined. Next, the SLA needs to be delivered on! This involves a number of aspects:

- The service needs to be set up—the network must be built out and resources allocated so the service level objectives can be supported. Connections must be properly dimensioned, ports must be reserved, the network topology must be planned, and of course, the service must be provisioned.

- When the service is operational, it must be constantly monitored to ensure that service level objectives that were promised are being met. The related activities are commonly referred to as *service level monitoring*. If there are indications that service levels are deteriorating, preventive action needs to be taken to reverse those trends before they lead to a violation of the agreement.

- Finally, statistical data must be collected as proof that the agreed-to service level is being delivered.

How to manage a network and services to meet service level objectives is by the nature of things of great concern to the provider of that service. However, even customers of networking services need to think about if and how they want to ensure that they are actually getting what they pay for. Do they simply take the service provider's word for it? Or do they share Lenin's adage that trust is good but control is better? If it's the latter, customers will be interested at least in service level monitoring as well.

The purpose of performing service level monitoring is, of course, different for customers of a service than for the networking service provider: Customers want to be able to complain when service levels drop below what was agreed to. After all, there was a reason they demanded a certain service level to begin with. Depending on the terms of the agreement, they want to also be able to request a refund. Of course, as so often in real life, if there is no accuser, there is no crime, so they need to make sure that they are not getting short-changed and collect the necessary evidence to support their claims.

We discuss each of these aspects in the following sections. Furthermore, to successfully manage a network so that it provides services at a certain service level, it is helpful to understand what the service consists of and which factors influence meeting the service level objectives. Therefore, let us start with this aspect.

Decomposing Service Level Parameters

In many cases, a service is realized by a combination of multiple pieces. We already encountered the example of a hosted application service depicted in Figure 11-4. In this example, an application service provider hosts a set of applications in a data center that is accessible over a network. Multiple pieces are involved in providing this service: A networking piece is used to provide connectivity to the host from the edge of the data center, with traffic possibly traversing a content switch that performs load balancing across a set of hosts. In addition, there is the host that the application runs on, the database that the application relies on, and the hosted application itself.

A second example is that of a global long-distance voice service, enabling users to call internationally (see Figure 11-5). Providing the service involves multiple pieces: an access network over which the customer premises is connected to a core network, a signaling and call-control component that is a part of the service provider's network and that makes the signaling and call-processing decisions (for example, where to route the call, when to play a busy signal, and so on), and, of course, the access network and customer premises on the other end. (We ignore the access network on the other end and depict the connectivity between customer premises and core simply as a link, realizing that this link might not always be simply a wire but might involve an entire network in its own right.) In some cases, calls might also be handed off to another party that handles the remote end of the call, perhaps a local traditional public switched telephone network (PSTN) provider.

Figure 11-5 *Global Long-Distance Voice Service*

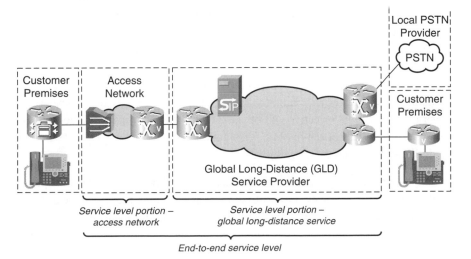

In general, service level parameters are influenced by the different parts that realize the service. For example, end-to-end response time for the hosted application will be influenced by the time that it takes for request and response to traverse the network, by the amount of time that it takes for the request to be processed by the application host, and possibly by the amount of time it takes to access required data from the database.

In many cases, service level parameters can accordingly be broken down into each of the components that factor into the parameter as a whole. In the example of the hosted application service, the end-to-end round-trip response time could be broken down into the network-traversal time of the request, the application-processing time, the database-access time, and the network-traversal time of the response.

As a service provider, it is therefore important to understand the different pieces that a service consists of and, consequently, the various factors that contribute to a service level parameter. Several potential benefits to this greatly facilitate service level management:

■   It helps in diagnosing the root cause for missed service level objectives or for an observed degradation of service level parameters. An understanding of what components factor into a service level parameter provides a good starting point for where to look when a problem with the service is observed. This way, potential causes can be more easily identified, and troubleshooting and diagnosis can be more targeted than would otherwise be the case.

■   It is easier to assess the impact of a failure (or of a drop in performance) in the network on a service and to identify which services and SLAs might be affected. This helps the service provider react proactively and take preventive counter measures, ideally before customers are even impacted.

■   It provides guidance to plan and design the network for a given service level. By understanding how different factors contribute to a service level parameter, a service provider can divide the overall service level objective into several subobjectives, one for each component that factors into the overall objective. For example, different components that contribute to a delay could be assigned a "budget" for their permissible delay contribution. Subsequently, the network can be planned and provisioned so that each component will remain within its allocated budget. In doing so, the service provider can be confident that the overall service level objective will be met. This is a classic case of divide and conquer, with a higher-level goal broken into a set of smaller, more tangible goals that can each be tackled individually to reach the overall goal.

■   Finally, understanding the different pieces that contribute to a service level parameter can be helpful to devise a strategy for how to monitor it. In some cases, it can be difficult to measure a service level parameter directly, but the infrastructure for measuring the individual pieces that the service level parameter is composed of could be readily in place. Although it is always preferable to monitor the actual service level parameter itself, monitoring factors that contribute to it instead and aggregating the respective measurements can be a reasonable alternative.

It should also be mentioned that it is not uncommon for consumers of one networking service to themselves be the providers of another service. If the SLA of the service they are dependent on is violated, they might not be able to keep their own commitments and might violate the SLAs of their customers.

Building on the example from Figure 11-5, the provider of global long-distance voice services might depend on another service provider for an international transmission line, meaning that, in reality, the scenario depicted in Figure 11-6 is more accurate. Of course, to the customer, the fact that the international link is subcontracted to another service provider is invisible. It is of no concern to the customer, as long as the global long-distance provider still can meet the agreed-upon service level objectives. To be able to do so, the global long distance provider will have a separate SLA in place with the provider of the international link, which contains the service level objectives for the transmission services that are associated with that link.

Note that Figure 11-6 also depicts other components that factor into the overall service level. In the example, the customer's end-to-end service level is also influenced to some degree by the access network portion, which is outside the global long-distance provider's responsibility. The customer might maintain a separate SLA with the access network provider.

Figure 11-6 *Global Long-Distance Voice Service, Examined More Closely*

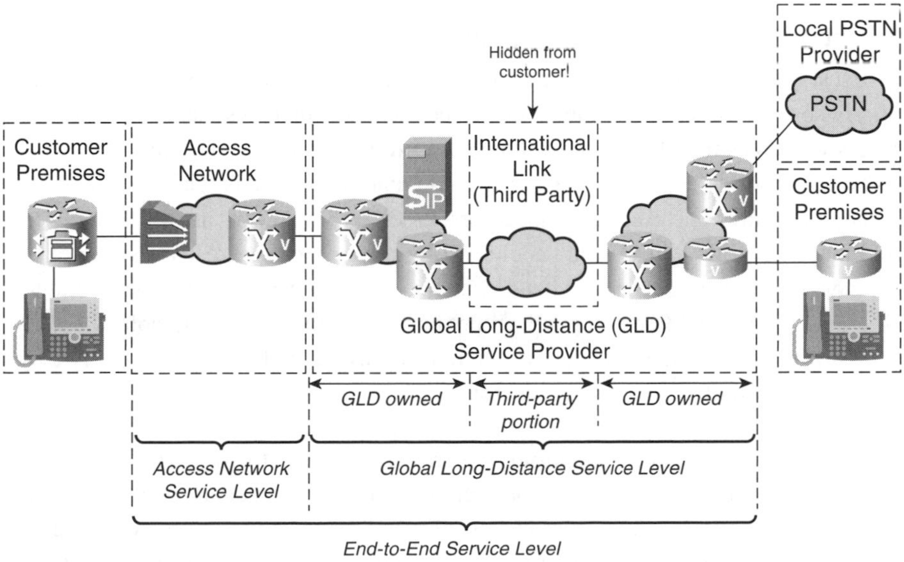

Figure 11-7 depicts the different business relationships of the example. Cascading relationships between service providers are not uncommon. The fact that this leads to cascading service level objectives is an excellent illustration of the fact that service level parameters are the result of a combination of factors, aggregated from the different pieces that a service consists of. Again, the customer does not care and, in most cases, is not even aware that these relationships exist—much as the buyer of a car does not care that the antilock braking system, the instrument panel, or the tires are not actually built by the car manufacturer, but bought from outside suppliers.

Figure 11-7 *Business Relationships and SLAs for Global Long-Distance Example*

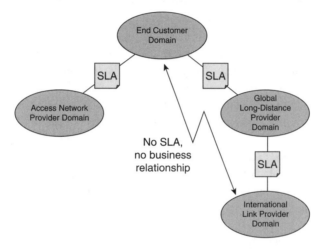

Planning Networks for a Given Service Level

The first step toward successfully meeting service level objectives consists of setting up the service properly so that service level objectives can be met. This involves identifying the devices and network resources that the service will be mapped onto and provisioning them accordingly. However, applying the proper configurations so that the service is functional is only one aspect. Just as important is ensuring that enough resources in the network are available so that service level objectives will be met, which could involve reserving those resources. For example, when setting up a video service, enough bandwidth and network capacity must be available to carry the additional video traffic that will result. If not enough bandwidth is available, the network might end up dropping too many packets, which, in turn, results in deteriorated quality of service and possible violation of service level objectives.

In many cases, SLAs that users and service providers enter into are fairly standard. Ideally, the service provider has a number of "cookie-cutter" configurations that can be readily applied and that are known to support the required level of service. Such configurations can be developed once, refined over time, and reused many times. Whenever a service with a particular SLA is ordered, it is checked whether enough network resources to support the required service level are still available, the required network resources are marked as reserved, and the respective configurations are applied to the devices that have to support the service.

In some cases, a cookie-cutter configuration might not (yet) exist. In such cases, it might not be clear how the underlying resources need to be dimensioned. Dimensioning involves determining how many resources need to be allocated to support the service level objectives, whether those resources involve ports, connection bandwidth, processing power, or amount of host memory. Proper dimensioning is perhaps the most critical factor when setting up a network to meet service level objectives. Therefore, let's discuss this aspect in a little more detail.

Dimensioning Networks to Meet Service Level Objectives

When dimensioning a network to meet service level objectives, it helps to decompose the service into its individual components, as discussed in the previous section. Subsequently, the required dimensioning for each component is established, depending on its role and contribution toward meeting service level objectives.

How to dimension—that is, to determine which and how many resources to allocate for a given service instance—is perhaps the most crucial aspect in provisioning a network for a particular service level. The most straightforward way is to simply reserve all the resources that are required if the customer always uses the service to its fullest capacity. This way, barring unforeseen failures, the provider of the service will never violate any service level objectives.

It turns out that, in reality, users do not generally use their services all the time or to the fullest extent of the capacity they purchased. For example, an enterprise might have purchased a link with 10 Mbps of bandwidth between two sites but rarely actually uses all of that bandwidth, certainly not all the time. This means that a service provider that reserves network resources assuming that the service will always be used to the fullest will find that generally a significant portion of the resources is idling. This is a problem because a network involves cost, and having network resources that are chronically underutilized and inefficiently used is a luxury that few can afford.

When it is unlikely that a service will constantly be utilized to the fullest, and if a service level objective does not involve a hard guarantee but a statistical guarantee, it might be possible to *oversubscribe* resources. This means that the service provider might be able to allocate the same resource to multiple service instances at the same time, in the hope that not every service instance will need the same resource at the same time. In effect, this allows the service provider to sell the same resource multiple times.

Consider the following example of a service provider that has a pool of bandwidth, consisting of 50 units of bandwidth, one unit of which is required for each service instance. In theory, this means that only 50 service instances can be provisioned. However, the service provider observes that many customers do not use the service all the time, so, on average, only 50 percent of services (and, hence, only 50 percent of allocated bandwidth) are used. The service provider might therefore decide to sell 80 service instances, in the hope that no more than 50 will be used at any one point in time. This principle is also called statistical multiplexing. This allows service providers to squeeze more out of their existing infrastructure. As a result, the service is provided more efficiently and economically. Cost advantages can be passed on to the customer, so everybody benefits. The situation is analogous to that of airline carriers who sell more seats than they actually have on the plane.

Managing Oversubscription Risk

Of course, oversubscribing network resources can be risky. At times every user might simultaneously access the service. In such cases, something will have to give. Also, sometimes the usage of service between different users might not be as statistically independent as the service provider would like.

An example of such a usage pattern might be in case of digital TV subscribers at a time when the Soccer World Cup final is on. When this scenario occurs, not only is a larger percentage of users than normal likely to watch TV at the same time, but to make matters worse, they also all want to watch the same program. Digital TV signals are compressed to reduce their bandwidth requirements, taking advantage of the fact that there is generally only a small difference between successive picture frames. However, cuts between scenes lead to temporary bandwidth spikes because an entire new picture needs to be transmitted, not just a delta of it. With different people generally watching different programs, the occurrence of spikes is somewhat distributed, which leads to a statistical effect that can be exploited. However, when everybody watches the same program, everybody requires simultaneously the same spike in bandwidth. This means that picture quality is likely to suffer if the underlying network connections are oversubscribed and not all bandwidth requirements can be satisfied.

Depending on the service, service providers can use a variety of techniques to mitigate those risks; for example:

■ **Reprovisioning**—In the course of monitoring current service levels and service consumption (see next section), a growing problem related to overusage often can be detected. In such cases, the service provider might be able to temporarily increase available capacity in some circumstances. For example, if core network bandwidth is running low, bandwidth on a network backbone might be increased by temporarily buying additional capacity from another service provider. If in the case of a web-hosting provider server capacity is running low, it might be possible to temporarily bring other servers online.

- **Imposing admission control**—A service provider might be able to impose a scheme in which users do not get access to a service if usage is above a certain level and admission of more users would lead to deterioration of everyone's service level. The idea is that sometimes it is better to make one or a few users unhappy instead of everyone. An example is telephone service, in which a user might experience a "busy out" when trying to place a call when a large number of calls already are in progress. The service provider essentially decides to block the call attempt instead of having everyone's call quality deteriorate.

  Simple admission-control schemes operate according to a first-come, first-served manner. More sophisticated schemes can make further differentiation based on a policy. For example, they might assign priorities or weights to certain categories of users—a "gold" user gets preferred treatment over a "bronze" user. Ideally, an admission-control scheme takes individual customers' service level objectives into account and gives priority to those customers that the service provider can least afford to disappoint.

In the end, oversubscribing resources in the network is a calculated gamble. Its purpose is to achieve a good balance between utilization of resources (which, if left idling, increase the cost of providing instances of the service) and keeping within agreed service levels (which, if violated, lead to decreased profitability, not just because of the cost that is associated with penalties, but because of lower customer satisfaction and the resulting loss of revenue).

Figure 11-8 depicts this situation. The figure also illustrates how the trade-off can be assessed and hence how the gamble can be calculated:

- Part (a) of the figure depicts the drop in service level in relation to the degree of oversubscription. By superimposing the service level objective on the curve, the level of oversubscription that is still acceptable can be obtained. (A different interpretation of the same curve that leads to similar conclusions is that the curve depicts the probability that a certain service level will be met at a given degree of oversubscription. The threshold indicates the probability that is still just acceptable.)

- Part (b) of the figure depicts the increase in utilization that can be achieved by oversubscription. Taking the degree of oversubscription that is still acceptable as was just identified using curve (a), it is possible to derive the level of resource utilization that can be accomplished with this degree of oversubscription. This yields important information about how the network needs to be dimensioned and how to calculate the cost basis for guarantees of a particular service level.

Figure 11-8   *Trade-Off Assessment—Acceptable Level of Oversubscription and Achievable Level of Utilization*

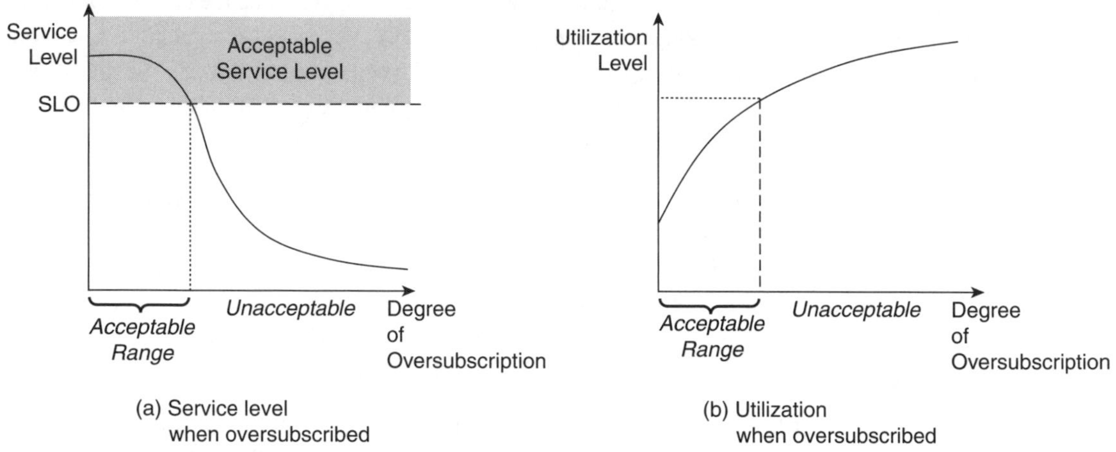

(a) Service level
      when oversubscribed

(b) Utilization
      when oversubscribed

What all of this also implies is that whenever a service level objective really, truly, positively requires an absolute guarantee, not just a probabilistic or statistical one, the required resources need to be dedicated to this particular instance of the service. Of course, this has its price and is a main reason why services with hard-and-fast guarantees tend to be much more expensive than services with softer guarantees.

Network Maintenance Considerations

Finally, a few remarks on network maintenance: Maintenance operations such as routine backups or hardware or software upgrades can potentially be disruptive for services running over the affected equipment. However, unlike sudden failures or shifts in usage patterns that fall outside the control of the service provider, how to perform maintenance is completely within the providers' control. Care should be taken to do the proper homework in this area because unintended or unanticipated service disruptions from maintenance are hard to excuse—basically, there is no one else to blame. Therefore, it should go without saying that when network maintenance needs to be scheduled, the services and customers that would be affected should be identified in advance. The affected services should be switched over to alternative resources if at all possible, or ample warning should be given to customers.

As mentioned earlier, the need to perform maintenance should be anticipated at the time the SLA is articulated. It might result in spelling out certain "blackout" periods during which a service might not be available because of maintenance. When calculating service levels such as availability over a period of time, it is important to factor out time intervals of planned network maintenance.

Service Level Monitoring—Setting Up Early Warning Systems

When a service is up and running, it needs to be monitored to ensure that it is running according to specification—that is, without violating any of the service level objectives. Impending problems should be detected early enough that there is still enough time for countermeasures.

Service level monitoring can accordingly roughly be divided into two aspects:

■ Monitoring service level parameters

■ Detecting when problems are about to occur

Let's take a closer look at how both aspects are addressed. Most of the underpinnings were already discussed earlier in this book because service level monitoring builds heavily on network management techniques and technologies that were introduced in earlier chapters. Service level monitoring thus serves as a good illustration of how those concepts can be applied to an important application area.

Monitoring Service Level Parameters

Different techniques exist for monitoring performance and quality of service level parameters that are the subject of service level objectives:

■ Analyzing management information. This includes the following:

— NetFlow and IPFIX records, which contain a lot of information about network flows

— SNMP MIBs, which include many objects with information about device state and device performance, and which therefore may be regularly polled for this information

— syslog messages, which could indicate certain problems in the network

Management information that is readily available—specifically, operational data and state information, as well as logged events—offers a wealth of information that is relevant for service level monitoring. Of course, in many cases information about service level parameters is not available directly—specifically, when end-to-end parameters are involved. Interpreting the management information that exists and trying to deduce service levels from it can sometimes resemble forensics. Once again, knowing how service level parameters are decomposed into different components and which statistical data factors into it can greatly facilitate this task.

■ Passive measurements. In some cases, operational performance statistics that would really be needed are not readily available. In such cases, special management tools might need to be introduced into the network with the specific purpose of observing network traffic to take certain service level measurements. This often involves using a separate device, a sniffer, that attaches to the network and "sniffs" what is going on. Sniffing often involves inspecting packet headers of network traffic for what they contain in search of certain patterns. This way, packets that belong to one particular application—a voice or a video stream, perhaps, or a data transfer—can be identified and various measurements can be taken. For example, such measurements might include throughput (how many packets are observed) and jitter (differences in interarrival times), and possibly also round-trip response times by matching packets that contain an application response with earlier packets that contained a request. (Incidentally, there are other uses for such techniques, such as in intrusion-detection systems that assess whether there are suspicious communication patterns indicative of an ongoing hacker attack.)

■   Active measurements involve injecting test traffic that simulates a service user, with the specific purpose of measuring service level parameters. In a network service setting, active measurements involve a probe from which test traffic is generated, just like traffic that would be generated from a legitimate service user. The traffic is directed at a second probe on the other side of the network that receives the test traffic and records the observed results. In some cases, where the parameters involve round-trip performance, the remote probe might also simply reflect the test traffic back to the sending probe and let the sending probe evaluate the performance. In this case, the remote end is also called a *responder.* A very simple yet famous example in networking for this concept is the Internet Control Message Protocol (ICMP) echo request, better known as a ping. This enables a network manager to ping a remote destination and measure the time until a response is returned.

Although they are not based on actual traffic and are instead synthetic in nature, active measurements have the advantage that they can be very well tailored to measure a wide variety of end-to-end service level parameters. The same parameters can often be quite difficult to measure using just passive measurement techniques. Also, active measurements do not face some of the security-related issues that passive measurements often have to deal with. For example, passive measurement techniques often cannot be applied to secure connections such as the ones used in Virtual Private Networks, where traffic is encrypted and packet inspection becomes impossible. On the downside, active measurements generate additional traffic, which can increase the network's load, thus potentially affecting the service level that they help ensure.

Anticipating Problems Before They Occur

Being able to monitor current service levels is nice, but when it is detected that service level objectives are violated, the damage is already done. Therefore, it would be nice to also anticipate a problem before it occurs. This way, it might still be possible to take countermeasures to avert service level objective violations. Accordingly, what is needed is a "service level forecast," not unlike a weather forecast—of course, in this case, the course of forecast events can still be influenced.

A number of techniques can be applied to anticipate problems before they occur, including the following:

■ Trend analysis. Users can regularly poll or collect critical service level data and track it over time. Using mathematical extrapolation techniques, it is possible to establish a trend to predict the most likely scenario if current trends continue, as illustrated in Figure 11-9.

Figure 11-9 *Trouble in the Making?*

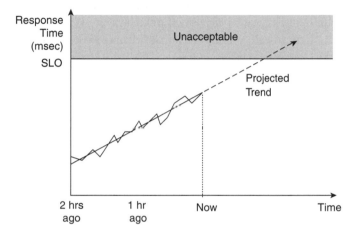

■ Anomaly detection. Often service usage patterns and fluctuations in service levels that are observed repeat over time. In many cases (but not always), this is a consequence of human behavior. For example, most people watch TV between 9 and 11 at night or make most of their business phone calls between 10:30 and 11:30 in the morning. As a consequence, networks get stressed during those times, which can lead to temporary drops in service performance. Using historical data, it is possible to establish what those patterns are. For example, lower and upper bands of service levels that are typically observed at any given time can be identified. This can be distilled into a digital footprint. Comparing what is currently being observed with these footprints can be a good technique to spot if anything unusual is occurring that requires attention.

Obviously, these techniques rely on continuous monitoring of service level parameters. As described in Chapter 9, "Management Organization: Dividing the Labor," relying on techniques that minimize the number of management exchanges is key to being able to perform these functions efficiently and in a way that scales. For example, instead of relying on continuous polling, the network should ideally be set up to automatically report the observed value periodically or, better yet, make it event driven to report only when the monitored values fall outside the ordinary. Of course, in many cases, such functions are not supported directly by the device being monitored. Alternatively, the task of polling can be distributed and delegated to a number of subordinate systems, which, in addition to polling, can preanalyze and aggregate the data before feeding it to a central application.

In fact, it needs to be mentioned that threshold-crossing alerts (TCAs), which we discussed in Chapter 7, "Management Communication Patterns: Rules of Conversation," play a central role in allowing service providers to react early to impending trouble. Properly set up, TCAs can effectively become service level alerts. Using the RMON MIB, for example, a service provider can define thresholds for MIB objects that are related to critical service level parameters. By setting a threshold to a value that is a little below the point where the actual service level violation occurs, a service provider can set up an early warning system. When the threshold is crossed, the service provider is automatically alerted and might still have enough time to take countermeasures as required.

Service Level Statistics—It's Fingerpointin' Good

In addition to monitoring and ensuring service levels, it is also important to keep a record of the service levels that are experienced over the course of time. Why? Because such a record can prove of tremendous value if a dispute between service provider and customer occurs. That's why historical service level statistics are often also referred to as fingerpointing data.

If a customer complains to a service provider about service level violations, the service provider might simply admit to it, to keep the customer happy. The service provider might even provide the customer with the statistics that enable the customer to make a claim in the first place—in some cases, service level reports are a part of the service package. However, a service provider might not always be so forthcoming. In such a case, it can be tremendously helpful for a customer to have a record of what service levels were observed at what time, to back up the claim. Likewise, if a service provider feels wrongfully accused, it can be tremendously helpful to have a record that proves to the customer that service levels were indeed adhered to. After all, the service provider has a reputation to defend, and building a reputation of violating SLAs can severely impede future business. As in other walks of life, if two people can settle a disagreement out of court, all the better. However, if a matter does need to go to court, hard evidence rules.

For statistical records to really be useful, they must provide an accurate and truthful picture of service levels that were delivered. For this to be the case, a few aspects must be considered when such statistics are collected and maintained. Likewise, when being presented with statistical data that is supposed to "prove" that a certain service level objective was either met or violated, a number of questions must be asked pertaining to those aspects to ascertain whether the presented data is indeed relevant. Here are the most important aspects to consider:

■ Are the collected samples statistically relevant? Often it is not feasible or simply impossible to measure and keep a complete record of service levels that were provided at every point in time. Instead, a sample needs to be kept. When selecting a sample, a key aspect to consider is how to ensure that the data points in the sample are statistically relevant.

Figure 11-10 shows an example of a sample that would probably not be considered statistically relevant because it misses the fact that service level objectives were violated during several periods of time. Accordingly, there needs to be a sufficiently large number of data points to paint a picture that is reasonably accurate. Ideally, it should be possible to state the degree of confidence with which the actual value of a service level parameter was within a given interval from the sample taken—say, "Our statistical data indicates that, with a 95 percent confidence level, response time on December 17 was 55 ms or better for at least 98 percent of the time." The larger the sample, the more accurate it should reflect the service level that was actually delivered, and the higher the confidence level should get. In the end, it must be ensured that the correct conclusions are drawn from the sample.

Figure 11-10 *Statistical Relevance of Samples*

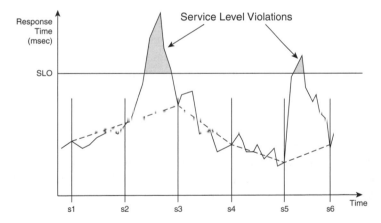

■ Does the collected data indeed accurately reflect the service level parameter it is supposed to contain? It must be clear what the sample represents and how the measurements were performed. To illustrate the types of considerations that must be made, consider the scenario that Figure 11-11 depicts. If there is a parameter named "network delay," the question needs to be asked whether the delay measured from the edge router of the customer, or from the access router of the service provider—in this example, is the delay defined as T1 + T2 + T3 (measured by the customer) or as T2 (measured by the service provider)? How is the delay measured? Do the measurements reflect a delay in one direction, or do they reflect a round-trip delay that is divided in half? For example, if it is measured using a ping that is issued from edge router 1 to edge router 2, what is measured is not really T1 + T2 + T3, but instead the sum of T1 through T6, which can then be divided in half. If this is the case, it must be ensured that it is a realistic assumption that "downstream" and "upstream" delay are the same and do not need to be distinguished. Also, does any time for processing in the responding node need to be taken into account?

Figure 11-11   *Measuring Delay of a VPN Service*

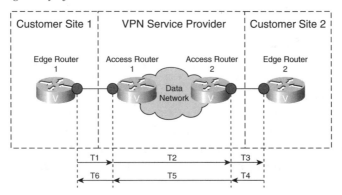

- Is the data authentic? Finally, the question might arise whether data being presented is indeed what it seems to be—for example, how can it be ensured that statistical records were not improperly deleted to skew the picture, and how can it be verified that the data was indeed taken at the measurement points and at the times that are claimed in the record? Often there are no fast and easy answers. Maintaining a bulletproof statistical record involves sophisticated digital authentication and signature schemes to be applied to the data that is being collected. Such schemes can ensure that data recorded did indeed originate from a certain piece of equipment at a certain time, and that a store of statistical data has not been tampered with. However, in most cases, such capabilities are not readily available. The consequence is that when entering an SLA, the relationship between service provider and customer needs to be such that there is at least a basic level of trust. Without it, it is probably not advisable to maintain a business relationship in the first place.

Chapter Summary

Service level agreements are often at the core of the business relationship between the provider and the customer of a service. An SLA specifies a set of service level objectives, how those objectives will be tracked and verified, and the course of action that needs to be taken along with possible consequences if service level objectives are violated.

A service level objective sets a target for a service level parameter—generally, a parameter that is related to the performance, capacity, or availability of a service. It is important to select parameters that truly characterize the service and capture properties that are important to users of the service. Specifically, in the case of higher-layer services that go beyond providing raw data connectivity, those parameters go well beyond typical network performance parameters such as throughput, delay, and jitter. In addition, service level objectives need to be defined so that they are truly relevant to the user of a service in terms of the target values set. They also need to be measurable and verifiable. Otherwise, including them in an SLA is a waste of energy.

When setting up a network (or another managed domain such as a data center) to provide services that meet a given service level, a service provider needs to find the right balance between not letting too many resources lie idle, which might require oversubscribing resources, and not overcommitting resources to a degree that would lead to violations of service level objectives. Whenever resources are oversubscribed, it is possible for resource contention to occur under certain circumstances, meaning that situations can arise in which the service level of one or more users will be adversely impacted. One strategy for dealing with resource contention is to establish admission-control policies. In some cases, those policies might be sophisticated enough to prioritize between users based on their SLA and current service level.

Service level monitoring involves monitoring and analyzing operational and state data that provides an indication of the service level that is currently being experienced. It also can involve techniques to measure service level parameters end to end. Passive measurement techniques involve analyzing actual network traffic, whereas active measurement techniques involve probes that simulate service users and measure the service level from synthetic test traffic or service transactions.

It is important to spot developing problems early, to be able to take countermeasures in time. A key technique involves threshold-crossing alerts, which can notify service providers of conditions in the network that indicate possible service level problems. Finally, data about the service level that is currently experienced should not be discarded, but collected. Such data might later prove useful as "fingerpointing data" if a dispute between service provider and customer arises about the level of service that was actually delivered and received.

Chapter Review

1. Both the provider and the customer of a service should be concerned with service level monitoring. Why is this so?

2. Assume that you are a service customer and are about to enter an SLA with a service provider to provide you with video phone service across your enterprise network. Can you think of some service level parameters that you might want to include in service level objectives of the SLA? (Pick three.)

3. In addition to a set of service level objectives, what else should an SLA spell out?

4. Give an example of a voice service level parameter that cannot be derived from an underlying network parameter.

5. Give an example of a service level parameter of a voice service that, when decomposed, contains a network service level parameter as a component.

6. Assume that your SLA specifies a maintenance interval of 1 hour per month. When measuring the availability of your network, you forget to take this maintenance interval into account and accidentally include 30 minutes that your service was not available during this interval. How much is your availability number skewed?

7. Name a technique that can be used to set up an early warning system for impending service level violations.

8. Assume for a moment that you are a service provider. A customer complains about the level of service he received. Your first impulse is to give little credibility to that complaint—you are quite certain that the level of service that you provided was well within the targets set by the service objectives. However, the customer produces as evidence a log file with service level measurements that were taken over the past month. Which three questions might you want to go over in your mind to assess the validity of the customer's claims?

9. What trade-off does a service provider need to assess when deciding whether and by how much to oversubscribe resources?

10. What strategy might a service provider take when realizing that resource contention occurs, to prevent everybody's service level from dropping?

CHAPTER 12

Management Metrics: Assessing Management Impact and Effectiveness

When we set the stage at the beginning of the book, we emphasized network management's business significance as a primary motivation and driver for network management technology. In this final chapter, we return to the business proposition of network management to close the circle, so to speak. Specifically, we take a look at how the impact of network management can be assessed and (because individual circumstances and goals can vary widely) how such an assessment might be methodically approached. Of course, the more effective management is, the greater its impact will potentially be. Therefore, we also discuss how to assess management effectiveness.

Assessing the effectiveness and impact of network management is important in a number of ways. For example, it helps in deciding where to direct investment into network management technology and which specific aspects to tackle first. It provides a basis for developing return on investment (ROI) models that help evaluate where such investment will have the biggest impact and whether it will even be justified from a business perspective. This is relevant not just for users of management technology, such as IT departments and service providers that operate networks, but also to developers of management technology, such as system integrators, equipment vendors, and management application software vendors; it allows them to assess where their development efforts will deliver the biggest bang for the buck. Also, although this is a technical book, a good understanding of the impact that technical choices have on the related business does matter, even from a technical perspective.

After reading this chapter, you will be able to do the following:

- Articulate the ways in which network management has a business impact

- Understand factors that impact management effectiveness

- Use metrics to quantify network management value propositions and measure the effectiveness of network management technology and organization

- Develop and apply metrics to help you evaluate technical alternatives and assess progress in management effectiveness over time

Network Management Business Impact

Network management is a competitive factor in a number of ways. As Figure 12-1 illustrates, network management affects the following:

■ The total cost of ownership (TCO) of a network

■ Revenues that can be generated from communication services

■ Certain properties of the network itself that increase its value—most importantly, network availability

We quickly review these three aspects before getting into factors that influence them and metrics to assess them.

Figure 12-1 *Network Management Business Impact*

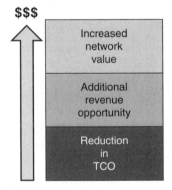

Cost of Ownership

Of the three factors just listed, the impact of network management on the cost equation is the one that generally receives most attention. Because it is also the most obvious, we keep its discussion brief.

Most obviously, network management affects the operational expense of running a network. An effective operations support organization, coupled with an effective operations support infrastructure, facilitates the job of the operations staff, allowing the staff to do more with less, increase its responsiveness, and potentially reduce the need for hard-to-find skills and training.

Very importantly, network management also affects the required investment in the network itself. Proper management tools can help plan a network and provision a network so that it becomes better utilized. This avoids dimensioning the network to a size that is larger than is required to meet service level objectives and helps to squeeze more out of each network investment dollar.

Other cost effects are more subtle. For example, using service level monitoring capabilities verifies the level of service that is received from other service providers. This can lead to the recovery of cost when service level objectives are violated. More important, the "threat" of verifying the service level that is delivered can lead to better service being provided in the first place. Another example of a subtle cost effect is associated with the capability to monitor communication resource consumption in an enterprise. When users or user groups are confronted with their communication service consumption (for example, by letting them known when they are a "top talker"), internal waste of communication services can be discouraged.

Enabling of Revenues

Less obvious, but just as important as the cost side of the equation is the fact that network management is also a big factor in increasing revenues that can be generated from a network investment. This occurs in a number of ways.

Perhaps most important, network management can accelerate service rollout—the speed at which new services can be introduced over a network and the speed at which they can be deployed. Service provisioning systems have a big role to play here. Obviously, the faster a rollout of services occurs, the sooner customers can be charged and revenues can be collected. An intangible side benefit of swift service rollout lies in creating the appearance of crisp responsiveness, which helps build confidence in the product with the customer.

By the same token, network management can help avoid revenue loss from inadequate network planning and dimensioning that impedes service rollout. As many companies can tell, few scenarios are worse than having a product that customers want but not being able to deliver. Proper network management tools for planning and statistics collection and analysis can decrease the likelihood of network provider organizations finding themselves in such situations.

Network management can also impact how much can be charged for a service. For example, with proper service level management in place, a service provider might feel confident guaranteeing higher service level objectives, for which it can then charge more. At a minimum, it provides a competitive advantage over competitors that cannot provide equivalent guarantees.

In some cases, network management itself might be a feature of a service that might be charged for at a premium. Examples include the capability to generate a unified bill for multiple services, or providing service statistics for users to access over the web. A famous example concerns the "family and friends" service plans, offered by some telecommunication service providers well over a decade ago. The capability to charge for calls differently depending on who was being called was a service feature that was enabled not by the network, but by the billing and accounting systems—in other words, management technology. Customers loved this plan, and service providers whose operations support infrastructure offered no comparative capabilities underwent serious struggles to maintain market share.

Network Availability

Finally, network management plays a significant role in improving certain properties of the network itself that increase the network's effectiveness and value. Of course, it might be argued that this additional value can be translated into additional revenues and hence be subsumed under the previous category, "Enabling of Revenues"; nevertheless, this aspect is relevant enough to stand on its own.

The most important aspect here concerns network availability. To improve network availability, a network provider might decide to invest in highly available networking equipment, at a cost. However, an equivalent or even greater impact on network availability can in many cases be achieved by investing in network management instead. Network management plays a significant role in reducing the number of errors that network operators and administrators make and that can lead to unintentional outages. An example is a service that is accidentally improperly configured, or the application of conflicting configurations to network devices that cause communications to be disrupted. Service provisioning and policy-based management are just two of the many techniques that contribute this way to network availability. In addition, network management can help reduce the impact that operational errors can have on the network and recover from those errors.

During operations, network management plays a major part in being able to spot impending trouble quickly and thereby ideally enables preventive action before problems occur. Performance trending and threshold-crossing alerting are examples of techniques that can be applied. Likewise, when failures do occur, network management facilitates quick identification of failure root causes and corrective action.

Trading Off the Benefits and Costs of Network Management Investments

Of course, network management's positive impact, described previously, is partly offset by the cost of network management itself: the cost for additional operational support infrastructure and, to a much lesser extent, the additional management traffic and load on network devices that could otherwise be used for production traffic.

Clearly, investment in network management technology needs to be directed in such a way that the incremental return exceeds the incremental cost. This incremental return consists of reductions in operational expense, increases in revenue, and increases in the network's value (which can be translated into some monetary value).

In addition to the immediate return, other factors need to be taken into consideration. One such factor concerns the cost of managing the operations support infrastructure itself as the underlying network evolves. This cost needs to be taken into account also as part of the decision for the network investment itself.

A second factor concerns economies of scale. Network management needs for a smaller network are not proportionally less than for a larger network. Of course, the scale is smaller, but the management functions that need to be provided and systems that require investment to support them in many cases might be largely the same as for the larger network. All other factors being equal, the incremental cost of network management should hence be expected to decrease as the scale of the network grows. Again, this could impact investment decisions: An investment that might not be feasible for a smaller network might become more feasible for a larger one because it can be amortized over a larger number of devices (or ports, or instances of end-user services, or whatever measure for network scale is used).

Factors that Determine Management Effectiveness

The effectiveness of management is influenced at multiple levels, as Figure 12-2 shows:

■ At the level of the managed technology itself. This is often also subsumed under the term *manageability*, referring to the ease with which managed systems and devices allow themselves to be managed.

■ At the level of management applications and operations support infrastructure.

■ Finally, at the level of the management organization itself that uses the tools and infrastructure.

Figure 12-2 *Multiple Levels of Management Effectiveness*

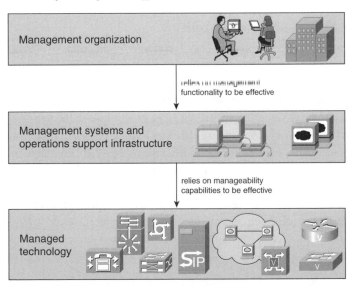

Shortcomings at one level can often be overcome—at least, to a degree—at a higher level. For example, consider a scenario in which operations support personnel want to be notified whenever utilization on an important link surpasses a critical level. One way to support this function is by configuring a threshold-crossing alert for link utilization on the affected equipment. If a managed device does not offer the capability to configure a corresponding threshold-crossing alert, a management application on top might resort to polling the device and emulating the threshold-crossing alert to make up for that capability. This enables operations support personnel to still be notified when an important threshold is crossed.

Of course, as we learned in previous chapters, letting the management application resort to polling comes at a price: For one, it increases the management load on network and devices. In addition, it decreases the scalability of the management application that now has to perform the polling because effectively complexity is pushed farther up to the level of the operations support infrastructure. Also, it can never completely substitute for true threshold-crossing alerts at the device because a crossed threshold will be reported after the next polling cycle, not when it occurs, so a delay will be incurred. This indicates that there are some limitations to how far shortcomings at one level can be made up at a higher level.

Hence, it does make sense to look at factors that affect management effectiveness at different management levels—the level of the managed technology, the level of the operations support infrastructure, and the level of the management organization. Understanding those factors is the first step in determining what measures can be taken to increase management effectiveness. In addition, those factors form the basis for the articulation of metrics that can be used to assess management effectiveness, discussed later in the chapter.

Managed Technology—Manageability

Manageability refers to the collective set of properties of an entity (that is, a device or a network) that allow it to be managed. Those properties can largely be attributed to the entity's management instrumentation—the management interfaces that it exposes and the capabilities that those interfaces provide. However, it involves other properties as well that make the entity easier to manage, such as capabilities that reduce the need of a device to be managed in the first place. Manageability is not binary in nature (either you have it, or you don't); instead, it represents a continuum that consists of a multitude of different factors that can make management easier or harder. No single factor determines manageability.

Therefore, we take a look at some of the factors that influence manageability. There are other factors besides those presented here. However, the discussion should provide a good notion of what types of aspects to look for in networks and managed devices that make them easy to manage.

We begin with manageability factors that affect cost of ownership. Two aspects are associated with cost of ownership: the cost of integrating the managed devices into an operations support environment, and the cost of operating and maintaining the device.

The cost that is involved with getting managed devices supported by management applications is often also referred to as the "integration tax." Higher manageability results in decreased development time and faster time to market of management applications, leading in turn to devices that are more widely supported by management application vendors. (Clearly, other factors influence this cost, including the ease of maintaining the management applications themselves.)

Here are examples of how various aspects of manageability can impact the integration tax:

- Consistency of (machine) management interfaces facilitates design and code reuse for application development and device integration, and is hence crucial to containing the integration tax. Consistency can be an issue at multiple levels—the consistency of management interfaces across different devices, across different revisions of the same device type, and even across different but related functions of the same device type. In each case, consistency means that the same management feature, instrumented in different places, works and behaves in the same manner. For example, if a device supports two kinds of network interfaces, it would be considered consistent if the aspects that are common to both can be managed using the same interface MIB. On the other hand, it would be considered inconsistent if both types of interfaces were represented by entirely different MIBs, or if one network interface would need to be managed using SNMP and the other through Netconf. Likewise, if two different devices both support the same routing protocol but they are managed in different ways with regards to that routing protocol, that would be inconsistent.

- Adherence to management standards, such as support for standardized MIBs, is one technique for ensuring consistency of management interfaces. This is not surprising: The very purpose of management standards is to promote consistency of management interfaces.

- Reliable events facilitate event-driven design of management applications. They reduce the amount of exception handling that management applications must implement to deal with the possibility that important events are missed, and they obviate the need for additional polling mechanisms.

- Self management of certain functions reduces their need to be managed (and to be supported by management applications) in the first place. An example is a capability for devices to exchange certain configuration parameters about each other through a mutual handshake instead of needing to have the configuration parameters provisioned by a management application.

- Introspection capabilities allow applications to obtain information about the management interface and capabilities that are supported by a device, without requiring this information to be coded into the application. Such information consists of metainformation (that is, information about information) concerning data revisions, management parameters, and commands supported. Introspection capabilities can thus facilitate data-driven design of management applications that makes maintaining the applications easier.

- Threshold-crossing alerts help management applications avoid the need to implement elaborate polling schemes and make it easier for them to scale.

The second aspect of cost of ownership concerns lowering operational cost. Loosely speaking, this refers to the cost that is required for operations personnel to support networking equipment. Of course, in many cases, operations personnel does not interact with the managed devices directly; instead, it interacts with management systems in the operations support infrastructure that hide many of the device intricacies. Nevertheless, there are examples of instances in which improved manageability at the device level directly impacts operational cost. It turns out that many are related to the same factors that influence the integration tax:

- Consistency of (human) management interfaces (for example, the CLI) facilitates the task of network administrators when interacting with the device directly, not through a management application. Consistency reduces training cost and increases the pool of personnel that can manage different pieces of networking equipment.

- Support for management policies allows network managers to configure only a few management policies instead of requiring tuning of many low-level parameters. An example is the capability to configure parameter defaults that will be applied to all ports on a given line card (for example, an echo-cancellation setting for voice ports) instead of requiring each port (possibly hundreds of them) to be configured individually. It might still be possible to override such policies on an individual basis, but chances are that most settings that need to be applied are the same. Admittedly, this is an extremely simple example of a policy, yet one that will clearly make life easier for network managers.

- Comprehensive diagnostics capabilities allow a network manager to more easily troubleshoot a device or network.

- Self management of certain functions reduces the need for management intervention, clearly simplifying life not just for application developers, but for network administrators as well.

Everything listed so far relates to lowering the total cost of ownership. However, as previously mentioned, manageability can also impact the revenue side of the equation. For example:

- Threshold-crossing alerts allow early and proactive reaction to performance degradation. This can result in higher service levels and ultimately higher revenues.

- Comprehensive data-collection capabilities in the device to provide detailed data about service levels can be used in accounting and dispute resolution.

- Support for resource partitioning enables network providers to divide a device into multiple logical devices and might facilitate providing new types of service altogether, such as a "virtual router" service.

Finally, manageability can be a factor that contributes to the availability of networks and services. Manageability features can help reduce the possibility of availability being affected by accidental operational errors. They also help accelerate problem diagnostics and repair, to minimize downtime. Increased availability in turn increases customer satisfaction and leads to increased revenues as well. Here are some examples of such features:

■ Concurrency support within a device and across devices facilitates coordination between competing management applications. Concurrency support includes the capability of management applications to lock parts of the configuration for their exclusive use. This helps avoid situations that result in inconsistent network configurations and service outages from multiple management applications that unintentionally conflict with each other.

■ Integrity checksums help avoid outages from corrupted configuration files. An integrity checksum is a number that is computed from the rest of the file contents and then appended to the file. The basic idea is that if the file has been altered, this can be easily recognized because recomputation of the checksum will lead to a different number that does not match the one that was originally appended.

■ Input validation—syntax and semantic checks—before actually attempting command execution helps avoid outages that are caused by invalid commands sent to a device. This is particularly important when there are groups of commands that can be submitted to a device for execution at the same time. For example, if there is an obvious error in the fifth command down the line, it would be nice to know before attempting to execute the commands. This way, the situation can be avoided in which it becomes necessary to back out of the first four commands, leaving the network in an inconsistent state in the meantime.

■ Rollback capabilities allow managed devices to automatically fall back to the last-known working configuration in case of a configuration error. This allows devices to recover from errors that were not caught or avoided by other means.

■ Self management capabilities decrease the dependency on external network managers and management applications, which also avoids operational errors or untimely management actions that could affect availability.

■ And again, threshold-crossing alerts allow early reaction to degradation of performance before availability is impacted.

As can easily be seen from the examples, in many cases the same manageability features contribute simultaneously to several goals. For example, support for threshold-crossing alerts affects not just operational cost, but also the capability to generate revenue as well as network availability.

Management Systems and Operations Support Infrastructure

We now take a look at management applications and identify what types of properties affect management effectiveness at that level.

As we did in the case of manageability, we turn to the cost side of the equation first. It must be recognized that management systems are themselves a cost factor, even if that cost is (hopefully) more than offset by the benefits they provide. The following are some of the aspects that affect the cost associated with management infrastructure—most of them completely unsurprising and in line with that of other business software applications:

■ The capability of a management application to scale. Management applications that scale well might reduce the number of hosts that are required as part of the operational support infrastructure. This lowers the secondary cost of needing to manage that operations support infrastructure itself. Management applications that scale well also facilitate buildout of the network itself because this buildout is less hampered by issues relating to the capability of the operations support infrastructure to keep up.

■ The capability of a management application to be distributed across multiple hosts. This can be one cost-effective way of allowing applications to scale because it is possible to simply add hosts instead of needing to upgrade to a larger (and potentially much more expensive) host.

■ Use of low-cost operating systems, hardware platforms, and databases.

■ Capabilities that facilitate management of management systems themselves. It is important that the task to manage the operations support infrastructure does not unduly distract from the management of the production network.

■ Features that facilitate integration into operations support environments. Perhaps most important, this includes support for comprehensive northbound interfaces. Properties that those interfaces should possess to facilitate an application's integration with other systems largely mirror those of management interfaces of the managed devices themselves. For example, integration cost can be reduced if interfaces adhere to standards as it leads to greater consistency among the interfaces of different management systems that might all have to be integrated as part of the same operations support infrastructure. Likewise, support for events to facilitate event-driven management simplifies the job of systems at higher layers.

In addition to features that lower the cost of the operations support infrastructure, other features lower the operational cost that is associated with using that infrastructure. Here are some examples—it should be clear, however, that specifics often depend on the specific function that the management system is trying to fulfill:

■ The capability of a management system to integrate with different systems can simplify workflows and avoid the need to enter and maintain redundant data.

■ Productive user interfaces can help network managers accomplish more. One aspect to consider is that, in many cases, the productivity of an interface depends on the target user. Occasional users require interfaces that are easy to learn and understand, often relying on drop-down menus, GUI wizards, and elaborate graphical displays. Power users, on the other hand, might find that the same interfaces slow them down, preferring interfaces that are more character based and that offer plenty of keyboard shortcuts.

■ Programmability and customization of management functions enables network managers to automate routine management tasks.

■ Features that assist users (and other systems) to sift through large volumes of management information enables management by exception and further increases productivity of network managers. Examples of such features include these:

— Functions to sort, search, and filter information according to a wide variety of criteria

— Graphical representation of large data sets—for example, through diagrams, curves to visualize trends, and the like

— Visual highlighting of information that seems out of the ordinary

Just as in the case of manageability, management applications are not only about reducing operational cost. There are also ways in which management application features can help increase revenue. For example, management applications can play an important role in raising service levels (for example, service level monitoring applications). This allows service providers to charge more for their services than they would otherwise. Another example concerns programmability of applications, which allows users to customize operations sequences. This can accelerate the deployment of services, as can service provisioning applications. One technique to improve provisioning throughput is to support concurrent communication with multiple devices, which allows the provisioning application to direct provisioning requests at multiple devices simultaneously instead of having to serialize requests.

In addition, in some cases, network management can itself be a service feature that a service provider might be able to charge for. For example, a service provider can make statistical data about a service available to customers, allowing them to track service levels and service usage themselves. In addition, a service provider might offer facilities that allow customers to provision certain aspects of their service; for example, to add bandwidth to a link in a Virtual Private Network in a self-service fashion. Such capabilities are sometimes marketed using labels such as "customer network management."

Finally, many management system features can help increase network robustness and availability. In fact, arguably this is one of the very purposes of many network management applications, such as fault management applications. However, other examples apply to a much wider range of management systems. For example, checkpointing, audit logs, and backup and restore functions allow management systems to more quickly recover from failures. In addition, management systems can perform a significant number of syntax and semantic checks before sending requests to managed devices, thereby decreasing the chance of introducing inconsistent network configurations.

Management Organization

Because this is a book on network management technology, we focus on the effectiveness of that technology, not on the management organization itself. Of course, effectiveness of the management organization that uses management technology is an equally important factor in the running of a network. Here lessons of general organizational effectiveness apply. Providing services and operating networks constitutes one particular scenario to which methodologies developed in that space can be applied.

One example of such a methodology is the Balanced Scorecard. This methodology suggests viewing the organization from four distinct perspectives—learning and growth, business process, customer, and financial—and developing metrics, collecting data, and analyzing the organization with respect to each of these perspectives.

A second example is the Performance Prism, a methodology that focuses more on optimizing organizational effectiveness than assessing it. The Performance Prism distinguishes among five perspectives: stakeholder satisfaction (identifying the stakeholders and what they want), strategies (satisfying the stakeholders), processes (executing the strategies), capabilities (supporting the processes), and stakeholder contribution (helping develop and maintain the capabilities).

Other methodologies exist. It is interesting to observe that this is the blind men and the elephant all over again—one aspect that many of those methodologies have in common is that they all identify a set of different dimensions that are used to characterize the problem space. Of course, there is no single way to assess organizational effectiveness, but there are multiple ways to skin the cat. Accordingly, different methodologies come up with different ways to divide and conquer the problem.

Assessing Network Management Effectiveness

Now that we have reviewed the factors and management features that contribute to management's business impact, how can we actually assess how well management is working? What is needed is a set of metrics by which the effectiveness of management can be measured. An understanding of such metrics, along with an understanding of the different ways in which management technology contributes to those metrics, can provide invaluable guidance for determining priorities in the development and deployment of management technology.

Ultimately, what counts is the bottom line—hence, metrics used for network management should include the same type of metrics that would be used for any other type of business. We therefore start by taking a look at some metrics that capture business impact. As we shall see, those metrics alone cannot capture the entire picture; they need to be augmented by other metrics that capture how effective various factors are that contribute to the bottom line. That aspect is discussed later in the chapter.

In effect, there is a management value chain. This chain starts with individual management features, such as threshold-crossing alerts, programmability, and sort and search functions. As discussed previously, those features contribute to various factors in management effectiveness, such as user productivity, operational robustness, and scalability of operations. Those factors in turn influence the bottom line, as Figure 12-3 shows.

Figure 12-3 *Management Value Chain and Associated Metrics*

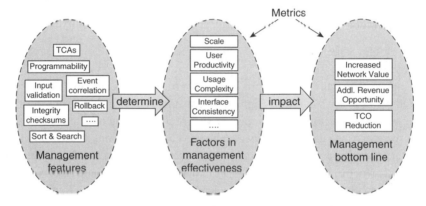

Management Metrics to Track Business Impact

As mentioned earlier, the business impact of network management consists of its contribution to cost savings, revenues, and improved network services themselves, specifically regarding reliability and availability. We start with metrics that can be applied to assessing the cost side of the equation. The metrics that are presented here do not constitute a complete list. Instead, they are intended to provide a sense of the areas on which management has an impact and how this impact can possibly be captured.

For one, there is the total cost of operations. This includes the cost of the operations staff and the amortization cost of the operations support infrastructure. The more effective the management, the lower the total cost.

Of course, total numbers can be hard to compare because the total cost does not take into account the complexity and scale of the network being managed. Normalized metrics that put the cost into perspective regarding what is actually being achieved are often more meaningful. For example, total cost of operations can be normalized over the following:

- Number of devices (operational cost per device). Because devices can be vastly different in nature and scale, this metric is not always meaningful unless dealing with very homogeneous environments.

- Number of ports (operational cost per supported access port). This provides a more level playing field and allows operational cost to be compared across different types of equipment. For example, this measure should reflect better economies of scale if large-scale pieces of equipment are used. Such equipment will likely involve a higher operational cost per device; however, taking into account the additional capacity paints a more appropriate (and favorable) picture.

- Number of service instances—for example, operational cost per voice extension.

- Number of end users—for example, the operational cost per employee in an enterprise.

Other metrics track the contribution of individual cost factors. An obvious set of metrics concerns operator productivity, measuring the number of devices, ports, service instances, or end users that a single network operator can support. A variation of this is the amount of service revenue supported per operator. Another example concerns the number of truck rolls—for example, truck rolls per service activation or truck rolls per year of maintaining an already activated service. Truck rolls refer to the need to send personnel to a customer (in many cases, driving in a truck) to activate and maintain a communications service. Not only are truck rolls very expensive, but they also inconvenience customers and negatively impact customer satisfaction. A third example concerns the number of customer calls to a help desk that are required to resolve a case. Clearly, the number of calls should be as low as possible because each call costs money and inconveniences customers.

Sometimes the ratio between different cost factors can provide useful information as well. A telling metric in that regard concerns the ratio of operations support infrastructure amortization cost to personnel cost. A high ratio could be an indication that there is a high buildout of operations support infrastructure, leading to potentially diminished returns on further investment in that area. A low ratio, on the other hand, could be an indication that investment is too low and that operators could be better leveraged by beefing up infrastructure, particularly if the normalized cost of operations is relatively high.

There are also metrics concerning network management's impact on revenue. The problem with many of those metrics is that although management is a contributing factor, how much revenue can really be attributed to management is not always clear. In many cases, there are also many other factors at work. Nevertheless, there are metrics that are still useful, such as the following:

- Customer loss rate from dissatisfaction with the service level. (This is similar to the popular business metric of customer retention rates, but it focuses on aspects that might be attributable to poor management of the service.)

- Mean time to fill customer orders—time from service order to service activation. The shorter the time, the better because the revenue potential of a service is more fully exploited.

- Average size of customer order backlog. Again, this number can be translated directly into customer dollars. The smaller the average backlog size, the better.

- Customer defections from slow order fulfillment (services cancelled and, hence, revenue lost from customers canceling services before they were activated).

- Total penalties for service level agreement violations, reflecting total lost revenue.

- Ratio between penalties and (theoretical) service revenue, reflecting the portion of revenue that was lost from violated SLAs.

Finally, reliability and availability of the network and services need to be assessed. The classical metrics here are the following:

- **Availability**—The percentage of time during which a service is functioning properly. Two aspects of availability should be distinguished: availability as a whole and availability that factors scheduled maintenance into the equation. The second aspect is much more relevant than the first because it captures only unavailability that comes as a negative surprise.

- **MTBF**—Mean time between failures. A classical measure of reliability, this gives an indication of how often a service or device becomes unavailable, regardless of the duration of the failure. Imagine a case in which a service is overall highly available, but occasional very brief glitches occur that require users to redial a phone call. Clearly, this is much less acceptable than if there is just one outage, even if that outage lasts slightly longer. Figure 12-4 depicts this situation.

- **MTTR**—Mean time to repair. Another classical measure, this indicates how long it takes for services that are impacted by failures to be restored.

Figure 12-4   *Availability and MTBF*

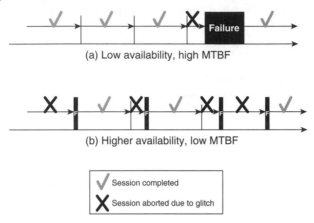

Of course, for all these metrics, the question needs to be asked: "Availability/MTBF/MTTR of what?" The metrics can be applied to individual devices in a network and to the service as a whole. However, it is quite clear what counts from the perspective of the customer: that customer's service. It is important to realize that availability of a service and of a device in the network that carries the service are not the same. The good news is that service availability can be much higher than availability of the network or network devices. For example, when a device fails, services might automatically be switched over to other devices in the network. Nevertheless, it is also important to keep an eye on these measures at the device level because poor reliability and availability of network equipment could ultimately affect services as well. In addition, it leads to negative impact on operational cost because failures must be dealt with.

As with many other metrics, it often makes sense to further differentiate these metrics and distinguish between different types of devices, different types of services, different geographical regions, and different domains of responsibility between organizational subgroups. This can yield data for interesting comparative evaluations. For example, if one group in the organization consistently scores higher on certain management metrics, it might be possible to learn important lessons from that group and apply them to other parts of the organization.

Finally, in the eyes of the customer, maintenance is another factor that impacts availability. Needing to account for maintenance operations is an inconvenience, although, of course, it is by far preferable to unexpected service outages. One meaningful metric with regard to the effectiveness of maintenance is the ratio between unplanned outages and scheduled (maintenance) intervals—for services and for managed devices. Clearly, this ratio should be as close to 0 as possible. Another metric is mean time to maintenance. Although the ratio between unplanned outages and scheduled maintenance intervals might be improved simply by increasing the number of maintenance intervals, doing so would come at the expense of this metric. In addition to being a factor in availability, how often maintenance needs to be performed is a cost factor.

Management Metrics to Track Contribution to Management Effectiveness

Metrics that can be used to assess management business impact are one way to assess management effectiveness. However, those metrics do not tell the entire story. Many factors impact management effectiveness, each of which is the result of a combination of features. For example, some features of management applications make network managers more productive. Other features improve operational robustness by making it harder for network managers to introduce inconsistent configurations, the operational equivalent of shooting themselves in the feet. An important question, therefore, concerns whether it is possible to assess the individual contribution of each of those features to management effectiveness. Although the metrics that have so far been discussed allow assessment of the *impact* that management features collectively have, they provide no indication of their individual effectiveness. In some cases, it is possible to do better. This is the topic of the following discussion.

Metrics for Complexity of Operational Tasks

Perhaps the most important aspect that contributes to management effectiveness concerns the complexity of operational tasks that network managers are faced with. Reducing complexity is important for a number of reasons: It reduces operational cost because operators generally have fewer steps to perform for a given task and those steps may be simpler, requiring less training. It allows the completion of more of the same task in the same time, thereby increasing operational throughput. It reduces the opportunity to introduce errors, which might impact availability and demand complicated recovery. The management metrics that we have encountered so far allow us to see the impact of complexity on business. However, they do not allow us to assess complexity directly.

Complexity of operational tasks can be assessed in a number of ways, many of which were first articulated in a paper by Brown, Keller, and Hellerstein that was published at the IM 2005 conference (the reference is listed in Appendix B, "Further Reading"). Three different categories of complexity are distinguished:

- *Execution complexity* consists of two aspects:

  — The number of steps that the task involves.

  — The number of context switches involved in a task. Roughly, this reflects how many different targets (for example, different pieces of networking equipment, or different types of device interfaces) the steps are directed at.

- *Parameter complexity* concerns the complexity of the parameters that are required as part of each step. This complexity is determined by several aspects, including the following:

  — The number of different parameters that are required for all steps, in total.

> — The average number of parameters that are required in each step. (Some parameters are required in more than one step.)

> — The ease with which a network manager can obtain those parameter values. For each parameter, a corresponding score is assigned. A high score is applied when a parameter represents an obscure value that requires a good deal of experience to choose; a low score is applied for parameters that are "obvious" or that require only a simple lookup. The scores of all parameters are aggregated.

■ *Memory complexity* concerns the amount of memory that is required in the mind of a network manager to perform the steps. It takes into account the number of parameters that must be remembered, the length of time they must be retained in memory, and how many intervening items were stored in memory between uses of a remembered parameter. Memory complexity can be expressed by the largest depth of a stack that would be required to hold the required items.

To obtain management metrics from these complexity measures, a number of benchmark tasks should be selected for which complexity is assessed according to the mentioned criteria. For example, tasks such as the following are good candidates:

■ Adding a device to the network in a rudimentary configuration.

■ Adding a device to the network in an advanced configuration, such as a redundant failover configuration.

■ Configuring all interfaces of the device with the same set of parameters. For example, this could be configuring all DS0 ports on a line card for voice service with a certain echo-cancellation setting.

■ Configuring a loopback on an interface.

■ Configuring an IPSec tunnel (for a reference network topology).

■ Adding a subscriber to a service.

Clearly, it is possible for different management applications to score quite differently when their operational complexity is evaluated against those benchmarks. For example, consider the operational complexity that is involved in adding a subscriber to a service. An operations support environment that includes an application that offers cookie-cutter templates to facilitate this task will achieve a much better score than an operations support environment in which every aspect of the service has to be configured individually (because more steps would need to be performed and more parameters would have to be remembered). Of course, we expected this outcome, but it is nice to have it backed up by quantifiable data.

Related to metrics that are intended to capture operational complexity for network managers are metrics that attempt to capture operational complexity for management applications. Instead of the number and complexity of individual operational steps, key in this case are the number and complexity of communication exchanges that need to take place. As before, it is advisable to select a number of benchmark tasks that are representative for tasks that management applications face. Here are some examples:

- Keeping an application synchronized with the actual device configuration, with mean time between configuration changes 48 hours and maximum permissible time lag to reflect a changed configuration 15 minutes

- Collecting a set of performance counters periodically, every 15 minutes over an interval of 24 hours

- Running a diagnostic test pattern every 15 minutes over the period of 24 hours, and being notified when an abnormal result occurs

Subsequently, the complexity of exchanges between managed network and management applications is assessed.

- The number of communications exchanges that are required.

- The number of dependencies between those exchanges, measured by number of exchanges that need to be serialized as one exchange relies on a piece of information provided by another. This also indicates the complexity of rainy-day scenarios in which things go wrong and need to be recovered from.

Again, different capabilities of systems in the agent role yield vastly differing results. For example, those results show that to keep a management application synchronized with a managed device, a much lower number of communication exchanges is required when reliable configuration change events are supported, compared to cases in which periodic synch-up with devices is required.

Metrics for Scale

Another aspect that is important to management effectiveness concerns scale. Scale is an area in which the need for metrics is widely recognized and often many different metrics are available.

Not all metrics that are offered to support claims of great scale are meaningful, even though they might sound reasonable and impressive at first. A good example is the "number of managed objects supported" by a management application. Several terms in that metric are quite fuzzy: What exactly is meant by a "managed object"? Is it an object in the object-oriented sense that abstracts a managed resource (such as a line card) on a device? If so, how complex is the model? How many managed objects are used to model a device? Or does every attribute count as its own managed object? What about data types? Can they be complex, such as structs or arrays, or are they simple only, such as strings or integers? And even if the meaning of the term "managed object" is clarified, what is exactly meant by "supported"? Does it simply mean that an application will not crash when populated with so many objects? If it indeed means that a network manager will still be able to do actual work, with what performance?

However, there are many excellent metrics for scale that are more appropriate. Here is a small sample:

■   Time to provision 1000 instances of a particular type of service.

■   Provisioning throughput, which is basically the inverse of the previous metric: Number of service instances that can be provisioned per time unit (minute, hour).

■   Time to synchronize a management application with a network of a given size.

■   Number of events that can be sustained per second without dropping events.

■   Number of managed devices of a given type (or a given mix) that are supported, accompanied by a meaningful performance measure—for example, while being able to perform a complete network audit within 60 minutes. (Note the difference to the less meaningful metric of the "number of managed objects supported.")

Other Metrics

Many other aspects contribute to management effectiveness. For example, one aspect concerns the effectiveness of events that are reported from the network and of events that management applications bring to the network manager's attention. It is important that the reported event information be rich enough to convey what is going on, while focused and relevant enough not to distract from the real problems. One metric that is useful in this context is the number of observed alarms per root cause—effectively, a "management signal to management noise" ratio. We would like to see this number go down—ideally, to 1, in which case there is no noise and each alarm is indeed indicative of a distinct problem. In some cases, it might make sense to exclude events from the ratio that are explicitly used to report the impact of a root cause and that refer to other events that point to the root cause. An example is service alarms that indicate which and how many customers are impacted by a service outage, which is caused by a failure that is indicated by a separate alarm.

Another aspect concerns operational robustness and the error-proneness of management interfaces. An interesting metric here is the percentage of network outages from operational error. This is a number that every network provider wants to see trend down over time.

There are other aspects still, such as the consistency between management interfaces of different managed systems, or between interfaces of management applications. As mentioned previously, the discussed metrics are by no means intended as a comprehensive list, but as an illustration of how the contribution of different factors to management effectiveness can be captured in a quantifiable manner. We leave this discussion at this point and turn to the topic of how to determine which metrics should be applied in a particular situation.

Developing Your Own Management Benchmark

By now, it should be clear that no single metric can be used to assess management effectiveness or the business contribution that management provides. Instead, many metrics should be looked at collectively to obtain the overall picture. (Of course, it is possible to combine different metrics into one aggregate using some formula.) In the end, the goal is to provide a set of criteria that can be used to assess the effectiveness and business contribution of management and management technology under different criteria.

Because there are so many metrics, which ones should you use in *your* particular case? The answer is: It depends. And: Use common sense. Obviously, when assessing the effectiveness of fulfilling telephony service orders, a metric to assess provisioning throughput will be more meaningful than a metric to measure the capacity of processing alarms. To identify meaningful metrics, it helps to think about the properties that are most important in the particular context. For example, is the main concern cost or improved availability? Depending on the answer, focus on metrics that provide information on one versus the other, and combine them into a management benchmark, custom-tailored to your specific situation. Also, be creative—do not hesitate to invent your own metrics as needed. Usually, a good question to ask is, "What *use cases* need to be assessed?"

Use case analysis is a software-engineering technique that is used to identify system requirements. In a nutshell, use-case analysis works as follows: First, a set of "actors" is identified. Actors are entities that derive value from the system being analyzed—network operators, for example. Then a set of basic scenarios called use cases is identified. For each use case, the individual steps and interactions that need to occur between the actors and the system are specified, along with preconditions and post-conditions that are supposed to hold before and after a use case is executed, and an explanation of exceptions that can occur.

Nothing prevents use cases from being used not only to derive requirements, but also to capture the factors that best characterize how effective the use case is executed. The result is a set of metrics that is custom-tailored to a particular context. One way in which metrics can be derived is to apply the complexity measures that were discussed earlier to the operational task that corresponds to the use case. For example, it can be meaningful to compare different systems with regard to the number of steps that are required for a given use case, along with the complexity of information that needs to be exchanged at each step.

Assessing and Tracking the State of Management

Now that we know what types of metrics can be applied, what values should these metrics indicate? What constitutes a "good" or "acceptable" value versus one that is "bad" and "needs improvement"? The general answer here again is, it depends.

What is perhaps most significant about those metrics is not their actual value at any one moment in time, but the fact that they can serve as a basis for quantifiable comparisons.

Those comparisons can be conducted between alternatives. For example, metrics can be used to compare management effectiveness between different service providers or IT departments, providing insight into their relative strengths and weaknesses. It might not be really all that interesting to know that it takes a service provider organization 8 hours to provision 1000 instances of a particular type of service, until you hear that it takes the competition only 15 minutes ("What are they doing that we don't?") or 15 days ("Wow, we're way ahead of them!"). Other metrics can be used to compare the effectiveness of different management applications, and of different device types and devices from different vendors that play a similar role in the network.

Comparisons can also be conducted over time, allowing assessment of progress. Again, the absolute value of a metric is often of lesser significance, as long as its trend points in the right direction. If your ratio of customer-reported incidents to incidents overall stands this month at 20 percent, this might be good news if it was 21 percent last month and 30 percent a year ago because it means you have gotten better at identifying problems yourself before they impact customers. However, it is bad news if it used to hover around 15 percent.

Another aspect to consider is that no single metric tells the whole story, but many metrics combine to provide an overall picture. It is easy to get lost in the amount of data that can be collected. What can be extremely helpful in such situations is a way to graphically visualize the data. No one common established technique exists for this. Figures 12-5 and 12-6 depict one way in which this can be accomplished. Figure 12-5 represents a management metrics coordinate system with multiple axes: one axis for every metric. Axes should be arranged so that axes of metrics that relate to similar factors are adjacent. For example, metrics that relate to operator productivity are in one quadrant, metrics related to availability as impacted by management are in a second quadrant, metrics that relate to the integration tax in are a third quadrant, and so on. Then the value for each metric is assessed. The corresponding coordinates are connected and the enclosed area is shaded. The result is a visual profile, as depicted in Figure 12-6. To compare different alternatives, their respective profiles can be superimposed to identify areas where over- and underlap occur, exposing their respective strengths and weaknesses. As management effectiveness improves over time, the values of the coordinates increase and the overall enclosed area grows.

Figure 12-5 *Visualizing Management Effectiveness: A Metrics Coordinate System*

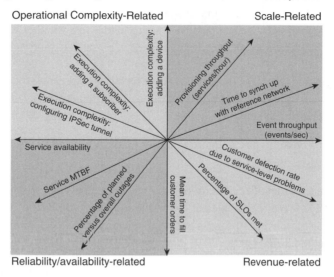

Of course, it is also possible to compile a single value across a set of metrics according to some formula. For example, each metric might be assigned a weight factor that it is multiplied by, before being added up. Although this approach is easy to use and convey, one drawback is that some information is lost in the course and the resulting picture is less differentiated.

Figure 12-6 *A Management Effectiveness Profile*

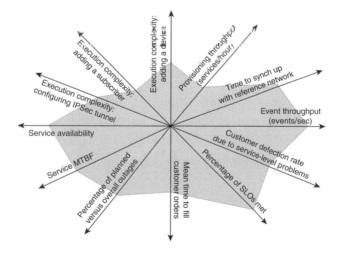

Using Metrics to Direct Management Investment

Metrics such as those discussed in this chapter can be of tremendous help when trying to determine where to direct management investment and to assess whether a particular management investment might even be worth the while. A general approach to take is as follows:

- In the beginning, establish the objectives for further investment—for example, is the most important goal to reduce operational cost, or to increase network availability, or to accelerate rollout of a particular service?

- With the objectives in place, identify metrics that can be used to assess the degree to which those objectives are met.

- With the metrics identified, determine different alternatives that will have an impact on those metrics. We saw many examples of this in the subsection on factors that determine management effectiveness. Assess and try to quantify the expected impact of those factors in terms of the identified metrics.

- Finally, select the alternative that yields the most attractive return on investment (ROI)—that is, the highest benefit in relation to the cost. Additional investment should be made as long as the expected ROI is deemed favorable.

  ROI is generally determined by dividing the benefit expected from an investment by the investment amount. A related measure calculates the time until the benefit will have paid for the investment. In our case, the benefit might not always be expressed in terms of dollars; however, the same general idea can be applied.

Chapter Summary

Network management is done not for its own sake, but to make networks, networked systems, and communication services run smoothly and efficiently. In the end, as interesting as network management is as a technology, the drivers behind it boil down to money. Hence, when dealing with network management, it is important to always keep this aspect in mind and understand the business ramifications of management technology. Management technology needs to be effective, which means that it provides tangible benefits for a network provider and delivers a good bang for the buck.

In this final chapter, we took a closer look at those aspects. One of the takeaways should be that network management is not just about reducing cost of ownership. It is also about revenues (of course, more so for service providers than for enterprise IT departments), about availability, and about getting the most out of your investment in communication services and technology. The effectiveness of management is influenced at every level at which management interactions occur: by the managed devices and systems and how "manageable" they are, by the operations support infrastructure and management systems and how productive they make their users, and by the management organization itself. Many factors contribute to management's bottom line.

To assess the effectiveness of management, management metrics are needed. Although there is no single established way to measure management in an objective manner, many metrics can be applied, both to measure management's business impact and to measure the effectiveness of different factors in management that are known to contribute to that impact. In addition to established measures for aspects such as scale and availability, many of the most relevant metrics are custom-developed to pertain to the particular context in which management occurs—for example, related to the efficiency of specific management tasks. In the end, such metrics can be used to track efficiency gains over time and to help direct investment as well as technical decisions concerning management technology.

Chapter Review

1. In what ways can network management impact a service provider's business?

2. Give an example of a network management technology or feature that can affect revenue.

3. Give an example of a network management technology that can affect availability.

4. At what levels can the effectiveness of network management be assessed?

5. Name two different contexts in which an elaborate GUI of a management application does very little to increase management effectiveness.

6. Imagine that you have decided to invest in the development of custom rules for your event-correlation system. The goal is to improve automated diagnosis of failures in the network. The development can be carried out by one consultant who can incrementally introduce new rules into the system, which will make the system gradually more effective. You decide to give it a try, but you want to make continuation of the project dependent on it indeed fulfilling your expectations as you go along. Can you think of some metrics to use to assess whether the system fulfills expectations?

7. Imagine that you need to decide whether to invest in a new service provisioning system. That system is expected to carry a significant price tag—in particular, when taking into account the cost of integrating the new system with the existing operations support infrastructure. What metrics might help you decide whether this is a worthwhile investment, and how would you do the math to arrive at a go/no-go decision?

8. What is the difference between MTBF and availability?

9. Which three aspects determine the complexity of operational tasks?

10. A management application vendor boasts about the scale of its management system, claiming that it can support 10 million managed objects. What are some questions that you might want to ask in return?

Part V: Appendixes

Answers to Chapter Reviews

Chapter 1

1. Explain the term *network management* in one sentence.

    Answer: Network management refers to the activities, methods, procedures, and tools that pertain to the operation, administration, maintenance, and provisioning of networked systems.

2. We used a patient in intensive care as one analogy to explain network management. Can you think of areas in network management that this analogy does not capture?

    Answer: For example, the analogy does not effectively capture the administration and provisioning aspects of network management.

3. Can you think of other areas in which you would expect analogies to network management to apply?

    Answer: Monitoring, planning, and control are involved in many areas—for example, running a railroad, controlling a space mission, and controlling a nuclear power plant.

4. Give two examples of how network management can help an enterprise IT department save money.

    Answer: One example concerns the capability to more efficiently localize network failures. This means that less time (and money) is spent on troubleshooting and network technicians are dispatched more effectively. Another example involves the automation of routine tasks to offload operating personnel.

5. Give two examples of how network management can help a service provider increase revenue.

    Answer: For example, the capability to turn up service for more customers faster means that more revenue can be collected earlier. A second example concerns being able to offer new communication services that result in new revenue streams, whose cost would be prohibitive without corresponding management capabilities.

6. A famous requirement for availability is "five nines." This refers to the requirement that a device or a service must be available 99.999 percent of the time. Assume that you have a device with hardware availability of 99.9995 percent. Now assume that an operational error is made that causes the device to go offline for 5 minutes until the error is corrected. Calculated over a period of a month, how much has the operational error just caused availability to drop?

Answer: Availability dropped from five nines to three nines. That means the system would be considered two orders of magnitude less available than before. ($30 \times 24 \times 60 \times 60 = 2,592,000$ seconds in a month. The rate of 99.9995 percent means that the system would have been available for 2,591,987 seconds had the operational error not occurred. With the 5 minutes of additional downtime, it was available only for 2,591,687 seconds, or 99.988 percent—in other words, three nines.)

7. How does the perspective under which network management is approached often differ for an enterprise IT department compared to a service provider?

Answer: Network management is a competitive differentiator for service providers—the service provider that runs the network in the best possible way wins in the marketplace. Therefore, there is a tendency for service providers to invest heavily in operations support infrastructure, including custom development where necessary, because this is critical to their business. On the other hand, network management is viewed more under cost considerations in the enterprise IT department—accordingly, there is greater reliance on commercial off-the-shelf management applications.

8. Name at least two factors that can be important to the business success of a third-party management application vendor that potentially has to compete with a network management offering of a network equipment vendor.

Answer: Factors that could be important include the capability to support multiple vendors, application extensibility to provide easy support for new types of equipment for faster time to market, and orientation more toward management of communications services and operational processes than network equipment.

9. What does the term *swivel-chair syndrome* refer to, and why is this undesired?

Answer: It refers to the problem of a lack of integration between management applications, requiring network operators to use multiple terminals at once and thereby needing to "swivel the chair" to switch between those terminals to perform their job. Swivel-chair syndrome is undesirable for many reasons, including the capital and administration expense for additional terminals, additional training cost, lack of qualified personnel, potential for things to "fall through the cracks," and general operational inefficiencies.

10. Name two or more reasons for network management applications to be approached as distributed systems.

Answer: Management applications are inherently of a distributed nature because they involve communication among multiple systems (management systems and network equipment). In addition, distributed systems help to address scaling requirements that might require the capability to add hardware to increase horsepower, resilience requirements that might require support for failovers between systems in case individual systems fail, and requirements to support follow-the-sun operations across geographically diverse regions.

Chapter 2

1. Is running a network only a matter of network management technology, or are there other considerations?

Answer: No, it is also a matter of organization, procedures, and human factors.

2. What does Pat's employer use to track the resolution of problems in the network?

Answer: Problems are tracked through trouble tickets that are managed through a trouble ticket system. Trouble tickets contain all the information pertaining to the problem and the steps that have been taken to resolve it.

3. How does the integration of the work order system with the trouble ticket system make Pat's job easier?

Answer: It saves her from having to enter redundant information, possibly introducing errors along the way. It automatically notifies her when the work order has been fulfilled. Presumably, the integration also allows her to more easily check on the status of the resolution of the problem in the trouble ticket, which links to the work order and its current status.

4. Which network provider do you think will be more vulnerable to human failures by operations personnel, Pat's or Chris's?

Answer: Clearly, Chris's. In Pat's case, everything is regulated by well-defined procedures. Every step along the way is clearly tracked, and automated systems check that nothing falls through the cracks. Chris, on the other hand, pretty much gets to run his own show; if Chris does not do his job properly, disruptions in his company's operations are likely.

5. Which of the following can be used as management tools? A. alarm management system, B. spreadsheet, C. pencil and piece of paper, D. all of them.

    Answer: The correct answer is D. Chris used a spreadsheet to plot performance statistics and identify trends and aberrations; in addition, he used a pencil and paper to track the assignment of phone numbers. The point is, tools other than management systems can be extremely useful in managing networks.

6. In how many different places does Chris need to maintain the same phone number, and why could this be an issue?

    Answer: In four places (IP PBX, voice-mail system, phone number inventory, company directory). Chris's processes are not optimized and could be improved through integration. Because Chris's network is small, this might not yet matter much, but it will as its scale increases.

7. When Chris is worried about compromised security of his company's network, does the threat come from outside attackers or from within the network?

    Answer: The threat comes from within the network. In fact, when managing the security of a network, internal security treats demand as much management attention as outside security threats, although outside threats dominate public perception.

8. Connectivity between different company sites is provided by an outside MSP. Why is Chris nevertheless concerned with monitoring traffic statistics across these outside connections?

    Answer: The need still exists to validate that Chris's company is getting what it pays for.

9. When Sandy wants to implement a security policy for the Internet Data Center, at what different levels does she take security into account?

    Answer: At the user/application level for the data itself, as well as at the networking level (VLANs, firewalls) used to connect to the system on which data is hosted.

10. Why is Sandy interested in "old" performance data and traffic statistics, even though she is not monitoring actual network operations?

    Answer: She uses this for network planning, to see how she needs to dimension the different components in the data center. In network management, there are many potential uses for any individual management function and set of data.

Chapter 3

1. Name the two contexts in which the term *agent* is used in network management.

   Answer: 1) The agent role—that is, the role of the managed network element, as opposed to the managing system.

   2) The management agent—that is, the software component of a network element that implements a management interface and handles management communication for the network element.

2. Compare the manager/agent and client/server paradigms. What are the commonalities, and what are the differences?

   Answer: In both cases, communication between the two roles is asymmetric. Manager and client roles are analogous, in that both own the initiative in the relationship and both send requests to the system in the other role. Agent and server roles are analogous, in that they are both subservient to the requests sent by the system in the other role. However, the manager/agent paradigm differs from the client/server paradigm because general managers manage many agents (each one managed by only one or very few managers), whereas servers serve many clients.

3. The chapter stated that a network element can contain more than one management agent and that a management agent can contain embedded management intelligence. Taking these statements literally can lead to the conclusion that the same management intelligence might have to be implemented redundantly in a network element, once for each management agent. Clearly, this would be a wasteful approach. What would be an appropriate refinement of the model of a management agent?

   Answer: The management intelligence should be shared between different management agents, making the same intelligence accessible across several management interfaces. One way would be to move the intelligence into the layer of the real resource. However, embedded management intelligence is not part of the function of the network and should, hence, not be considered a real resource. This implies that the implementation of management agents itself results in a layered subsystem architecture inside the network element. This architecture needs to separate functions and "intelligence" that are generically applicable across management interfaces (and that should therefore be implemented only once) from functions that are genuinely tied to the particular management interface and the way the agent represents management information.

4. Explain the term *MIB*—what does the acronym stand for, what is it, and who provides it?

Answer: *MIB* stands for Management Information Base. It is a conceptual data store that represents an abstraction of a network element for management purposes. It is provided by a system in an agent role.

5. Name one difference between a MIB and a database.

Answer: The MIB represents a view of real resources, not a set of passive data items that need to be maintained from the outside.

6. Tell whether the following statement is true: "If a network is required to have availability of 99.999 percent, its management systems need to also be 99.999 percent available." Why or why not? Please elaborate. For extra points, factor in the influence of the type of application that the management system is used for.

Answer: A network functions independently of its need to be managed. Accordingly, the 99.999 percent availability should not be affected if the management system's availability is less. Therefore, to achieve five nines, five nines availability of the management system is generally not required. However, we need to distinguish between the types of management applications that the management system supports: Availability of a management system used for monitoring the network should not be allowed to drop much below five nines because the lack of monitoring capability could adversely affect the network's availability. On the other hand, availability of a management system used to add new users to a network is less critical. Finally, management systems used to collect accounting data that is used to bill for services by a service provider does need to be as highly available as the network—not for reasons of network availability, but because any loss of accounting information can result in loss of revenues because customers cannot be billed.

7. Management traffic is different from other communication traffic, in that the NE itself is a destination and originator of traffic. However, it is not the only type of traffic for which this is true. Name an example of other network traffic that the NE does not just switch or route, but actively participates in.

Answer: Control and signaling traffic, such as traffic from routing protocols.

8. What could be the most important reason for using a dedicated management network instead of a shared one?

Answer: The most important reason generally concerns reliability. In case of network failures and congestion, it is important to communicate with network elements to diagnose what happened and apply reconfigurations to remedy the situation remotely. Without a dedicated management network, in those cases it will be hard to get through to the network element, just when it is needed the most. A second reason concerns avoiding interferences with other network traffic, with which management traffic would compete for networking resources.

9. Which other term do service providers use to refer to management systems?

   Answer: Operational support systems (OSS).

10. Would you expect a management system to provision services to be located at a NOC or at a Central Office? Why?

   Answer: At a NOC. The NOC is the Network Operations Center from which network management involving operations personnel takes place. Central Offices, on the other hand, resemble remote branch offices in an enterprise. They terminate local lines and might not even be staffed.

Chapter 4

1. What are the different aspects, or "subdimensions," of management interoperability?

   Answer: Communication, function, and information

2. Why is a management protocol needed between managers and agents, and why isn't mere connectivity between them sufficient?

   Answer: It is possible for people to hear each other but not understand each other. In the same fashion, mere connectivity would allow managers and agents to send messages to each other but not to understand and know how to interpret those messages or what to do in response. A management protocol is needed to define the "rules of conversation" between managers and agents, including the syntax and meaning of messages to be exchanged.

3. Why is it important for interoperability that a manager understand the functions provided by an agent?

   Answer: If a manager did not understand the functions provided by an agent, the manager might get unexpected return codes when sending a request or, worse, not understand the effects of an operation. Either situation could lead to unintended consequences. For example, a manager might send a group of commands assuming that they would be treated as a "transaction," but the agent might support only "best effort" semantics. If an error occurred, the manager might assume that none of the commands had taken effect, whereas some of them actually did, and it would be the manager's responsibility to undo their effects.

4. Assume that you need to manage a network that contains three different types of devices. To avoid dependence on a particular vendor, you have two suppliers for each type of device. Explain some of the ways in which management standards are important in this situation.

    Answer: Without management standards, chances are, you must support six different types of interfaces for your network. If you develop tools or scripts, you need to be well versed in six interfaces instead of only one. In addition, it will take you longer to develop them. Likewise, network management suppliers incur higher costs that they will want to recover from their customers—in other words, from you.

5. What does TMN stand for?

    Answer: Telecommunications Management Network, a set of standards that defines a network used to manage telecommunications networks.

6. Would the layers of the TMN reference model apply to application management? Why or why not?

    Answer: The TMN reference model applies specifically to the management of telecommunications networks, not to application management. The network management layer, for example, is not directly applicable to application management. Having said that, the concept of a hierarchical set of management layers applies also to application management—for example, a distinction between management of individual applications and business management can certainly be made. This hierarchy will likely be sliced a little differently than the TMN reference model.

7. Name three phases in a typical network management life cycle.

    Answer: Three phases in a typical network management life cycle are network planning, network deployment, and network operations.

8. If an upgrade in a network is not carefully planned, service outages can occur. Name three ways in which upgrade operations might impact network availability.

    Answer: Disconnecting and reconnecting physical cabling, during which equipment is offline; loading a new software image (such as a new operating system revision) that might require an equipment reboot, during which it is unavailable; and downloading and activating an updated configuration that resembles the configuration that was in place before the upgrade. All of these can lead to impact on network availability that can be avoided or minimized with proper upgrade planning as part of the management life cycle of the underlying network. For example, services and network traffic need to be switched to other parts of the network before maintenance and upgrade operations are performed.

9. Give three reasons why cookie-cutter procedures can be useful in network management.

    Answer: These reasons include the following: (1) Greater efficiency in performing a given repetitive task. The efficiency comes from eliminating the step of repeatedly figuring out how to perform the task. (2) Easier troubleshooting. When problems are encountered with services, it is clear what configurations are supposed to look like, making it easier to spot problem areas. (3) Key personnel are freed up for more advanced tasks instead of being bogged down by routine tasks.

10. An enterprise organizes network operations as follows: Group 1 is responsible for telephony services. Group 2 is responsible for interactions with end users. Group 3 is responsible for maintaining the network infrastructure. Can you see potential problems with this organization?

    Answer: This is an open-ended question with many aspects to consider. In the example, potential problems can exist regarding whose responsibility it is to forecast demand for voice services and plan network upgrades in a timely manner. Another problem is the efficiency with which a voice problem would be resolved because this could involve all three organizations (group 2 to take the call, group 1 to determine what's wrong, and group 3 to address the problem and fix it). Generally, it helps to identify key scenarios and play through them, asking whether responsibilities in those scenarios are clearly defined, and whether the number of parties involved and exchanges between them could be reduced.

Chapter 5

1. What does FCAPS stand for?

    Answer: Fault, Configuration, Accounting, Performance, and Security.

2. What does OAM&P stand for?

    Answer: Operations, Administration, Maintenance, and Provisioning.

3. What is the difference between alarm filtering and alarm correlation?

    Answer: Alarm filtering lets alarms pass only if they meet a certain criteria, such as if they have a certain severity. The alarm itself is left untouched. If alarms do not meet the criteria, they are simply dropped. Alarm correlation, on the other hand, preprocesses information from alarms and, in the process, modifies alarms that are sent. For example, alarm correlation might generate additional information that is added to the original alarm, such as information that one alarm is likely related to another, or might replace alarm information, such as sending an alarm about a suspected root cause instead of alarms for each symptom that is believed to be caused by that same root cause.

4. The management functions discussed in this chapter pertain not only to the element management layer that deals with individual pieces of equipment, but really to any management layer. Give an example of a fault at the element management layer, an example of a fault at the network management layer, and an example of a fault at a service management layer.

    Answer: Element management layer: Failure of a card

    Network management layer: Loss of connectivity between two devices—for example, cannot ping system A from system B

    Service management layer: Degraded service—for example, for a voice service, no dial tone or excessive post-dial delay (time from dialing a phone number to hearing a ring tone)

5. Give an example of a configuration operation at the element management layer, a configuration operation at the network management layer, and a configuration operation at the service management layer.

    Answer: Element management layer: Configure a host name

    Network management layer: Establish a permanent virtual circuit (PVC) between systems A and B

    Service management layer: Add telephony service (Voice over IP) for employee Smith, including caller ID, a voice-mail box, call forwarding, and international calling privilege

6. Give an example of an event sent by a network device that supports an accounting management function. Give an example of an event that supports a security management function.

    Answer: Example of an event that is relevant for accounting management: call proceeding, start time = xxx, called party number = yyyy, call ID = zzzzz

    Example of an event that is relevant for security management: failed logon attempt, origin identification = yyyy

7. Provide a technical reason, not a marketing reason, for why a service provider might choose to provide flat-rate billing.

    Answer: The service provider might not have the technical capability to reliably collect usage-based accounting information and provide an itemized bill to end customers.

8. Performance and accounting management are similar, in that both are interested in collecting usage data from the network. Describe an important way in which the use of this data and the requirements for its collection differ.

    Answer: The purpose of collecting the data is different. Performance management is interested in using the data for statistical purposes, such as getting an idea of overall load and utilization of the network and detecting statistical trends. Accounting management is interested in using the data as the basis for billing and attributing usage data to the actual users. Accordingly, the data-collection requirements for accounting management are much more stringent than for performance management. The data collected must be complete— after all, each piece of accounting data that is lost could result in lost revenues. Performance management, on the other hand, can generally afford to lose some data, as long as the remaining sample is statistically relevant.

9. "I have no need for security management functions because I am using a dedicated and secure management network." Please comment on this statement.

    Answer: Although a dedicated and secure management network goes a long way toward securing the management of the network, it does not protect against all security threats, some of which could come from the inside. In addition, it does not address how to manage security threats that are directed at the production network (that is, the network that is being managed) itself, such as denial-of-service attacks. By turning a blind eye to these aspects, the network is left dangerously exposed.

10. Provide a rough sketch of how OAM&P and FAB relate.

    Answer: The following table provides a rough sketch of the relationship between OAM&P and FAB.

	O	A	M	P
F	—	—	—	X
A	X	—	X	—
B	—	X	—	—

Chapter 6

1. What does the acronym MIB stand for?

   Answer: Management Information Base.

2. Name four categories of management information and tell what distinguishes them.

   Answer: State information reflects the current state of physical and logical resources. It is used mainly for monitoring. It tends to be dynamic in nature and subject to constant change, and it cannot be modified by management applications.

   Physical configuration information is static in nature, changing rarely, if at all; it cannot be modified by management applications.

   Logical configuration information concerns parameter settings that are subject to modification by network administrators and management applications. It provides the management "knobs" for the managed device.

   Historical information contains periodic past snapshots of state information, as well as logs of events that have occurred in the past. It is less common than other categories of management information and is often retrieved in bulk from the device.

3. In what ways does a MIB differ from a database management system?

   Answer: It is an abstracted view of an "active" real-world system, not a set of information that is actually stored somewhere in a file system. It is optimized for management requirements—for example, omitting general-purpose database capabilities such as joins—and has a smaller footprint. Also, the managed objects contained in a MIB tend to be much more heterogeneous in nature than data maintained by database management systems.

4. Name two of the different paradigms that can underlie a MIB definition language.

   Answer: Table orientation and object orientation.

5. Can you think of a MIB object for which it would make sense to define a maximum access of write only?

   Answer: An example is security-sensitive information such as a password.

6. What is the name of the language for the definition of management information used with SNMP?

   Answer: Structure of Management Information (SMI)—specifically, SMIv2.

7. In SMI, what is an important difference between an OID designating an object type and an OID designating an object instance?

   Answer: An OID that refers to an object type definition is globally unique. An OID that refers to an object instance is unique only within the MIB that it is contained in.

8. Why are SNMP MIB objects not considered objects in an object-oriented sense?

   Answer: They lack features that are commonly associated with object orientation. One such feature is inheritance (the capability to derive specializations from existing object class definitions). Other object-oriented features that SNMP MIB objects lack but that were not mentioned in the chapter include polymorphism (the capability for instances of a subclass to be treated as if they are instances of a superclass) and the inclusion of methods as part of the object class definition, commonly associated with the property of encapsulation. SNMP MIB objects are essentially simply MIB variables.

9. SNMP MIBs use a hierarchical naming structure very similar to the structure many operating systems use to name files and folders. In which way is the object identifier tree of SNMP MIBs different from a naming tree for a file system?

   Answer: The naming tree in a file system represents a containment hierarchy between the objects. If you delete an object that contains other objects—that is, that are in a subtree underneath the object—those other objects will be deleted as well. The object identifier tree of SNMP MIBs, on the other hand, does not reflect a hierarchy between objects. Instead, it reflects the structure of the underlying MIB definition, or the way in which the definitions of the object types are grouped that are instantiated by objects in the MIB. The objects in the MIB themselves are flat; every one of them is a leaf node in the MIB object identifier tree.

10. What does the granularity of a model refer to?

    Answer: It refers to the degree to which management information is aggregated and lumped together (coarse granularity), or to which every individual real resource is separately accounted for (fine granularity). Generally, a coarse-grained model is more efficient but offers less detailed control capabilities than a fine-grained model.

Chapter 7

1. What are the fundamental interaction patterns between the management agents?

   Answer: Manager-initiated request and response, and agent-initiated events.

2. Assume that you have a network with 1000 devices and 1500 links. Assume that a performance management application is interested in 18 performance parameters per link and 7 performance parameters per device. Assume that with incremental information-retrieval requests, you can retrieve 5 parameters at a time. Someone asks you to build an application that will keep a database of historical information of those parameters, using 15-minute intervals. What rate of management requests and responses must your application support per second? Furthermore, if it takes an average of 5 seconds to receive a response from a device, how many requests must the application be capable of handling in parallel?

    Answer: Polling the link parameters requires four requests per link, and polling device parameters requires two requests per device. This means that $1500 \times 4 + 1000 \times 2 = 8000$ requests and responses need to be handled per 15-minute interval. Fifteen minutes have 900 seconds, so assuming that there will be some request timeout and retries, the sustained rate needs to be approximately 10 requests and responses per second. If it takes 5 seconds to receive a response from the device, the application needs to be capable of handling an average of 50 outstanding—or parallel—requests at any given point in time.

3. What do you call the capability to apply the same management operation to multiple managed objects simultaneously, using only one management request?

    Answer: Scoping.

4. One important technique that could be supported by devices to facilitate management transactions involves locking the device—that is, allowing a single management session to take management "ownership" of the device and allow no one else to modify the configuration during that time. Such a capability is very powerful, but in what ways does it still fall short of true management transaction support? For bonus points, can you think of new management issues that it introduces?

    Answer: The capability to lock a device is not the same as a management transaction. For example, it does not include rollback capabilities.

    The capability to lock a device imposes performance limitations if multiple management applications and users want to configure different aspects of the device simultaneously—operations need to be serialized instead of being executed concurrently. To be effective, locking requires applications to be fair and not "hog" a device—that is, apply a lock without releasing it. It also requires a mechanism to break locks, for example, if an application is no longer capable of releasing a lock (or forgets to do so).

5. One technique that can be used to roll back management transactions involves reverting to an earlier configuration file. Discuss advantages and drawbacks of this technique.

   Answer: Advantages:

   - Very effective

   - Simple, straightforward application logic and semantics

   Drawbacks:

   - Performance overhead in persisting configuration file at the beginning of a transaction, as well as reverting to a configuration file in case of rollback, which could make the system too slow to be practical

   - Does not provide "locking," and may result in also rolling back configurations done independently by someone else at the same time during which the transaction took place

6. Why can management actions never be subjected to management transactions?

   Answer: They might involve real effects that cannot be undone as part of a rollback, such as an action that leads to a reboot.

7. In network management, what is an alarm?

   Answer: An alarm is an event that indicates the onset or the remission of an alarm condition.

8. Does a TCA have more in common with a configuration-change event or an alarm? Why?

   Answer: A threshold-crossing alert is essentially a special type of alarm. Like an alarm, it is used to notify the onset (or remission) of a condition—in this case, the crossing of a threshold.

9. Is it possible to support polling-based alarm management? If so, why is alarm management generally event based?

   Answer: It would be possible if devices maintain the current alarm state on the device. A management application would repeatedly need to poll the devices for their alarm information. Of course, in practice, this is infeasible for several reasons: It would imply an extremely high load on an alarm management application (compare this with the earlier question on polling-based performance management). In addition, there will be a delay between polling cycles that prevents alarm management in near–real time and that practice is unacceptable. Event-based alarm management is therefore the only feasible option.

10. Name three techniques that can be used to make events reliable.

    Answer: Use of a reliable transport protocol, consecutive sequence numbers and replay capability, acknowledgment of events and retransmission capability.

Chapter 8

1. Why is SNMPv1 not considered secure? How could a hacker exploit its security holes?

   Answer: SNMPv1's only security mechanism is a community string that is part of SNMP messages, which is communicated in the clear. For example, it does not offer authentication, which would enable an agent to ascertain the identity of a manager, or encryption, which would prevent SNMP messages from being seen by others or tampered with. A hacker could exploit the lack of authentication by sending unauthorized commands to a device that might alter its configuration, for example, to steal service or to sabotage the network. For this reason, many agents do not allow their configurations to be modified through SNMP and limit SNMP's use to monitoring, where exposure to security holes is less critical.

2. One of the advantages of SNMPv1 lies in the simplicity of its agent implementations. Does this simplicity also have drawbacks?

   Answer: The simplicity means limited power, which, in turn, means that management applications have to do more work. Note also that SNMPv3 is much more powerful and, hence, less simple than the original SNMPv1.

3. Explain the difference between an SNMP trap and a syslog message.

   Answer: The information that is conveyed as part of a trap is formally defined in a MIB specification. A syslog message is much more ad hoc and informal; the contents carried in its body part are typically not formally defined.

4. What is the most important reason CLI is hard to use for management applications?

   Answer: Screen scraping—that is, interpreting the returned results, which can take vastly different formats and, therefore, are difficult to parse and process in a generic manner.

5. In what way do CLI and syslog complement each other?

   Answer: CLI provides for request-response–based management interactions and does not address events, whereas syslog addresses events but not request-response–based management interactions.

6. SNMP has a specific concept of MIBs. Where is the MIB in Netconf?

   Answer: The MIB consists of the datastore that contains the management information of the device, which can be subjected to the Netconf operations. Specifically (for configuration management information), the MIB is the running config.

7. One criticism in conjunction with SNMP concerns reliability because SNMP in general uses UDP as a transport, in which packets (and, hence, SNMP management requests or responses) can be dropped. Describe an obvious way of handling reliability in Netconf.

   Answer: Specify reliability as a requirement for the Netconf transport in the application protocol layer.

8. File transfer protocols allow the transfer of files between two locations. Netconf operations have some resemblance to file transfer protocols, in that they allow the copying, transfer, and deletion of config files. Name three ways in which Netconf differs from a simple file transfer protocol for configuration files.

   Answer: 1) **edit-config** of a running config causes commands within a configuration file to be executed, not merely transferred. 2) Additional capabilities, such as validation of config files or (again, linked to the execution of commands within a config file) rollback on failure. 3) Subtree filtering, allowing to process only subconfigurations within a configuration file.

9. What is a flow in Netflow?

   Answer: A flow is a set of IP packets that traverse a router and that apparently belong to the same communication context, as defined by seven parameters: the source IP address and port, the destination IP address and port, the protocol type, the type of service (TOS), and the interface that the IP packets were received on.

10. We stated that Netflow can help you identify the top talkers in your network. How? (You may assume that each talker connects to your network using a static IP address—that is, an IP address that does not change.)

    Answer: You collect flow information from all your access routers. For each router, you aggregate the flow information for each source IP address, adding the traffic totals from each flow. At the end of this exercise, you can stack rank the addresses from which the most amount of traffic originated. Clearly, with the volume of Netflow records, a lot of number crunching will be required. (Note that in the case of dynamic IP addresses, you also need to reconcile the flow information with the records of who had what IP address at what point in time.)

Chapter 9

1. Assume that you have to manage an enterprise network with several remote branch locations. You are told that you need to collect performance data from each remote location to assess the total traffic that goes to headquarters, that is directed to other enterprise locations, and that goes to destinations outside the enterprise. Your low-bandwidth WAN connection that leads back to your network operations center doesn't seem to have enough bandwidth to allow for the export of all the Netflow data from the remote locations. What other options do you have?

   Answer: You can deploy a management solution with a remote subordinate management application that collects Netflow data at the remote site, aggregates the desired information, and sends back only the aggregated information to the NOC.

2. What is RMON?

   Answer: RMON stands for remote monitoring MIB. It refers to a capability to delegate certain management functionality to so-called RMON probes using SNMP. RMON probes reside near the monitored network elements, sometimes in the devices themselves. They offer functions that include threshold-crossing alerts, periodic polling and statistics collection of performance-related MIB variables, and event filtering and subscription capabilities, all of which are remotely controlled through a MIB.

3. Give an example of a management task that a management appliance could provide.

   Answer: One example is tasks associated with RMON—RMON probes.

4. If management by delegation is such a great idea, why don't we simply delegate all management tasks to the network?

   Answer: There are limitations in the processing horsepower that is available, such as CPU and memory. The primary purpose of devices in the network is to provide communication functions; making the job easier for management applications is a distant second. In addition, many tasks don't lend themselves to delegation, such as tasks that require additional information (for example, customer information) that is not readily available to devices in the network.

5. What do the acronyms PDP and PEP stand for?

   Answer: Policy Decision Point and Policy Enforcement Point.

6. How can policy-based management help scale management?

Answer: Policies provide guidelines for what behavior is expected under certain conditions, without requiring intervention by the upper-layer management system, similar to reflexes in the human nervous system that do not require conscious thought. This frees the upper-layer management system from routine tasks, allowing it to scale better and to cover a larger domain.

7. What are the main limitations of syntactical management mediation?

Answer: For one thing, in many cases, not all aspects of the underlying source interface can be hidden. This concerns, for example, the way in which management information is exposed across the interface. In addition, not all features of the target interface can be leveraged. This is specifically the case for functions that are not supported on the source interface, which cannot be emulated using syntactical management mediation alone.

8. Why is stateful mediation more complex than stateless mediation?

Answer: Stateful mediation is more complex for a variety of reasons. For example, single operations might need to be broken into multiple operations, their execution kept track of, and results aggregated. The management gateway needs to deal with exceptions when some of the operations fail, having to provide the semantics of a transaction for what are only single operations on the target interface. Also, the management gateway might need to cache information about the underlying network elements, bringing about the need to deal with all the issues usually associated with synchronizing management information. In contrast, stateless mediation requires none of this; it's a translate-and-forget kind of deal.

9. Assume for a moment that you have two fictitious management protocols, SIMP and COMP. SIMP is a very simple protocol, providing only a small set of the most basic management primitives. COMP is much more powerful; it offers all the capabilities that SIMP offers, plus additional functionality. For example, COMP enables you to apply the same management operation to a group of managed objects that meet a certain criteria, and it offers a threshold-crossing alerting capability, whereas SIMP does not. Now assume that you are asked to build two management gateways, one for SIMP managers to manage COMP agents, the other for COMP managers to manage SIMP agents. Which of the two do you expect to be simpler? Why?

Answer: The gateway that allows SIMP managers to manage COMP agents will be much simpler. The reason is that COMP provides a much richer interface than SIMP. SIMP primitives can most likely be mapped directly to COMP operations. The reverse is not true: Many COMP capabilities will not have an SIMP counterpart. The difference in capabilities will need to be made up by the gateway, requiring functionality that goes well beyond translating from one management message to another.

10. Would you expect semantic mediation of management information that involves CLI as the source (agent) interface to be simple or hard? Why?

Answer: This is likely to be difficult. The reason is that interpreting the responses to CLI commands requires screen scraping to properly populate responses for the target interface, and this must be done for a large number of CLI commands.

Chapter 10

1. Imagine that you are a service provider. An equipment vendor offers you an integrated management system. Which aspects of management integration will such a system be unlikely to address, even if the equipment vendor's claims are, from his perspective, entirely correct?

Answer: It might not provide multivendor support or integration with service and business management functions that are specific to the service provider's operational support environment.

2. Which factor has perhaps the most significant impact on management complexity?

Answer: Heterogeneity complexity.

3. Provide an example of how management integration as a technical issue mirrors management integration as an organizational issue.

Answer: For example, clear roles and responsibilities need to be defined, and clear chains of commands need to be established.

4. Give three examples of management application infrastructure that is commonly provided by management platforms.

Answer: A common database for information storage, common system administration facilities, and network-discovery services.

5. Why can functional overlap between management applications in an operational support environment be a problem?

Answer: It violates the principle that there should be clear ownership for different functions. As a result, information between applications might be harder to synchronize and problems might be harder to troubleshoot because it will be harder to trace requests to their source.

6. Provide two examples of technical obstacles that can increase a management solution's footprint.

Answer: Different operating system requirements might prevent applications from running on the same hosts; incompatible database management system requirements might result in the need to deploy multiple database management systems.

7. Which industry consortium concerns itself with the standardization of interfaces between management systems in operations support environments?

Answer: The TeleManagement Forum (TMF).

8. Contrast shallow with deep integration of applications at the user interface level.

Answer: Shallow integration allows functions of different applications to be launched from the same screen, but boundaries between the applications are clearly noticeable and navigation between different application functions is not seamless. Deep integration, on the other hand, makes it difficult if not impossible for users to tell that the functions are actually provided by different systems.

9. Name three ways in which complexity that is caused by heterogeneity can be reduced.

Answer: Reduction of the number of vendors and types of equipment in a network, separation of equipment of different type and vendor that provides similar functions into different network regions or administrative domains, utilization of cookie-cutter topologies and configurations for network deployments across different sites.

10. How do cookie-cutter deployments make network management easier? Are there any downsides?

Answer: They make it possible to devise and test a configuration only once and deploy it multiple times, making deployment and provisioning much more efficient and reducing the risk of introducing configurations that do not work as intended. They also facilitate troubleshooting and fault management because different deployments do not have to be custom-analyzed. One downside can be that possible optimizations cannot be exploited as they could be with custom deployment, but this drawback is often easily offset with simplified management.

Chapter 11

1. Both the provider and the customer of a service should be concerned with service level monitoring. Why is this so?

    Answer: The customer might not know for sure whether he is indeed getting the service level that was agreed to.

2. Assume that you are a service customer and are about to enter an SLA with a service provider to provide you with video phone service across your enterprise network. Can you think of some service level parameters that you might want to include in service level objectives of the SLA? (Pick three.)

    Answer: Examples might include picture resolution, picture jerkiness, time to set up a video call when dialed, overall video call quality (a video call mean opinion score that captures also factors such as whether the voice and audio are synchronized).

3. In addition to a set of service level objectives, what else should an SLA spell out?

    Answer: An SLA should also spell out how service level objectives are measured and what happens when service levels are violated. The latter includes the course of action that is to be taken when service level violations are detected, financial penalties that are incurred, and possible legal ramifications, for example, regarding early termination of service agreement.

4. Give an example of a voice service level parameter that cannot be derived from an underlying network parameter.

    Answer: For example, the time to set up a call. This involves a sequence of signaling activities and processing that the underlying transport has no notion of. Another example is the mean opinion score, which judges the voice quality of a call that is impacted by aspects such as static, echo, and clipping.

5. Give an example of a service level parameter of a voice service that, when decomposed, contains a network service level parameter as a component.

    Answer: Voice delay. Although it is influenced also by dejitter buffers, network delay is the main variable component of the voice delay that is experienced during a call.

6. Assume that your SLA specifies a maintenance interval of 1 hour per month. When measuring the availability of your network, you forget to take this maintenance interval into account and accidentally include 30 minutes that your service was not available during this interval. How much is your availability number skewed?

Answer: One month has 30 days with 24 hours, with 60 minutes, for a total of 43,200 minutes—excluding the maintenance interval of 43,140 minutes. Of that, 30 minutes constitutes roughly 0.07 percent by which the availability number is now skewed. Even if availability had otherwise been perfect, that would result in 99.93 percent availability—not bad for many scenarios, but two orders of magnitudes off from the coveted five nines carrier-class availability.

7. Name a technique that can be used to set up an early warning system for impending service level violations.

    Answer: Threshold-crossing alerts, to indicate when service levels get dangerously close to missing service level objectives and when components of service level parameters are exceeding their allotted budget.

8. Assume for a moment that you are a service provider. A customer complains about the level of service he received. Your first impulse is to give little credibility to that complaint—you are quite certain that the level of service that you provided was well within the targets set by the service objectives. However, the customer produces as evidence a log file with service level measurements that were taken over the past month. Which three questions might you want to go over in your mind to assess the validity of the customer's claims?

    Answer: Are the measurements statistically relevant, or is it possible that they paint a picture that is skewed? How were the measurements taken—are they sure to accurately reflect the service level parameters? Is the data authentic, or could important samples have been inadvertently left out or manipulated?

9. What trade-off does a service provider need to assess when deciding whether and by how much to oversubscribe resources?

    Answer: The trade-off is between cost and revenue. Cost is associated with resource utilization, which needs to be high because having resources idling is expensive. Revenue is associated with service levels that are achieved, which need to be high to charge top dollar for a service and keep customers satisfied. A service provider needs to find the spot at which maximum resource utilization is achieved without violating service level objectives.

10. What strategy might a service provider take when realizing that resource contention occurs, to prevent everybody's service level from dropping?

    Answer: Until the resource-contention situation passes, impose some form of admission control to prevent additional users from generating additional load on the network and underlying resources.

Chapter 12

1. In what ways can network management impact a service provider's business?

    Answer: It affects the cost of ownership of a network, revenues that can be generated from communication services, network availability, and the quality of the communication services that are offered.

2. Give an example of a network management technology or feature that can affect revenue.

    Answer: Service provisioning systems are one example. They enable faster rollout of services and hence allow sooner collection of revenues from customers. A second example concerns service level monitoring, which enables you to offer higher service level guarantees, for which a higher price can be charged. A third example is offering unified billing and service statistics as a premium feature of a service itself, which might attract additional customers.

3. Give an example of a network management technology that can affect availability.

    Answer: Here are a few examples: Performance trending combined with threshold-crossing alerting brings impending problems to the attention of network managers, who might be able to take preventive action and avert problems before availability is affected. Well-designed user interfaces can reduce their tendency to err during configuration changes—as many as half of all network outages can be attributed to preventable user error. A reduction in user errors hence implies an increase in availability. Event correlation enables network managers to spot the root cause of problems more quickly, which leads to sooner repairs.

4. At what levels can the effectiveness of network management be assessed?

    Answer: Network management effectiveness can be assessed at the following levels: the managed technology itself, which is subsumed under the term *manageability*; management applications and operations support infrastructure; and the management organization that makes use of this infrastructure.

5. Name two different contexts in which an elaborate GUI of a management application does very little to increase management effectiveness.

    Answer: One context is that of a management application that is driven primarily through its northbound interface from other applications in an operations support environment, not by network managers sitting in front of a screen. The second context is that of an application that is used by power users who are more efficient typing command shortcuts than performing point-and-click operations in a GUI, which slows them down.

6. Imagine that you have decided to invest in the development of custom rules for your event-correlation system. The goal is to improve automated diagnosis of failures in the network. The development can be carried out by one consultant who can incrementally introduce new rules into the system, which will make the system gradually more effective. You decide to give it a try, but you want to make continuation of the project dependent on it indeed fulfilling your expectations as you go along. Can you think of some metrics to use to assess whether the system fulfills expectations?

   Answer: The metrics should indicate whether the quality and accuracy of diagnosis is actually improving. Possible metrics might include mean time to repair (which should get shorter), the average number of steps an operator must perform to diagnose a problem (which should get smaller), and the percentage of events that are correctly diagnosed and attributed to a root cause by the system without requiring further operator intervention (which should increase).

7. Imagine that you need to decide whether to invest in a new service provisioning system. That system is expected to carry a significant price tag—in particular, when taking into account the cost of integrating the new system with the existing operations support infrastructure. What metrics might help you decide whether this is a worthwhile investment, and how would you do the math to arrive at a go/no-go decision?

   Answer: You might consider the number of truck rolls (per service order), the mean time to fill customer service orders, and the average size of customer order backlog as useful metrics.

   What needs to be compared is the value that those metrics have today versus the value that those metrics are expected to have in the future with the new system in place. This difference needs to be translated into a monetary value. For example:

   - The monetary value yielded by the reduction in truck rolls can be calculated as follows:

     Let *rtrso* be the expected reduction in the number of truck rolls per service order, *ctr* the cost per truck roll, and *nso* the number of service orders per month. The value per month of the reduction in truck rolls is $rtrso \times ctr \times nso$.

   - The monetary value yielded by the reduction in mean time to fill service orders can be calculated as follows:

     Let *rmtso* be the expected reduction in the mean time to fill a service order, *rso* the revenue per service order that can be collected during a time period of length *rtmso*, *cso* the cost of the resources that are required to provide service during a time period of length *rtmso*, and *nso* the number of service orders per month. The value per month of the reduction in mean time to fill service orders is $(rso - cso) \times nso$.

The combined benefits are then juxtaposed with the cost of the system, using standard business metrics to assess the return on investment. One simple measure is calculating the time until the investment pays for itself—basically, dividing the cost by the additional revenue and operational cost savings.

Of course, these are back-of-the-envelope calculations. To increase the accuracy of those calculations, other factors (such as interest cost and other costs associated with the additional revenue) need to be taken into the equation.

8. What is the difference between MTBF and availability?

    Answer: Availability denotes the percentage of time during which the service or system is available (that is, functioning properly and capable of being used) over a time period. Mean time between failures denotes the frequency of failures, without regard to how long the failures last. Hence, it is possible to have a service with high availability but with low MTBF, meaning that the overall user experience despite high availability can still be pretty bad.

9. Which three aspects determine the complexity of operational tasks?

    Answer: The three aspects are: execution complexity, which is determined largely by the number of steps of the task; parameter complexity, which is determined by the number of parameters required in those steps and the ease of obtaining them; and memory complexity, which involves how much data a user must retain in memory at any one time during the task.

10. A management application vendor boasts about the scale of its management system, claiming that it can support 10 million managed objects. What are some questions that you might want to ask in return?

    Answer: What do you consider a managed object, and how does it translate to managed network size? For example, would you require one managed object per managed device, or per configuration parameter, or per port? How long does it take you to initially populate the system with those 10 million objects? How long does it take you to synchronize your 10 million objects with the network, and what is the maximum time lag that a managed object can have until it reflects changes in the managed resource that the managed object represents? How many events can your system process, and is this sufficient to keep up with the managed network size that corresponds to 10 million objects without dropping events?

Further Reading

Books on Network Management

■ Alger, D. *Build the Best Data Center Facility for Your Business*. Cisco Press, 2005. A how-to guide on setting up and operating a data center, providing insight on how to apply network management in the context of data centers.

■ Claise, B., R. Wolter. *Network Management: Accounting and Performance Strategies*. Cisco Press, 2007. As indicated by its title, this book provides an in-depth look at accounting and performance management.

■ Deveriya, A. *Network Administrators Survival Guide*. Cisco Press, 2005. Another "how-to book," geared toward network administrators in enterprise environments, providing a perspective on how people manage network equipment from the ground up.

■ Hegering, H. G., S. Abeck, B. Neumair. *Integrated Management of Networked Systems*. Morgan Kaufmann, 1999. A broad survey of network management technology and network technologies to be managed. This book lacks the more recent developments, but it is still one of the most relevant in the field.

■ Lewis, L. *Managing Business and Service Networks*. Kluwer Academics/Plenum Publishers, 2001. This book focuses on the process of managing networks in enterprise and service provider environments. It illustrates the use of a management platform (Aprisma's Spectrum) in this process and builds around three extensive case studies to convey the big picture.

■ Martin-Flatin, J. P. *Web Based Management of IP Networks and Systems*. John Wiley and Sons, 2002. This book describes the application of web techniques to network management, such as the use of embedded web servers as management agents, and makes a case for the use of XML instead the more prevalent SNMP. Although it is perhaps the only book on this particular topic, it predates Netconf and is hence partly overtaken by more recent developments.

- McConnell, J., E. Siegel. *Practical Service Level Management.* Cisco Press, 2004. This book delves into the topic of defining and monitoring service-level agreements, with specific emphasis on web services.

- Misra, K. *OSS for Telecom Networks.* Springer, 2004. A brief introductory-level book with particular focus on telecommunications service providers and their operational support environments.

- Stallings, W. *SNMP, SNMPv2, SNMPv3, RMON 1 and 2* (3rd ed.). Addison-Wesley, 1998. As the title indicates, this book provides an in-depth look at the gory details of SNMP in its different versions and the RMON MIBs.

- Strassner, J. *Policy-Based Network Management.* Morgan Kaufmann, 2003. This book offers an in-depth treatment of policy-based network management, drawing on concepts of a technology known as next-generation Directory Enabled Networks (DEN-ng).

- Subramanian, M. *Network Management: Principles and Practice.* Addison-Wesley, 2000. This book offers a fairly comprehensive discussion of selected management technologies and protocols, such as TMN (whose relevance is fading) and SNMP, as well as a discussion of management tools available to operate a network.

- Terplan, K. *Operations Support System Essentials.* John Wiley and Sons, 2001. This book is geared specifically toward telecommunications service providers and deals with the operations support infrastructure that is needed to support their business processes and practices.

Standards and Industry Recommendations

SNMP:

- McCloghrie, K., D. Perkins, J. Schoenwaelder, J. Case, M. Rose, S. Waldbusser. *Conformance Statements for SMIv2.* IETF RFC 2580, April 1999. (http://www.ietf.org/rfc/rfc2580.txt)

- McCloghrie, K., D. Perkins, J. Schoenwaelder, J. Case, M. Rose, S. Waldbusser. *Structure of Management Information Version 2 (SMIv2).* IETF RFC 2578, April 1999. (http://www.ietf.org/rfc/rfc2578.txt)

- McCloghrie, K., D. Perkins, J. Schoenwaelder, J. Case, M. Rose, S. Waldbusser. *Textual Conventions for SMIv2.* IETF RFC 2579, April 1999. (http://www.ietf.org/rfc/rfc2579.txt)

  These above three references specify SMIv2. RFC 2578 is the SMIv2 specification itself, RFC 2579 defines a set of textual conventions (in effect, predefined data types that can be used with SMIv2), and RFC 2580 specifies how SMIv2 conformance statements are written, which allow developers to specify which parts of an SMIv2-based MIB an agent implementation actually contains.

- Presuhn, R., J. Case, K. McCloghrie, M. Rose, S. Waldbusser. *Version 2 of the Protocol Operations for the Simple Network Management Protocol (SNMP)*. IETF RFC 3416, December 2002. (http://www.ietf.org/rfc/rfc3416.txt)

  SNMPv3 is specified in RFCs 3410 through 3418; RFC 3416 is the core RFC, which specifies the protocol itself (don't let the title deceive you—this is SNMPv3, not v2).

- Levi, D., P. Meyer, B. Steward. *Simple Network Management Protocol (SNMP) Applications*. IETF RFC 3413, Dezember 2002. (http://www.ietf.org/rfc/rfc3413.txt)

  Another RFC in the SNMPv3 series, this one is noteworthy and hence mentioned specifically here because it contains an overview of the ways in which SNMP is deployed in management architectures.

- Case, J., M. Fedor, M. Schoffstall, J. Davin. *Simple Network Management Protocol*. IETF RFC 1157, May 1990. (http://www.ietf.org/rfc/rfc1157.txt)

  This is the "original" SNMP and no longer has the status of a standard.

- McCloghrie, K., M. Rose. *Management Information Base for Network Management of TCP/IP-Based Internets: MIB-II*. IETF RFC 1213, March 1991. (http://www.ietf.org/rfc/rfc1213.txt)

  MIB-II can be considered the "mother" of all MIBs. It is an example of a MIB specification that has enjoyed very widespread implementation.

- White, K.: *Definitions of Managed Objects for Remote Ping, Traceroute, and Lookup Operations*. IETF RFC 2925, September 2000. (http://www.ietf.org/rfc/rfc2925.txt)

- Frye, R., D. Levi, S. Routhier, B. Wijnen. *Coexistence between Version 1, Version 2, and Version 3 of the Internet-standard Network Management Framework*. IETF RFC 2576, February 1999. (http://www.ietf.org/rfc/rfc2576.txt)

  This RFC is not a normative standard, but an RFC that has been put out for "informational" purposes—an authoritative whitepaper, if you will, that explains how the different SNMP versions relate.

RMON:

RMON consists of SNMP MIBs that are used for delegating certain remote monitoring logic to SNMP agents that serve as RMON probes and are defined in their own set of RFCs. The two "classical" RMON MIBs are as follows:

- Waldbusser, S. *Remote Network Monitoring Management Information Base*. IETF RFC 2819, May 2000. (http://www.ietf.org/rfc/rfc2819.txt)

- Waldbusser, S. *Remote Network Monitoring Management Information Base Version 2 using SMIv2*. IETF RFC 2021, January 1997. (http://www.ietf.org/rfc/rfc2021.txt)

RMON 2 extends the work of the original RMON by extending the scope of what is being monitored beyond the networking layer to the application layer. Curiously, you will notice that the RFC for version 2 of RMON predates the RFC version 1. However, there was an earlier and semantically equivalent version of RFC 2819 that was specified in SMIv1 (which does predate RFC 2021) until it was updated with the more modern SMIv2 notation.

NetFlow:

As mentioned earlier, strictly speaking, NetFlow is not a standard—it is a specification that Cisco owns. For information on NetFlow, search for "NetFlow" on http://www.cisco.com/. Here are some of the resources you can find:

■ NetFlow documentation and list of whitepapers: http://www.cisco.com/en/US/products/ ps6601/prod_white_papers_list.html

■ NetFlow Version 9 Flow Record Format: http://www.cisco.com/application/pdf/en/us/guest/ tech/tk362/c1550/ccmigration_09186a00800a3db9.pdf. Cisco Systems, 2004

IPFIX:

At the time this book goes to press, IPFIX is not yet an official standard. It still has the status of an Internet draft, meaning that it is subject to change. An RFC has been issued listing the requirements that the IPFIX specification must meet.

■ Quittek, J., T. Zseby, B. Claise, S. Zander. *Requirements for IP Flow Information Export (IPFIX)*. IETF RFC 3917, October 2004. (http://www.ietf.org/rfc/rfc3917.txt)

The following are the core Internet drafts for protocol and information content of the flow records. Bear in mind that Internet drafts have a limited shelf life and are subject to frequent updates. For the most current document version, refer to the IETF website (http://www.ietf.org/).

■ Claise, B. *IPFIX Protocol Specification*. Internet draft (work in progress) <draft-ietf-ipfix-protocol-22.txt>, June 2006.

■ Quittek, J., S. Bryant, B. Claise, J. Meyer. *Information Model for IP Flow Information Export*. Internet draft (work in progress) <draft-ietf-ipfix-info-12>, June 2006.

Syslog:

Currently, two RFCs relate to syslog: RFC 3164 describes syslog as it is implemented by BSD (Berkeley System Distribution) UNIX systems, without having the status of a standard, whereas RFC 3195 describes a mapping of syslog messages to a reliable transport protocol called BEEP.

The syslog protocol itself still has the status of an Internet draft. Again, because of the limited shelf life of Internet drafts, refer to the IETF website (http://www.ietf.org/) for the most current version.

■ Lonvick, C. *The BSD syslog Protocol.* IETF RFC 3164, August 2001. (http://www.ietf.org/rfc/rfc3164.txt)

■ New, D., M. Rose: *Reliable Delivery for syslog.* IETF RFC 3195, November 2001. (http://www.ietf.org/rfc/rfc3195.txt)

■ Gerhards, R. *The syslog Protocol.* Internet draft (work in progress) <draft-ietf-syslog-protocol-17.txt>, June 2006.

Netconf:

Like IPFIX and Syslog, at the time this book goes to press, Netconf has not yet reached the status of an RFC. A series of Internet drafts has been written; the most important contains the specification of the Netconf architecture and the protocol itself that is listed herein. Refer to the IETF website for the most current version (http://www.ietf.org/). Other drafts not listed here include transport mappings that specify how Netconf is to be carried over various transport protocols such as SSH or SOAP.

■ Enns, R. NETCONF Configuration Protocol. Internet draft (work in progress) <draft-ietf-netconf-prot-12>, February 2006.

eTOM:

TeleManagement Forum's enhanced Telecom Operations Map is documented in a set of specifications that, like all TMF documents, can be accessed on the document library on TMF's website (http://www.tmforum.org/). eTOM has also been co-published by the International Telecommunication Union as a set of ITU-T standards in the recommendation series ITU-T M.3050. The following documents should be of particular interest:

■ *Enhanced Telecom Operations Map—The Business Process Framework for the Information and Communications Services Industry Release 6.0 GB 921.* TeleManagement Forum, November 2005.

This is the main document, which is supplemented with a series of addenda.

■ *Enhanced Telecom Operations Map (eTOM)—The Business Process Framework for the Information and Communications Services Industry Release, Addendum P: An eTOM Primer.* Release 4.5 GB921 P. TeleManagement Forum, November 2004.

One of the addenda to the main document, this document provides a tutorial-style introduction and overview of eTOM and is hence the best document in the eTOM set of specifications to start with. (The release of the document is still 4.5, not 6.0, like the main document, because it has not been necessary to provide an update for this primer.)

■ *Enhanced Telecom Operations Map (eTOM)—The Business Process Framework for the Information and Communications Services Industry Release 6.0, Addendum D: Process Decomposition and Descriptions.* TeleManagement Forum, November 2005.

Another addendum, this specification contains a detailed description of service provider end-to-end processes, starting from the top at the level of service- and business-management–related tasks.

NGOSS:

■ *The NGOSS Technology-Neutral Architecture—NGOSS Release 6.0.* TMF053, November 2005.

TeleManagement Forum's next-generation OSS (NGOSS) initiative has produced a series of specifications for an overall architecture of operations support environments that will consist of multiple systems that need to interact with each other to support the processes and roles that are defined as part of eTOM. Like eTOM, NGOSS is independent of particular managed services and technologies, and geared toward very large service providers. This document represents the core ngOSS specification.

TMN:

TMN is defined in a set of standards issued by the standardization branch of the International Telecommunication Union (ITU-T). The following is a (noninclusive) list of some of the core specifications:

■ *Overview of TMN Recommendations.* ITU-T Recommendation M.3000, February 2000.

Provides an overview of the way in which the standards are structured and how they relate.

■ *Principles for a Telecommunications Management Network.* ITU-T Recommendation M.3010, February 2000.

This specification is the "classic" of the TMN specifications and defines the overall management reference architecture, including the different management layers. Its most recent update was in 2000, although earlier revisions have been around since the early 1990s.

■ *Telecommunications Markup Language Framework (tML).* ITU-T Recommendation M.3030, August 2002.

A relatively little-known specification, this document contains an XML schema that can be used to define management information. Its intent is to propel TMN into the XML age and offer an alternative to an earlier notation called Guidelines for the Definition of Managed Objects (GDMO) that, while powerful, has not gained widespread industry acceptance. However, whether tML itself will gain industry significance remains to be seen. M.3100 (see reference below) is TMN's core standard with regard to management information but is itself not yet available in a tML version.

■ *Generic Network Information Model.* ITU-T Recommendation M.3100, April 2005.

Another "classic" TMN standard that has been around since the early 1990s, M.3100 received a recent face-lift that specifies the management information in the technology-neutral Unified Modeling Language (UML) notation, with the formerly used GDMO and ASN.1 notations still available. M.3100 contains an information model—that is, a generic management information schema that can be used to model telecommunications networks that provide connection-oriented services; it is not geared toward packet-oriented data networks and services. It provides the starting point to define more specialized management information for specific technologies and telecommunications services.

■ *TMN Management Functions.* ITU-T Recommendation M.3400, February 2000.

This document contains a detailed rundown of individual management functions in each of the FCAPS functional areas.

■ *Information technology—Open Systems Interconnection—Systems Management: Alarm Reporting Function.* ITU-T Recommendation X.733, February 1992.

Strictly speaking, this document is not a part of the TMN suite of standards but it is closely related to it; it defines information that is contained in alarms.

The DSL Forum is representative of several industry consortia that have their own set of network management standards to be applied for a particular network technology. We did not discuss their concepts in this book because they are used only in a particular niche (DSL for service providers); however, looking at those standards that are a little "off the beaten path" can provide interesting insights.

■ Bernstein, J., T. Spets (eds.). *CPE WAN Management Protocol.* DSL Forum Technical Report TR-069, May 2004. (http://www.dslforum.org/aboutdsl/Technical_Reports/TR-069.pdf)

As the title indicates, TR-069 actually defines its own management protocol. So why did they not simply adopt one of the existing protocols? The answer lies in a combination of factors, most important of which is the fact that there are sometimes specifics to the particular subject domains that can be more effectively addressed by a custom-tailored solution than a generic one. In the case of DSL, this concerns specifically the need for service providers to manage DSL modems at customer locations in private networks and behind firewalls, scenarios in which traditional management techniques encounter limitations because the devices are hard to reach by a manager using a traditional request-response paradigm.

■ Abbi, R. (ed.). *Protocol Independent Object Model for Managing Next Generation ADSL Technologies.* DSL Forum Technical Report TR-090, December 2004. (http://www.dslforum.org/aboutdsl/Technical_Reports/TR-090.pdf)

This is an example of a specification that lists a set of requirements for what needs to be presented as part of the management information, regardless of the actual representation of that management information as part of a MIB.

Conferences and Workshops

Network management conferences and workshops constitute the best source of information about the current forefront of network management technology. There are several noteworthy conference series; for each, proceedings are published that contain a wealth of papers describing current research projects. (Proceedings are essentially books whose chapters consist of papers that are also presented in talks at the event.) By nature, they focus mainly on the academic and research-oriented crowd. Those series include the following:

■ The IFIP/IEEE International Symposia on Integrated Network Management (IM) (http://wwww.ieee-im.org/). This can be considered the premier event in the field; it takes place in odd-numbered years and takes turns with its sister conference, NOMS.

■ The IFIP/IEEE Network Operations and Management Symposia (NOMS). NOMS is IM's sister conference, with which it takes turns by being held in even numbered years. It is very similar in nature and enjoys the same excellent reputation.

■ The International Weeks on Management of Networks and Services (Manweek). Manweeks are umbrella events that comprise several conferences and workshops that are otherwise independent. They include the IFIP/IEEE International Workshops on Distributed Systems: Operations and Management (DSOM), the IEEE International Workshops on IP Operations and Management (IPOM), and the IFIP/IEEE International Conferences on Management of Multimedia and Mobile Networks and Services (MMNS). Manweeks are smaller than IM and NOMS and cater more to an expert crowd; attendees are usually also presenters. Despite the unfortunate title, Manweeks are of course also open to women.

With the exception of IM, the web addresses of those events vary from year to year. An Internet search on the conference names should yield links to the most current event.

Here is a list of some of the more recent proceedings:

■ Goldszmidt, G., J. Schönwälder (eds.). *Integrated Network Management VIII—Managing It All. Proceedings of the 2003 IEEE/IFIP International Symposium on Integrated Network Management.* Colorado Springs, Colorado. Kluwer Academic Publishers, March 2003.

■ Brunner, M., A. Keller (eds.). *Self-Managing Distributed Systems. Proceedings of the 14th IFIP/IEEE International Workshop on Distributed Systems: Operations and Management.* Heidelberg, Germany. Lecture Notes in Computer Science LNCS 2867, Springer, October 2003.

■ Boutaba, R., S. B. Kim (eds.). *Managing Next Generation Convergence Networks and Services. Proceedings of the 2004 IEEE/IFIP Network Operations and Management Symposium.* Seoul, Korea. IEEE, April 2004.

■ Sahai, A., F. Wu (eds.). *Utility Computing. Proceedings of the 15th IFIP/IEEE International Workshop on Distributed Systems: Operations and Management.* Davis, California. Lecture Notes in Computer Science LNCS 3278; Springer, November 2004.

■ Clemm, A., O. Festor, A. Pras (eds.). *Integrated Network Management IX—Managing New Networked Worlds. Proceedings of the 2005 IEEE/IFIP International Symposium on Integrated Network Management.* Nice, France. IEEE, May 2005.

■ Schönwälder, J., J. Serrat (eds.). *Ambient Networks. Proceedings of the 16th IFIP/IEEE International Workshop on Distributed Systems: Operations and Management.* Barcelona, Spain. Lecture Notes in Computer Science LNCS 3775; Springer, October 2005.

■ Hellerstein, J., B. Stiller (eds.). *Management of Integrated End-to-End Communications and Services. Proceedings of the 2006 IEEE/IFIP Network Operations and Management Symposium.* Vancouver, Canada. IEEE (CD-ROM only), April 2006.

In addition to those research events, some events cater more to an industrial crowd that is interested in current product offerings and best practices. Two noteworthy events are the following:

■ Cisco Networkers. Networkers is a product-oriented series of conferences that are sponsored by Cisco, focusing on networking technology as it relates to Cisco's product portfolio. Network management is also covered. Information can be found at http://www.cisco.com/networkers/.

■ TeleManagement World (TMW). TMW is organized by the TeleManagement Forum (TMF) and takes place twice a year. It is centered on the standards activities of the TMF and focuses particularly on operations support infrastructure of service providers, featuring presentations as well as vendor exhibits. Information about TMW can be found on the TMF website, http://www.tmforum.org/.

Web Resources

The Web has many excellent sources of information. Readers are encouraged to conduct their own Internet searches. Just try a Google search on terms such as "network management," "command-line interface," "SNMP," and "service-level management." Searches on the various topics discussed in this book are sure to yield a wealth of information, as are the websites of vendors engaged in management technology. Here is a very short list of links that you may want to try.

■ http://www.simpleweb.org/ contains a wealth of resources that are related to SNMP and SNMP MIBs.

■ http://www.ibr.cs.tu-bs.de/projects/snmpv3/ contains more information about SNMP—specifically, SNMPv3—along with a comprehensive list of vendors supporting SNMPv3 in their products.

■ http://www.artofnm.com/, maintained by the author of this book, provides a web portal related to network management.

■ http://www.ietf.org/ is the home page of the Internet Engineering Task Force and the entry point to locating the numerous RFCs and Internet drafts that relate to network management.

■ http://www.tmforum.org/ is the home page of the TeleManagement Forum, which contains a wealth of information on TMF initiatives and the topic of interoperability of operations support systems.

■ http://www.dmtf.org/ is the home page of the Desktop Management Task Force, another standards organization concerned mainly with management information and the Common Information Model (CIM), for the management of networked systems.

■ http://www.dslforum.org/ is the home page of the DSL Forum and, among other things, contains specifications that pertain to the management of DSL technology.

■ http://www.mfaforum.org/ is the home page of another industry consortium that includes a number of specifications related to the management of MPLS, Frame Relay, and ATM technology. (The MFA Forum succeeds the ATM Forum.)

■ http://www.packetcable.com/specifications/ is the entry point to specifications of the Packet Cable consortium, filling a role analogous to the DSL Forum in the case of DSL for cable-based access network technology. Several documents deal specifically with management.

Other Material Related to This Book

■ Bichsel, P. *There Is No Such Place As America: Stories.* Delacorte Press, 1970. This book contains the short story "A Table Is a Table," mentioned in Chapter 6.

■ Brown, A., A. Keller, J. Hellerstein. *A Model of Configuration Complexity and Its Application to a Change Management System.* In *Proceedings of the 2005 IEEE/IFIP International Symposium on Integrated Network Management,* p. 631–644, 2005. This paper contains an analysis of operational complexity that is associated with configuration activities, as was mentioned in Chapter 12.

■ Kaplan, R., D. Norton. *The Balanced Scorecard: Translating Strategy into Action.* Harvard Business School Press, 1996. Not a network management book, this book contains information on assessing business performance that applies also to network providers as discussed in Chapter 12.

■ Neely, A., C. Adams, M. Kennerly. *Performance Prism: The Scorecard for Measuring and Managing Stakeholder Relationships.* Financial Times Prentice Hall, 2002. Having nothing to do with network management, per se, this book discusses the Performance Prism methodology used to measure business performance that was mentioned in Chapter 12.

■ Wustenhoff, E. *Service Level Agreement in the Data Center.* Sun BluePrints Online, 2002, http://www.sun.com/blueprints/0402/sla.pdf. A technical whitepaper that contains an excellent treatment of service-level agreements.

AAA Authentication, Authorization, Accounting.

ACL Access control list. A list of rules that specify filters for network traffic, used to specify security policies in routers.

agent (i) A role that is assumed by a system that is being managed. Counterpart to a manager role. (ii) A software entity that implements a management interface that allows a system or a device to be managed by a management application. A management server.

alarm An event message that indicates the onset of an alarm condition.

alarm clear An event message that indicates the remission of an alarm condition.

alarm condition A state of an entity (typically, a network element) that indicates distress that typically requires management attention and whose onset is notified through an alarm.

alarm correlation Event correlation applied to alarms.

announcement An event message that announces the presence of a managed entity.

API Application programming interface.

application management The management of applications that are deployed on systems that are interconnected over a network.

ASN.1 Abstract Syntax Notation One. A standard for the specification of data types that are to be exchanged over a communications protocol, used in conjunction with SNMP.

ATM Asynchronous Transfer Mode. A networking technology.

audit trail A log that records activity, particularly management requests, at a managed entity (for example, a device), used to help reconstruct the management history of a device.

auditing   Retrieval of management information from a managed entity (such as a device) by a management application, typically for reconciliation or discrepancy-reporting purposes.

authentication   The act of verifying whether a message or a request is authentic—that is, verifying the identity of the originator and ensuring that the message or request was not altered.

authorization   The act of determining whether a requestor has sufficient privileges for a request.

autodiscovery   The process of automatically detecting network elements that are connected to a network.

CDR   Call detail record. A record of a call, typically a voice call, that is recorded by network elements that serve the call. CDRs are used to account for service use.

central office   A local facility of a telecommunications service provider that houses network equipment used to connect customers to the service provider's network.

CIM   Common Information Model. A management information model standardized by the DMTF.

CLI   Command-line interface. A management interface that human administrators use to interact with networking equipment.

client   An entity that is being served by a server. A client directs requests to a server and processes responses and event messages from the server.

columnar object   An object in a table in an SNMP MIB.

configuration   A set of configuration settings for a managed device, often persisted in a configuration file.

counter   A management variable representing a statistical value that monotonically increases (for example, number of transmitted packets).

CPE   Customer premises equipment. A piece of networking equipment that is physically located at an end customer outside the network provider's domain.

craft technician   A human administrator who uses a craft terminal to interact with a piece of network equipment, often in conjunction with turning up, troubleshooting, or decommissioning equipment.

craft terminal   A data terminal (for example, a notebook computer) with management software that enables craft technicians to view and configure a device and that can plug into a device's data port.

CRM   Customer relationship management. The management of all aspects that relate to interaction with customers, including but not limited to service ordering or help desk.

customer   The term a service provider uses to refer to a user of its communication services.

DBMS   Database management system.

discovery   The process of identifying how a given managed entity (typically, a network element) is configured.

discrepancy reporting   The process of calling out differences between information stored about a managed entity (typically, a network element) in a management application and information obtained by auditing the network element. Discrepancy reporting is typically part of a user-directed synchronization function; it is up to an end user to decide whether the reported discrepancies should be reconciled (updating the management application database with information from the managed entity) or reprovisioned (applying the view of the management application to the managed entity).

DMTF   Desktop Management Task Force, the standardization organization that defines CIM.

DoS attack   Denial-of-service attack. An attack on a network that attempts to shut down a communication service by overwhelming it with bogus requests, to prevent legitimate requests from getting through.

DSL   Digital subscriber line. An access-network technology to connect residential customers to a data network.

DSP   Digital signal processor. A chip that performs specialized communications functions in a piece of networking equipment.

element management system   A system for the management of devices ("network elements") in a network.

EMS   *See* element management system.

entity   In the context of this book, used synonymously with *managed entity*.

eTOM   Enhanced Telecom Operations Map. A standardization effort of the TMF concerning business processes of (telecommunications) service providers, including the operations support environments needed to support those processes, the different roles that management systems and applications are expected to play in those environments, and the interactions between them.

event   An occurrence of something in the "real world." Events can be indicated to managers through an event message. Note that the term *event* is often overloaded and is used to refer both to an event and to an event message.

event correlation   An activity that analyzes event messages to identify which ones are likely related, for example, because they have the same underlying root cause. Multiple events that have been correlated are sometimes consolidated in an additional, correlated event that replaces the original events, to reduce the number of events that event receivers get exposed to.

event deduplication   A simple form of event correlation whose purpose is to identify and be able to remove duplicate event messages from a stream of event messages. When duplicate event messages occur, in many cases, a separate event message is sent to indicate the number of duplicates that were removed.

event filtering   An activity that drops event messages that do not meet a certain criteria and that lets event messages that do meet the criteria pass unaltered.

event message   An unsolicited message that an agent emits to notify a manager of an occurrence of an event.

event subscription   A service that an agent offers to allow a manager to subscribe to events—that is, to allow a manager to indicate during runtime that it wants to receive event messages from the agent. Often event subscription is combined with event filtering, allowing a manager to subscribe to only those types of event messages (based on a filter criteria) that it is interested in.

FAB   Fulfillment, Assurance, Billing. Three categories of service management functionality defined by the TMF as part of eTOM.

fault   A state of an entity in which an error or malfunction is present. If the state is reported through an alarm, the fault also constitutes an alarm condition.

FCAPS   Fault, Configuration, Accounting, Performance, Security. The five categories of management functionality defined by TMN.

gauge   A type of management variable that represents a statistical value that can increase or decrease (for example, utilization).

GUI Graphical user interface.

ICMP Internet Control Message Protocol. A protocol defined by the IETF that includes the echo request, better known as ping.

IDS Intrusion detection system. A special type of management application intended to detect and, if possible, prevent attacks on a network or data center.

IETF Internet Engineering Task Force. An organization responsible for standardizing communication protocols used in the Internet, such as IP or SNMP.

image management The management of distribution and activation of software images on network devices.

inheritance An object-oriented concept that represents an "is a kind of" relationship, allowing a (more specific) subclass to inherit the properties of its (more generic) superclass.

interface A set of rules according to which other entities can interact with the entity that is providing the interface.

introspection A feature of a management agent that enables a manager to discover the management capabilities that the agent supports.

inventory Information about physical properties of a network or a device, such as chassis and line cards, or logical assets of the device, such as a software image or license. Inventory does not include information related to logical configuration parameters that are configured by users, or to state or operational data of the device.

IP Internet Protocol. The network layer communications protocol that is at the core of the Internet.

IPFIX IP Flow Information Exchange. An IETF-defined version of NetFlow, a format for the export of IP flow records.

IP flow A set of IP packets of the same type, originating from the same source and directed toward the same destination, indicative of a connection (at a higher communications layer) between source and destination.

ISO International Standardization Organization.

IT Information technology. An enterprise's IT department is generally the internal provider of communication services for that enterprise.

ITU-T   International Telecommunications Union–Telecommunications Standardization Sector. The organization that standardizes TMN.

LAN   Local area network.

loopback   A diagnostic test that involves a device reflecting back a signal that is received through a particular port across a link, allowing the initiator of the test to compare the original signal with the signal that was received back.

MAC address   Media Access Control address. The physical (hardware) address of a network interface of a device.

manageability   The collective set of properties of an entity (typically, a network element) that allow it to be managed.

managed entity   An entity that is subjected to management, such as a network device or an end system that is connected to a network or a data center. Often, *managed element* is used as a synonym.

managed object   A management abstraction of a real resource; a piece of management information in a MIB. As a note, a managed object is not necessarily an object in the object-oriented sense.

management agent   An agent.

management appliance   A piece of equipment with management application functionality. Unlike management application software that is deployed on a host, a management appliance bundles management application functionality and the hosting equipment as an inseparable package.

management gateway   A management proxy that performs management mediation.

management information   Data that represents a managed entity.

management information model   A management abstraction that, when instantiated, represents a managed entity.

management mediation   The process of translating between different management protocols and management information models to allow managers and agents that speak different management languages to communicate with each other.

management network A network that is dedicated to carry management traffic; a network that connects management systems with the entities they manage.

management platform A piece of management software that provides a collection of management functions (typically related to the monitoring of data networks), that supports multiple device types of different vendors, and that provides infrastructure that makes it extensible, allowing third parties to provide additional management functions and support for additional managed entities.

management probe A piece of management software that is embedded in network devices, whose purpose is to collect management data. Examples are probes that collect statistics about network traffic, that conduct performance measurements, or that run diagnostic tests.

management proxy A system that manages a managed entity on behalf of another manager.

management transaction A set of management commands that are to be executed as if they were a single atomic unit.

manager An entity that acts in a manager role, either a user or an application. The counterpart to an agent. A management client.

metaschema A language for the specification of a schema—that is, of management information.

MIB Management Information Base. A conceptual data store, provided by a management agent, containing the management information of a managed entity.

MIB module A MIB definition, typically for a particular network technology feature, that constitutes a subtree in an object identifier tree. A MIB that is provided by a management agent is typically composed of multiple instantiated MIB modules.

MPLS Multiprotocol Label Switching. A networking technology.

MSP Managed service provider. A company that manages a network or a data center for other companies.

MTBF Mean time between failures. A measure for the failure rate of a device.

MTTR Mean time to repair. A measure for the average time that it takes to resolve a problem after it is first observed.

NE *See* network element.

Netconf   A management protocol that is geared toward managing network configurations by management applications.

NetFlow   A format for the export of IP flow data.

network control   Automated management tasks that are performed in near–real time and that are considered a function of a service and of the network itself, not of its management.

network element   A managed entity in a network that is, for management purposes, represented by a management agent. Typically, a network device.

network management   The activities, methods, procedures, and tools that pertain to the operation, administration, maintenance, and provisioning of networked systems.

network operations center   *See* NOC.

network provider   In the context of this book, the owner of a network that provides communication services; a service provider or an enterprise IT department.

NGOSS   Next Generation Operations Support System. A standardization effort by the TeleManagement Forum for management systems targeted at service provider environments.

NOC   Network operations center. The command center from which a network is managed.

northbound interface   The interface or API exposed by a management system to other management applications; on architecture diagrams, these are typically depicted "on top of" or "to the north" of the system that exposes the interface.

notification   An event message.

OAM&P   Operations, Administration, Maintenance, Provisioning. Categorization of management functionality that is popular with telecommunications service providers.

object identifier   An identifier of a managed object or of a definition of a piece of management information in an SNMP MIB.

object identifier tree   A conceptual structure that is used to arrange the object identifiers of MIBs in hierarchical fashion.

OID   *See* object identifier.

operations support infrastructure   The technical infrastructure of a service provider, typically consisting of a multitude of operations support systems that are integrated to exchange data with each other and that are tuned to support a service provider's processes and workflows.

OSS   Operations support system. A management system that is part of the operations support infrastructure of a service provider.

PBX   Private branch exchange. A private telephone switch that provides telephony services in an enterprise.

PDP   Policy decision point. A component in a policy-based management architecture that makes policy decisions about requests, such as admission-control decisions.

PDU   Protocol data unit. A message with a data structure as defined by a protocol.

PEP   Policy enforcement point. A component in a policy-based management architecture that is responsible for implementing policy actions decided by a PDP.

ping   An ICMP echo request, used to check reachability of network devices and to measure network delay.

policy   A management policy is a declarative, high-level definition of a management rule or course of action.

polling   The act of sending a management request to a device to retrieve a piece of management information.

programmatic   A property of an interface that allows it to be used by an application—a program—instead of a human user.

protocol   A set of rules that, when followed, allow two entities (network devices, applications, systems) to communicate and exchange data.

provisioning   The act of assigning resources and configuring a managed entity, or a set of managed entities, for them to provide a service.

PTT   Post, telegraph, and telephone administration. A category of large-scale telecommunications service providers that is also often referred to as carriers.

subclass   In object-oriented models, a class that inherits from and hence specializes a more generic superclass.

superclass   In object-oriented models, a class from which subclasses that are more specific and less general are derived.

QoS   Quality of service. Generally refers to quality characteristics of network traffic, such as delay, bandwidth, or jitter.

real resource   The actual entity that is subjected to management, abstracted for management purposes by managed objects. The managed resource. Ultimately, the real-world entity that is to be managed and that is to be influenced by management operations.

reconciliation   Synchronizing management information of a manager with that of an underlying agent; the agent constitutes the golden store.

reprovisioning   Synchronizing management information of a managed entity (for example, a network device) with that of a management application. The manager constitutes the golden store, which means that sending configuration commands to the device might be required to get both in synch.

relay   A system that stores and forwards messages—for example (in network management), syslog messages.

RFC   Request For Comments. A document (typically, a specification) that is published by the IETF. An RFC is not synonymous with an IETF standard: Although IETF standards are published as RFCs, not all RFCs are standards.

RMON   Remote Monitoring. A MIB—or, rather, a series of MIBs—used to delegate simple monitoring tasks to SNMP management agents.

ROI   Return on investment. A measure for the profitability of an investment.

RPC   Remote procedure call. A communication paradigm that allows a client to invoke a procedure on a remote server as if it were local.

running config   The configuration currently in effect at a device.

scalar   An SNMP MIB object that is not part of a table.

schema   A definition of a model; in the context of network management, the definition of a management information model.

scoping   A capability that enables a manager to apply the same management operation to multiple managed objects simultaneously, using only one management request.

server   A provider of a service to a client. A server receives requests from a client and sends responses and event messages to the client.

service   A function that is provided to clients who derive value from it.

service level   The overall quality of a service, as defined by a set of service-level parameters.

service level management   Management activities that are geared at asserting a certain service level.

service level monitoring   Management activities that are geared at assessing the level of a service that users of the service experience.

service level parameter   A parameter that indicates a measure of quality of a service that is provided to a user of the service.

service order   A form that contains details about an order for a service that a customer or end user has placed.

session   A communication association between two communicating systems. An application layer connection.

shadow MIB   A cache, maintained by a management system, that replicates the MIB of a managed element or of a set of managed elements for application performance-tuning reasons.

SLA   Service level agreement. A contract between a service provider and a customer that is the basis of their business relationship and that defines the terms and expected service level of the provided service.

SLO   Service level objective. A component of an SLA that defines a target value for a service-level parameter that the service provider must meet for the SLA not to be violated.

SMIv2   Structure of Management Information Version 2. A metaschema for the definition of management information for SNMP.

SNMP   Simple Network Management Protocol.

SQL   Structured Query Language. A language for data query and retrieval in databases.

SSH   Secure Shell. A protocol that allows for secure and encrypted data transport.

startup config   A configuration that is applied upon startup of a device. Note that a startup configuration is typically persisted in a separate file and might be different from the running config.

stateful   Containing state—that is, information to perform a function. For example, a stateful management gateway is capable of matching data in a response against data in a request, or gathering additional data and performing multiple steps, the results of each of which it needs to retain to fulfill a request.

stateless   Without state—that is, not needing to retain information to perform a function. For example, a stateless management gateway needs to be capable of translating management requests and management responses without requiring data beyond what is contained in the request or response.

synchronization   The act of bringing two data stores into synch—that is, having them reflect consistent information.

syslog   A protocol and data format for the logging of system messages, commonly used for event messages in management.

system management   The management of end systems that are connected to a network.

tag   An element in an XML document that is used to delimit a piece of data.

TCA   Threshold-crossing alert. An alarm that is raised when a management variable, typically a counter or a gauge, crosses a predefined threshold value.

TCP   Transmission Control Protocol. A connection-oriented transport protocol.

TeleManagement Forum   An industry consortium that defines standards for operations support infrastructure in service provider environments, including eTOM and NGOSS.

TL-1   Transaction Language 1. A legacy standard for the management of telecommunications equipment, popular in North America.

TMN   Telecommunication Management Network. A framework by the ITU-T that defines standards for the management of telecommunications networks.

transaction   A single unit of interaction between two systems, such as (in databases) a client and a server, or (as it relates to management) a manager and a management agent. In some cases, a transaction groups multiple operations as one unit, which requires the capability to roll operations back in case of failures and to lock managed resources that are subjected to operations during the transaction.

trap   An SNMP event message.

trouble ticket   A form that contains a description of a problem, typically reported by an end user or customer.

UDP   User Datagram Protocol. A connectionless protocol on top of IP that is used by several management protocols as a transport, including SNMP.

UML   Unified Modeling Language. A methodology and a standard for the definition of data models.

user   The term an enterprise IT department uses to refer to an enterprise-internal customer of its communication services.

VLAN   Virtual LAN. A networking technology that allows network devices to behave as if they were connected to the same LAN, even though they might be physically located on separate LAN segments.

VoIP   Voice over IP.

VPN   Virtual Private Network. A private network that makes use of a public networking infrastructure, using networking tunnels that maintain privacy and security to interconnect network equipment.

WAN   Wide area network.

workflow management system   A system that manages workflows, generally centering on a workflow engine that automatically schedules and keeps track of the various steps that workflows are composed of.

XML   Extensible Markup Language. A popular language on the web, used to encode documents that are exchanged between computers and that is at the same time human-readable.

XSD   XML Schema Definition. An XML-based language that can be used to describe the contents of XML documents—for example, XML documents containing management information.

Index

A

X

SEARCH THOUSANDS OF BOOKS FROM LEADING PUBLISHERS

Safari® Bookshelf is a searchable electronic reference library for IT professionals that features more than 2,000 titles from technical publishers, including Cisco Press.

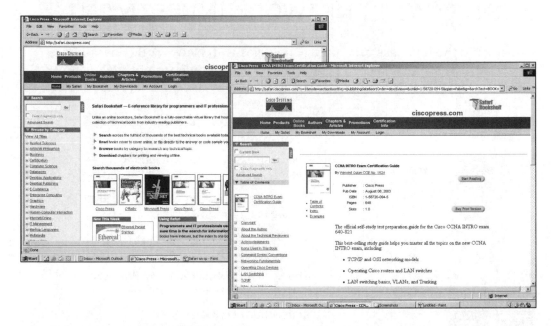

With Safari Bookshelf you can

- **Search** the full text of thousands of technical books, including more than 70 Cisco Press titles from authors such as Wendell Odom, Jeff Doyle, Bill Parkhurst, Sam Halabi, and Karl Solie.

- **Read** the books on My Bookshelf from cover to cover, or just flip to the information you need.

- **Browse** books by category to research any technical topic.

- **Download** chapters for printing and viewing offline.

With a customized library, you'll have access to your books when and where you need them—and all you need is a user name and password.

TRY SAFARI BOOKSHELF FREE FOR 14 DAYS!

You can sign up to get a 10-slot Bookshelf free for the first 14 days. Visit **http://safari.ciscopress.com** to register.

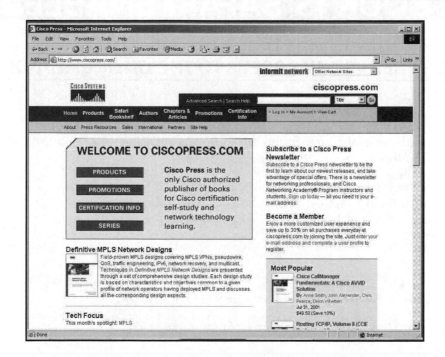
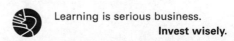

BOOKS ONLINE

ENABLED

THIS BOOK IS SAFARI ENABLED

INCLUDES FREE 45-DAY ACCESS TO THE ONLINE EDITION

The Safari® Enabled icon on the cover of your favorite technology book means the book is available through Safari Bookshelf. When you buy this book, you get free access to the online edition for 45 days.

Safari Bookshelf is an electronic reference library that lets you easily search thousands of technical books, find code samples, download chapters, and access technical information whenever and wherever you need it.

TO GAIN 45-DAY SAFARI ENABLED ACCESS TO THIS BOOK:

- Go to **http://www.ciscopress.com/safarienabled**
- Complete the brief registration form
- Enter the coupon code found in the front of this book before the "Contents at a Glance" page

If you have difficulty registering on Safari Bookshelf or accessing the online edition, please e-mail customer-service@safaribooksonline.com.